E. O Phinney

Letters on the Eucharist, Addressed to a Member of the Church of Rome

Formerly a Preacher in the Methodist Episcopal Church

E. O Phinney

Letters on the Eucharist, Addressed to a Member of the Church of Rome
Formerly a Preacher in the Methodist Episcopal Church

ISBN/EAN: 9783744779272

Printed in Europe, USA, Canada, Australia, Japan

Cover: Foto ©Lupo / pixelio.de

More available books at **www.hansebooks.com**

ON

THE EUCHARIST,

ADDRESSED TO

A Member of the Church of Rome,

FORMERLY

A PREACHER IN THE METHODIST EPISCOPAL CHURCH.

BY

E. O. PHINNEY, A. M., M. D.

'Ορᾷς γὰρ ὡς οὐ περὶ μικρῶν εἰσὶν ἡμῖν οἱ λόγοι· 'αλλ' ὅν τινα χρὴ τρόπον πεπιστευκέναι· καὶ γὰρ οὐδὲν οἶμαι τοσούτων κακῶν ἀνθρώπῳ γενέσθαι, ὅσον 'απὸ τῶν ἀναγκαίων ὁπόταν Ψευδῆ περὶ αὐτῶν δοξάζοι.   *Epiphanius adv. Hæreses.*

Thou seest that our reasonings are not about things of small importance, but in what manner it is necessary that any one should believe; for surely I think that nothing is of so great evil to man, as to believe falsely concerning things which are necessary.

BALTIMORE:

PUBLISHED FOR THE AUTHOR, BY D. H. CARROLL,

METHODIST BOOK DEPOSITORY.

1880.

Entered according to the Act of Congress, in the year 1880,

By E. O. PHINNEY,

In the Office of the Librarian of Congress at Washington, D. C.

PREFACE.

Circumstances, which it is not needful here to detail, induced the writer of the several Letters comprised in this volume, to investigate the claims of the Church of Rome to the example of the early church, in proof of the antiquity of her peculiar teachings.

As it respects her visible worship, no one of her dogmas is second in pretentious importance, to that which respects the Eucharist. "Numerous as are the differences between the Catholic and Protestant religions," says one of her earnest advocates, "we may safely assert, that not one is more frequently discussed, or made the touchstone of the two systems' respective claims, than their doctrine respecting the Sacrament of the Blessed Eucharist." And this writer expresses the belief, that more persons are brought to the faith of his church, by satisfying their minds with the Catholic belief respecting the Sacrament, than by being convinced upon many other subjects. Accordingly, we find the believers of a physical change, advocating it as an essentiality, and the sacrifice of the Mass, as the distinctive mark of the true Church of God. Should the discussion of this subject, and the presentation made, in these communications, contribute somewhat to the exposure of error, and the vindication of the truth, the object of the writer will be realized.

Most of the testimonies produced from the writings of the ancient Christian Fathers, have been copied personally, and a faithful representation of their meaning is believed to be given, as deduced both from the text itself, and the subject of discourse. In discussing collateral topics, it has been necessary, in a few instances, to refer to passages previously quoted, when such repetition was required to prove a relative point. And so much only of the original languages of our authors is published, as foot notes, and in the form of an Appendix, as seemed desirable to enable the reader to form a satisfactory judgment of the propriety and correctness of the use made of their productions. If it be true, as an American Statesman of a former generation, has said, that "Opinion is the queen of the world," we shall do well to be always ready to give a reason of our religious belief, and be prepared to defend it, against the sophistical attacks of misguided opposers. And as ability and opportunity involve responsibility, so no one is excusable, who, so far intrusts the keeping of his spiritual interests to the care of another, as to neglect the legitimate exercise of his own understanding.

Deeply impressed with a sense of the responsibility that attaches to the dealing with a subject affecting infinite issues, this endeavor is devoutly committed to the direction of Him, who out of weakness ordains strength, and makes the creature's well-meant effort, contribute to the accomplishment of the ends of His own high administration.

E. O. P.

Baltimore, April, 1880.

CONTENTS.

LETTER I.

SEVERAL TOPICS BRIEFLY NOTICED.

[1] Exclusive claims of the Church of Rome. [2] Evangelical Faith and Christian Doctrine not the same. [3] Transubstantiation and Worship of the Eucharist. Of such a special presence of Christ's Divinity in the Sacrament as to authorize its worship, we have no sufficient evidence either from Scripture or Reason. [4] Church-Infallibility not a Christian doctrine. That of the Church of Rome unlike that of the Bible. Disproved by matter of fact. But supposing the doctrine revealed, it can be ascertained only by private interpretation. Romanists therefore self-condemned.................Page 1

LETTER II.

TRANSUBSTANTIATION STATED, AND THE DISCUSSION OF JOHN VI INTRODUCED.

I. [1] Eucharistic elements denied to have been called by the ancient Fathers the FIGURE of Christ's body and blood, and Transubstantiation affirmed to be true. [2] REAL PRESENCE and Transubstantiation, how different. II. Discussion of the sixth of St. John's Gospel introduced. [1] Circumstances which occasioned our Lord's Discourse, and his method of instruction. [2] Character of his hearers. [3] FAITH the subject of the "sacred lecture.".................................p. 18

LETTER III.

DISCUSSION OF JOHN VI CONTINUED.

I. Were our Lord's Discourse explained as referring primarily to the Eucharist, it would not follow necessarily, that a manducation of his real flesh and a drinking of his real blood were intended. Reasons for not explaining this Discourse of the Eucharist. [1] The word here used is FLESH, while BODY is elsewhere employed. [2] Christ's flesh not given when this sacrament was instituted. [3] St. John, in his Gospel, gives no account of the institution. [4] The Eucharist not instituted when Christ delivered this Discourse. His conversation with Nicodemus touching Baptism, does not invalidate this argument. [5] The consequences of partaking or not partaking, too momentous to be referred to "sacramental feeding." [6] The circumstances of delivering this Discourse, not favorable for proposing the doctrine of a Christian sacrament. II. [1] The true doctrine of the Discourse shown. [2] Christ explains his own language. Augustine and Athanasius quoted.....p. 33

LETTER IV.

PATRISTIC VIEWS OF OUR LORD'S DISCOURSE IN JOHN VI.

Opinion of the Fathers respecting the Discourse of Christ at Capernaum. [1] Ignatius. [2] Irenæus. [3] Tertullian. [4] Cyprian. [5] Clement of Alexandria. [6] Origen. [7] Eusebius. [8] Athanasius. [9] Cyril of Jerusalem. [10] Basil, Bishop of Cæsarea. [11] Jerome. [12] Augustine. Pope Innocent III. Pope Pius II. Gabriel Biel.............................p. 52

LETTER V.

THE WORDS OF INSTITUTION.

[1] The words of Institution. Method of discussing them. Clement's general Rule for interpreting the Holy Scriptures. Horne's Rule quoted. [2] Institution of the Jewish Passover illustrative of that of the Eucharist. Dr. Wiseman's Objections examined......................................p. 74

LETTER VI.

NECESSITY OF THE FIGURATIVE INTERPRETATION.

The words, "This is my body," how understood by the modern advocates of a corporeal presence. Reasons for rejecting the literal interpretation of the words of institution and the necessity of adopting the figurative. [1] The words themselves do not indicate the operation of any change in the substance of the bread and wine. [2] The expressions, "which is given," and "which is shed," forbid the literal interpretation. [3] The words, "I will not drink henceforth of this fruit of the vine," also forbid it. [4] The disciples were commanded to celebrate the REMEMBRANCE of Christ. [5] The eucharistic elements CORRUPTIBLE, Christ's real body is not. [6] The real body of Christ not multipresent. [7] Christ has been offered but ONCE, and therefore not REPEATEDLY sacrificed. [8] The Scriptures regard the evidence of the senses as reliable and certain. Archbishop Tillotson quoted. [9] Scripture is not repugnant to reason, but this dogma is. [10] Omnipotence cannot be urged in defence of this doctrine, as its advocates presume to do. Paschasius, Hughes and Wiseman quoted. Tertullian and Origen quoted against this heretical practice. [11] Several Romish divines, as Cardinal Alliaco, Scotus, Cardinals Bellarmine and Cajetan, Fisher, Bishop of Rochester, and some others, confess the doctrine cannot be clearly proved from Scripture..................................p. 89

LETTER VII.

VIEWS OF THE ANTE-NICENE FATHERS.

I. Early corruption of Christianity. Tertullian and Cyprian's testimony. The Fathers of the Church to be regarded not as our judges in matters of faith, but as credible witnesses of facts. Ignatius, Origen, Cyril of Jerusalem, Augustine and Jerome quoted. II. Testimony of the early Fathers respecting the body and blood of Christ in the Eucharist. [1] Ignatius. [2] Justin Martyr. [3] Irenæus. [4] Tertullian. [5] Clemens Alexandrinus. [6] Origen. [7] Cyprian....................p. 117

LETTER VIII.

VIEWS OF THE POST-NICENE FATHERS.

I. Patristic testimonies continued. [1] Eusebius. [2] Macarius. [3] Cyril. [4] Nazianzen. [5] Ambrose. [6] Jerome. [7] Augustine. [8] Facundus. [9] Isidore. II. That the bread and wine do not lose their proper substance in virtue of consecration is expressly taught by, [1] Ephrem of Antioch. [2] Chrysostom. [3] Gelasius. [4] Theodoret. III. The change believed to be effected in these elements is compared to other changes where confessedly no transmutation of substance takes place, by, [1] Irenæus. [2] Cyril of Jerusalem. [3] Gregory of Nyssa. [4] Theodotus..p. 136

LETTER IX.

SECRET DISCIPLINE OF THE ANCIENT CHURCH.

Undue importance attached to the Secret Discipline. I. Its Origin. It may be traced back to the age of Tertullian. II. Its Nature. The things kept secret were, [1] Baptism. [2] Chrism. [3] Ordination of the clergy. [4] The Liturgy, or solemn prayers of the Church. [5] The Eucharist. [6] The doctrine of the Trinity and Incarnation, the Creed of the Church and Lord's Prayer. III. Its Reasons. [1] To guard the plainness and simplicity of the Christian rites from being despised. [2] To secure a veneration for the mysteries of the Church. [3] To excite a curiosity to become acquainted with them. [4] The inexperienced were not prepared for the reception of some of the sublime doctrines of Christianity. [5] Other things kept secret were considered inappropriate to the condition of the unbaptized. [6] The good of unbelievers thereby promoted. The Fathers to be interpreted as other writers..............................p. 155

LETTER X.

SEVERAL TERMS APPLIED TO THE EUCHARIST.

I. According to Roman Catholics the ancient Fathers applied the terms FIGURE, SIGN, SYMBOL, TYPE, ANTITYPE AND IMAGE to the Eucharist, with reference to the external appearances only, of the bread and wine. II. Objections to this interpretation. ¹ Such a sense of the terms when applied to sensible objects, is not sustained by good use. ² The Fathers themselves give them a meaning different from this, when they apply them to other things, besides the Eucharist. ³ They apply them to the *substance* of the elements. ⁴ They distinguish the *figure, sign,* &c., from the reality, and make the former inferior to the latter. III. Romanists also apply the term *species* to the external appearances of the bread and wine,— the Fathers, to their substance. IV. The former affirm that *accidents* exist without a subject,—the latter deny this. V. The Church of Rome differs from the ancients, in ascribing to the Eucharist properties and mode of being which the latter deny of all bodies.................................p. 175

LETTER XI.

THE TERMS BODY AND BLOOD OF CHRIST, AND THE EXPRESSION, MAKING THE BODY AND BLOOD OF CHRIST.

I. Several considerations showing that the Fathers, when speaking of the Body and Blood of Christ in the Eucharist, use these terms in a sense different from that given them by the Romish Church. ¹ They sometimes connect with them an indefinite and restrictive term, showing that they are not used in their full and proper sense. ² They give their *Reasons* for so calling them. ³ They sometimes point at something different from Christ's real Body and Blood. ⁴ They speak of his Body in the Eucharist as being sanctified, when the sacrament is consecrated; ⁵ Also, as being broken and divided into parts, neither of which can be true of his real and glorified Body. II. What is meant when the Fathers speak of *Making* the Body and Blood of Christ.......................p. 192

LETTER XII.

SEVERAL OTHER POINTS RELATING TO THE EUCHARIST.

I. When the ancients say the bread and wine are *changed* into Christ's Body and Blood, they are not to be understood as meaning a transubstantiation of them. For, ¹ They distinguish the change of a thing from the abolition of its substance. ² They use the same language when speaking of other changes, in which confessedly no transmutation of substance takes place. II. Other considerations confirmative of the foregoing. ¹ According to Romanists the wicked eat the real body of Christ,—the Fathers affirm the contrary. ² They differ also, when they distinguish the several ways of eating Christ's body. ³ The ancients teach Christ's corporal absence from the earth...................................p. 205

LETTER XIII.

EVIDENCE OF THE SENSES PATRISTICALLY CONSIDERED.

The Church of Rome rejects the evidence of the senses in the matter of the Eucharist. That the ancient Church did not is evident from the following. ¹ The Fathers argue the certainty of the evidence of the senses. ² They distinguish the outward sign from its invisible signification. ³ When they treat of Baptism and confirmation, they express themselves in the same manner, as when they speak of the Eucharist. ⁴ In express terms, they affirm the certainty of the evidence of the senses. ⁵ Augustine appeals to their evidence in the matter of the sacrament. ⁶ The language of Cyril and Chrysostom, apparently contradictory of this, reconciled...p. 221

LETTER XIV.

HALF-COMMUNION.

¹ Communion in one kind is contrary to the practice of the ancient Church. ² The Roman Church not excusable on the plea of her practice being one of mere discipline. ³ The ancient practice of communicating in both kinds, continued more than a thousand years. ⁴ The same usage proved from the practice of intinction, sucking the wine through quills, and, more anciently, the using of milk, instead of wine, by

some errorists. [5] Introduction of Half-Communion. [6] Arguments offered in defence of this usage examined. [7] The reasons assigned for it. [8] Some things *circumstantial* and others *essential*, to the right celebration of the sacrament. Roman Catholics omit what is *essential* and therefore do not rightly and fully celebrate it.................................p. 245

LETTER XV.

SACRIFICE OF THE MASS.

Sacrifice of the Mass stated, according to the Council of Trent. The word *sacrifice* figuratively used in scripture and by the ancients. That the term, when applied to the sacrament by the Fathers, is not used in its full and proper sense appears from the following. [1] They apply the same to the offerings made by the people. [2] They expressly designate the Eucharistic sacrifice, by the terms bread and wine. [3] The Eucharist is called a sacrifice, on account of those religious acts performed by the communicants. [4] And because it is a commemoration and sign of the sacrifice of Christ upon the cross. [5] The Jews and heathen reproached the early Christians for their want of *altars and sacrifices*. [6] When the Fathers call the Eucharist a sacrifice, they add such qualifying epithets as plainly indicate that they did not regard it as a proper sacrifice. The Apostles not made sacrificing priests at the institution of the Eucharist.................p. 269

LETTER XVI.

WORSHIP OF THE SACRAMENT.

Worship of the sacrament stated, as found in the standards of the Church of Rome. I. The practice is not authorized by any Scripture precept. II. In view of the uncertainties of due consecration and the contingencies to which the sacrament is confessedly liable, such worship is unreasonable. III. It has no sanction from the ancient Church as appears [1] From the universal silence respecting any such practice.

² From several usages wherein the ancient Catholic differed from the present Church of Rome. ³ From the objections made by the Christians against the inanimate and helpless objects of heathen worship, and the silence of the heathen respecting any worship of the sacrament. ⁴ From their teaching, expressly, that none but God is either invoked or worshiped. IV. Discussion of those passages usually quoted from the Fathers, to prove the worship of the Eucharist, and of the terms employed. V. Romanists argue a continued succession of miracles in this sacrament, such as are not claimed by the ancient and universal Church of Christ...p. 295

LETTER XVII.

THE RISE, PROGRESS AND ESTABLISHMENT OF THE DOCTRINE OF TRANSUBSTANTIATION.

I. Romanists consider it impossible that the change in the doctrine of the Eucharist affirmed by us, should ever have taken place. The possibility shown from ¹ General ignorance. ² Immorality. ³ Clerical ambition. ⁴ Persecutions. ⁵ Superstitions. II. The Rise, Progress and Establishment of Transubstantiation. ¹ The Sacraments were early abused by being unduly exalted. ² The idea of a physical change of the bread and wine, was first suggested by the heresy of Eutyches. ³ It was first introduced in the *eighth* century upon the occasion of a dispute about the worship of images. ⁴ In the *ninth* century a warm controversy arose in the Latin Church, respecting the *manner* in which the Body and Blood of Christ are present in the sacred supper. ⁵ In the *tenth* century, little or no controversy on the subject. ⁶ It was revived in the *eleventh* century, Berengarius being the principal leader in the opposition. ⁷ The doctrine remained unsettled in the *twelfth* century. ⁸ It was established by Innocent III, in the year 1215, at the fourth Lateran Council................p. 328

LETTERS ON THE EUCHARIST.

LETTER I.

SEVERAL TOPICS BRIEFLY NOTICED.

DEAR BROTHER:—Since the providence of God has brought us within limits somewhat more narrow and fraternal, and especially since I have had the privilege of perusing your published letter to a brother, containing the "Reasons for embracing the Catholic Religion, or the Motives which lately influenced you to unite yourself with the Roman Catholic Church," I have felt a desire to avail myself of the opportunity thus afforded of presenting my salutations to one in whom the circumstances referred to have awakened no small degree of interest. And as there is no other subject which, in point of importance, can compare with that which relates to the salvation of the soul, I trust you will allow me to make a few suggestions relative to some of the sentiments advanced in your "Reasons." This liberty I take the more readily because, both from the language of those published "Reasons" and from the knowledge of your character derived from other sources, I believe you to be sincere in your professions, and a lover of the truth as you understand it to be in Jesus, the author and finisher of our faith.

As an honest man acting from a full persuasion of the rectitude of his cause, you have expressed yourself frankly and boldly. Allow me to do the same without violating good nature, brotherly affection or Christian charity.

1. Without attempting a formal review of your letter, permit me to say, that you appear to me to have assumed as true what requires stronger proof than you have produced; namely, that the Roman Church is the only true church, to which alone the promises were made, within whose pale alone salvation can be found, and whose pastors are the only successors of the apostles, and alone authorized to teach mankind the doctrines of the gospel: and are infallible in their teaching. Were all this true, it would certainly be a sufficient reason for uniting with that church with all possible haste. But so far from the truth are your assumptions, that I believe—and with good reason—that their opposites are rather true. And you are hardly as charitable toward us Protestants as are some of your modern theologians, who suppose that the sincere ignorance of a few of us may turn the scales in our favor. You should have told us what constitutes a true Apostolical Church, and then given the most satisfactory and incontrovertible reasons for considering the Roman Church as entitled to a claim so exclusive and important; which you have not done, unless a few notes played upon the old succession harp be intended as the proof of your Apostolicity. Supposing it to be true—which indeed I have never seen proved—that your church can trace back an unbroken succession of legitimate bishops who have governed the church of Rome, what has this to do with unchurching and damning all those churches that do not acknowledge her claim to universal dominion? Do you not know that, after the ascension of our Saviour, in the days of the Apostles, numerous churches were founded by those holy men in various places in Europe, Asia, and Africa, which, in regard to ecclesiastical authority, were in nowise inferior to that founded at Rome? And do you not know that several centuries elapsed before the union

of most of them under one system of government now denominated the "Romish hierarchy?" Do you suppose the conditions of human salvation were changed by this consolidation of power? If not, why may we not now have churches independent of the Roman as well as during the first six centuries? I will not stop to discuss this question here, only adding: I invite you to prove that I am required, on pain of eternal damnation, to submit to any particular form of church government prescribed in the Holy Scriptures. And this you ought to do before proceeding deliberately to consign to the regions of hopeless misery all who do not acknowledge your claims.

No more can my salvation depend upon a continued succession of priests and bishops duly ordained by those already in office.

Suppose, my brother, a ship stopping at an island of the ocean inhabited by heathen, and a pious sailor should chance to impart to them some of the great truths of the Bible; they become interested and wish him to remain and instruct them farther in the gospel way; he assents, and multitudes believe on the Son of God, would such be in a salvable state; and should they die without a priest would they be saved according to this declaration: "For God so loved the world that he gave his only begotten Son, that whosoever believeth in him should not perish but have everlasting life." (John, iii: 16.) If so, then salvation is *possible* without the pale of your succession. I value the Christian ministry perhaps as highly as yourself, and believe it to be of divine appointment, and necessary to the complete success of the gospel in the world, as the officers of an army are to instruct, direct and govern those under their supervision. But when you make the eternal salvation of my soul depend upon the regular ordination and office of bishops and priests, you give them an undue importance in the economy of divine grace, and make them the lords over God's heritage by making their interposition essentially necessary to the impartation of heavenly grace. The salvation of my soul is a matter to be determined between myself and my Maker; and if he saves me from sin and death, I am safe, though all earth and hell unite for my destruction. For "when a man's ways please the Lord, he maketh even his enemies to be at peace with him." (Prov. xvi: 7.) "And who is he that will harm you, if ye be followers of that which is good?" (1 Peter, iii: 13.) "Go ye, therefore, and teach all nations, baptizing them in the name of the Father, and of the Son, and of the Holy Ghost; teaching them to observe ALL THINGS WHATSOEVER I have commanded you: and lo, I am with you always, even unto the end of the world." (Matt. xxviii: 19, 20.) This constitutes the commission of Christ to his ministers. They are not, therefore, our saviours, but the teachers of the Saviour's gospel. What essential difference, whether I learn this gospel from their oral instructions or from the written word, provided I understand and obey it? "For by grace are ye saved, through faith; and that not of yourselves: it is the gift of God." (Ephes. ii: 8.) I conclude, therefore, that a man *may* be saved without being a member of any regularly organized body of Christians, or ever having been taught, by an ordained minister, the way of salvation; admitting at the same time the necessity of a duly authenticated ministry for the most successful propagation of the gospel, and the duty of all who have it in their power to sustain such ministry, and unite themselves with a Christian church: not because such a union is absolutely essential to individual salvation, but because it conduces to personal good, and the welfare of the church. Is it not even so? Where, then, is your authority for confining the Divine mercy to this succession of Romish prelates? Such a limitation of the blessings procured by the atonement of Christ, is altogether opposed to the spirit and letter of God's Word. Forbid us not, therefore, an entrance into the Kingdom of grace and of glory because we follow not with you; for "of a truth I perceive that God is no respecter of persons; but in every nation, he that feareth him and worketh righteousness, is accepted with him." (Acts, x: 34, 35.)

2. You appear to me also to err when you represent religion and faith as consisting essentially in doctrine. The necessary consequence of this is, that all who do not receive this doctrine are destitute of saving faith, or true religion, than which nothing can be more dangerously false. St. Paul defines faith to be: "The substance of things hoped for, the evidence of things not seen." (Heb. xi: 1.) You say: "It is to believe, receive, and practice ALL that Jesus Christ has revealed, both great and small." Again this same Apostle says: "With the heart man believeth unto righteousness." (Rom. x: 10.) Your faith will doubtless lead to a Pharisaical righteousness, a simple reception and observance of the externals of Christianity, the letter of the gospel. St. Paul goes farther than this, and makes evangelical faith depend upon the exercise of the heart, or moral affections. His faith embraces the things "hoped for" and "not seen," yours, the things possessed and seen, to wit, the revealed word, and, by consequence, not "hoped for." You make it necessary for a man to "believe, receive, and practice ALL that Jesus Christ has revealed:" but what will be the final condition of those who may have heard only a part of what is revealed? Your definition makes it necessary for a man first to become thoroughly acquainted with ALL God's revela-

tion before he can exercise saving faith! Would not this exclude from salvation the mass of your own church, who, by being denied the free use of the Bible in their vernacular tongue, remain in ignorance of much of it till death? Happy for them, and others ignorant, that your definition is not an inspired one.

You will doubtless agree with me that the promise, "Lo, I am with you always, even unto the end of the world," applies only to those who teach "whatsoever" Christ "has commanded;" and if they teach things not "commanded," or contrary to the injunctions of God's Word, they have no claim to the promise, and are not true successors of the Apostles. For the succession of men in office without the succession of faith and doctrine scarcely deserves the name of succession.

3. Again: Why was not the doctrine of transubstantiation authorized by the church before the fourth Lateran Council, held A. D. 1215? After a considerable examination, I can find nothing of this doctrine, as now taught amongst you, for some six or seven centuries after Christ. On the contrary, the Fathers of those ages speak of the eucharistic elements as the *figure* of Christ's broken body and shed blood.

Now, if these elements are not really and truly the flesh and blood of Jesus Christ, comprehending his soul and divinity, according to your standards, are you not guilty of the dreadful sin of idolatry whenever you bow before the elevated wafer and worship it?

Dr. Milner's solution of this important and solemn question I consider a mere evasion. If the doctrine of transubstantiation be not true, he would excuse his church on the ground that they believe what they worship to be God. But may we not be as charitable toward those Israelites who worshiped the golden calf? Do not the heathen also worship what they believe to be the Supreme Being in the universe? Wherein, then, are they idolators more than the worshipers of the sacrament? "Thou shalt worship the Lord thy God, and Him only shalt thou serve," is the language approved by our Divine Redeemer. Now suppose the bread of the eucharist to become by consecration, the real and true body of Christ according to your literal interpretation of the words of institution, THIS IS MY BODY. Are you quite certain that the divine nature of our Lord is so associated with that newly created body and dwelling in it as to render it a proper object of supreme worship? You may say, that *reason* teaches that, on the principle of concomitance, wherever the body of Christ is, there also must be his divine substance. True, but what has *reason* to do with this dogma which, at every turn, contradicts all reason and sense, and transcends all human comprehension? If, contrary to the general laws of material bodies, the flesh of Jesus Christ can be in more places than one at the same time; if ten thousand individual and separate bodies can, at the same moment, be one and the same body; if a part of a thing can be equal to the whole, and the whole no greater than each of a thousand parts, when a separation is made, who can affirm any thing of its mode of existence?

If the presence of Christ's material and human flesh cannot be determined by reason and sense according to the usual mode of determining the presence or absence of things material, how shall the presence or absence of the divine essence be ascertained by reason? I mean such a presence as to authorize especial and local worship, supposing it to be right thus to contemplate the Deity.

It is vain to introduce our reason to ascertain an extraordinary presence of Christ's divinity, whose mode of existence infinitely transcends all human conception, and then set aside that reason—when we come to investigate what more properly belongs to it.

There being nothing revealed in the Holy Scriptures in regard to an especial presence of Christ's divinity in the eucharistic elements, we cannot from any exercise of our reason be more certain of such presence than, from the exercise of that same reason, we are of the absence of his natural flesh in this sacrament. If, therefore, we Protestants cannot, by an exercise of the reasoning faculty, certainly know that Christ's natural flesh is absent from the eucharist, much less can you certainly know that his divine substance is there present in a manner extraordinary. But if his divine substance is not thus present, then you incur the guilt of idolatry by worshiping the creature but not the Creator. How are you involved in doubtful uncertainty? If you employ your reason in order to ascertain the divine presence which is all the guide you have here, then you must use the same reason when you investigate the natural presence. But this faculty denies the natural presence with a thousand times more certainty than it affirms such a divine presence. So that whether you exercise your reason or not, you run the fearful risk of idolatry: for when you exercise this faculty, it tells you that Christ's natural flesh is not present in this sacrament; and if his flesh is not present, then his especial and divine presence is not there by concomitance. But if you reject reason altogether then you know nothing of the divine presence. And thus it is that "you worship you know not what."

Brother, I beseech you to review this whole matter in the light of God's Word and an enlightened reason, and see whether you can reconcile your multiplicity of Divinities under the form of wafers with the One Only God of the Bible. I say, an enlightened reason; for I believe the Bible to be addressed to our reason; and if it cannot by any just interpretation be reconciled with it, we may be allowed to entertain a doubt of its divine origin; for we may venture to affirm, that a wise and benevolent God would never require rational man to believe a revelation of facts contrary to his enlightened reason.

4. I perceive that you have also embraced the the doctrine of the infallibility of the church, because you find it "grounded on the infallible promises of God recorded in Holy Writ." For the same reason do I believe the church of God to be infallible; that is, never failing to exist, and never failing to hold and teach the essential doctrines of Christianity. Such a people has ever been upon earth since the day of Pentecost, and such a people will continue to inhabit this globe till Christ "shall come to be glorified in his saints, and to be admired in all them that believe." (2 Thess. i: 10.) This is the only infallibility that I can find "recorded in Holy Writ." Thus Christ said to his disciples: "Go ye, therefore, and teach all nations.... teaching them to observe all things whatsoever I have commanded you; and lo, I am with you always, even unto the end of the world." (Matt. xxviii: 19, 20.) "He saith unto them, But whom say ye that I am? And Simon Peter answered and said, Thou art the Christ, the Son of the living God. And Jesus answered and said unto him, Blessed art thou Simon Bar-jona; for flesh and blood hath not revealed it unto thee, but my father who is in heaven. And I say also unto thee, That thou art Peter; and upon this rock I will build my church; and the gates of hell shall not prevail against it." (Matt. xvi: 15–18.) "But the Comforter, the Holy Ghost, whom the Father will send in my name, he

shall teach you all things, and bring all things to your remembrance, whatsoever I have said unto you." (John, xiv: 26.) "Howbeit when he, the Spirit of Truth, is come, he will guide you into all truth .... and he will show you things to come." (John, xvi: 13.) Here our Lord enjoins upon his disciples to teach all nations all his commands with the annexed promise, that in so doing he will be with them all days even to the end of time. It is with them, and them only, that Christ continually abides, who receive and teach *all things whatsoever* he has enjoined; and against such the gates of hell shall never prevail, neither shall any pluck them out of his hands. For our Lord and Saviour declared to Peter: *upon this rock*—this confession of thine of my Messiahship, which indeed did not originate with thee, a feeble mortal, but was revealed to thee as a celestial idea from my father in heaven—*I will build my church, and the gates of hell shall not prevail against it.* This is one of those things to be taught, in order to enjoy Christ's presence, that we are built UPON THIS ROCK, the Son of God; "For other foundation can no man lay than that is laid, WHICH IS JESUS CHRIST," (1 Cor. iii: 11,) not St. Peter, as you would fain have us believe, unless by a metonomy we put Peter for the doctrine which he taught. Thus the Apostle Paul says: We "are built upon the foundation of the apostles and prophets, Jesus Christ himself being the chief corner-stone." (Eph. ii: 20.) In this sense only can we be said to be built upon Peter, together with the other apostles and those ancient and holy prophets, who spoke as they were moved by the Holy Ghost, and said: "The stone which the builders refused is become the head of the corner;" (Psal. cxviii: 22.) And, "Behold I lay in Zion for a foundation a stone, a tried stone, a precious corner-stone, a sure foundation." (Isa. xxxviii: 16.) This stone which God has laid "in Zion for a foundation" is no other than Christ "The Lord of hosts himself," (Isa. viii: 13,) who is a sanctuary for his people and a rock of offence to his enemies that reject him.

The two passages cited from the gospel according to St. John were addressed to the Apostles and intended to apply to them particularly as divinely inspired, as it is evident from the expressions: "Bring all things to your remembrance whatsoever I have said unto you," and "Show you things to come." The former can apply only to those to whom Christ spoke whilst upon earth, and the latter to those only who should be endowed with a prophetic spirit. But confessedly there is no one now living upon earth who conversed with Christ more than eighteen hundred years ago, or can justly claim the power to foretell future events; therefore these promises apply to none now living in their most enlarged sense, and cannot be used to prove an infallibility in teaching in the church, unless it can also be shown that those in whom such infallibility resides have the power of foretelling future events, and of calling to remembrance *all things whatsoever* Christ said unto his disciples whilst upon earth with them; both which are impossible. I conclude, therefore, that such an infallibility as you vainly profess is not to be proved from the records of Holy Writ, and has not existed in the world since the decease of the Apostles, who, for the establishing of the infant church, were endowed with the supernatural gifts of speaking divers tongues, working miracles, foretelling future events, and declaring infallibly what was according to the will of God, so that what they bound or forbid on earth was bound in heaven, and what they loosed or permitted on earth was also loosed in heaven. But you profess to work miracles and infallibly to bind and loose, why not speak in divers tongues and prophesy? It is remarkable that you should inherit a part of the supernatural gifts bestowed upon the Apostles, but not the whole. Let your Apostolical successors speak with tongues and foretell coming events, and then we will believe that they can work miracles and bind and loose, *but never before.* Your professed infallibility differs subjectively very much from that of the Apostles. They were individually inspired and infallible, but yours is a kind of collective infallibility, dependent for its operation upon certain conditions necessary to constitute an œcumenical council; as if the Holy Spirit cannot now operate as formerly upon individual mind and soul.

Your infallibility then requires a combination of human wisdom and judgment, otherwise it confessedly has no existence; but the infallible teaching of the Bible has come to us through individual mind, and our inward persuasion of its divine origin depends upon personal obedience and holiness. "If any man will do his will, he shall know of the doctrine, whether it be of God." (John, vii: 17.) "He that is of God heareth God's words." (John, viii: 47.) "And the sheep follow him; for they know his voice." (John, x: 4.) "And I give unto them eternal life; and they shall never perish, neither shall any man pluck them out of my hand." (John, x: 28.) "But ye have an unction from the Holy One, and ye know all things." (I Epist. John, ii: 20.)

We must then do his will if we wish to arrive at a knowledge of his doctrine; we must follow him if we will escape death and receive the gift of eternal life; we must have an unction from the Holy One if we will know all things necessary to be understood in order to be saved infallibly in heaven. And there is no difference whether he be Papist or Protestant; for it is written, IF ANY MAN will do his will HE SHALL KNOW of the doctrine whether it be of God; he shall have the Spirit himself bearing witness with his spirit that he is a child of God, if a child, then an heir of God, and joint heir with Christ.

This divine assurance that we are right is infinitely better than all the canons of all the councils ever held in Christendom: and without it all your pretensions to infallibility are but a sounding brass and a tinkling cymbal. But with it, be assured that you are infallibly saved from all fatal error, and thus continuing, will be finally and infallibly saved in heaven.

If these views be just and scriptural, then you have fallen into several very grave errors when discussing the infallibility of the church.

1. You apply the promises made to the Apostles only, in their full sense, to the whole church of God in all succeeding ages.

2. You call the Church of Rome the catholic or universal church which only is infallible in her teaching.

3. And then you confine the exercise of this prerogative to a definite circle of bishops convened after a certain manner, in a certain place, at a certain time, and for a certain purpose.

But your theory of church infallibility is overthrown by matter of fact.

The Council of Nice, held A. D. 325, and that of Ephesus, held A. D. 431, decreed with an anathema "That no new article *forever* shall be added to the creed or faith of Nice." But the Council of Trent, in A. D. 1545, added twelve new articles to this creed, and anathematized all who will not embrace them. The Council of Laodicea, held during the fourth century, determined on the canon of Scripture now received by Protestants. The council of Trent added to this canon the books of the Apocrypha.[1] Not less contradictory has been the legislation of councils respecting image worship, a sketch only of which can I now give, which, for the sake of convenience may be arranged tabularly. It was:

CONDEMNED.	ORDAINED.
By Council of Elvira, held between 300 & 400	By the Second Council of Nice, A. D., 787
By Council of Constantinople, held A. D., 754	By a Council at Constantinople, convened by Theodora during the minority of her son, - - - - A. D., 842
By Council, Frankfort, assembled by Charlemagne, - - A. D., 794	
By Council at Constantinople, assembled by Leo, A. D., 814	By another Council, held at Constantinople, - A. D., 879, the decision of the Second Council of Nice was confirmed and renewed.[2]
By Council at Paris, assembled by Louis, the Meek, A. D., 824	

Such contradictory legislation quite destroys your pretensions to infallibility. But I must notice your mode of argumentation whereby you arrive at results so convincing and satisfactory to your own mind.

In your letter of "Reasons" and "Motives" you say, p. 10: "Thus you perceive that my belief of the Church's infallibility, is grounded on the infallible promises of God, recorded in Holy Writ." And again, p. 18, you say: "It is evident, that the rule of faith left by the Saviour to the world, is the Word of God, whether *written* or *unwritten*, as interpreted by that infallible authority established by *Him*, viz: the Church, that is, the Apostles and the lawful successors of the Apostles in all ages, to the consummation of the world." After this you undertake to point out the "dreadful and tremendous results" of the Protestant rule of faith em-

[1] See Elliot on Romanism, vol. 1.
[2] See Faber's Difficulties of Romanism, note, pp. 41–44.

bracing the principle of private interpretation; and having attributed the great evils of Protestantism, and the "bold and alarming strides" which infidelity is making "through our beloved country;" to this principle, you add, p. 22, "I might thus trace and pursue this principle through a thousand other consequences equally alarming, but what I have advanced will suffice to show its natural, awful and horrid tendencies." From this language of yours two things are obvious.

First, that the doctrine of the infallibility of the Church is founded upon Scripture testimony.

Second, that the Scriptures are not to be interpreted by private and fallible judgment, but viz: "by that infallible authority established by God, the Church."

Now let me ask: In what manner could you, a private individual and fallible mortal, ascertain the meaning of those "infallible promises recorded in Holy Writ," except in the exercise of that very principle of private interpretation which you condemn and denounce? In other words, how could you ascertain from the written word of God that the church is infallible, except by your private and fallible reasoning? I answer, in no possible manner.

For you will observe that, at your starting point, you are required to prove that the Holy Scriptures teach the fact that such an infallible authority has been established, in order to be perpetuated "in all ages to the consummation of the world." And you cannot here assume that infallible authority to prove its own existence. You must prove this before you can introduce it into your argument as a thing known, unless it be a fact so self-evident that like axioms in science, it is incapable of being made more plain by any demonstration. But this is not the case, as all men know, and as you confess; for you say that it "is grounded on the infallible promises of God recorded in Holy Writ," and therefore, not upon itself as a self-evident verity. You have therefore, in denouncing the principle of private interpretation of Scripture, written out the sentence of your own condemnation, brought down your own boasted rule of faith to a level with that of Protestants, and sapped the very foundation of your pretended prerogatives.

For if what you know of the existence of such a divine attribute depends primarily upon the exercise of your private and fallible judgment, you cannot be made more certain of its existence than I am of its non-existence. The above reasoning holds good if you cast the proof of the Church's infallibility upon herself: for she cannot assume to be an infallible interpreter of Holy Scripture until she demonstrates her infallible authority from the Scripture.

Thus it is that the knowledge of your infallibility rests upon your private and fallible interpretation of the Holy Scriptures.

By the very necessity of the case, are you driven back and compelled to adopt the very principle which you regarded as having given rise to the "dreadful and tremendous results" of Protestantism.

How do you know that, by adopting this same "principle" you have not, in this case at least, run into "results" equally "dreadful and tremendous?" And in view of your liability to err, how dare you sit in judgment upon the present religious condition and eternal destiny of millions of your fellow-beings, who may be quite as competent to judge of the truth as yourself. "Therefore thou art inexcusable, O man, whosoever thou art that judgest: for wherein thou judgest another, thou condemnest thyself; for thou that judgest doest the same things. But we are sure that the judgment of God is according to truth AGAINST them that commit such things. And thinkest thou this, O man, that judgest them that do such things and doest the same, that thou shall escape the judgment of God?" Nay, verily: "For with what judgment ye judge ye shall be judged." Cease then I entreat you to render yourself a candidate for the Divine displeasure, by your simple attempts to unchurch and consign to perdition all who do not adopt your symbol of faith, and consent to your private interpretation of Holy Scripture. That for having thus done, you may find repentance unto life, is the sincere prayer of

Your Brother,

E. O. P.

LETTER II.

TRANSUBSTANTIATION STATED AND THE DISCUSSION OF THE SIXTH CHAPTER OF JOHN INTRODUCED.

Dear Brother:—Your communication has been been duly received, and I perceive by its contents, that of the several doctrines of your church briefly noticed by me, you have chosen to enter upon the defence of your favorite dogma of transubstantiation. This you introduce in the following language: You ask "why was not the doctrine of transubstantiation authorized by the Church before the fourth Lateran Council, 1215." It was believed by the Church from the beginning: that is, the meaning and thing signified by the word, viz., the "Real Presence." The term, I grant, was not used before—the dogmas of the Catholic Church are fixed—there is no being on earth capable of making a new article of faith. If there is a new term introduced, it is in order to define more clearly the belief of the church on that point. You further say: "that you can find nothing of this doctrine as now taught for the first six or seven centuries; but, on the contrary, the fathers of those ages speak of the eucharistic elements as the *figure* of Christ's broken body and shed blood." This I deny *in toto;* and it is conclusive to my mind that you have never investigated the subject, or you never could have arrived at such results: results so diametrically opposed to all history. To this you presently add: "Our divine Redeemer has said:" "unless you eat my flesh and drink my blood, you shall not have life in you."—I trust in God that I shall be able to present to your mind such an amount of testimony of the truth of this dogma, that you will be obliged to confess, that it is the part of enlightened wisdom to admit that it was taught, believed, and practised by the Apostles themselves, and in every subsequent age, and consequently, that my views on this point are not singular, but in union with all Christendom in every age—and that I am more rational in believing it, than to reject it.— Christ our Lord instituted this sacrament when at his last supper "He took bread, blessed and broke, and gave to his disciples, saying, take, eat, *for this is my* body, which shall be [is] broken for you. In like manner he took the cup, blessed, and gave it to them saying: drink ye all of this, &c. &c. Again: "The bread which I will give is my flesh for the life of the world." St Paul says: "Whosoever shall eat this bread or drink the chalice of the Lord unworthily, shall be guilty of the *body* and *blood* of the Lord. For he that eateth and drinketh unworthily, eateth and drinketh judgment to himself, not discerning the body of the Lord." This comprises all your Scripture defence of the doctrine in question, from which you pass immediately to the ancient fathers.

Having denied *in toto* the correctness of my statement, that the fathers speak of the Eucharistic elements as the *figure* of Christ's broken body and shed blood, you have devolved upon me the task of verifying my assertion, which I hope to do in its proper place.

It will be necessary however first to consider the Scripture doctrine of the Sacrament of the Eucharist in order to show the inapplicability of the passages cited by you, to your purpose; and to render the reasons for my saying that "I can find nothing of this doctrine as now taught amongst you for some six or seven centuries after Christ."

For it is an undoubted fact, that the Scriptures of the New Testament contain the earliest record of the institution and doctrine of this Christian Sacrament; so that they constitute the starting point whether inquiries partake of the historical or theological. Nay, whatsoever is clearly demonstrated to be contained in the revealed Word of God must be acknowledged as decisive ; and the evidence gathered from other sources can be regarded only as auxiliary to the discovery of its divine, truth and confirmatory of the correctness of our deductions.

2. For what reason I know not, you appear to me as if you wish to change the point at issue when you say, that "the meaning and thing signified by the word" transubstantiation is the "Real Presence." The doctrine of transubstantiation does, indeed, necessarily embrace that of the Real Presence; but the doctrine of the Real Presence does not thus necessarily comprehend that of transubstantiation. God may, by his spirit and power, be really and effectively present in a thing without operating any substantial change in that thing. "If a man love me," says Christ, "he will keep my words: and my Father will love him, and we will come unto him, and make our abode with him." (John xiv: 23; compare Rom. viii: 22, and I Ep. John iv: 13, 15, 16.) So we may infer a Real Presence in that ancient inner Sanctuary into which the high priest alone entered once every year, not without blood, which he offered for himself, and for the errors of the people. (Heb. ix: 7.) But no one supposes hence a transubstantiation, either of man or the ancient Sanctum Sanctorum.

We may then admit a Real and sanctifying Presence of the Holy Spirit in the consecrated Eucharist, without subscribing to a transubstantiation of the elements of bread and wine. It would not, however, be an easy task to prove from Scripture any change whatever, except that of circumstance, in the consecrated elements; so that a considerable latitude of opinion may be allowed in a matter concerning which Holy Scriptures are silent. For who can tell whether, in virtue of consecration, any change at all is effected in the thing thus set apart for sacred purposes, and if any, what is its precise nature and extent? It is true that ancients did pray for the descent of the Holy Spirit upon the elements bread and wine, set apart for religious use; and they doubtless believed that the sanctifying spirit of God did descend, and so enter them as to constitute a Real and effectual Presence. I do not deny that some Protestants hold to such a presence of the sanctifying power of God in the Eucharist; but they do utterly renounce, as the leading heresy of your Church, the doctrine of transubstantiation; by which is meant not simply a Real Presence as above considered, but the change of the substance of the bread and wine, in virtue of the words: *Hic corpus meum est*, &c., into that real and substantial body and blood of our Lord Jesus Christ, who was born of the Virgin Mary, suffered under Pontius Pilate, rose again, and ascended into heaven, to be seated at the right hand of his Father, where he ever liveth to make intercession for us. Nay, your church teaches that Christ entire is contained in each species, and in every particle of the same when a separation is made, by reason of that natural concomitance which is supposed ever to subsist between his human and divine nature.

The Council of Trent, at its thirteenth session, holds the following language touching this dogma:

Canon I. "If any one shall deny that in the sacrament of the most holy Eucharist, there are truly, really and substantially contained the body and blood, together with the soul and divinity of our Lord Jesus Christ, and therefore whole Christ;

but shall say that he is in it only as in a sign or figure, or by his power; let him be accursed."

Canon II. "If any one shall say that in the most holy sacrament of the Eucharist the substance of the bread and wine remains together with the body and blood of our Lord Jesus Christ, and shall deny that wonderful and singular conversion of the whole substance of the bread into his body, and the whole substance of the wine into his blood, the species [appearances] of bread and wine only remaining; which conversion the Catholic Church does indeed most fitly call Transubstantiation; let him be accursed."

Canon III. "If any one shall deny that, in the venerable sacrament of the Eucharist, whole Christ is contained under each species, and under every part of each species when a separation is made; let him be accursed."[1]

It is this affirmed "wonderful and singular conversion of the whole substance of the bread into the body, and the whole substance of the wine into the blood" of our Lord Jesus Christ that Protestants deny; and it is this feature of the doctrine especially

---

[1] Can. I. Si quis negaverit in sanctissimæ eucharistiæ sacramento contineri vere, realiter, et substantialiter, corpus et sanguinem una cum anima et divinitate Domini nostri Jesu Christi, ac proinde totum Christum; sed dixerit tantummodo esse in eo ut in signo, vel figura, aut virtute; anathema sit.

Can. II. Si quis dixerit in sacrosancto eucharistiæ sacramento remanere substantiam panis et vini una cum corpore et sanguine Domini nostri Jesu Christi, negaveritque mirabilem illam et singularem conversionem totius substantiæ panis in corpus, et totius substantiæ vini in sanguinem, manentibus dumtaxat speciebus panis et vini: quam quidem conversionem catholica ecclesia aptissime Transubstantionem appellat; anathema sit.

Can. III. Si quis negaverit in venerabile sacramento eucharistiæ, sub unaquaque specie, et sub singulis cujusque speciei partibus, separatione facta, totum Christum contineri; anathema sit.

that constitutes the true point now at issue between us.

II. You quote the language used by our Saviour in that very remarkable discourse of his in the synagogue of Capernaum, in which he affirmed the necessity of eating his flesh and drinking his blood; and also that employed by him at the institution of this holy sacrament; and it might be supposed from your quoting these words of the Saviour without any remark, that you consider their literal acceptation so perfectly self-evident as to need neither qualification nor comment.

However well satisfied you may be in regard to receiving Christ's words on both these occasions in a literal sense, it is a well known fact that a very respectable portion of Christendom understand these words as spoken figuratively; and I will add that you would know, if rightly informed, that this sense has been attached to these words ever since they were uttered by our Lord and Saviour.

1. In his discourses to the Jews, it was usual with our divine Teacher to avail himself of well known practices and current modes of expression, in order to make himself understood, and give greater force to the truths delivered. And sometimes he seized upon recent or passing events, and employed the very words of the addressed to convey some grand doctrine of Christianity, giving to such language a sense more elevated and spiritual than what had just before been given it by his hearers. Somewhat such is the character of that discourse which he addressed to the Jews at Capernaum, recorded in the sixth chapter of St. John's Gospel; and it is therefore exceedingly important to keep in mind the particular circumstances that gave occasion to it, in order to ascertain its import and true meaning.

Having witnessed the miraculous cures wrought by Jesus upon them that were diseased, a multitude of five thousand men, besides women and children, assembled in a retired place near Bethsaida, and when the evening drew nigh the disciples advise their Master to dismiss the people and permit them to go into the villages and procure for themselves food; but he embraces the opportunity to perform one of the most extraordinary miracles that he ever wrought. From five loaves of barley bread and the flesh of two small fishes he feeds this large multitude of people, who, in consequence of this, said: "This is of a truth that Prophet that should come into the world;" and in their selfish and sensual worldliness they would fain have taken him and made him their King; but he dismisses them and retires to pray in a place of solitude. At even-tide his disciples embark in their vessel, in order probably to pass along the lake to some selected point from which, taking Jesus, they designed to cross over to Capernaum, which was situated on the western shore; but an unexpected storm of wind drove them far into the lake where Jesus appeared to them at the fourth watch of the night walking upon the water. Being received into the ship the sea became calm, and they soon reached their place of destination.

On the day following the excited multitude, not finding Jesus, and knowing that he did not embark with the disciples, and having seen no other vessel except that occupied by them, procure other boats and cross over to Capernaum in search of him who had so miraculously supplied them with food the previous day. Having found him, they exclaimed in apparent wonder: *Rabbi, when camest thou hither?* Discerning their real character, he accuses them of unworthy and selfish motives, and exhorts them to seek earnestly the spiritual and everlasting food which could be imparted only by himself, whose authority had been attested and approved by God. "Verily, verily, I say unto you, ye seek me, not because ye saw the miracles, but because ye did eat of the loaves and were filled. Labor not for the meat which perisheth, but for that meat which endureth unto everlasting life, which the Son of Man will give unto you; for him hath God the Father sealed;" (verses 26, 27.)

The figure selected by our Lord whereby to convey his exhortation, is evidently taken from the food which had been miraculously supplied to the multitude the preceding day. This agrees with his practice on other occasions, a striking illustration of which we have in his conversation with the Samaritan woman at Jacob's well, whom he asked for a drink, and to whom he immediately after recommends the blessings of the Spirit under the figure of living or running water. (John iv: 10.) On another occasion he relieved a blind and dumb demoniac, and afterwards illustrates the deplorable condition of the Jews under the idea of an evil spirit taking his seven companions, and returning with redoubled fury to the residence from which he had been expelled. (Matt. xii.)

This usage of our Lord, in improving recent or passing events to supply himself with figures appropriate for the impressive delivery of some important truth, deserves particular attention, as it may throw much light on some parts of this discourse. When his hearers, in evident allusion to his words, inquire: "What shall we do that we may work the works of God?" he immediately replies: "This is the work of God, that ye believe on him whom he hath sent," (verses 28, 29.) No work is more important for you to do, and none more acceptable to God than right faith in him whom my Father hath sent. This is the true principle and germ of all other works, that you assent to the evidence set before you, acknowledge and embrace me as your divine Messiah, sent by God to be the Saviour of a lost world. This is the introductory proposition laid down by Christ in this important discourse, first expressed in figurative language under the idea of *working for imperishable food*, and afterward stated in literal terms in reply to the proposed interrogation. And this leading idea of the discourse, this fundamental truth of Christianity, is continually kept before the mind and repeated again and again, with the same change of expression. Thus, he promises blessings to the believer when he says of him in a figure: "He that *cometh* to me shall never hunger;" and adds, in proper terms: "He that *believeth* on me shall never thirst," (verse 35.) A little after using the same figure, he says of the believer: "Him that cometh to me I will in no wise cast out," (v. 37;) and again, literally, he says: "Every one that seeth the Son and *believeth on him* may have everlasting life," (v. 40.) And yet again, in reply to their murmurings, he affirms the necessity of the Father's influence to produce this faith, and adds with the same figure: "No man can *come to me*, except the father who hath sent me draw him; and I will raise him up at the last day," (v. 44;) and, "every man therefore that hath heard, and hath learned of the Father, *cometh unto me*," (v. 45.) Then once more, without a figure, he promises to such the full blessings of the Gospel: "Verily, verily, I say unto you, he that *believeth on me* hath everlasting life," (v. 47.) True faith in Christ then is the main principle advanced in this divine discourse; and it is urged as the *sine qua non* of a glorious resurrection and life everlasting.

2. How do his carnal hearers receive this spiritual and sublime doctrine of our blessed Redeemer? Do

they show themselves prepared to give glory to God for the wisdom which they have heard, and to acknowledge that he who spoke to them and wrought such a notable miracle in feeding them, was indeed the Christ? On the contrary, although they had but the day before witnessed one of the most astonishing miracles ever wrought for the confirmation of the truth, they disregard it and demand another, that they might see and believe, (v. 30.) Such a miraculous supply of their wants as they had experienced for one day did not suffice to convince them of his unlimited power and goodness as the expected Messiah. They doubtless supposed that he would give them a continual supply of temporal delicacies, such as was afforded to their ancestors by the manna. This is rendered highly probable from the following: "Many affirm, says Rab. Mayemon, that the hope of Israel is this, That the Messiah shall come and raise the dead; and they shall be gathered together in the garden of Eden, and shall eat and drink and satiate themselves all the days of the world. There the houses shall be all builded with precious stones; the beds shall be made of silk, and the rivers shall flow with wine and spicy oil. He made manna to descend for them, in which was all manner of tastes; and every Israelite found in it what his palate was chiefly pleased with. If he desired *fat* in it, he had it. In it, the young man tasted *bread*, the old man *honey*, and the children oil. So shall it be in the *world to come*, (*i. e.* the days of the Messiah.) He shall give Israel peace, and they shall sit down in the garden of Eden, and all nations shall behold their condition; as it is said, *My servants shall eat, but ye shall be hungry*, &c., Isa. lxv: 13."[1] In the days of the Messiah they expected to enjoy a life of ease and

---

[1] Lightfoot, as cited by Clarke, in Comment on the place.

luxury, to lie on beds of silk, to recline and EAT in houses of precious stone. So that when our Lord, in allusion to the ancient manna, says: "The bread of God is he that cometh down from heaven, and giveth life unto the world," (v. 33,) they exclaim: "Lord, evermore give us this bread," (v. 34.) And when Jesus explains his language and tells them that he is the bread of life which came down from heaven, they murmur and inquire, "Is not this the son of Joseph, whose father and mother we know?" (v. 42.)

Such being the character of those to whom this discourse was addressed, we cannot fail to see the propriety of the repeated and varied *instruction* made use of by our Lord in order to disengage their minds from those carnal thoughts which they had learned to associate with the Messiah, and lead them to contemplate and understand the spiritual design of his mission, and the heavenly character of his doctrine.

Having premised thus much concerning the circumstances which gave occasion to this discourse, the usage of our Lord in conducting his addresses, the main principle here advanced, and the character of his auditors, let us with a little more particularity notice it throughout.

3. Our divine Redeemer, perceiving the sensual and unworthy motives of those Jews that followed him, opens his discourse to them with a severe rebuke. "Verily, verily, I say unto you, ye seek me, not because ye saw the miracles, but because ye did eat of the loaves, and were filled," (v. 26.) You have crossed the Tiberian sea, having witnessed the miracles wrought in proof of my Messiahship, not so much because you are interested in being redeemed from your sins and filled with spiritual grace, as you are in elevating me to distinction as a king to deliver you from temporal evil, and ad-

minister to the gratification of your animal appetites. For this purpose I have not appeared in the world; I exhort you therefore to "labor not for the meat which perisheth, but for that meat which endureth unto everlasting life, which the Son of man will give you; for him hath God the Father sealed," (v. 27.) They inquire: "What shall we do that we may work the works of God?" (v. 28.) Jesus immediately answered: "This is the work of God, that you BELIEVE on him whom he hath sent," (v. 29.) No work is so important, none so acceptable to God as right FAITH in him whom he has sent into the world, bearing the impress of his own seal, and duly accredited by incontestable miracles. Understanding him to speak of himself, they ask: "What sign showest thou then, that we may see, and believe thee? What dost thou work? Our fathers did eat manna in the desert; as it is written, He gave them bread from heaven to eat," (verses 30, 31.) "Thou hast fed five thousand men with five loaves and two small fishes, we acknowledge; but what is this in comparison of what Moses did in the desert, who for forty years fed more than a million persons with heavenly bread; do something like this, and we will believe on THEE, as we have believed Moses."[1]

To this unreasonable demand, our Lord replies that it was not Moses, but God, who gave the manna, that he now offers them the true bread of heaven, the manna being only a material symbol of the spiritual reality, which is intended, not like that ancient food, to contribute to the sustenance of a few in the present life, but to afford eternal life to the whole world. Having no internal character adapted to the perception of his meaning, and dwelling upon the carnal idea of corporeal food to be

[1] Clarke Com. in loco.

3*

continually imparted by their Messiah, by which the present life should be sustained without toil, they exclaim, "Lord, evermore give us this bread," (v. 34.)

He immediately corrects their error, declaring himself to be the bread of life just spoken of, and promises an exemption from spiritual want to the believer. He then, as at the beginning of his discourse, rebukes them for a want of FAITH in him, although they had been eye-witnesses of his miracles, which were sufficient to convince them of his Messiahship, provided their hearts were rightly disposed to appreciate his character and receive his doctrines. "But I said unto you, that ye also have seen me, and believe not," (v. 36.) In the verse following he teaches an important truth, namely, that those who receive his doctrine and believe in him are influenced so to do by his Father, which plainly intimates that their want of disposition to come to Christ and receive him as their Messiah arose from an unwillingness to be drawn by the gracious influences of the Spirit, they having resisted his drawings by passion, prejudice and worldly ambition. Now he assumes the prerogatives of the divine Messiah, and affirms that he will in no wise reject him who, through the influence of the Father, believes in him, but will raise him up at the last day according to the will of God, for the accomplishment of which he "came down from heaven," (verses 37–40.) Truths glorious and sublime—a Saviour engaging to "cast out" none that yield to the influence of the Father and believe on him; but promising to accord to such everlasting life, and a happy resurrection. At the announcement of these great consoling truths of Christianity, did they shout for joy and welcome the messenger? No. "The Jews then *murmured* at him, because he said, I am the bread which came down from heaven, And they said, Is not this Jesus, the son of Joseph, whose father and mother we know? How is it then that he saith, I came down from heaven?" (verses 41, 42.) What slowness of heart to believe. No wonder that Jesus, after checking their murmurings, insists on the necessity of the Father's gracious influence in order to the exercise of saving faith in their divine Redeemer.

The Father must draw and teach by his Spirit; and he that will be saved, must hear his instructions, and, with the docility of a diligent pupil, learn his will, accept the offered salvation, be justified by faith, and nourished continually by the bread of life in order to escape death, to be raised up at the last day, and to be made a partaker of eternal life, (verses 44-46.) All this is evidently to be understood by our Saviour's instruction to the unbelieving Jews.

The divine instructor now resumes the primary and leading topic of his discourse, which he introduces with the strong declaration, "Verily, verily, I say unto you, he that believeth on me hath everlasting life," (v. 47.) The proper object of your faith is he who being in the bosom of the Father, having seen him, and been sent by him from heaven with full authority and power to give eternal life to them that believe in him. He is the food that imparts and sustains this spiritual and everlasting life. However extraordinary was that manna which your fathers ate in the desert, it was incapable of sustaining even their animal life, whereas the antitype of that earthly food which has no association with this world but comes down from its own native heaven, is able to give and preserve a life which is beyond the reach of death. I who address you am that life-giving and unfailing food "which came down from heaven," (verses 47-51.)

Both Protestants and Romanists agree in interpreting the former part of this discourse of *believing in Christ*. But the latter contend that, at the forty-eighth or fifty-first verse, "a perfect transition is made from believing in him to a real eating of his body and drinking of his blood in the sacrament of the Eucharist," while "the generality of Protestants maintain that no such transition takes place."[1]

Do you ask, why I have discussed that part of this discourse, upon whose doctrine both parties are agreed? I answer: In order to point out the *circumstances* which occasioned the "sacred lecture," the *leading topic* of the discourse, our Lord's *method of instruction*, and the *character* of his hearers; a just knowledge of all which will greatly help to a proper understanding of what is contained in the sequel. It is hardly necessary here to remind you that the *leading topic* of discourse is FAITH in Christ inculcated to FAITHLESS Jews.

Yours truly,
E. O. P.

[1] Wiseman on the Real Presence, Section 1, p. 50.

LETTER III.

DISCUSSION OF JOHN VI CONTINUED.

DEAR BROTHER:—You are doubtless aware that if a transition in the discourse of our Lord could be proved, either from the structure, phraseology, or scope and evident intention of the language used by the speaker, it would not necessarily follow that a manducation of the real flesh, and a drinking of the real blood of our Lord in the Eucharist was intended. For, although the strong and very expressive language—"eat the flesh of the Son of man and drink his blood"—should be interpreted as relating to the Eucharist, it might be understood of an internal and spiritual feeding upon him by faith in the use of the mystic symbols of his body and blood. There are, however, several difficulties in explaining the latter part of our Lord's discourse as referring to the Eucharist in either sense.

The word used here is *flesh*, while *body* is always employed elsewhere in the New Testament, as in the words of institution as recorded by the Evangelists and quoted by St. Paul. Had the divine speaker intended in this discourse a particular reference to the eucharistic body, it is but reasonable to suppose that he would have employed the same word here as he subsequently did at the institution of this sacrament. It is true the thought, were it intended, might have been expressed by either term, and therefore the use of the word *flesh* might have been rather circumstantial than otherwise; still however we must feel that if the Eucharist had been intended the sense would have been clearer if the word *body* had been used as elsewhere.

2. In verse 51, Christ says: "and the bread that *I will give* is my flesh, which *I will give* for the life of the world." This cannot be interpreted of the Eucharist, for his flesh or body was not then given when this sacrament was instituted; for the inspired writers plainly declare that the offering of the body of Christ was made once for all by his death upon the cross. (See Heb. vii: 27; ix: 25-28; x: 10, 12, 14; 1 Pet. ii: 24.) If therefore Christ's body has been given but once as a sacrifice for sin when he made a voluntary offering of himself upon the cross, it is certain that verse 51 cannot be explained of the Eucharist, but must be interpreted of the *gift* which he made of himself at his death. And this exposition agrees with the use of the word in other places. Thus, it is said, "The Son of man came to *give* his life a ransom for many,"—"he *gave* himself a ransom for all,"—"who *gave* himself for our sins,"—"who *gave* himself." (Matt. xx: 28; Mark, x: 45; 1 Tim. ii: 6; Col. i: 4; Tit. ii: 14.) This meaning of the term accords with general usage and harmonizes with the context. If then the language of verse 51 must be explained of something different from the bread of the Eucharist, it follows that we must also understand the eating and drinking of Christ's flesh and blood afterward mentioned as relating also to something different, for the connection is so intimate that we are compelled to admit that both must be understood of the same topic.

3. If this discourse of our Lord be explained of the Eucharist, it is not easy to account for the fact that the writer of this gospel has elsewhere made no mention of the institution of this sacrament. Indeed it is wholly improbable, and seems quite unnatural, that St. John should give the relation he has done of

this discourse of Christ, if he understood it as spoken of the Eucharist, without taking any notice of its institution. And especially is this consideration strengthened when we reflect that the eating and drinking urged in this chapter is represented as absolutely necessary in order to obtain Christian privileges and receive spiritual and everlasting life. And, on the other hand, if this part of our Lord's discourse was understood by the other Evangelists as referring primarily to the Eucharist, it is remarkable that they should have given no account of it. So naturally would the institution have suggested the discourse, that it is difficult, on this theory, to assign any good reason for its omission.

4. Another difficulty, and closely connected with that just noticed, arises from the fact that the Eucharist was not yet instituted. The general tenor of our Lord's discourse plainly shows that when he urges the duty and necessity of eating his flesh and drinking his blood, he means that those very persons addressed should, without delay, do the thing enjoined. From the remarks made in a former communication (Letter II) it is evident that the whole discourse preserves a proper unity of subject. The words, "this is that bread which came down from heaven; not as your fathers did eat manna, and are dead: he that eateth of this bread shall live forever," verse 58, naturally refer us back to verses 50 and 51: "This is the bread which cometh down from heaven, that a man may eat thereof and not die. I am the living bread which came down from heaven;" and again to verses 31–33: "Our fathers did eat manna in the desert; as it is written, He gave them bread from heaven to eat. Then Jesus said unto them, Verily, verily, I say unto you, Moses gave you not that bread from heaven; but my Father giveth you the true bread from heaven. For the bread of God is he who cometh

down from heaven and giveth life unto the world." It being evident, therefore, that an indissoluble connection exists between these several parts of the discourse, it is clear that our Lord does not, in his most emphatic and solemn manner, here insist upon the necessity, in order to secure union with him here and eternal life in heaven, of observing an institution and obeying a command which were not to be promulgated until a full year after, but is urging an immediate observance of the command with which he introduces the discourse: "Labor for the meat which endureth unto everlasting life," (v. 27,) which he afterwards explains of believing on him whom God hath sent, (v. 29.)

To this argument of ours that the Eucharist was not yet instituted, Dr. Wiseman replies in the language of Dean Sherlock, that "our Saviour said a great many things to the Jews in his sermons, which neither they nor his disciples could understand when they were spoken, though his disciples understood them after he was risen," (p. 138.) Dr. Wiseman instances, as an example of similar conduct in our Lord, his conversation with Nicodemus which, he affirms, "took place before baptism was instituted, and yet the necessity of it is there declared." He continues, "Now, no one has ever yet thought of denying that the regeneration there mentioned referred to baptism, on the ground that this sacrament had not yet been instituted," (p. 140.)

He assumes here what he could not prove, namely, that the baptism of Christ was not instituted at the time of this interview with Nicodemus. For it is in the highest degree probable that the baptism of Christ was in use before the conversation with Nicodemus. The first direct mention that is made of our Lord's baptizing is, indeed, in the verse that follows the account of this interview; but the apparently incidental manner in which the practice is introduced, makes it extremely probable that he had already sanctioned the rite by using it in the introduction of his followers to discipleship. "After these things came Jesus and his disciples into the land of Judea; and there he tarried with them and baptized," (John, iii: 22.) "Behold the same baptizeth, and all men come to him," (v. 26.) And, "When therefore the Lord knew how the Pharisees had heard that Jesus made and baptized more disciples than John, (though Jesus himself baptized not, but his disciples,)" (iv: 1, 2.) These passages show the usage of this rite immediately or shortly after the interview with the Jewish ruler; and there can be no reasonable doubt that those disciples who had before witnessed his miraculous power and *believed on him*, (ii: 11,) made the same public profession of their faith as did they who became his disciples after the interview; in other words, that they received his baptism. When therefore Dr. Wiseman asserts that the discourse of our Lord to the Jews, recorded in the sixth chapter of St. John, "stands in the same relation to the institution of the Eucharist, as the conference with Nicodemus does to the institution of baptism," (p. 140,) he makes a statement which is entirely gratuitous, and without the shadow of a proof.[1]

Besides, Nicodemus must have been familiar with the rite of baptism, as it had, for a long time, been practiced among the Jews; "and for the very same *end*," says Lightfoot, "as it now obtains among Christians, namely, that by it proselytes might be admitted into the church; and hence it was called *baptism for proselytism*."

"All the Jews assert, as it were with one mouth, that all the nation of Israel were brought into

[1] Turner's Essay on our Lord's Discourse, p. 69.

covenant, among other things, by baptism. Israel (said Maimonides, the great interpreter of the Jewish law) was admitted into the covenant by three things, namely, by circumcision, baptism, and sacrifice. Circumcision was in Egypt, as it is said, 'None uncircumcised shall eat of the passover.' Baptism was in the wilderness, before the giving of the law, as it is said, 'Thou shalt sanctify them to-day and to-morrow, and let them wash their garments.' 'Whensoever any heathen will betake himself, and be joined to the covenant of Israel, and place himself under the wings of the Divine Majesty, and take the yoke of the law upon him, voluntary circumcision, baptism, and oblation are required; but if it be a woman, baptism and oblation.'" Maimonides, Issure Biah, c. 13.[1]

Should all this, however, be questioned, still it is a matter of fact that John, as the forerunner of the Messiah, had been publicly baptizing, and that crowds had flocked to him from Judea and Jerusalem. The use of water, therefore, in admitting to discipleship must necessarily have been known to Nicodemus, and he might readily have applied the well known fact as explanatory of our Lord's language of being born of water. Dr. Wiseman is therefore exceedingly unfortunate when he selects this allusion to baptism as an example illustrative of the affirmed incomprehensible language of the latter portion of the discourse at Capernaum. The answer of Nicodemus, *How can these things be?* was doubtless made with reference to the spiritual regeneration—the *heavenly things*—spoken of.

5. The consequences of partaking or not partaking the divine food as stated by our Lord, do not harmonize with the interpretation which refers this passage principally or wholly to the Eucharist.

---

[1] See Lightfoot's Horæ Hebraicæ, in Matt. iii and xxviii.

"If any man eat of this bread, he shall live forever," (v. 51.) "Whoso eateth my flesh, and drinketh my blood, hath eternal life; and I will raise him up at the last day," (v. 54.) "Verily, verily, I say unto you, except ye eat the flesh of the Son of man, and drink his blood, ye have no life in you," (v. 53.) Even admitting that, although this is said absolutely, yet right disposition and other conditions requisite to what is called *sacramental feeding* are implied; nevertheless, such great and glorious promises on the one hand, and so solemn a warning and formidable results on the other, are never set forth in the New Testament as the direct consequences of observing or neglecting any one outward institution. Certainly this is so in regard to the sacrament of baptism. We do not read, "He that is baptized shall be saved," but, "he that *believeth* and is baptized," while we do read, "he that *believeth not* shall be damned," and "whosoever shall call upon the name of the Lord shall be saved." And it is particularly worthy of notice, that when baptism is represented as *cleansing, purifying,* and *saving,* there is usually added some explanatory word or phrase, guarding us against attaching such effects to this sacrament however rightly performed.

Thus, when Ananias requires Saul to "arise and be baptized and wash away his sins," he adds, "calling on the name of the Lord," (Acts, xxii: 16,) which teaches the necessity of prayer in connection with outward profession. And when St. Paul speaks of Christ as "having purified his church by the washing of water," he adds, "through the word," (Ephes. v: 26,) implying the efficacy of the truth in producing the result. St. Peter also, when he speaks of "baptism saving us," is careful to introduce the caveat, "not the putting away the filth of the flesh, but the answer of a good conscience towards God," and adds, "by the resurrection of

Jesus Christ." (I Peter, iii : 21.) Here inward purity is presumed to exist with the external act, and Christ's resurrection is represented to be the procuring cause of the blessing.

At the institution of this eucharistic sacrament, our Saviour did indeed command its observance as a memorial of himself, but he did not then attach to an obedience of this injunction simply, the rewards of everlasting life and a resurrection from the dead; nor did he threaten a want of this life to those, who should never commemorate the sacrificial death of their Saviour God. Did the apostolic church believe that they ate the very flesh and drank the very blood of Christ in the Eucharist, it is difficult to conceive how the Corinthian Christians, at so early a period, could have made so strange a use of it as to connect it with an ordinary meal after the Jewish manner of celebrating the passover. And it is equally difficult in this view of the doctrine, to account for St. Paul's moderation in rebuking them for thus abusing this sacrament. (See 1 Cor. xi : 17, *et seq.*) Instead of quoting the strong language of our Saviour to the Jews at Capernaum, and reminding them of the great and precious rewards promised to those who rightly and worthily partake of the flesh and blood of Christ, he goes on to cite the language of institution, and reminds them that it is to be celebrated in remembrance of their crucified Lord, in order to show forth his death till he come. It is highly probable from the language of St. Paul, that these Corinthians did celebrate the Eucharist rather as a kind of historical commemoration of the death of Christ than they did as a memorial of his sacrificial death; and thus it was, that they ate the bread and drank the cup of the Lord in a sense inferior and unworthy, not discerning the Lord's body as sacrificed for the sins of a guilty world. By not keeping in view the sacrificial death of Christ in the observance of the Eucharist, they lowered, so to speak, the death of Christ and virtually represented him rather as dying a malefactor than a spotless and atoning victim: for there is no medium between the two. And thus, so far as their disorderly and perverted use of the sacrament was concerned, they were like the rejecting enemies of Christ, guilty of his body and blood, and ate and drank *judgment* to themselves; not *damnation*, for the Apostle goes on to say in substance, that if we would pass judgment upon our own disorderly conduct and humbly repent we should not be judged; but when we are judged we are chastened of the Lord for our good, that we should not be condemned with the world. There is therefore nothing in the whole passage that answers to the promise of everlasting life and a glorious resurrection, as the reward of observing the Saviour's command to eat his flesh and drink his blood; and nothing, that threatens a want of this life, to those that do not partake of these sacred emblems. If ever a suitable occasion was offered to set forth the exceedingly great rewards consequent upon a right observance of this holy sacrament, and thunder into the ears of heretical communicants the terrors of God's threatening against such as observe it not, or altogether pervert it, it was in the days of the Apostle Paul; and could the inspired Apostle have drawn his argument from our Lord's discourse at Capernaum, doubtless he would have so done, and struck alarm to the hearts and consciences of the schismatic and heretical Corinthians. I conclude, therefore, from the foregoing, that such exceeding great and precious, and life-giving promises as are contained in our Lord's discourse, are not annexed to sacramental feeding, however rightly done, this not being in harmony with the usage of the New Testament Scriptures.

4*

6. The circumstances which accompanied the delivery of this discourse of our Saviour, do not appear to be the most suitable for proposing the doctrine of a Christian sacrament. It seems quite unnatural that our Lord should propound, more than a year before its institution, the doctrine of the Eucharist.

We may venture to affirm, that in the annals of this world, there cannot be found a judicious, wise and benevolent legislator enforcing obedience to a law not yet enacted, or the observance of an institution not yet established, by the highest possible sanctions, remunerative and penal. Nor has such been the method employed by God with his rational and accountable creatures. We cannot, therefore, reasonably suppose that our blessed Redeemer would act contrary to all known precedent, both human and divine; nay, contrary to what seems to us ordinary wisdom, common prudence, and just conduct.

Nor, to my mind, was his audience the most suitable for the delivery of the doctrine of the principal and peculiar sacrament of a new dispensation. Of their unbelieving, sensual, and worldly character, enough has already been said. With our present evidence therefore, it is difficult to believe that our Lord would select the presence of such an assembly to announce, in terms the most unusual, the doctrine of the Eucharist. Dr. Wiseman therefore makes a most gratuitous assumption, when he says: "It will be acknowledged at once, that if our Saviour ever intended to propound the doctrine of the Real Presence, a more appropriate and favorable opportunity never occurred, in the course of his entire ministry, than the one exhibited in the sixth chapter of St. John." (Page 49.)

II. If the words in question cannot be referred primarily to the Eucharist, you may ask, "What then is their meaning?"

To this I reply in the language of another:[1] "The same as had already been conveyed by the phrases before employed; namely, the duty and rewards of a living faith in the Redeemer, with the fuller and more distinct development, however, than had been before made of the atoning sacrifice which was to be effected by his death, and the necessity of this faith acting on it, in order to secure the pardon of sin, the mystical union of the believer with his Lord, and, by consequence, his attainment of present spiritual life, of future resurrection, and of eternal happiness. The exercise of such a faith is what is meant by 'eating the flesh and drinking the blood of the Son of Man,' by whatever means of grace it may act, whether they were in existence and operation at the time when the discourse was uttered, or were subsequently developed or established.

"This view of our Lord's meaning is drawn from the occasion and whole tenor of the discourse as already presented. He begins by urging faith; he replies to the querulous objections of his opponents by inculcating faith; he proceeds by repeatedly stating the necessity of the Father's influence to produce faith; and, after he has finished his discourse, and corrected the gross error of some of his hearers, he introduces the same fundamental principle of faith, as effected by the Father's influence. 'There are some of you that *believe* not; for Jesus knew from the beginning who they were that *believed* not; and he said, therefore said I unto you, that no man can *come unto* me, except it were given him of my Father,' (verses 64, 65.) And, moreover, to the question, 'Will ye also go away?' the honest, the truly 'ardent and enthusiastic' Peter responds in his Master's own strain, "We believe and are sure that thou art the Christ, the

[1] Turner's Essay on John vi, *et seq.* To this Author the writer is indebted for much contained in the Scripture discussion of this question.

Son of the living God,' (v. 69.) The verbal difficulties which can set aside such an interpretation, sustained by the facts that gave occasion to the discourse, by its whole train and tenor, and by the leading idea pervading the mind of both teacher and disciple after it had been delivered, ought to be not only weighty, but overwhelming."

"It is granted that the expressions are unusually strong, and that the figure is developed with extraordinary boldness. At the same time, it is contended that it is the same sort of figure as had all along been employed, and to which the occasion gave rise. The words embodying the one thought are varied; and this, as has already been said, because our Lord adopts the very terms of his opponents, and because the general figure having been already repeatedly employed, these terms are an amplification well fitted to express the closeness of the union intended. The increased strength and boldness of the terms will appear natural to all who patiently attend to the circumstances. They are in analogy with other scriptural representations, of which I shall adduce a single instance. St. Paul, delineating the inward working of the natural mind, when reason is acting on the subject of religious obligation, and the conscience is in some measure alive to a regard to it, while, at the same time, the grace of the Gospel is wanting, uses the language, *I consent* unto the law that it is good. This simply expresses acquiescence in its excellence. But afterward, becoming more warmed with the subject, and desiring to state as fully as possible the completeness of this acquiescence of reason and conscience, he employs a stronger term, *sunedomai*, '*I delight in*,' or, '*am pleased with*' the law of God, after the inner man." (Rom. vii: 16, 22.) The expressions, "eat the flesh and drink the blood of the Son of Man," when considered in relation to the language "eat me," are similar to the latter word of St. Paul in relation to the former. In each case, both expressions designate the same thing, the one being only more fervid and energetic than the other.

"It is hardly necessary to remark, that words denoting food and beverage, and freely partaken thereof, have in all ages and nations been employed to signify an ardent attention to learning, a reception of doctrine, particularly when it engages the whole mind and interests the affections. This is admitted by all. The reason of the figure is evident. As the food is taken into the system, combines with the substance, nourishes and strengthens it and thus becomes a natural cause of its continued vitality; so does the learning or the doctrine embraced influence the intellectual or moral character of the recipient. Hence he is commonly said to *imbibe* its excellence, to *taste* and enjoy its sweetness, to *devour* the truth with greediness, or to *swallow* error with avidity. Perhaps no people were more accustomed to an extreme use of this figure than the Hebrews. It occurs very often in the New Testament, and abounds in the Old. 'If any man hear my voice, I will *sup* with him and he with me. (Rev. iii: 20.) I have *fed* you with milk, and not with *meat*. (1 Cor. iii: 2.) I have *eaten* my honey-comb with my honey; I have drunk my wine with my milk; *eat*, O friends, *drink*, yea, drink abundantly, O beloved, [or, *be drunken with love*. Margin.] (Sol. Song, v: 1.) The Lord of hosts shall make unto all people a *feast* of fat things, a *feast* of wines on the lees; of fat things full of marrow, of wines on the lees well refined.' (Isa. xxv: 6.) The same class of expressions is used to convey the idea of *enjoying* and *delighting in* any thing. Thus, for instance, 'Thy words were found and I did *eat* them, and thy word was unto me the joy and rejoicing of my heart.' (Jer. xv: 16.) Also for a hearty reception in contradistinction to an unwillingness to see and admit the truth: 'Thou, son of man, hear what I say unto thee: Be not thou rebellious like that rebellious house; open thy mouth and *eat* that I give thee. *Eat* that thou findest, *eat* this roll. So I opened my mouth, and he caused me to *eat* that roll; and he said unto me, son of man, *cause thy belly to eat, and fill thy bowels* with this roll that I give thee. Then *did I eat* it; and it was in my mouth as honey for sweetness.'" (Ezek. ii : 8, and iii : 1-3.) In the Apocryphal writings wisdom personified uses similar language: "They that *eat me* shall yet be hungry, and they that drink me shall yet be thirsty." (Ecclus. xxiv: 21.)

The same figure is employed by later Jewish writers. Thus the Rabbis say, that "every eating and drinking mentioned in the book of Ecclesiastes refers to the law and good works;"[1] and Maimonides employs similar language when he speaks of "filling the stomach with bread and meat," while he means to express the idea of "knowing what is lawful or unlawful."[2]

In that collection of ancient Jewish law, traditions and interpretations, called the TALMUD, we find passages which more nearly resemble the language of our Saviour. The Talmudist in giving certain comments of the Rabbis on Jer. xxx: 6, among other things furnishes the following: "And what (means) all faces are turned into paleness? Rabbi Johanan says, *the family which is above and the family which is below,* &c. The Jewish comment, printed in the margin, explains, "the family

---

[1] This is a quotation from the Midrash Koheleth.

[2] Jad Hazakah. Grounds of the Law, chap. iv, *ad finem*, fol. 7, vol. i, Amsterdam edition.

which is above and the family which is below," of "the angels and Israel." The Talmudist proceeds as follows: "Rab says Israel are about *to eat the years* of the Messiah. Says Rabbi Joseph, true, but who *eats of him?* Do Hillek and Billek *eat of him?*[1] in opposition to the words of Hillel, who said, there is no Messiah for Israel, for a long time ago *they ate him*, in the days of Hezekiah. Says Rab, he did not create the world except for David; and Samuel says for Moses; and Rabbi Johanan says for Messiah. What is his name?" Here follows the several answers given to this question, and a very preposterous application of several texts of Scripture to the Messiah, after which the writer remarks: "Rabbi Hillel says, not for them, for Israel is Messiah, for a long time ago *they ate him* in the days of Hezekiah."

From the foregoing, it is evident, that the Jews were accustomed to the use of such figures of speech, used to express a reception of truth in the mind and heart; and it is quite reasonable to suppose, that they might have understood our Lord to speak figuratively, had they been candidly disposed to learn of him, especially as they had, in the former part of his address, repeatedly listened to this kind of metaphorical discourse. It was, doubtless, their ignorance of the spiritual design of the Saviour's mission, their unjust prejudice, and worldly expectations, which prevented them from properly understanding him as teaching the sublime doctrine of faith in him as relating to the sacrificial death, or atoning sacrifice which he would make for the world; which death he had already symbolically

---

[1] Hillek and Billek are the names of certain judges in Sodom, according to Rabbi SOLOMON JARCHI, followed by LIGHTFOOT. Works, vol. ii, p. 554, fol. London, 1684. Buxtorf considers them as fictitious persons.—Lex. Talmud, p. 777.

predicted by, "Destroy this temple, and in three days I will raise it up," (John, ii : 19,) and which was prefigured through a long catalogue of generations by continued sacrifices. ST. AUGUSTINE attaches to the murmuring disciples the fault of their own unbelief. "If it be inquired of me wherefore they could not believe, I quickly reply, because they would not."[1]

2. It is doubtless true, that our Lord intended his remark to these as a solution of what he had before said: "Doth this offend you? If then ye shall see the Son of man ascend up where he was before? It is the spirit that quickeneth; the flesh profiteth nothing; the words that I have spoken unto you are spirit and are life." (Verses 61-63.) As if he had said: Does this afford an obstacle to your faith? What will you think when you see me ascend to my Father and take with me this very flesh which you erroneously suppose you have been exhorted to eat? Will you not then see that you have wholly misapprehended the meaning of my language? Be assured, it is the spirit that gives life. This material flesh of mine would profit you nothing in the way of obtaining life eternal, even were it possible for you to eat it corporeally, my words were designed to teach, not a carnal, but a spiritual manducation, the exercise of a firm faith in me as an atoning sacrifice for the sins of the world. That this is the meaning designed to be conveyed by his words, I have no doubt. And in order to show you that the same view was anciently taken of these explanatory words of our Saviour, I will adduce a testimony or two from the Fathers, though it be anticipating a little the line of argument which I intend in my next to follow.

[1] Quare non poterunt credere, si a me quæratur, cito respondeo, quia nolebant.—Tract. liii in Joan.

St. Augustine says: "'*For it is the Spirit that quickeneth, the flesh profiteth nothing.*' But then, when the Lord commended this, he spake of his flesh, and said, 'Unless any one eat my flesh, he shall not have eternal life in himself.' Some of his disciples, the seventy, for the most part, were offended, and said, 'This is a hard saying, who can understand it?' And they receded from him, and walked no more with him. It seemed to them hard that he said, 'Except any one eat my flesh he shall not have eternal life.' They understood this FOOLISHLY; they thought of it CARNALLY; and supposed that the Lord was about to cut off certain particles of his body and give them, and they said, 'This is a hard saying.' *They* were hard, not the saying. For if they had not been so, but had been meek, they would have said to themselves: Not without cause has he said this, [not] unless there were some latent sacrament there. They should have remained with him tractable, not difficult, and they would have learned from him what, themselves departing, they that remained learned. For, when the twelve disciples remained with him, themselves receding, they appeared as if lamenting their death because they were offended at his word, and had receded. But he instructed them, and said, It is the Spirit that quickeneth, but the flesh profiteth nothing; the words which I have spoken unto you are spirit and life. *Spiritually* understand what I have said; you are not about to eat this body which you see; and drink that blood which they that crucify me are about to shed. I have commended unto you a certain sacrament; *spiritually* understood, it shall quicken you. Although it is necessary that this be celebrated *visibly,* nevertheless it must be understood *invisibly.*"[A]

[A] Enarratio in Psal. xcviii: § 9.

From this language of St. Augustine, two things are obvious:

1. He considered the Jews to have understood Christ literally and carnally.
2. He condemns their carnal apprehension of his words as *foolish*.

With this orthodox view of the matter, let us compare, or rather contrast, the language of Dr. Wiseman. "Were the Jews *right*, in so understanding him, or were they *wrong?*" "If they were *right*, then so are the Catholics, who likewise take his words literally; if *wrong*, then Protestants are right, when they understand him figuratively." (Lecture iii, p. 102.) He having examined our Saviour's usual practice when his words were misapprehended, by being literally understood, as also when they were literally and rightly perceived, thus concludes: The objection of the Jews proves that they understood our Redeemer's words in their literal sense, of a real eating of his flesh; his answer illustrated by his invariable practice, demonstrates that they were right in so understanding. We, therefore, who understand them as they did, are right also. (Idem, p. 111.)

Dr. Wiseman may, if he please, enjoy all the honors of the society to which his literal and carnal interpretation entitles him, as for me, I prefer the sense which the learned Bishop of Hippo gives.

St. Athanasius also says: "When our Lord conversed on the eating of his body, and when he thence beheld many offended, he forthwith added: 'Doth this offend you? If then ye shall behold the Son of man ascending where he was before? It is the spirit that quickeneth: the flesh profiteth nothing. The words which I speak unto you are spirit and life.' Both these matters, the flesh and the spirit, he said respecting himself, and he distinguished the spirit from the flesh, that we might know those things which he spoke to be not carnal, but spiritual. For, to how many persons would his body suffice for food, even should it become aliment for the whole world? But that he might turn away their minds from carnal cogitations, and that they might learn that the flesh which he would give them, was heavenly and spiritual food, he, *on this account,* mentioned the ascent of the Son of man to heaven. 'The words, said he, which I speak unto you are spirit and life!' As if he had intimated: My body shall be given as food for the world; but then it must be imparted to each one only after a spiritual manner, that so it might be to all an earnest of the resurrection to eternal life."[B]

Those Fathers therefore understood Christ as *explaining* his language to his disciples, whereas Dr. W. contends that he only *repeated* it without explanation.

With the regards of your brother,

E. O. P.

[B] Athanas. Epist. ad Serapion., in illud, quicunque dixerit verbum, etc. Tom. ii, p. 710. Paris, 1698.

LETTER IV.

PATRISTIC VIEW OF OUR LORD'S DISCOURSE IN JOHN VI.

Dear Brother:—The importance attached by modern writers in your church to the language of our Saviour in his discourse at Capernaum, will be a sufficient apology for the somewhat protracted discussion of this topic which we have already made. According to Dr. Wiseman's language, cited near the close of my last, I understand him to rest his doctrine of a carnal manducation of Christ's flesh upon the literal meaning of the passage in question: if it be right to interpret the words of our Lord *literally*, then are Catholics right; but if it be right to interpret them *figuratively*, then are Protestants right. That we are right in the exposition which we give them is evident from the general scope and design of the whole discourse, Dr. W's learned subtleties to the contrary notwithstanding. In further proof of the correctness of our exposition, I now propose to consider the evidence drawn from the writings of distinguished authors, who have given us their views of the meaning of our Lord's discourse, beginning with the ancient Fathers of the church and confining myself principally to those writers acknowledged by you as standard authors.

You need not be reminded, that we look in vain for formal and critical interpretation of the Holy Scriptures in the writings of the first three centuries. The Fathers of those ages were interested in spreading a knowledge of the Gospel, and in cultivating its practical influence on their own character; and their expositions of Scripture are to be sought in various treatises, on topics of philosophy and theology, in their epistolary writings, and works composed in opposition to existing errors, commentary, in the later sense of the word, being hardly known. Modern theologians of extensive patristic learning, differ in their views of the exposition, given by the ancient Fathers, of the discourse of our Lord recorded in the sixth chapter of St. John's Gospel; some contending that they interpret it directly of the Eucharist, while others maintain, that they only make an application of it to this sacrament. With the settlement of this difference of opinion I am not so much interested, as I am to show from the writings of antiquity, that the ancient church understood by the words of our Saviour, not a carnal, but a spiritual manducation of the flesh of Christ, that is, a feeding upon him by an appropriating faith in the efficacy of his sacrificial death.

The worthy use of the Eucharist is, without doubt, one of the means whereby we are enabled to partake of this heavenly food, and the ancients were therefore right, when they applied the *general* doctrine in John vi, to the *particular* case of the Eucharist, considered as rightly and worthily received; because the spiritual feeding spoken of by our Lord, is the thing signified and performed in this sacrament. I submit the following quotations from the Fathers, with such remarks only, as seem needful to a proper understanding of them.

1. IGNATIUS, having his approaching martyrdom in view, after speaking of his desire to depart, and of a living principle within him, "which says, come to the Father," says: "I take pleasure neither in the food of corruption, nor in the pleasures of this life; I desire the bread of God, bread celestial, bread of life, which is the flesh of Jesus Christ, the Son of God, who was made of late of the seed of

David and Abraham, and I desire for drink his blood, which is love incorruptible and eternal life. No longer do I wish to live according to man."[A]

It is evident that IGNATIUS here alludes to our Lord's discourse at Capernaum; and from the circumstances under which it was written, from the connection in which it was found, as well as from the language itself, it is obvious that this spiritually-minded bishop has in mind, not a participation of the Eucharist, but a spiritual and eternal enjoyment of Christ after his martyrdom.

Were we, however, to allow this author to refer to the Eucharist, instead of proving a partaking of Christ's real blood, it plainly teaches the contrary, namely, a participation of "love incorruptible and life eternal." In like manner are we to understand by the expression, "The bread of God," the heavenly and life-giving food procured by the sacrifice of our Lord and Saviour Jesus Christ. So that, allowing him to allude to the Eucharist, which is altogether improbable, his language is to be explained as referring to a spiritual feeding upon Christ in the sacrament, but not to a participation of the corporeal flesh and blood of our Lord.

2. There is a passage in IRENÆUS, which may be thought to allude to the discourse recorded in the sixth chapter of St. John. He says that our Lord did not come to us, as he might have done, in his incorruptible glory, which we could not have borne; but "the perfect bread of the Father supplied us with himself, as babes with milk, which was his advent according to man, that we, nourished, as it were, by the breast of his flesh, and accustomed by such lactation to eat and drink the Word of God, might be able to retain in ourselves the bread of immortality, which is the Spirit of the Father."[B]

[A] Epist. ad Romanos, cap. vii, p. 88.
[B] Adv. Hæres. lib. iv, cap. 74.

If this be an allusion to John vi, it is evident, that the author does not consider the discourse there recorded, as relating directly to the Eucharist, for he is speaking of the incarnation of Christ, by which are effected the eating and drinking of which he speaks. Indeed his language plainly teaches that it is a spiritual union with Christ that is intended by the expression, "to eat and drink the Word of God."

3. TERTULLIAN, when proving that the words of our Lord, "The flesh profiteth nothing," do not militate against the doctrine of the resurrection, says: "Although he says that the flesh profits nothing, the sense is to be drawn from the matter of the declaration. For, because they considered his word as hard and intolerable, as if he had determined that his flesh was truly to be eaten by them, he premised, *It is the Spirit that quickeneth*, in order that he might arrange the state of salvation according to the Spirit. And to the same effect he subjoined: *The flesh profits nothing*, that is, for quickening. Because also he will have the Spirit to be understood, it further follows: *The words which I have spoken unto you are Spirit, and are life. As also above; he that heareth my words and believeth on him that sent me, hath eternal life, and shall not come into judgment, but shall pass from death unto life.* Constituting, therefore, the Word the vivifier, because the Word is Spirit and life, he called the same his flesh also; and because the Word was made flesh, he is therefore to be sought for the sake of life, and to be devoured by the hearing, and to be ruminated by the understanding, and digested by faith. For a little before he had pronounced his flesh to be celestial bread also, everywhere enforcing, by the allegory of necessary foods, a remembrance of their fathers who preferred the bread and flesh of the Egyptians to the divine calling. Adverting there-

fore to their thoughts, because he perceived that they were scattered, he said, *The flesh profits nothing.* What is there in this to destroy the resurrection of the flesh?"[c]

Again, this author remarks in his exposition of the Lord's Prayer: "How fitly has the divine wisdom arranged the prayer! that after things celestial, that is, after the name of God, the will of God, and the kingdom of God, it has also made place in the petition for terrestrial necessities; for the Lord has also said: *Seek first the kingdom* [of heaven] *and then these things shall also be added unto you.* We may, however, rather understand, GIVE US THIS DAY OUR DAILY BREAD, in a SPIRITUAL sense. For Christ is our bread; because Christ is life, and bread is life. *I am,* he says, *the bread of life.* And a little before: 'the bread is the Word of the living God who descended from heaven.' Moreover, because also by bread his body is understood; THIS IS MY BODY. Therefore, by asking for daily bread, we pray for a perpetuity in Christ, and an inseparability from his body [spiritually understood.] But although this word [or expression] is admitted CARNALLY, it cannot be done without the religion of spiritual discipline."[D]

In the former passage quoted from this author, he clearly appears to have had no idea of expounding the sixth of John directly of the Eucharist; much less of a carnal manducation of the food there spoken of. In the latter passage, though allusion is made to this sacrament, it is very evident that Christ's body is to be received spiritually, but not carnally.

4. CYPRIAN, who regarded TERTULLIAN as his master, in his treatise on the Lord's Prayer, makes use

[c] Tertul. de Resurrectione Carnis, cap. 37. Edit. Rigalt. p. 347.
[D] Idem de Oratione, cap. vi, p. 131.

of the following language: "GIVE US THIS DAY OUR DAILY BREAD. This may be understood both spiritually and simply, each sense, by the divine blessing conducing to salvation. For Christ is the bread of life, and this is not the bread of all, but it is ours. And as we say, OUR FATHER, because he is the Father of [us] who understand and believe, so also we call [him] our bread, because Christ is the bread of us who are connected with his body. But we pray that this bread be given us daily, lest we, who are in Christ, and receive the Eucharist daily as the food of salvation, should, by the intervention of some more grievous fault, be separated from the body of Christ, whilst debarred, and not communicating, we are prohibited from the heavenly bread, he himself declaring and admonishing: 'I am the bread of life which came down from heaven. If any one shall eat of my bread he shall live forever. But the bread which I will give is my flesh for the life of the world.'

"When, therefore, he says, if any one shall eat of his bread, as it is manifest that they live who belong to his body, and receive the Eucharist with a right of communicating, so, on the other hand, it is to be feared, and we are to pray that no one remain far from salvation, whilst debarred, he is separated from the body of Christ, who himself threatens and says: 'Except ye shall eat the flesh of the Son of man, and drink his blood, ye shall not have life in you.'"[E]

This passage affords another example of applying the language of our Lord in John vi, to a right participation of Christ in the Eucharist. But from his language, we are by no means to conclude, that our author considered the discourse as originally and directly intended of this Sacrament. So also

[E] De Orat. Dom.

the application of the Lord's prayer for daily bread to the Eucharist, says Dr. Turner, "is almost universal with the Fathers, and yet it is hardly to be supposed that they understood this as the direct and original purport of the petition, as taught by our Lord to his Apostles during his life-time. Being a prayer for sustenance of the whole man, both soul and body, they understood it to *comprehend a reference* to all the means by which such sustenance might be obtained." [1]

And thus, in the quotation which has been made, CYPRIAN *regarded* Christ himself as spiritually our food, and *considering* this as given especially in the Eucharist, directs the attention to this sacrament.

5. CLEMENT, of Alexandria, after speaking of those who are called *carnal* and *spiritual*, [I Cor. iii: 1,] and of the difference between *milk* and *meat* [verse 2] as symbolically used to designate spiritual food, continues: "Elsewhere also the Lord in the Gospel according to John, has explained this by symbols, saying, 'eat my flesh and drink my blood,' plainly speaking in allegory of the drinking of faith and the promise, by which the church, as a man, consisting of many members, is watered and increased, is closely united together and composed of both; of faith as the body, and of hope as the soul, as also the Lord [was composed] of flesh and blood. For, in reality, the blood of faith is hope, with which faith is connected as it were by a living principle." [F]

Subsequently in the same chapter he thus expresses himself: "The Word is all things to the babe, both father and mother, schoolmaster and nourisher. *Eat*, says he, *my flesh and drink my blood*. These appropriate nourishments for us, the

---

[1] In Opere citat. p. 119.

[F] Pædagog. lib. I, cap. vi, p. 121. Edit. Oxon. 1715.

Lord supplies. He reaches forth flesh and pours out blood, and nothing is wanting for the increase of his little ones. O wonderful mystery! He commands us to put off the old fleshy corruption, as also the old nourishment, that we, partaking of other new food of Christ, and receiving, may, if it be possible, lay him up within ourselves, and enclose the Saviour in the breast in order to set aright the affections of our flesh.

"But not for this reason will you understand, that it is in like manner, of less value. And therefore give ear. As to [the word] flesh [in the passage just quoted from John vi,] it allegorically signifies to us the Holy Spirit, for by him has the flesh [of Christ] been made. As to [the word] blood, it intimates to us the Word, for as rich blood, the Word is poured into [our] life; but the Lord, the mixture of them both, is the nourishment of his babes; the Lord, Spirit and Word: the food, that is, the Lord Jesus, that is, the Word of God, the Spirit incarnated: the sanctified heavenly flesh; the food, the milk of the Father, by which alone we babes are nursed."[G]

After this, on the words, *And the bread which I will give is my flesh,* he makes the following sufficiently mystical remarks: "But flesh is irrigated by blood, and blood is allegorically called wine. It must therefore be known that, as bread, broken into a mixture of wine and water, absorbs the wine but leaves the water, so also the flesh of Christ, the bread of heaven, drinks up the blood, nourishing heavenly men unto incorruption, but leaving to corruption those fleshly desires alone." And then he adds what is more important: "Thus in many ways the Word is allegorically represented as meat, and flesh, and nourishment, and bread,

[G] Ibid, pp. 123-4.

and blood, and milk. The Lord is all things for the enjoyment of us who have believed in him."[H]

After this he repeatedly teaches the figurative signification of the term blood. Thus, "He declares that he will adorn the body of the Word in his own spirit, as he will assuredly nourish with his spirit those that hunger for the Word. But that the blood is the word, the blood of righteous Abel, which speaks with God, is witness."[I] And, "therefore both blood and milk are a symbol of the Lord's passion and doctrine."[J]

In the next book he tells us that "the blood of Christ is two-fold, for the one is his fleshly, by which we have been redeemed from corruption; the other his spiritual, that is, by which we have been anointed. And this is to drink the blood of Jesus, to partake of the Lord's incorruption."[K]

Again, in his "Miscellanies," after quoting 1 Cor. iii: 1, 2, 3, he says: "If therefore *milk* is called by the Apostle the nourishment of babes, but *meat* the food of the perfect, then milk will be understood [to be] the first rudiments of instruction, as if the first nourishment of the soul; but meat, the visible contemplation [1] [of the Christian mysteries.] And this is the flesh and blood of the Word, to wit, the apprehension of the divine power and essence. Taste and see that Christ is the Lord, says [the Psalmist, xxxiv : 8;] for in this manner he imparts himself to those who, after a more spiritual manner, partake of such food."[M]

[H] Ibid, p. 126.   [I] Ibid.   [J] Page 127.
[K] Idem Prædagog., lib. ii, cap. 2.
[1] This is evidently an allusion to the discipline of the early church, whereby the catechumens were made to undergo a course of primary instruction before their initiation by baptism; after which they were, with the rest of the faithful, admitted to be present at the celebration of the sacraments.
[M] Stromat., lib. v, cap. 10, prope ult.

These several passages I have produced from the writings of this author, who is regarded as one the most pious, learned, and orthodox of the earlier Christian Fathers, not because they comprise any very lucid exposition of our Lord's discourse, but because, of the various interpretations given by him, in no one instance does he explain the terms, *flesh* and *blood* used in John vi, literally. And to me the testimony of this great philosopher and master of the Alexandrian school, at the close of the second century, is instead of a myriad modern witnesses for a literal interpretation of our Saviour's discourse.

While the latter dwell upon the gross idea of eating and drinking the real flesh and blood of the Son of God, his thoughts and devout affections rise, far above the mere letter, to the blessed person thereby signified, the participation of whose flesh and blood is no other than the feeding upon Christ after a spiritual and heavenly manner,—to partake of his incorruption, to receive the gift of the Holy Ghost, to apprehend the divine power and essence. The former idea is sensual, profitless, and revolting; the latter is spiritual, life-giving, and soul-inspiring. The one tends to degrade the mysteries of our holy religion, and reduce to contempt their divine author; the other gives them their proper position in the economy of grace, and shows forth the dignity and sublime character of the Redeemer.

6. In passing to consider the testimony of ORIGEN, it may not be improper to remark, that although he was distinguished for his great abilities and extensive learning, he nevertheless fell into several important errors, which were made the subject of stricture and condemnation by other and later Fathers of the Church. This remark, however, does not apply to the views entertained and taught

by him in regard to the doctrine of the Eucharist, nor to any exposition given by him of the discourse of our Lord as contained in John vi. Having been regarded as orthodox on these points by those that flourished in the ages immediately succeeding him, I shall therefore indulge no scruple in producing his testimony.

The first which I will offer seems, in few words, to embody a general canon for interpreting John vi. "If we speak those things that are perfect, that are forcible, that are more strong, we set before you the flesh of the Word of God to be eaten."[N]

Very like this is another passage. *Man did eat angels' bread, &c.* The Saviour says, "I am the bread that came down from heaven. This bread, therefore, angels formerly ate, but now men also. To eat here signifies to know. For the mind eats what it knows, and what it does not know it does not eat."[O]

Speaking of a spiritual understanding of the law, he says: "Therefore we go out from the letter of the law; but being constituted under the power of a spiritual law, spiritually celebrating we fully perform all things which are there commanded to be corporally done. For we cast out the old leaven of malice and wickedness, and celebrate the passover with the unleavened bread of sincerity and truth; Christ supping with us according to the will of the lamb, who says; Except ye shall eat my flesh and drink my blood, ye shall not have life in you."[P]

Here is doubtless an application of the language of our Saviour to the Eucharist, of which he after-

[N] In Num., Hom. xxiii, Opera tom. ii, p. 359.
[O] Selecta in Psal. lxvii, Opera tom. ii, p. 771.
[P] Comment. in Matt. Tract. xxxv, tom. iii, pp. 895-6.

ward discourses at some length in the same Tract. And the fact that he thus spiritually applies these words of our Lord's discourse to the Eucharist, is important, not only as showing that he does not interpret them literally, but also as proving that, in this sacrament, he does not understand the body and blood of Christ to be corporally present and received.[1] And this agrees with his subsequent teaching, "that the bread, which God the Word, confesseth to be his body, is the nutrient word of souls," "the word that nourishes and gladdens the heart."

Again, on the words of the Apostle: "For he is not a Jew who is one outwardly; neither is that circumcision which is without, in the flesh; but he is a Jew who is one inwardly; and circumcision is that of the heart in the spirit, not in the letter;" (Rom. ii : 28, 29,) he remarks, "For they feast upon the inward and unleavened bread of sincerity and truth, which is invisible. They also eat Christ, the passover, who was slain for us, who said: 'Except ye eat my flesh ye have not life abiding in you.' And with this true drink, which they drink as his blood, they anoint the lintel over the door of the house of their soul, seeking, not as they, [the Jews,] glory of men, but of God, who seeth in secret."[Q]

When passing from the discussion of drinking wine to the consideration of foods, our author remarks: "But now let us consider somewhat that is read concerning those things which are clean and unclean, or of foods, or animals. And as in the explanation of the cup we ascended from the shadow

---

[1] This remark will apply to others of the Fathers, who also interpret our Lord's language spiritually, or figuratively, and at the same time extend its application to the Eucharist.

[Q] Ubi Sup. Tract. xxiv, p. 837.

to the truth of the spiritual cup, so also in respect of the foods which are spoken of by a shadow, let us ascend to those which by the Spirit are the true foods." After quoting several passages of Scripture, (I Cor. x: 2, *et seq.;* Acts, x: 9, *et seq.;* Matt. xiii: 47, *et seq.*) which speak of spiritual nourishment under the idea of corporeal food, he adds: "But that what we say may appear the more clearly to thy understanding, let us take an example from the greater, that descending thence gradually we may come even to the less. Our Lord and Saviour says: 'Except ye shall eat my flesh and drink my blood ye shall not have life in yourselves. My flesh is meat indeed, and my blood is drink indeed.'

" Therefore, because Jesus is all clean throughout, all his flesh is meat, and all his blood is drink, [Why?] because every WORK of his is holy, and every WORD of his is true. Moreover therefore, both his flesh is the true meat and his blood the true drink.

" For, with the flesh and blood of his WORD, as with clean meat and drink, he gives to drink and feeds the whole race of mankind.[R] In the second place, after the flesh, Peter and Paul and all the Apostles are clean food. In the third place, their disciples; and so each one in proportion to his *deserts*, or the purity of his *thoughts*, is made clean food to his neighbor. He who cannot hear these things, carps, perhaps, and turns away his ear as did they who said, 'How will this man give us his flesh to eat? Who can hear him? And they departed from him.' But if you are sons of the Church, if you are imbued with the Gospel mysteries, if the Word made flesh dwells in you, then do you know what we say, because they are the Lord's, lest he who is ignorant should be ignorant."

[R] In Levit., Homil. vii, No. 5, tom. ii, p. 225.

The whole scope and design of this passage, as well as its language, clearly show that ORIGEN understood the words of our Lord in John vi, in a spiritual sense. For the object of his discourse is to ascend from the shadow to the substance—from the letter to the thing signified; in other words, to give the practical and spiritual meaning of the inspired word. And he quotes, by way of illustration, what he considers a most striking example of the figurative use of Scripture phraseology.

Indeed, comment is unnecessary; for he goes on to say: "Know you that those things which are written in the divine volumes are FIGURES, and, therefore, as spiritual, and not as carnal, do you examine and understand what is said. For if as carnal you understand these things, they injure you, and do not nourish. For there is in the Gospels a letter that kills; not only in the Old Testament is there a letter found that kills. There is also in the New Testament a letter that kills him who does not understand spiritually what is said. For if you follow according to the letter, this itself that is said; Except you shall eat my flesh and drink my blood, this letter kills." [S]

"Moreover, when the Lord said, 'The bread which I will give is my flesh for the life of the world,' when the Jews strove among themselves, saying: 'How can this man give us his flesh to eat?' We prove that they were not so stupid who heard as to suppose that the speaker invited his hearers to come to him and eat his flesh." [T]

Lastly, "We are said to drink the blood of Christ, not only in the rite of the sacrament, but also when we receive his words in which life consists, as he says, 'The words which I have spoken are spirit

---

[S] (Ibid.)
[T] Com. in Joan., Opera tom. iv, p. 364.

and life.' He, therefore, was wounded, whose blood we drink, that is, receive the words of his doctrine." ᵁ

7. EUSEBIUS, paraphrasing upon the words of John vi, says: "Think not that I speak of that flesh with which I am compassed, as if it were necessary to eat this, neither suppose that I command you to drink this sensible and bodily blood. So that those very words and speeches are his flesh and blood. For these things understood according to sense profit nothing, but it is the quickening Spirit that profits those who are able to understand these things spiritually." ⱽ

8. ATHANASIUS, when treating of the human nature of Christ, says: "Unless the Holy Spirit were of the substance of that which is only good, it would not have been called good, since the Lord refused to be called good, as far as he was a man, saying: 'Why callest thou me good? There is none good except the one God.' But the Scripture does not scruple to call the Holy Spirit good, according to David, who says: 'Thy good Spirit shall lead me in the right way.' Again, the Lord says concerning himself: 'I am the living bread which came down from heaven.' Elsewhere he has called the Holy Spirit heavenly bread, saying: "Give us daily our daily bread.' For he has taught us in the prayer to ask now for daily bread, that is, for that which shall be, the first fruits of which we have in the present life, being partakers of the flesh of Christ; as he said, 'And the bread which I will give is my flesh for the life of the world.' FOR THE FLESH OF THE LORD IS A QUICKENING SPIRIT." ᵂ

ᵁ In Num., Hom. xvi, tom. ii, p. 334.
ⱽ Eccles. Theol., lib. iii, cap. 17.
ᵂ De Humanâ Naturâ Susceptâ, Opera Paris, 1627, tom. i, p. 607.

In the former part of this passage this author distinguishes the Holy Spirit from the human nature of Christ; subsequently, however, he explains the term *bread* as used in the Lord's Prayer and John vi, as signifying the same thing, that is, the Holy Spirit, or flesh of Christ; which shows most conclusively that he did not understand our Lord's discourse literally.

9. CYRIL of Jerusalem, in one of his lectures to the recently baptized, briefly refers to this discourse of our Lord. "When Christ formerly addressed the Jews, he said: 'Except ye eat my flesh and drink my blood, ye have not life in yourselves.' But they, not spiritually understanding his sayings, were offended and went back, thinking that he exhorted them to eat his flesh."[x]

Observe: the offence of the Jews and their departure from Christ, is attributed to their "not spiritually understanding" our Lord's words.

10. BASIL, Bishop of Cæsarea, remarks: "'He that eateth me,' he says, 'shall live by me.' For we eat his flesh and drink his blood, being made partakers, through his incarnation and perceptible life, of the Word and wisdom. For he denominated his whole mystical sojourn, flesh and blood; and he made manifest his doctrine, by which the soul is nourished, consisting of practical, and natural, and theological."[y]

11. "We read the Holy Scriptures," says JEROME: "I suppose the Gospel to be the body of Jesus, the Holy Scriptures his doctrine. And when he says, 'He that shall not eat my flesh and drink my blood,' although it may be understood in the mystery, nevertheless, the word of the Scriptures, the divine doctrine, is more truly the body of Christ and his

---

[x] Catech. Mystagog. V, § 1, Opera, Oxon. 1703, p. 293.
[y] Epist. cxli.

blood. If, when we go to the mystery—he that is faithful understands—if one fall into sin, he is in peril. If, when we hear the word of God, and the word of God, and the flesh of Christ, and his blood is poured into our ears, and we are thinking of something else, into how great danger do we run!"

He relates that, according to a Jewish tradition, the taste of the manna in the desert corresponded to the individual desire of the consumer, and adds: "So also in the flesh of Christ, which is the word of his doctrine, that is, the interpretation of the Holy Scriptures, as we will, so we also take meat. If thou art holy, thou findest refreshment; if thou art a sinner, thou findest torment." z

"By a figure of speech we may say that all lovers of pleasure, more than lovers of God, are sanctified in gardens and in dwellings, because the mysteries of truth cannot enter, [them] and they eat the food of impiety while they are unholy in body and spirit; they neither eat the flesh of Jesus nor drink his blood, concerning which he says, 'He that eateth my flesh and drinketh my blood hath eternal life.' For Christ our passover has been sacrificed, who is eaten not without, but in one house and within"[a] — in the one house of the Church, and in the soul of the believer is his probable meaning. That he intends a spiritual manducation of Christ's flesh, in this passage, is evident from the antithetic relation in which it is put to the eating of the food of impiety by the lovers of pleasure.

12. In his treatise on Christian Doctrine, AUGUSTINE comments on the fifty-third verse of John vi as follows: "If the discourse is preceptive, whether

[z] Hieron. Com. in Psal. cxlvii, v, 5. Tom. iv, p. 894.

[a] Idem Com. in Isa. Proph. lib. xviii, tom. iii, p. 506. See also a passage cited below, Letter viii, where he plainly distinguishes Christ's divine or spiritual blood from his real blood.

forbidding a wicked act or crime, or enjoining beneficence, it is not figurative. But if it seem to command a wicked act or crime, or to forbid something useful or beneficial, it is figurative. 'Unless ye shall eat the flesh of the Son of man and drink his blood ye have not life in you,' seems to enjoin a crime or wicked act, it is therefore a figure, commanding to communicate in the Lord's passion, and sweetly and profitably to lay up in the memory that his flesh has been crucified and wounded for us." [b]

"They said to him, 'What shall we do that we may work the work of God?' For he had said to them, 'Labor for the meat that perisheth not, but endureth to eternal life.' 'What shall we do?' say they; 'by observing what, shall we be able fully to perform this precept?' Jesus answered and said to them, 'This is the work of God, that ye believe on him whom he hath sent.' This, therefore, is to eat the meat that doth not perish, but endureth to eternal life. Why dost thou prepare the teeth and stomach? BELIEVE AND THOU HAST EATEN." [c]

"Finally, he now explains how that may be done of which he speaks, and what it is to eat his body and drink his blood. 'He that eateth my flesh and drinketh my blood abideth in me and I in him.' To abide in Christ, and to have him abiding in us, this is, therefore, to eat that food and drink that drink. And for this reason he who does not abide in Christ, and in whom Christ does not abide, without doubt does neither spiritually eat his flesh nor drink his blood, although he carnally and visibly press with his teeth the sacrament of Christ's body and blood; but he rather eats and drinks the sacrament of so great a thing to his condemnation." [d]

[b] De Doct. Christi, lib. iii, cap. 16.
[c] In Johan. Evang., cap. vi. Tract. xxv, §12.
[d] Idem Tract. xxvi. § 18.

From these quotations it is very evident that the ancient Fathers understood a spiritual participation of Christ, and a union with him by faith, to have been intended by our Saviour in his discourse to the Jews at Capernaum.

It was doubtless a thorough acquaintance with the writings of antiquity that compelled the learned ERASMUS, in his notes on the fifty-first verse of John vi, to acknowledge that "the ancients interpret this place of heavenly doctrine."[e]

Whilst all this remains true, it is granted that some of them apply the language of our Lord in question to the Eucharist as the means by which, in a great degree, faith is promoted and a union with Christ effected and maintained. Thus CLEMENT, of Alexandria, teaches that the eucharistic "mixture of wine and water feeds unto faith;" and, "they that partake of the Eucharist in faith are made holy in body and soul."[f] And CYRIL of Jerusalem, exhorts: "Wherefore with all assurance let us partake of the body and blood of Christ; for in the type of bread his body is given to thee, and in the type of wine his blood is given to thee; so that partaking of the body and blood of Christ thou mayest be made of the same body and blood with him."[g]

Entertaining such views of the efficacy of the Eucharist when duly received by faith, it is by no means strange that the Fathers should apply the language of our Saviour in John vi to this sacrament, since it expresses, in the most forcible manner, the very union supposed to be effected through the instrumentality of this eminent means of grace. Such an application of our Lord's words is, without doubt, in perfect keeping with orthodoxy.

[e] Crit. Sac. in Johan, tom. vi, p. 115. Edit. Amst. 1698.
[f] Lib. ii, cap. 2.
[g] Catech. Mystag. iv, p. 292.

With such an amount of testimony, gathered from the writings of the most distinguished Fathers that flourished during a period of more than four hundred years from the Christian era, and embracing the purest ages of ancient Christianity, it is not a little remarkable that men of acknowledged ability and extensive research; that men, avowedly claiming the inheritance of ancient doctrine as peculiarly theirs; and above all, that men, nursed at the breast of a professedly holy and infallible mother, and sworn to interpret the Sacred Scriptures according to the unanimous consent of the holy Fathers, should, in these latter days of reading and intelligence, have the boldness to urge the literal interpretation as the only allowable and consistent meaning of our Saviour's discourse at Capernaum. The exclusive pretensions of those who advocate this carnal exposition, remind us of the professions of its original interpreters, who, on one occasion, vaunted themselves as being the children of Abraham. (John, viii: 39.)

In estimating our relationship to the ancient Christian family, we shall do well to keep in mind the principle then sanctioned by our Saviour, and look for a family resemblance in that vital principle and distinctive feature of Christianity, an EVANGELICAL FAITH, and its legitimate and necessary fruits. Such is the characteristic mark of God's household in all ages of the world.

But before closing the historical representation of our subject, I must produce the testimony of a few more recent witnesses, both Papal and Protestant.

INNOCENT III, the very Pope of your church, who is regarded as the establisher of the dogma of transubstantiation, treating of the mysteries of the Mass, says, "The Lord saying, 'except ye eat of the flesh of the Son of man, and drink his blood, ye have no life in you,' speaks of the spiritual manducation: in this manner the good only do eat the body of Christ." [1]

Pope Pius II says, "The sense of the Gospel of John is not such as you ascribe to it, for there it is not commanded to drink at the Sacrament, but a manner of *spiritual drinking* is taught. The Lord, when he says, 'It is the spirit that quickeneth, the flesh profiteth nothing,' by these words declares, in that place, the secret mysteries of the spiritual drink, and not of the carnal."..... "'The words that I speak unto you, they are spirit and they are life;' wilt thou know openly, the Evangelist speaks of the *spiritual manducation* which is made by faith, (not by the mouth.) Consider the Lord's words, 'He that eateth and drinketh,' are words of the present tense and not of the future; at that very instant, therefore, (more than a year before the last supper,) there were some that did eat him and drink him." Again, "Ye must not wonder at some doctors speaking of the sacramental communion, and counseling the people to it, who employ St. John's words; yet, it does not, on this account, follow, that such is the true and proper meaning of this place." [2]

GABRIEL BIEL says, "the doctors hold, with a common consent, that in the sixth of John, no mention is made but of the spiritual manducation." [3]

And STAPLETON affirms that, "St. John writes nothing of the eucharistic supper, because the other three Evangelists before him had fully described it." [4]

---

[1] Lib. iv. cap. 14. This and the three authors following are cited by Ousley. Old Christianity against Papal Novelties, p. 202.

[2] Pius ii, Ep. 130, ad Cardinalem Carvialem.

[3] Gabriel Biel, in Lesson xxxvi, can. Missæ.

[4] Johannes de eucharistica cœna nihil scribit, eo quod cæteri tres evangelistæ ante eum, eam plene descripsisent. In promp. Cath. Ser. 1. Hebd. Sanct.

To add farther remarks upon the testimony of this "cloud of witnesses" would be but a needless multiplication of words. I therefore submit, for your careful examination, the foregoing, with the request that you consider well the force of the whole argument before you proceed to set it aside, and produce something better, before you ask me to abandon my own convictions, and the concurrent testimony of the ancient writers of the church. For, "An honest man's the noblest work of God."

To possess the consciousness of such a character is the constant aim of him who is permitted to subscribe himself.

Your unworthy Friend and Brother,

E. O. P.

LETTER V.

DISCUSSION OF THE WORDS USED BY OUR LORD WHEN HE INSTITUTED THE SACRAMENT OF THE EUCHARIST AND THE FIGURATIVE INTERPRETATION SHOWN TO ACCORD WITH SCRIPTURE USAGE.

DEAR BROTHER:—We now come to the consideration of the words used by our Saviour when he, in presence of his twelve disciples, instituted the Eucharistic Sacrament.

You are aware that the history of this institution is given by the first three Evangelists, Matthew, Mark and Luke, and also by St. Paul in the eleventh chapter of his first Epistle to the Corinthians. By comparing the several descriptions given by these sacred writers, it will at once be seen that they agree substantially in the account which they give, notwithstanding the slight difference of phraseology employed. It is, therefore, sufficient to cite, for the sake of convenient reference, the words recorded by the Evangelists, Matthew and Luke:

"And, as they were eating, Jesus took bread, and blessed *it*, and brake *it*, and gave *it* to the disciples, and said, Take, eat, this is my body.

"And he took the cup, and gave thanks, and gave *it* to them, saying, Drink ye all of it, for this is my blood of the new testament, which is shed for many for the remission of sins." Matt. xxvi: 26, 27, 28.

"And he took bread, and gave thanks, and brake *it*, and gave unto them, saying, This is my body which is given for you: this do in remembrance of me.

"Likewise also the cup after supper, saying, This cup is the new testament in my blood, which is shed for you." Luke xxii: 19, 20.

The question is, what did our Lord mean when he said of the Eucharistic elements, THIS IS MY BODY—THIS IS MY BLOOD? You suppose that he intended to convey the idea, and was understood by those present to affirm, that those elements were no longer in their physical substance, bread and wine as when first taken, but the real and substantial body and blood of Christ himself; that is, you take the words in question in their literal and grammatical sense.

On the contrary, I understand these words in their metaphorical sense, which, by consequence, excludes the idea of a corporeal presence of Christ's flesh and blood in the Eucharist.

In discussing these words of our Lord our line of argument will be *first:* to prove that the words of institution *may* be taken figuratively, and, *secondly:* to demonstrate that, to avoid great difficulties and plain contradictions, we are *compelled* to adopt this figurative interpretation.

The most ancient rule with which I am acquainted for the discovery of Scriptural truth, is that given by CLEMENT of Alexandria. After speaking of the perfection and fullness of Scripture, he adds: "But the truth is not discovered by changing the signification of things, for, in this manner, do they overturn all true doctrines; but by considering thoroughly what is perfectly proper and fitting to the Lord, and to God the Creator, and, by confirming each of those things demonstrated, according to the Scriptures, from those Scriptures which again are similar."[A]

From which we may observe: 1. We are not to change the meaning of words from that sense intended to be given them by the author. 2. Our interpretations of Scripture must so accord with the

---

[A] Stromat., lib. vii, cap. 16. Edit. Oxonii, 1715, vol. ii, p. 891.

well known character of our Lord and Saviour, and of God the Creator, as not to conflict with the revealed attributes of either, considered as Redeemer or Creator. 3. Our proofs must be strengthened by the concurrent testimony of other and similar Scriptures, which evidently implies, that they are not to be such as may be weakened or destroyed by other Scriptures. As a general rule of interpretation, the above may be regarded as sufficiently correct, and we shall do well to have it constantly in mind in our Scriptural expositions; but in order to have some more *particular* standard, by which to regulate our present inquiries, and to determine the correctness of our results, I think you will agree with me in adopting the following rule, viz:

The literal meaning of a text is to be retained, when it can be done, without conflicting with natural reason, and without being repugnant to any other Scripture clearly revealed, or to the general spirit and scope of the revealed Word of God; but that the literal meaning of words is to be given up, if it be either improper, or involve an impossibility; or when words, properly taken, contain any thing contrary to the doctrinal or moral precepts delivered in the other parts of the Scriptures.[2]

2. In view of the method already suggested, and the principles of interpretation adopted, let us inquire whether any corresponding examples of figurative language, are furnished us in the Holy Scriptures.

I am free to admit that the expressions, THIS IS MY BODY, and, THIS IS MY BLOOD, are, abstractly considered, capable of the interpretation given them by either party: for, as no one will deny, that, on the strictest principles of grammar, they may be understood literally, so no one of common intelli-

[2] See Horne's Introduction, vol. i, p. 356.

gence can deny, that, on the principles of rhetoric, they may be understood figuratively.

These expressions, however, are not isolated; they constitute a part of the whole revealed Word of God. The true point of our present essay is, therefore, to answer this simple inquiry: *From Scriptural usage, may the words in question, be understood figuratively?*

When God was about to deliver his chosen people from their Egyptian servitude, he found it necessary to inflict severe judgments upon those that held them in bondage, and refused obedience to his command to let the oppressed go free. After having afflicted the land with several distressing plagues, without affecting the heart of Pharaoh sufficiently to induce him to permit the Israelites to depart, he resolved, with one terrible blow, to strike alarm to the heart of Egypt's cruel slaveholders, by cutting off at a stroke, in one dismal night, all the first-born of the land. But he commanded his people to take a lamb, without blemish, a male of the first year, and, on the evening before he inflicted his last and fearful plague, to slay it, and strike the blood thereof on the two side-posts, and on the upper door-posts of the houses in which they should eat it. And this blood was for a *sign* upon their dwellings, seeing which, God promised to PASS OVER them and destroy them not. Now the act of God in *passing over* the children of Israel constituted the real passover. But he says of the lamb: *It is the Lord's pass-over.* (Exod. xii: 11.)

Here God instituted a feast to be observed once a year, forever, throughout the generations of Israel, for a *memorial* (v. 14) of their miraculous deliverance from Egypt. But the lamb slain, which was a type of the Lamb of God our passover, and intended to be afterward for a commemoration of the deliverance of Israel from Egypt, is declared to be the Lord's passover. Here then we have the *sign* called by the name of the *thing signified*. And this circumstance is of additional importance to us, in the solution of our question, from the fact, that the feast of the passover was to the Jew, under the old dispensation, what the feast of the Eucharist is to the Christian, under the new. As the ancient passover was instituted the night before the actual deliverance of the children of Israel from the bondage of Egypt, so was the Lord's Supper instituted the night before the redemption of the world from the bondage of sin, by the death of the Lamb of God, our passover.

Moreover, when the modern Jews celebrate thsi feast of the passover, the master of the family, and all the guests, are said to take hold of the dish containing the unleavened bread, previously broken, and exclaim:—"*Lo this is the bread of affliction which all our ancestors ate in the land of Egypt.*" The antiquity of the phrase, *bread of affliction*, as applied to the Jewish passover, is evident, from its occurrence in the sixteenth chapter of Deuteronomy. "Seven days shalt thou eat unleavened bread therewith, even the bread of affliction." [v. 3.] But, in the use of these words, no Jew ever entertained the most distant idea of his eating the identical bread of affliction which his ancestors ate in Egypt. And this manner of expression is perfectly analogous to that used in Exod. xii: 2, "It is the Lord's passover."

Now suppose, what is highly probable, that our Saviour, when he ate the paschal supper with his disciples, made use of the same mode of expression as that employed in the Jewish ritual, it is perfectly certain, that they could not be so stupid, as to suppose the bread broken by the Lord and given to them, to be the identical bread which their fathers ate in Egypt. Now whilst they were at the table, eating the passover, and thinking of the circumstances of the delivery of their ancestors from servile bondage, with the words of God, used at the time of its institution, fresh upon their minds, and, very probably, similar words spoken at the time by their Divine Master, Jesus took bread, and having pronounced the blessing, broke it, and gave it to them, saying, THIS IS MY BODY. Is it at all probable, that the disciples, under these circumstances, and with such commemorative associations pressing upon their mind, would suppose, that the food last given was different in its nature from that given at the first? In other words, would they be likely to understand by the words, THIS IS MY BODY, that Christ had, by an exercise of his omnipotent and miraculous power, annihilated the substance of the bread, and, in its place, with all its sensible properties, created something entirely different, to wit, his own real human flesh, and bones, and nerves, and sinews, a thing never before intimated in the Holy Scriptures, unlike any other known exhibition of God's almighty energy, contrary to the united testimony of the senses of smell, taste, touch, and sight, and repugnant to natural reason? Considering the words of the Eucharistic institution in connection with the circumstances in which they were pronounced, the corresponding relation which the Eucharist and the Jewish passover were designed to sustain to their respective dispensations, and the well known mode of figurative expression employed at the celebration of the latter, I can, by no possible stretch of probability, suppose, that the disciples understood their Lord to speak literally on that occasion. On the contrary, it appears to me morally certain, that they must have understood the words of the eucharistic institution in the same manner that they did those of the paschal institution. Indeed, we have not the least intimation on record that the Apostles called in question, doubted, or even hesitated to receive, with the fullest satisfaction, these words of our Lord. Nor did they subsequently ask for an explanation of them, as they had done before when his language was not well understood. We are not, therefore, to doubt that they correctly understood the divine Teacher on this occasion.

Now I hold it to be a moral impossibility, that the twelve disciples should have understood our Lord literally, and not have felt or expressed the least surprise at such extraordinary sentiment.

They must, at least, have thought: How can these several morsels of food be that flesh and blood which lives and acts before us? How is it possible that our Lord, who has always, in the indubitable evidences which he has given us of his Messiahship by miracles, assumed the infallibility of our bodily senses, now delivers to us a doctrine which entirely sets aside their testimony, and thus destroys all the former proofs of his character as the Messiah? How can our Saviour thus contradict himself and overturn the whole fabric of Christianity? Nay, it is altogether repugnant to reason itself, to suppose, that even omnipotence can make a plurality of things to be at the same time one and the same, in their physical substance. Had such thoughts occupied the mind of the disciples, the Saviour's omniscient mind would have detected them, and, in conformity with his usual practice, he would have silenced their misgivings, by insisting upon the necessity of submission to the dogma, had they rightly understood his words, or corrected their imaginations had they been wrong.

Dr. Wiseman's attempt to do away these difficulties, is truly pitiful. He observes: "We must, in the first place, remember that the Apostles were illiterate, uneducated. and by no means intellectual men at that time; consequently we must not judge of their mind or of its operations as we should of a philosopher's, but we must look for its type among the ordinary class of virtuous and sensible, though ignorant men."[1]

Alas for the cause, that requires such an imputation of ignorance touching those holy men who had for years followed the Saviour, and listened to him who taught as never man taught, and to whom their Master had already said, "Unto you it is given to *know* the mysteries of the kingdom of God." (Mark iv: 2.) It is doubtless true, therefore, that the Apostles understood the doctrines into which they had been initiated by the Saviour's instruction, sufficiently well, at least, to know whether they were inconsistent the one with the other, unsuitable to the revealed attributes of God, or contrary to natural reason. We may not then assume, that, because they were unlearned in the wisdom of human science, they were not acquainted with those doctrines of Christianity, by the teaching of which they were soon to go forth and disciple all nations.

If they were not philosophers themselves, it should be borne in mind, that they were the very men chosen to teach philosophers. But Dr. W., afterward, on the supposition that "the Apostles had some notions of the repugnance of certain conceivable propositions to the unchangeable laws of nature," labors industriously to show, that they were not "likely to form, in an instant, decision to that effect on the literal import of their Divine Master's words;" and that they would not have been right in so doing.

His whole argument proceeds upon the assumed ground, that transubstantiation involves no farther departure from the established laws of nature, than those miracles which were wrought by Christ, dur-

[1] In Opere Citato Lect. vi, p. 210.

ing his earlier ministrations. But, as I have already indicated, the latter are as unlike the former as light and darkness, as truth and error. This subject will be discussed hereafter in its more appropriate place; we may therefore pass it over for the present, having remarked thus much to show only, that the doctrine in question is unlike any other known doctrine in the universe; and secondly, on the supposition of its being true, that the ignorance of the twelve Apostles is not to be presumed as the reason of their acquiescence in its difficulties, when it was originally propounded by Christ.

Before taking leave of the Jewish passover, however, whose institution and rites we have noticed, as illustrative of the meaning of the words of Christ, used at the Eucharistic institution, it will be in place to consider the objections, offered by Dr. W., against thus employing the expression, *It is the Lord's passover.* He remarks:

"1. I say, then, in the first place, that if the words in question signify, 'This represents the passover,' the many ceremonies and peculiar rites prescribed in eating the paschal lamb, of which they were spoken, were of a character to prepare the Jews for a symbolical explanation of them." [1]

Very true. How much more, therefore, must the disciples have been prepared "for a symbolical explanation" of our Lord's words, since they had just witnessed the performance of these very "ceremonies and peculiar rites," in the celebration of a feast, now disappearing with its dispensation, to give place for the Eucharist, corresponding to it, and so changed from it as to be better adapted to a new economy. Our author continues:

"2. Again, granting the point at issue that the paschal sacrifice is called the Lord's passover, mean-

---

[1] Lecture v, pp. 195-6.

ing that it was only its symbol, this might be a figure easily allowed; because it was familiar to the Hebrews to call sacrifices by the name of the object for which they were offered. Thus a peace-offering and a sin-offering are known in Hebrew by the simple designation of *peace* and *sin*. This, in fact, was so usual, as to have given rise to several peculiar images, as in Osee, iv: 8, where the priests are said 'to eat the sins of the people;' and II Cor. v: 21, where St. Paul says of God, 'Him who knew no sin, for us he hath made sin,' that is, an oblation for sin. In like manner, therefore, the sacrifice of the Lord's passover might by the same familiar image be called his passover." (p. 196.)

All this simply shows that it was a well understood practice among the Jews to call one thing by the name of another; so that, from this usage, they would be very likely to understand our Lord to speak in like manner when he said, *This is my body*.

Dr. W. is entitled to our thanks for furnishing us this and the foregoing argument, as proving our symbolical interpretation.

We re-assert, therefore, the perfect applicability of the words of the institution of the ancient passover to the illustration of the words of the eucharistic institution. As the former were confessedly used in a figurative sense, we fairly infer from this fact a figurative meaning of the words, *This is my body*, and *This is my blood*.

Having shown from Scriptural usage that these expressions *may* be understood figuratively, we might here rest this part of our argument, but we have no necessity of limiting ourselves to a single passage however decisive.

The Scriptures abound with this kind of expression. Thus, "The seven good kine ARE seven years; and the seven good ears ARE seven years."

(Gen. xli : 26.) "The ten horns ARE ten kings." (Dan. vii : 24.) "He that soweth the good seed IS the son of man: the field IS the world: the good seed ARE the children of the kingdom; but the tares ARE the children of the wicked one: the enemy that sowed them IS the devil: the harvest IS the end of the world; and the reapers ARE the angels." (Matt. xiii : 37–39.) "They drank of that spiritual Rock that followed them: and that Rock WAS Christ." (I Cor. x : 4.) "These ARE the two covenants—For this Agar IS Mount Sinai in Arabia." (Gal. iv : 24, 25.) "The seven stars ARE the angels of the seven churches: and the seven candle-sticks which thou sawest, ARE the seven churches." (Rev. i : 20.)

These passages are cited by Dr. Wiseman, (p. 175,) who groups them together as "strictly parallel one with another," and forming a class by themselves. It is hardly necessary to remark that these are quoted by Protestants as illustrative of the words of our Saviour. Dr. W. attempts to deprive us of their use by undertaking to prove that they are not parallel to the eucharistic formula. He very clearly and satisfactorily shows that, to constitute a parallelism between two or more passages of Scripture, it is not enough that the same *word* occurs in both, but that the same *thing* or object must be intended. In the application of this rule he urges that, in the above cited texts, the *same thing* is intended, namely, the "*explanation of a symbolical instruction,*" and adds: "But then it follows, likewise, that in order to thrust the words 'this is my body,' into the same category, and treat them as parallel, we must show *them* also to contain the same *thing*—the explanation of a symbolical instruction. Till this be done, there is no parallelism established." (Page 180.)

Had the learned author given a true and impartial definition to his *"res eadem,"* he might have saved himself the drudgery of racking his brain to extort from it an assemblage of quibbling distinctions without a difference and erudite unintelligibilities. For I suppose it requires more labor and pains-taking to invent artful subtleties, and study out biased definitions of things, than it does to give utterance to plain and candid verities. He should have defined the "same *thing*" in the quoted passages to be, *Instruction by symbolical imagery,* or *metaphorical language;* not, "the explanation of a symbolical instruction."

In his usual and sophistical manner, Dr. Wiseman argues their want of parallelism by "observing, that in no one of the instances heaped together by our opponents, are we left to conjecture that an explanation of symbols is meant to be conveyed, but the context in each, expressly informs us of the circumstance. This is evident of the examples from Joseph, Daniel, and our Saviour, for they are clearly said to be giving or receiving interpretations. St. Paul to the Galatians is equally careful to let us see the same; for this is his entire sentence: 'Which things are an *allegory;* FOR these *are* the two covenants.' After the expression, 'the rock was Christ,' he is careful to add, (v. 6,) 'now these things were done *in figure of us;*' and in the very sentence he tells us that it was a *spiritual* rock whereof he spoke. In fine, the instance from the Apocalypse is equally explicit: 'Write down the things which thou hast seen . . . the mystery (*allegory* or *symbol*) of the seven stars . . . and seven golden candle-sticks. The seven stars ARE the angels of the seven churches.' And with passages so explained by the very writers, it is pretended to compare the simple narrative, 'Jesus took bread, and blessed and brake, and gave to his disciples, and said, Take ye and eat; *this is my body!*'" (pp. 180, 181.)

Who ever read a more artful and carefully wrought sophism? From the tenor of these remarks one might infer that the subsequent explanation of a symbol or metaphor destroys the *fact* of the symbol or metaphor. The interpretation which followed Daniel's vision of beasts, does not at all invalidate the *fact*, that the vision was symbolical; nor did the explanation of the parable of the sower, make it less a parable. Facts are immortal. The expression, "The seven good kine are seven years, and the seven good ears are seven years," "the ten horns are ten kings," "The seed is the word of God," are metaphors, and will forever remain such. In the number and resemblance of the points of similitude to the thing signified, they may vary, but they must ever remain essentially the same, that is, figures of speech. One metaphor may be so unusual and obscure, as to require explanation, another may be so common and patent, as to be easily apprehended.

The figurative use of the language, touching the passover, must have been so familiar to the disciples, as to prepare them in an eminent degree for symbolical instruction. The circumstances attending the institution of the Eucharist, and the language employed, were such, as would naturally lead the disciples to apprehend the figurative words employed. It is expressly recorded that Christ took *bread*, which, after giving thanks, he *broke*, and gave to his disciples. He did not take some strange and unusual thing and pronounce it to be his body, but in the presence, and sight of the twelve, he took BREAD. This identical BREAD he broke and gave to them:—this same BREAD they received into their hands, looked upon it, conveyed it to their mouths, and, tasting, ate it. Neither reason nor sense could have allowed them to understand our Lord otherwise than figuratively, when he said of that visible BREAD, *This is my body.* Under these circumstances there existed no necessity for our Saviour to add, "These things are *symbols* or *figures.*" Such an affirmation would have been a useless redundancy: nay, an undeserved reflection upon the intelligence and good sense of his chosen and beloved disciples. These observations will receive still greater strength, from the remarks hereafter to be made on those other portions of our Lord's words, "This do in remembrance of me," and, "I will not henceforth drink of this fruit of the vine," &c.

The principal objections advanced by Dr. Wiseman, as designed to prove a want of parallelism, in the several passages cited, to the words of institution, have now been considered. Those that remain are undeserving a serious refutation.

To his repeated endeavors to range the doctrine of transubstantiation by the side of Christ's divinity, it is enough, at present, to reply, that the former has no Scriptural authority, according to the opinion of several distinguished divines of his own church; whereas the latter is clearly and fully taught in the Word of God, as he himself more than intimates, when he says: "The texts whereby any dogma is proved, may be so clear, that they demonstrate it, at first sight, yet may consistently be submitted to the most rigid examination. For instance, is not the Divinity of our Lord so clear in the Scripture, that an unprejudiced mind is satisfied with the simple recital of the texts relating to it?" (p. 43.) I apprehend the two doctrines have nothing in common, except a lodging-place in the mind of their common advocates. Finally, I have abundantly proved what was proposed to be done in the early part of this communication, namely, that from Scripture usage the words of the eucharistic institution *may* be understood figuratively.

The *necessity* of such an interpretation will constitute the subject of my next.

With sentiments of esteem allow me to subscribe myself as heretofore,

Yours truly,

E. O. P.

LETTER VI.

NECESSITY OF THE FIGURATIVE INTERPRETATION OF THE
WORDS OF INSTITUTION SHOWN.

DEAR BROTHER:—We have now arrived at the point in our discussion which I regard as the most important. It is not enough for us to show from Scripture usage, that the words of our Lord *may* be understood in a figurative sense; in order to decide the matter it is necessary to prove, that to avoid great difficulties and plain contradictions, we are *compelled* to adopt this figurative interpretation. If I succeed in doing this, you will perceive that a point of no small importance is gained in our favor: for your church has defined, that these words teach the doctrine of transubstantiation. Indeed, the Council of Trent declares it to be "a most heinous crime, that they should be turned by certain contentious and wicked men into pretended and imaginary figures, to the denial of the truth of the flesh and blood of Christ."[1] And Dr. Wiseman says: "We entrench ourselves behind the strong power of our Saviour's words, and calmly remain there, till driven from our position." (p. 168.) These words understood literally, are, therefore, regarded by your church, as the strong defence of the doctrine in question. Safe, however, as you may feel behind this your fancied "strong power of our Saviour's words," I shall venture to approach, and prove the strength of your position by wielding a few of those weapons which the God of battles has

[1] Sess xiii, cap. 1, De Reali Præsentia Domini nostri, etc.

put into the hands of his militant followers, premising a few general propositions, as forming a sort of groundwork of much that may follow.

1. The Being whom we call God, is an uncaused, unoriginated, and, by consequence, eternal existence; all his attributes, both those called natural, and moral, are likewise eternal, infinitely perfect, and therefore unchangeable.

2. It necessarily follows from his eternal and immutable perfections, that there are some things which are morally, and, therefore, naturally impossible to be done by God; for we cannot suppose that his omnipotence can consistently be exerted to do what is repugnant to his eternal and infinite holiness; because, if it could, he might be at variance with himself, and, therefore, imperfect.

Hence, God cannot lie; which necessarily implies, that He cannot make that which is essentially and eternally wrong, to be essentially and eternally right; He cannot contradict himself, either in his Word, or his Works; He cannot make that which is already made, for that would imply that it was not made, though it was made; He cannot make things which are essentially different the one from the other, to be essentially the same; He cannot make a part of a thing equal to its whole, at one and the same time, otherwise he might operate contradictions, which is impossible and absurd.

3. More particularly: A revelation for the good of his creature, man, proceeding from this infinitely good and perfect Being, must be perfectly consistent with all his attributes, adapted to the nature and wants of the being to be benefited, and consistent in all its parts.

Having stated these fundamental truths, I proceed to notice the difficulties which forbid the literal interpretation of our Lord's words, at the institution of the Eucharist. And this I will endeavor to do, with special reference to the doctrine of transubstantiation in general, and to those consequences and teaching, in particular, which necessarily or constructively result from it. For I regard this doctrine and its appendants, as standing or falling with the literal interpretation of the words of institution, or its opposite.

1. The words themselves do not indicate any change whatever. They are declarative of what already exists, but not effective of what is not. We might as well argue from the expressions, "It is the Lord's passover," "the ten horns are ten kings," that some change was effected by virtue of them, as to affirm, that by the words, "this is my body," a change of substance is effected. But no one contends, that the pronunciation of the former operated any change of substance; so we affirm, that the enunciation of the latter, is not operative of any change whatever. Had our Lord intended by words to transubstantiate the bread in his hands into his own body, it is reasonable to suppose, that he would have said, "Let this become my body," or some other equivalent words. From an expression of this kind, we might argue for some kind of change. When God displays his omnipotent energy through the medium of words, His language is indicative of something effected. Thus he says: "Let light be," "Lazarus, come forth," "Tabitha, arise," and the like.

If words simply declarative of a fact, like those of our Lord, may be supposed to indicate a new creation, then I see no reason, so far as the mere words are concerned, against supposing a change, or new creation of substance, wrought in virtue of the words of the paschal institution, and the numerous other passages already cited in the connection; which is not true. Nay, might we not bring into the category those words of the beloved disciple, when giving expression to the unerring spirit within him, *In the beginning was the Word*, and argue thence the creation of the second person in the Trinity?

It is doubtless true, that Christ's whole act, in taking bread, blessing, breaking and distributing, did constitute the consecration of the bread, or setting it apart for sacred use, and that the words, *This is my body*, are to be considered as expressive of what was already effected. I can therefore see no reason for the teaching of your church, when she declares, that Christ, in virtue of these words of consecration, transubstantiated the bread and wine into his own body and blood.

Moreover, admitting for argument's sake, that the transubstantiation is *effected* by the words under consideration, it will thence follow that the change or conversion must *follow* their use; for all *effects* must of necessity *follow* their *causes*. Now, however closely this conversion may follow, it is certain that it cannot exist prior to its cause, that is, before the utterance of all the causative words. Hence, our Saviour affirmed the eucharistic elements to be his body and blood, before they were his body and blood. Your doctrine therefore gives the lie to our Divine Master, and must therefore be rejected, as false and impossible.

Do you reply, that the present is sometimes put for the future by the inspired writers, when the thing spoken of is near or certain? (See John, v: 25; xii: 23, 31; xvii: 4, 11, 12; Isa. liii: 3–10.) Such I admit to be a frequent usage when *acts* or *events* are the subjects of prophetic affirmation, but not when the *esse* of things real is spoken of. When God affirms of any substantial existence that it *is* this or that, he means that it is such *when* he speaks, and not that it will *afterward* be such.

2. The difficulty of the literal interpretation is increased, by the addition of the words, *which is*

given, and *which is shed,* to those just considered. According to this exposition of his language, the real human body of Christ was actually given as a sacrifice, and his blood shed, when he instituted this sacrament; but this is contrary to the history given by the Evangelists, and the repeated declaration of the Apostles. The same sacred historians that record the Saviour's own predicted delivery, (Matt. xx: 19, and Mark x: 33,) put this delivery subsequent to the eucharistic institution. (Matt. xxvii: 2, and Mark, xv: 1.) This delivery up to the Gentiles Peter associates with his crucifixion, (Acts ii: 23,) when he "bore our sins in his own body on the tree." (I Pet. ii: 24.) And the Apostle Paul teaches, that he "was delivered for our offences;" (Rom. iv: 25;) "for when we were yet without strength, in due time Christ died for the ungodly," (v: 6; viii: 32,) and thereby offered, through the eternal Spirit, a sacrifice, once for all, to God for us. (Heb. vii: 27; ix: 14, 27; x: 10.)

When therefore our Saviour says, "This is my body which is *given* for you," and, "This is my blood which is *shed* for you," he is to be understood as saying: "This is my body which is offered for you upon the cross," and, "This is my blood which is there poured out for the world." But his real body was not then offered, nor was his real blood then shed, when he uttered these words. It follows hence that what he called his body was not his real and human body, but only a symbolical representation of it. This exposition of our Lord's words removes these difficulties which stand in the way of the literal interpretation; for it is easy to understand, how the bread broken, and wine poured out, were a symbol of the crucified body and shed blood of Christ. The evident meaning of his words may be thus briefly paraphrased: "This bread now given you, to be distributed amongst yourselves, is a symbol of my body which is about to be given, as a sacrifice for you, upon the cross; and this cup poured out is a symbol of my blood as being shed for you, for the remission of sins." So certain and present was the whole tragedy in the mind of the divine Saviour, that he speaks of the transaction as already taking place, whilst representing it by the symbols of bread and wine. So in another place, to which reference has been made, he speaks of having finished his work, and being no longer in the world, (John, xvii: 4, 11,) even before his crucifixion and ascent to heaven. Our exposition, therefore, harmonizes with Scripture usage, and agrees with the matter of fact in the case, but yours is repugnant to both; for having affirmed the literal explanation to be the meaning of our Lord, when he says, *This is my body*, you cannot ascribe to the words, *which is given* or *broken* a future signification; because, if what he called his body were his real body, it was then already broken and given; which, as just shown, was not the fact.

3. At the institution of the Eucharist, Christ is represented by the first two Evangelists, Matthew and Mark, as saying of what was contained in the cup subsequently to its consecration, that he would no more drink of that *fruit of the vine* until that day that he should drink it new with them in the kingdom of God. That same substance which he had before called his blood, he afterward denominated the *fruit*, or *product* of the vine. If the words, *This is my blood*, are interpreted literally, it is difficult to account for his calling that real blood of his the *fruit of the vine*.

It is sheer sophistry to undertake to do away the force of these considerations, by affirming, that Christ spoke these words with reference to the nature of the wine prior to its consecration, because St. Luke arranges a like expression before the words of benediction. In addition to the fact that Matthew and Mark place them after the words of consecration, so-called, you will observe that when Christ spoke of the *fruit of the vine*, he spoke of what was *drank*, which was no other than the liquid contained in the cup, after its consecration to the use of this holy sacrament. If then, what was drank by the twelve disciples, was the fruit of the vine, it could not, at the same time, have been human blood; for they are not one and the same thing, either in their substance, or sensible properties. But how perfectly does this expression of our Lord agree with the Protestant view, which regards the elements, not as the real, but symbolical body and blood of Christ.

4. The disciples were commanded to celebrate this institution of their Lord, in REMEMBRANCE of him. Now memory never has respect to what is either present or future, but always refers to what is past. If the divine speaker used language in its ordinary acceptation, he could have meant no more in this injunction, than to command the Apostles, and with them the whole church, to celebrate this sacrament as a means of calling to mind, afterward, certain truths or facts of which they had before a knowledge, such as his incarnation and death as an atoning sacrifice upon the cross. But the literal interpretation of this text, makes Christ say: Do this, not as a remembrance of my incarnation and death simply, but also, as actually making a repeated incarnation and perpetual sacrifice of me; which is most evidently inconsistent with the express words of our Lord. Your church teaches, that Christ entire, embracing his body, soul and divine substance, is really and substantially present in the Eucharist. According to this doctrine how can this sacrament be observed in *remembrance* of Christ, he being really and sub-

stantially present? It is impossible to do so. The literal interpretation of the words of institution, I therefore conclude, to be quite irreconcilable with the proper signification of this term employed by the Saviour; and, by consequence, such exposition must be false.

In illustration, suppose your friends should gather about your person and perform certain kindly acts, and being interrogated by a friendly visitor about the significance of those ceremonies, they should reply, "we are doing this in remembrance of our friend."

Do you suppose that your guest would understand what was meant by such a reply? Would you not even correct your friends for perverting the use of common and plain language?

We have before remarked, that the passover under the Jewish dispensation, was to be observed, as a memorial of the Lord's passing by the children of Israel; but no Jew ever supposed that anniversary to be the same day, in which they were preserved from the destructive plague. Why then should the Christian suppose the consecrated bread to be really Christ's body, when he expressly commands this sacrament to be observed in remembrance of himself?

5. From the literal interpretation of Christ's words, we are compelled to admit the *corruptibility* of his real and true body. This is a matter of fact so undeniable, and cognizable by any man's senses, that your church does not attempt to conceal it, but, on the contrary, even makes provision how to dispose of it when corrupted. The Roman Missal teaches: "If the Priest vomit the Eucharist, if the species appear entire, they are reverently to be taken, unless nausea be produced; in this case the consecrated species are to be carefully separated and laid aside in some holy place until they are

CORRUPTED, and afterward cast into the sacristy. But if the species do not appear, [distinguishable from the other vomited matter] the vomit must be burned, and the ashes cast into the sacristy."[1] This is the language which Rome puts forth to the world, and which necessarily follows her literal exposition of the words of institution. How does it agree with the Holy Scriptures?

David says: "Therefore my heart is glad, and my glory rejoiceth; my flesh also shall rest in hope. For thou wilt not leave my soul in hell; NEITHER WILT THOU SUFFER THINE HOLY ONE TO SEE CORRUPTION." (Psal. xvi, 10.)

At the very opening of the new dispensation, upon the day of Pentecost, Peter quotes this passage from David and observes, that he "being a prophet, and knowing that God had sworn with an oath to him, that of the fruit of his loins, according to the flesh, he would raise up Christ to sit on his throne; he seeing this before, spake of the resurrection of Christ, that his soul was not left in hell, NEITHER DID HIS FLESH SEE CORRUPTION." (Acts, ii: 30, 31.)

Observe, It was the flesh of Christ which proceeded from the loins of the patriach David that SAW NO CORRUPTION; but that body of Christ in the Eucharist continually sees corruption, in the process of human digestion and other animal processes, as also according to the ordinary laws of decomposition, recognized by your Missal. It follows hence, that what Christ called his body at the institution

---

[1] Si sacerdos evomet eucharistiam, si species integrae appareant reverentur sumantur, nisi nausea fiat; tunc enim species consecratae caute separentur, et in aliquo loco sacro reponantur donec corrumpantur, et postea in sacrarium projiciantur; quod si species non appareant, comburatur vomitus, et cineres in sacrarium mittantur. De Defectibus in Missa. Art. x, No. 14.

of the Eucharist, was not his real and substantial body, that body which proceeded from the loins of David, and was born of the Virgin Mary; but it was his symbolical body. For he has no body holding a medium place between his human and sacramental body. Your literal interpretation necessarily leads to consequences perfectly contradictory to plain explicit Scripture, and must therefore be false.

6. Whilst upon the earth, our divine Lord very plainly taught the doctrine of his omnipresence, when he promised his disciples, that "where two or three are gathered together in my name, there am I in the midst of them:" (Matt. xviii : 20;) "and lo, I am with you always, even unto the end of the world." This must be understood of his divine and spiritual presence; for, at another time, when speaking with reference to his human body, he says to the Jews: "Ye shall seek me and shall not find me." (John, vii : 34.) He afterward repeats the same to his disciples. (xiii : 33.) Again he says: "Yet a little while and the world seeth me no more." (xiv : 19.) "For the poor ye always have with you, but me ye have not always." (xii : 8, Matt. xxvi : 11, and Mark, xiv : 7.)

The comment of ST. AUGUSTINE on these last words, is worthy of notice. "He speaks," says he, "of the presence of his body; ye shall have me according to my providence, according to my majesty and invisible grace; but according to the flesh which the Word of God assumed, according to that which was born of the Virgin Mary, ye shall not have me; therefore because he conversed with his disciples forty days, he is ascended up into heaven, and is not here."[A]

But the doctrine of transubstantiation most unqualifiedly contradicts these plain words of our

---

[A] Aug. Tract. L, in Joan. tom. ix, p. 152.

Lord, since it makes his real body and blood present in the Eucharist, whenever the words of consecration are canonically pronounced. Again, therefore, we affirm your literal interpretation to be false.

Moreover, from these same Scriptures, we argue the *non-multipresence* of Christ's natural body. Our Saviour evidently teaches, that he is ever divinely present in the midst of his faithful ones, though his body be absent from the world; from which we conclude, that there is no such inseparable and necessary union between his divine and human natures, that the former cannot operate without the presence of the latter. This truth seems to me perfectly established by the words of Christ under consideration, which, at the same time, totally destroy your doctrine of concomitance. If then Christ is perpetually and divinely present with his Church on earth, but his body is perpetually absent from us in heaven, we may fairly infer, in the absence of contrary testimony, that his body is local in heaven and never elsewhere present.

Again, if we admit that Christ's natural body may be present in more places than one, at the same moment, then we must allow that it may be in a thousand, and consequently that it may be omnipresent and divine. Thus directly does the doctrine of transubstantiation lead to the heresy of the ancient Eutychians, who taught that the human nature of Christ was destroyed by being taken up, or absorbed into his divine substance when he ascended. This error, however, was opposed by the orthodox Fathers, and condemned by the Council of Chalcedon, which defined, that "the differences of the two natures in Christ were not destroyed by the union; but that their properties were preserved distinct, and concur to one person." [B]

[B] Concil. Chalcedon., Act. v, A. D. 451.

Before you undertake, as some have done, to prove the multipresence of Christ's human body from the exclamation of a dying Stephen: "Behold; I see the heavens opened, and the Son of man standing on the right hand of God;" (Acts, vii: 56;) you ought to be able to locate heaven, and make it appear, that Christ was not then in that place when Stephen saw him. This may be a severe task, like making brick without straw, but you must do it before you can prove, by this passage, the ubiquity of Christ's human body, which necessarily results from that favorite doctrine of a corporeal presence in the Eucharist.

7. Your church teaches that the eucharistic offering, denominated the Sacrifice of the Mass, "is the sacrifice which was figuratively represented by the various sacrifices offered in the times of nature, and of the law; since it includes every good which was signified by them, and is the consummation and perfection of them all."[1] "For the sacrifice which is now offered by the ministry of the priests, is one and the same as that which Christ then offered on the cross, only the mode of offering is different."[2] "And, Whoever shall affirm, that a true and proper sacrifice is not offered to God in the mass, or that the offering is nothing else than giving Christ to us, to eat: let him be accursed."[3]

[1] Hæc denique illa est, quæ per varias sacrificiorum Naturæ, et legis tempore, similitudinem figurabatur, utpote quæ bona omnia per illa significata, velut illorum omnium consummatio et perfectio complectitur. Concl. Trident. Sess. xxii. cap. 1.

[2] Una enim eademque est hostia, idemque nunc offerens sacerdotum ministerio, qui scripsum tunc in cruce obtulit, sola offerendi ratione diversa. Idem, cap. 2.

[3] Si quis dixerit, in Missa non offerri Deo verum et proprium sacrificium, aut quod offerri non sit aliud, quam nobis Christum ad manducandum dari; Anathema sit. Sess. xxii, De Sacrificio Misbæ, Can. i.

According to this the sacrifice of Calvary is repeatedly and continuously offered, and that too, "not only for the sins, punishments, satisfactions, and other necessities of living believers, but also for the dead in Christ, who are not yet thoroughly purified."[1] By the "dead in Christ," is meant those detained in purgatory, not yet being fully purged.

Let us compare this doctrine with the inspired word of God. St. Paul says, that Christ our high priest "needeth not daily, as those high priests, [under the law] to offer up sacrifice, first for his own sins, and then for the people's; for this he did ONCE, when he offered up himself." (Heb. vii: 27.) "Neither by the blood of goats and calves, but by his own blood, he entered in ONCE into the holy place, having obtained eternal redemption for us." "For Christ is not entered into the holy places made with hands, which are the figures of the true; but into heaven itself, now to appear in the presence of God for us: nor yet that he should offer himself, often, as the high priest entereth into the holy place every year with the blood of others; for then must he often have suffered since the foundation of the world; but now ONCE, in the end of the world, hath he appeared to put away sin by the sacrifice of himself. And as it is appointed unto men ONCE to die, but after this the judgment: so Christ was ONCE offered to bear the sins of many; and unto them that look for him shall he appear the second time, without sin, unto salvation." (Heb. ix: 12, 24–28.) And "We are sanctified through the offering of the body of Jesus Christ ONCE for all." "For by ONE offering he hath perfected for

[1] Quare non solum pro fidelium virorum peccatis, pœrnis, satisfactionibus et aliis necessitatibus, sed et pro defunctis in Christo, nondum ad plenum purgatis, ritè juxta Apostolorum traditionem, offertur. Ubi Sup. Cit. cap. 2.

ever them that are sanctified. (ch. x: 10, 14.) From which we are clearly taught the following truths:

1. Christ needs not to offer up sacrifice for sin daily, or continuously, as the high priests did under the law.

2. When he offered himself upon the cross, that ONE sacrifice was the only proper sacrifice ever made, or that ever will be made for sin.

3. No other sacrifice is required for the putting away of sin, because by this he has "obtained eternal redemption for us," and "perfected forever them that are sanctified."

The Apostle makes it just as certain that Christ has been offered but ONCE, as it is that it is appointed unto men to die ONCE, and to be judged ONCE. Your doctrine of the mass is, therefore, perfectly contradictory to that taught by an inspired Apostle, and, by consequence, false.

Again, more particularly, the sacred penmen concur in teaching that no true and proper sacrifice for sins was ever made before Christ offered himself upon the cross. By a *true* and *proper* sacrifice is meant, a *full* and *perfect* sacrifice, such as God is pleased to accept as an atonement for the sins of men. But the imperfection of the Jewish sacrifices is evident from the following: "Hath the Lord as great delight in burnt offerings and sacrifices, as in obeying the voice of the Lord? Behold, to obey is better than sacrifice, and to hearken than the fat of rams." (I Sam. xv: 22, compare Matt. ix: 13, and xii: 7.) Sacrifice and offering thou didst not desire ... burnt-offering and sin-offering hast thou not required." (Psal. xl: 6, compare li: 16, and Hosea vi: 6.) "Be it known unto you therefore, men and brethren, that through this man is preached unto you the forgiveness of sins; and by him all that believe are justified from all things, from which they could not be justified by the law of Moses." (Acts, xiii: 38, 39.) "For by the law is the knowledge of sin, [but not a propitiation for it.] But now the righteousness of God without the law is manifested, being witnessed [or testified to] by the [sacrifices of the] law and [the predictions of] the prophets. Even the righteousness of God, which is by faith of Jesus Christ unto all, and upon all them that believe." "Being justified freely by his grace, through the redemption that is in Christ Jesus: Whom God hath set forth TO BE A PROPITIATION THROUGH FAITH IN HIS BLOOD, to declare his righteousness for the remission of sins that are past." (Rom. iii: 20-25.)

"In whom we have redemption THROUGH HIS BLOOD, even the forgiveness of sins. For it pleased the Father that in him should all fullness dwell; and, having made peace THROUGH THE BLOOD OF HIS CROSS, by him to reconcile all things unto himself." (Colos. i: 14, 19, 20; compare Ephes. ii: 13-16.) "And every priest standeth daily ministering and offering oftentimes the same sacrifices, which can never take away sins; but this man, after he had offered ONE sacrifice for sins, forever sat down on the right hand of God." ... "Now, where remission of these is, there is NO MORE OFFERING FOR SIN." (Heb. x: 11, 12, 18.) "Knowing that Christ being raised from the dead, dieth no more; death hath no more dominion over him. For in that he died, he died unto [for] sin ONCE." (Rom. vi: 9, 10.) "For Christ also hath ONCE suffered for sins, the just for the unjust, that he might bring us to God, being put to death in the flesh, but quickened by the Spirit." (I Pet. iii: 18.)

It is therefore plain that no true and proper sacrifice for sin was made before Christ, "through the blood of his cross," offered that ONE SACRIFICE FOR sins when "he suffered, the just for the unjust," by "being put to death in the flesh."

But the Eucharist was instituted before Christ's death; it could not therefore have been a real and propitiatory sacrifice for sin; hence your sacrifice of the Mass, which is confessedly but a repetition of that sacrament which Christ celebrated before his death, cannot be a true, proper and propitiatory sacrifice for the sins of the living and the dead, as you pretend. Your literal interpretation of our Saviour's words, therefore, which gives rise to the doctrine of the Mass, must be false.

The Council of Trent holds the following language: "And since the same Christ who once offered himself by his blood on the altar of the cross, is contained in this divine sacrifice which is celebrated in the Mass, and offered without blood, the holy council teaches that this sacrifice is really propitiatory, and made by Christ himself. . . . And the fruits of that bloody oblation are plentifully enjoyed by means of this unbloody one."[1] And this unbloody sacrifice is said to be properly offered for the sins, punishments, satisfactions, and other necessities of the living and the dead.

In this remarkable article we are told, that "the same Christ, who once offered himself by his blood on the altar of the cross, is contained in this divine, propitiatory, and bloodless sacrifice of the Mass; that it is the same sacrifice that was offered upon the cross." It is the same sacrifice offered in a different manner only, and yet it is not the same, for the former was *bloody*, but the latter *unbloody!* It is said to be propitiatory, though bloodless, whereas the Holy Scriptures teach that "without shedding of blood there is no remission!" Christ is said to

---

[1] Cujus quidem oblationis (cruentæ inquam) fructus per hanc incruentam uberrimæ percipiuntur. Sess. xxii, cap. 2.

offer this sacrifice of the Mass himself, whereas the Apostle declares that "after he had offered *one* sacrifice for sins, he forever sat down on the right hand of God!"

May the God of mercy and truth open the eyes of your Mass-worshipers, discover to them the folly of arraying the human against the divine authority, and give them repentance unto life.

8. In order that the believers of transubstantiation be not naturally led to suppose this sacrament to contain nothing more than bread and wine, your church requires their minds to be withdrawn, as much as possible, from subjection to the senses, and excited to the contemplation of the stupendous power of God. But it has pleased God at divers times, to reveal his will to man, and, in so doing, to confirm the truth of his revelation by miracles. These supernatural proofs of the Divine Being, were so made, as to be cognizable by the bodily senses of those that witnessed them. He changes the rod of Aaron into a serpent, divides the waters of the Red Sea and of Jordan, raises the dead, feeds multitudes with a few loaves and small fishes, turns water into wine, and the like. For our knowledge of these divine pooofs of the truth of God's word, we are indebted to the testimony of the senses of those that witnessed them; and our knowledge is certain, in proportion to the certainty and infallibility of the evidence of their senses. But God has not selected an insufficient and uncertain medium, through which to communicate a knowledge of his will to the world; for the testimony of the senses is infallible.

In this light the inspired writers themselves regarded the evidence of the senses, as we learn from the following: "Forasmuch as many have taken in hand to set forth in order a declaration of those things which are MOST SURELY BELIEVED amongst us, even as they delivered them unto us, who were EYE-WITNESSES and ministers of the word; it seemed good to me also, having had PERFECT UNDERSTANDING of all things from the very first, to write unto thee in order, most excellent Theophilus, that thou mightest know the CERTAINTY of those things, wherein thou hast been instructed." (Luke, i: 1–4.) "That which was from the beginning, which we have HEARD, which we have SEEN with our eyes, which we have looked upon, and our hands have HANDLED of the Word of life; that which we have SEEN and HEARD declare we unto you, that you also may have fellowship with us. And these things write we unto you that your joy may be full." (I John, i: 1, 3, 4.)

From these passages it appears, that the things seen and heard, were most surely believed by the Evangelists and primitive Christians. Thomas was cured of his unbelief by seeing and feeling, and so might every Romanist in the world, if he would submit, like the first Christians, to the indubitable evidence of his own natural senses. And now allow me to inquire in the language of Archbishop TILLOTSON, "Whether it be reasonable to imagine that God should make that a part of the Christian religion, which shakes the *main external evidence* and confirmation of the whole, I mean the *miracles* which were wrought by our Saviour and his Apostles, the assurance whereof did at first depend upon the certainty of sense. For if the senses of those who saw them were or could be deceived, then there might have been no miracles wrought, and consequently it may be justly doubted, whether that kind of confirmation which God hath given to the Christian religion would be strong enough to prove it; for, supposing transubstantiation to have been a part of it, every man would have had as great evidence that it was false as that the Christian religion is true.

"Of all the doctrines in the world, this of transubstantiation is peculiarly incapable of being proved by a miracle. For if a miracle were wrought for the proof of it, the very same assurance that any one could have of the truth of the miracle, he hath of the falsehood of this doctrine: that is, the clear evidence of his senses. For that there is a miracle wrought to prove that *what he sees in the sacrament is not bread, but the body of Christ,* there is only the evidence of sense, and there is the same evidence to prove that what *he sees* in the sacrament is not *the body of Christ, but bread.* So that here would arise a new controversy, whether a man should rather believe his senses giving testimony against the doctrine of transubstantiation, or bearing witness to a miracle wrought to confirm that doctrine; there being the very same evidence against the truth of the doctrine which there is for the truth of the miracle. And then the argument for the *doctrine* and the objection against it would balance one another, and consequently transubstantiation is not to be proved by miracles, because that would be to prove to a man by *something that he sees* that *he doth not see what he sees.* And if there were no other evidence that transubstantiation is no part of the Christian religion, this would be sufficient, that what proves the one doth as much overthrow the other; and that miracles which are certainly the best and highest external proof of Christianity, are the worst proof in the world of transubstantiation, unless a man can renounce his senses at the same time that he relies upon them, for a man cannot believe a miracle without relying on his senses, nor transubtantiation without renouncing them. So that never were any two things so ill coupled together as the doctrine of Christianity and of transubstantiation, because they draw several ways and are ready to strangle one another; for the main external evidence of the doctrine of Christ, which is miracles, is resolved into the certainty of sense, but this evidence is clear, and point-blank against transubstantiation."[1]

9. "Come now, and let us reason together, saith the Lord." It is an argument of no small weight in favor of the truth and divine origin of our holy religion, that it is perfectly adapted to the physical, intellectual, and moral nature of man. Its holy requisitions are exactly suited to the constitution and laws of the human mind. Nothing short of omniscience could have devised, and nothing but omnipotence could have carried into effect, such a harmonious exhibition of creative power and wisdom, as we find displayed in the economy of our whole man, and his redemption from sin. The Author of our being, and of the Christian religion, is that same God whose "way is perfect," and "all whose works are done in truth." He cannot deny himself; his very nature requires him to act with perfect consistency in whatever his goodness moves him to do. He who adapted the eye to the light and the ear to sound, has, with, at least, equal wisdom and benevolence, addressed his revealed word to the understanding of his rational creatures. Throughout the Bible man is regarded as a being of reason; and the Author of this sacred book appears constantly to have had in mind this least impaired and noblest faculty of his intellectual creatures. True it is, however, that God, in his Word, has revealed to us truths, whose mode of existence and ultimate nature far transcend the comprehension of finite intelligences; though the *fact* of their existence is not repugnant to natural reason. For instance, we are taught that in the *one divine nature*, JEHOVAH, there are *three persons*, co-equal and co-

---

[1] Tillotson on Transub. Cited by Ousley, pp. 193-5.

eternal, yet not three and one in the same sense, hence not involving any contradiction, and therefore not contrary to reason though above it.

It being true, therefore, that God's revelation to man is addressed to him as an intelligent being, and adapted to his noblest faculty, REASON, it must follow that if any doctrine be proposed for our belief as the Word of God which is repugnant to the very nature of this faculty, it is to be rejected as spurious and false.

In this light I view the doctrine of transubstantiation; for it involves the following impossibilities: that the natural qualities of bread and wine subsist without their subjects; that the *whole* of a material thing is no greater than one of its parts when a separation is made; that what is already made and perpetually remains so can be repeatedly made again; that our Lord gave himself with his own hands to his disciples to be eaten and drunken, still keeping himself to himself; and, that his same numerical and material body may be in a thousand different places at the same time, and exist under as many different forms. All which is impossible even to God; for he cannot do what he wills not to do; and he will not work natural contradictions; for this would be to act contrary to himself, contrary to the fixed and immutable principles of Him who cannot lie.

10. It is in vain, therefore, for the advocates of this doctrine, to resort to the omnipotence of God, in order to prove its possibility, and screen it from the unpalatable charge of impossible, and absurd. This was the method employed by the ancient heretics, who could not screen their errors, except by taking refuge under the broad cover of almighty power. And the reply given to them by the more orthodox Fathers of the church, may now be made, with great propriety, to the defenders of transub-

stantiation, a doctrine not excelled, in unreasonableness, by the most extravagant reveries of ancient heresy. Indeed, the unlikeness of this dogma to anything else within the range of human knowledge, is clearly perceived and felt by those who attempt to shelter it from its confessedly apparent absurdities, by pretending the broad shield of God's omnipotence. Thus PASCHASIUS RATBERT, the father of transubstantiation, in the very commencement of the first treatise ever written in defence of this doctrine, argues the omnipotence of God in its proof, in the following manner: "Since without the power of God nothing exists, therefore all things are possible [to him.] For God the maker of all things has not so ordained the nature of things, that he should take from them his own volition: because every creature subsists by the same will and power from which it has its cause, not only that it should subsist as something, but also that it should so exist as the very will of God decrees, which is the cause of all creatures. In no other manner does any creature subsist, except by the will of Him from whom flows its entire being; and therefore as often as the nature of the creature is changed, increased, or subtracted, it is not diverted from that Being in whom it exists; because it so is, and is made as he in whom it exists, decrees. It appears therefore that nothing is possible without, or contrary to the will of God, but all things wholly obey him. And for this cause let no one be moved in regard to this body and blood of Christ, that it is, in a mystery, true flesh and true blood, whilst he who created so willed. For all things whatsoever he hath willed, he hath done, both in heaven and in earth. And because he hath willed, although the figure of bread and wine are here, we are to believe that they are no other than the flesh and blood of Christ after consecration. Whence the Truth himself said to the disciples: This is my flesh for the life of the world. And though I speak wonderfully it is plainly no other than what was born of Mary, suffered upon the cross, and rose again from the sepulchre. This, I say, is that very flesh which even to this day is offered for the life of the world and therefore it is Christ's." c

Passing by the savor of fatalism in this passage, it needs no extraordinary skill in the art of reasoning, to detect the fallacy of Paschasius' pretended argument. It is a simple begging of the question. For he assumes as true the very point to be proved; namely, that it is the will of God to change the bread and wine into the real body and blood of Christ. The proof for God's will in any operation, either real or supposed, must be sought in his revealed word, or deduced from his works so interpreted as not to conflict with other known truths, established principles, or certain phenomena. But we are not left to conjecture whether that doctrine be true and according to God's will, which contradicts plain Scripture, saps the foundations of Christianity, by rejecting the infallible testimony of the senses, sets reason at defiance, and challenges omnipotence to measure the lists with eternal truth and divine propriety.

In imitation of their illustrious hero, the modern champions of this doctrine still hold out this ancient shield of their faith, time-worn, and pierced a thousand times, by the burning darts of truth.

"To *creatures* deputed by God," says Mr. Hughes, "some *power* was given, but to Christ ALL POWER both in heaven and on earth: and it was in the eucharist alone that this ALL POWER was exercised."[1]

---

c De Corp. et Sang. Dom. in Euch., lib. cap. 1, Edit. Paris, A. D. 1575.

[1] Controversy with Breckenridge, No. xxvii, p. 220.

And Dr. Wiseman labors hard to make it appear that the Apostles, "simple minded men," having witnessed the miracles wrought by their Master, would not have used, "to interpret his simple words, 'This is my body,' any idea of the impossibility of their literal import."[1]

To the propounders of such reasonings we may reply, as did TERTULLIAN to those who affirmed, that "because the things which are impossible with men are possible with God, it was not difficult to Him that he should make himself both father and son, contrary to the form delivered to human things." He answers: "Plainly nothing is difficult to God. But if we make use of this opinion so inconsiderately in our presumptions, we shall be able to pretend anything whatever respecting God, as if he would do it because he has the ability. But not because He can do all things are we therefore to believe that he has done all things; nay, the question is not what he might do, but whether he will do it. God could, pardon me the expression, have provided man with wings for flying as he has furnished them to birds; nevertheless, not because he could, did he forthwith do it. He could have immediately extinguished Praxeas and all heretics in like manner; nevertheless, not because he could, did he put an end to them..... In this manner there will be somewhat that is difficult even to God; to wit, whatsoever he will not do; not because he could not, but because he would not: FOR GOD'S POWER IS HIS WILL, AND NOT TO HAVE POWER IS NOT TO WILL."[D]

So ORIGEN says: "We do not retreat into that most absurd subterfuge, saying that all things are possible to God.... We say that God cannot act

---

[1] In Op. Cit., pp. 211–218.
[D] Adv. Praxeam, cap. x, p. 505.

wickedly, otherwise he who will be God, is not God.... and we affirm that GOD WILL NOT DO THOSE THINGS WHICH ARE CONTRARY TO NATURE, nor those that spring from wickedness and folly. But if things are done according to the word of God and his will, THEY ARE OF NECESSITY NOT CONTRARY TO NATURE; NEITHER ARE THOSE THINGS WHICH ARE WROUGHT BY GOD CONTRARY TO NATURE; although they may be paradoxical, or seem paradoxical to some. But if we must specify, we will say that, as to our nature, considered in its impure state, there are some things which God does that are above nature, when he elevates man above his human nature, and causes him to change to a nature better and more divine."[E]

No labored argument will be required, I apprehend, to show that the proper instrument by which to ascertain what is "according to the word of God and his will" what is "above nature" and what is "contrary to it," is the human reason. It is by the exercise of this faculty, that we have endeavored "to discover the truth," according to the rule of CLEMENS ALEXANDRINUS, "by considering thoroughly what is perfectly proper and fitting to the Lord and to God the Creator, and by confirming each of those things demonstrated according to the Scriptures from those Scriptures which again are similar." We have also endeavored to show the correctness of that other proposition included in the same rule, namely, that "by changing the signification of things," they, [who advocate the literal interpretation of Christ's words,] "do overturn all true doctrine."

You will also doubtless recollect that, according to the rule given by HORNE, "The literal meaning of

---

[E] Contra Celsum, lib. v, No. 23. Opera, vol. 1, p. 595. Edit Paris, A. D. 1759.

words is to be given up, if it be either improper, or involve an impossibility; or when words, properly taken, contain any thing contrary to the doctrinal or moral precepts delivered in the other parts of Scripture."

That all these difficulties necessarily follow the literal interpretation of our Saviour's words, has been clearly and fully shown; it must therefore be given up. And so fully persuaded am I, that this your exposition is wrong, that I could just as soon believe that God can be guilty of falsehood or self-contradiction, as believe your doctrine.

11. In conclusion, several very distinguished divines in your own communion, have acknowledged that the doctrine of transubstantiation is not taught by the word of God.

Cardinal Alliaco says, "It appears that this doctrine [which teaches that the substance of bread remains after consecration] is possible; nor is it repugnant to reason or the authority of the Bible, nay, it is easier to be understood and more reasonable than any other."[F]

Scotus says, "There is no place to be found in the Scripture that may compel a man to believe the transubstantiation had not the church so determined it."[2]

Cardinal Bellarmine admits this declaration of Scotus to be "not altogether improbable; for though the Scripture we have alleged seems to us so plain that it may compel a man not froward, yet it may be justly doubted whether it be so, when the most learned and acute men, such especially as Scotus, held a contrary opinion."[G]

[F] In Sent. iv, qu. vi, art 2. Cited by Ousley, p. 198.
[2] In Dist. xi, qu. 3.
[G] Lib. iii, cap. 33, de Eucharist.

Cardinal CAJETAN, in his notes on Aquinas, remarks: "The other point which the Gospel has not expressly unfolded, we have received from the church, that is, the conversion of the bread into the body of Christ, we have not plainly in the Gospel." Again, "there appears from the Gospel nothing which compels to understand these words THIS IS MY BODY, in a proper sense. Nay, that presence in the sacrament which the church holds, cannot be proved from these words of Christ, unless the declaration of the church be also added."[H]

And FISHER, Bishop of Rochester, and a martyr of your church, affirms, "That there is not one word in the institution, from which the true presence of Christ's flesh and blood, in our mass, can be proved."[1]

VASQUEZ,[2] OCHAM,[3] ALPHONSUS DE CASTRO,[4] DURAND,[5] GABRIEL BIEL,[6] MELCHIOR CANUS,[7] and Cardinal CONTARENUS,[8] also agree with the foregoing, that the doctrine of transubstantiation cannot be proved from the Holy Scriptures.

It is proper here to remark, that these authors flourished in those ages when the authority of the Church of Rome stood higher in the public estimation than at the present day. Intelligent men are now losing their undue regard for the mere authority of their predecessors, and are beginning to look for themselves into the grounds of their faith; and it requires not the spirit of a prophet, to forsee the fate of the doctrine in question, when mankind shall have burst those spiritual bonds, which, for

[H] Cajet. in Thom. p. iii, q. 75, art. 1.
[1] Contr. Captiv. Babylon, cap. x, No. 2.
[2] Part. iii, Disp. 180.
[3] Sent. iv, q. v.
[4] De Hæres. lib. viii.
[5] In Sent. lib. iv, dist. 11, q. 1.
[6] In Canon. Miss. Lect. 43.
[7] Loc. Theol. lib. iii, cap. 3.
[8] De Sacram. lib. ii, cap. 3.

many ages, have bowed their souls to the authority of a human institution.

How significant is the testimony of these distinguished writers. It is no other than a plain confession that their church obliges them to a doctrine which is not taught in the Gospel, and therefore to a new doctrine, a heresy!!!

And this is a doctrine that occupies no ordinary place in your creed. Indeed, Mr. Hughes in his controversy acknowledges, that the sacrifice of the Mass is the principal business of Romish priests. Can it be true, that the chief employment of your clergy is no other than the celebration of a mere human institution?

And is it possible, as you inform me, that your "heart burns for the conversion of your dear friends" to such a faith, and to the observance of such an unscriptural ceremony, as the sacrifice of the Mass? I greatly suspect that you never received your fire from heaven's altar. Beware, I entreat you, lest that come upon you which was long since threatened to all those "that kindle a fire, that compass themselves about with sparks;" (Isa. 1: 11,) and to such as trust in man and make flesh their arm. (Jer. xvii: 5.)

That we may be found in the day of eternity the true worshipers who worship in spirit and in truth, is the sincere desire and humble prayer of him who subscribes himself,

Your friend and brother,

E. O. P.

LETTER VII.

VIEWS OF THE ANTE-NICENE FATHERS RESPECTING THE BODY AND BLOOD OF CHRIST IN THE EUCHARIST.

DEAR BROTHER:—Having shown from the sacred writings of the New Testament, the earliest and most authoritative history of the primitive church, that the doctrine of transubstantiation is not deducible from our Saviour's language, either in his discourse to the Jews at Capernaum, or to his disciples at the institution of the Eucharist, it remains for me to verify my early affirmation, that "the Fathers of the first six or seven centuries, speak of the eucharistic elements as the *figure* of Christ's broken body and shed blood."

But in what light are we to regard the writings of the early Fathers of the Christian Church?

From the acquaintance which I have been able to make with them, I make free to say, that I regard the Fathers as very unsafe guides, in many matters relating to the Christian religion. Their interpretations of Scripture are often wanting in sound judgment, fanciful, and even puerile. At no very remote period from the ascent of our Lord, superstitious usages and heathenish practices began to make their appearance in the church; among which may be enumerated, the signing of the cross on the forehead in baptism, the mixing of water with the sacramental wine, reserving a part of the eucharistic bread to send to the sick, the using of holy water, incense, and tapers, the adoption of monasticism, and the honoring of deceased martyrs by ceremonies performed at their graves. Of this class of disciplinary usages says one, "If you demand Scripture authority, you will find none. Tradition is pretended as their author, custom their confirmer, and faith their observer."[A] None but vague tradition could be found capable of measuring back their years; and even he refuses to tell their age, or birth-place; custom however had given them confirmation, and faith in their supposed utility, had secured a cordial observance. No wonder when such usages had become common in the church, that the dove-like spirit of a true and rational piety fled from the society of professing Christians, and left them to a cold and formal ritualism, to a lifeless sacramentarianism: So that "the Church of God and spouse of Christ had fallen to that state of evil, that, for celebrating the heavenly sacraments, light borrowed discipline of darkness, and Christians did what anti-christ practised."[B] Notwithstanding these disciplinary corruptions, it is doubtless true that, for several ages after Christ, the fundamental doctrines of Christianity, as now held by the Protestant Churches, continued to be the creed of the ancient Christians. The Holy Scriptures were their only and sufficient rule of faith. But laxity of discipline did not long exist, without being followed by laxity and innovation in doctrine. The very questionable practice of praying *for* the dead was succeeded by praying *to* the dead; the employment of images as aids and incentives to devotion, was at length followed by their worship; and clerical celibacy, at the first approved and lauded only, has in the Church of Rome passed into an unyielding law. The same law of progressive development, is observable in other doctrines and institutions of the ancient

[A] Tertul. de Cor. Milit., c. iv, p. 102.
[B] Cyprian, Epist. 74, ad Pompeium.

Church, especially in the value and necessity of the sacraments.

Convinced, therefore, as we are, of the errors of the early church, we do not embrace their doctrines and adopt their usages any farther than they are found to agree with those of the New Testament Scriptures. The revealed word of God is our rule of Christian faith; and from this we make no appeal to the Fathers, as possessing any decisive authority in the premises. We do not refer to them as our judges, but as credible witnesses of usages practiced, and doctrines believed, in their own times. We do not try the Scriptures by them; but we try them by the Scriptures, as they did one another. "Not as Peter and Paul do I command you," says IGNATIUS. "They were the Apostles of Jesus Christ, but I am the least."[C]

To a supposed objector to his explanation, says another: "I do not require any belief in these my words, unless I shall give suitable witnesses. I will give you the Lord himself, even our Saviour Jesus Christ as their witness and author."[D]

"Believe me not," says CYRIL, "simply delivering these things to thee, unless thou find the proof of those things spoken, in the divine Scriptures: for the preservation of our faith is not grounded upon the eloquence of language, but upon the proofs derived from the divine Scriptures."[E]

AUGUSTINE, speaking of those books which we write, says: "As for this kind of books, we are to read them, not with the necessity of believing, but with the liberty of judging them. . . . . In no way do they equal that most sacred excellence of the canonical Scriptures, although in some of them

---

[C] Epist. ad Rom. No. 38, p. 85. Ed. Oxen. 1644.
[D] Origen, Hom. vii, in Levit., No. 5.
[E] Cyril. Hieros. Catech. Illum. iv, c. 12, p. 56.

the same truth is found, nevertheless, they are of very unequal authority. Therefore, if by chance we here meet with such things as seem contrary to the truth, because they are not understood, the reader or hearer has the liberty to approve what he likes, or to reject what offends. And therefore, unless all things of this kind be defended by some certain reason, or canonical authority, and it be made to appear, that what is disputed or narrated, either really is, or might have been, he that shall be displeased or not believe the same, is not to be reprehended."[F]

Writing to Theophilus, Patriarch of Alexandria, JEROME says: "I know that I hold the Apostles in a rank distinct from other writers; the former always speak truth, the latter sometimes err, as they are men."[G] Again, "Some, both Greeks and Latins, have erred in points of FAITH; whose names I must not produce, lest we might seem to defend ORIGEN by the errors of others, rather than by his own worth."[H]

Much more might be cited from these Fathers themselves, and from several distinguished writers of your own church, to prove that the writings of the ancients possess no decisive authority, in matters of Christian doctrine; but thus much will suffice to show, in what light we are to consider their productions.

From the nature of the case, therefore, ours must be regarded as a historical inquiry, not of mere curiosity, but of intense interest, and no inconsiderable degree of relative importance. For, although the Fathers were fallible men like ourselves, and may have entertained many errors in discipline and

[F] Aug. Ep. ad Hieron. lib. xi, contr. Faust., cap. 5.
[G] Hieron. Epist. lxii, ad Theoph. Alex.
[H] Idem, Ep. lxv, ad Pancm. et Oceanum.

doctrine, nevertheless, being credible historians, if they generally concur in recording the existence of any usage or doctrine, in preference to another and totally different, we are not only bound to believe their testimony, but we must also admit that such concurrent evidence, in regard to a Scriptural matter, of a disputed, yet practical nature, is an important aid in arriving at the truth in the case.

II. Let us then see what they say in regard to the eucharistic sacrament, and ascertain whether they speak of the elements employed as the *figure* of Christ's broken body and shed blood.

1. In the few epistles left by IGNATIUS, we find but little that relates to the Eucharist; and this seems to have been chiefly written by way of exhortation to its use as a means of grace, whereby the love and unity of believers is to be promoted. "Hasten therefore," says he, "to come together more frequently to the Eucharist of God, and unto glory; for, when the same is continually done, the powers of Satan are destroyed, and his weapons, burning unto sin, are turned back ineffectual; for, your concord and consonant faith are his destruction, and the torment of his armor-bearers."[1] And near the close of the same epistle, he again exhorts: "Stand firm, therefore, brethren, in the faith of Jesus Christ, and in his love, and in his passion and resurrection. And do ye all assemble in the grace of his name, in the one common faith of God the Father, and Jesus Christ his only-begotten Son, and the first-born of every creature; but, according to the flesh, of the race of David. Directed by the Comforter, do you obey your bishop and the presbytery, with undistracted mind, breaking one bread which is the medicine of immortality, the antidote, that we should not die, but live in God through

[1] Ep. ad Ephes. No. 56, p. 40.

Jesus Christ."ᴊ   "Do you therefore, resuming a gentle forbearance, renew yourselves in faith, which is the flesh of the Lord, and in charity, which is the blood of Jesus Christ. Let no one of you have aught against his neighbor."ᴋ

By the expression, *breaking one bread*, we are without doubt, to understand Ignatius, as exhorting to use one Eucharist, and thereby preserve the unity of the Spirit in the bonds of Christian love: and when he denominates it the *medicine of immortality, the antidote against death*, he attributes to the outward sacrament, or sign, the immortalizing qualities of the thing signified, whose purifying and preserving influence is thereby procured and maintained in the soul in an eminent manner. This being the meaning of the author, the term BREAD must be taken in its literal sense, otherwise we cannot properly connect with it the word BREAKING. For, if we suppose the term BREAD here to signify *spiritual food*, then it were wholly unwarrantable to exhort those addressed to *break*, or *impart* it, because this is God's prerogative. If therefore the term BREAD be used here in its proper sense, as it evidently is, then it is certain that Ignatius had no idea of its being Christ's real body, but his symbolical body only.

2. Justin, who was martyred about the year 167, and sixty years after the death of Ignatius, has, in his first Apology to the Emperor Antoninus Pius, for the Christians, left us a somewhat minute description of the manner in which the early church celebrated the Eucharist. After mentioning the prayers made at the introduction of one newly baptized, he continues: "When we have made an end of these prayers, we embrace one another with

---

ᴊ Idem, No. 94, p. 46.
ᴋ Idem, Ep. ad Trallasios, No. 72, p. 208.

a kiss. Then is brought to the president of the
brethren bread, and a cup of water and wine mixed;
and he, receiving it, sends up praise and glory to
the Father of the universe, through the name of his
Son, and the Holy Spirit; and he gives thanks at
much length, that we are thought worthy of these
things from him. He having made an end to these
prayers and giving of thanks, all the people present
respond, saying, Amen. Amen signifies in the
Hebrew language, So let it be. When the president has given thanks, and all the people responded,
those called by us deacons, give to each of those
present to partake of the bread, for which thanks
have been offered, and the wine and water; and
they send it to those not present. And this food is
called by us the Eucharist, of which it is permitted
to no other to partake, except him who believes
those things taught by us to be true, and has been
baptized for the remission of sins, and unto regeneration; and so lives as Christ has delivered. For
we do not receive these as common bread and common drink, but as our Saviour Jesus Christ, who
was made flesh by the word of God, took flesh and
blood for our salvation, so also we have been taught
that the food for which thanks have been made by
the prayer of his word, and by which our flesh and
blood are nourished in the change, is the flesh and
blood of that Jesus who was made flesh. For the
Apostles, in the memoirs which were made by them
and called Gospels, have so delivered, that when
Jesus had taken bread and given thanks, he gave
them command, saying: 'Do this in remembrance
of me, this is my body;' and in like manner, when
he had taken the cup and given thanks, he said:
'This is my blood.' And to them only did he impart [them.]"[L]

[L] Justin. Mart. Apol. I, pro Christianis ad Ant. Pium. Ed.
Lond. 1732, pp. 95-97.

In regard to this passage I remark. (1.) Our author denominates the eucharistic elements, both before and after the prayer of consecration, by the same terms, BREAD, and WINE and WATER. (2.) He says, "We do not receive them as common or ordinary bread and drink;" which implies, that, although they were not common bread and wine, yet they were really bread and wine. (3.) By these elements, he affirms that our flesh and blood are nourished in the change which they undergo, after being received. On the supposition that transubstantiation be true, our flesh and blood are nourished, according to JUSTIN, either by the mere accidents of bread and wine, which is impossible, or by the real body and blood of Jesus Christ, which is blasphemous.

From these considerations it appears perfectly certain, that JUSTIN Martyr could have had no idea of a corporeal presence in the Eucharist.

3. IRENÆUS, who lived till the year 202, uses, in several places, language similar to that just quoted from JUSTIN Martyr. He remarks: "Since then we are Christ's members, and are nourished by the creature; but he gives us the creature, making his sun to rise and sending rain as he will; that CUP, which is of the creature, he confessed [to be] his own blood, by which our blood is increased, and that BREAD which is of the creature, he confirmed [to be] his own body, by which our bodies are increased. When, therefore, the mixed cup and the wrought bread receive the Word of God, they become the Eucharist of the blood and body of Christ, and by these the substance of our flesh is increased and consists." M

In order properly to understand this and like passages from several others of the Fathers, we

---

M Iren. Adversus Hæreses, lib. v, cap. ii, Edit. Lond. 1702.

must have in mind the ancient heresy against which they were writing. This passage was penned against those who denied the proper humanity of Jesus Christ. In a former book, this author tells us of "some, who suppose that Christ was manifested as a transfigured man, but was neither born, nor incarnated. But others say that he did not assume the form of man, but that he descended like a dove upon that Jesus who was born of Mary."[1] They said that the flesh in which Christ appeared was not his own, but belonged to some other than the *proper* Christ. And they not only denied the proper incarnation of Christ in particular, but in general they also "denied the salvation of the flesh, scoffed at its regeneration, and said that it was not capable of incorruptibility." It was against these fundamental errors, that our author penned this chapter; and he shows, that, according to this, the Lord has not redeemed us by HIS OWN blood, neither is the cup of the Eucharist the communication of HIS blood, nor the bread which we break, the communication of HIS body." From these observations we see the propriety and force of the words *his* and *his own*, as used in connection with the terms, body, and blood. Hence, also, the appropriateness of the words, *he confessed* to be *his* blood and *confirmed* to be *his* body; by which he intended to indicate the certainty of these eucharistic elements representing the body of Christ himself and of no other.

That IRENÆUS does not intend the proper and real body and blood of Christ, when he designates the eucharistic elements by those epithets, is evident from the latter part of the passage cited, wherein he expressly declares the BREAD and CUP to be the Eucharist of his body and blood, by which the sub-

[1] Lib. iii, cap. xl, p. 219.

11*

stance of our flesh is increased, and consists. Indeed, it was the opinion of IRENÆUS, together with several others of the Fathers, that Christ himself drank of the cup at the institution of this sacrament. Thus he says: "When he had given thanks, taking the cup he drank of it, gave it to the disciples, and said to them: DRINK YE ALL OF IT."[N]

He could not therefore have believed that cup to be the real and proper blood of Christ; for, the idea of Christ's drinking his own blood, is too abhorrent for a sane mind to entertain for a moment. Every nobler feeling of our nature repels the thought.

4. The force of the remarks which have been suggested, as explanatory of the passage cited from IRENÆUS, will farther appear from a few passages from TERTULLIAN, his contemporary. This author also wrote largely against Marcion, who, as IRENÆUS tells us, in the twenty-ninth chapter of his first Book against Heresies, blasphemed God, rejected the Gospel according to Luke, and those parts of our Lord's discourses "in which he manifestly declared his Father to be the maker of the world." "And, in like manner, he cut from the Epistles of Paul the Apostle, taking away whatever was said manifestly by the Apostle of that God who made the world, that he is the Father of our Lord Jesus Christ; and whatever the Apostle taught from the prophecies which foretold the advent of the Lord." In short, he emphatically denied Christ's incarnation and his passibility, or capability of suffering. To him, therefore, TERTULLIAN objects: "'For unto us a child is born, and unto us a son is given.' What know I if he does not speak of the Son of God, whose government was laid upon his shoulder? Who bears a kingdom, the sign of his power, upon his shoulder, and does not also bear either a diadem

---

[N] Adv. Hæres., lib. v, cap. 33.

upon his head, or a sceptre in his hand, or some proper mark of dress? But Christ Jesus, the only new King of the new dispensation, has borne upon his shoulder the power and sublimity of his new glory, to wit, his cross; so that, according to the above prophecy, the Lord henceforth reigns from the tree. This tree Jeremiah also intimates to thee when speaking of the Jews who said, 'Come let us cast away the tree with the bread of it,' with his body assuredly. For in your Gospel also God has revealed it calling bread his body, that you may understand, that he has given to the bread to be a figure of his body; whose body the prophet had before figured by bread; the Lord himself being about to interpret this sacrament afterward."[o] "But indeed he does not, even to this present time, reject the water with which he washes his people, nor the oil with which he anoints them, nor the union of honey and milk with which he feeds his infant ones, nor the BREAD with which he REPRESENTS his own body, even in his own sacrament needing the beggarly things of the Creator."[p]

Again he says: "The bread which he took and distributed to his disciples, that he made his body, by saying, 'This is my body,' that is, a *figure* of my body. But it would not have been a figure, unless his body had been a true one. But a void thing, as a phantasm, cannot take a figure. Moreover, if he had feigned bread for his body, because he was destitute of a true one, then he ought to have delivered bread for us. That bread had been crucified, would have been practising after Marcion's vanity. But why does he call BREAD his body and not rather [call it] the gourd—*peponem*—which Marcion had in the place of a heart, not un-

[o] Adv. Marcion, lib. iii, cap. 19.
[p] Id., lib. i, cap. 14.

derstanding that this was an ancient figure of Christ's body; who said by Jeremiah: 'Against me have they devised devices, saying; Come let us cast away the tree with the bread thereof;' to wit, the cross with his body. And thus the illuminator of antiquity sufficiently declared what he then wished to signify by bread, calling his body bread. So ALSO by the mention of the cup, when he constituted the testament sealed with his blood, HE CONFIRMED THE SUBSTANCE OF HIS BODY. For of no body can there be blood, except of flesh. And if any kind of body not fleshly be opposed to us, certainly it shall not have blood except it be fleshly. Thus the proof of the body depends upon the testimony of the flesh, and the proof of the flesh upon the testimony of the blood."[Q] You see that TERTULLIAN was not very well versed in the doctrine of the *unbloody* sacrifice of the body of Christ in the Mass. He lived too early to be initiated into its mysteries.

The whole scope and design of TERTULLIAN, in the passages quoted, is evidently to prove the reality of Christ's human flesh, against the error of Marcion, from those Scriptures which point to his flesh and blood by certain figurative expressions, in which the term BREAD was understood to indicate the body of Christ, and the term WINE his blood.[R] In doing this he makes use of the words of institution. THIS IS MY BODY, and the passage of Jeremiah to prove the same thing, namely, that bread is a figurative representation of the body of Christ. And he produces the mention of the cup, at the eucharistic institution, together with two other passages from the Old Testament, immediately following the last passage above cited, to show

[Q] Adv. Mar., lib. iv, cap. 40, p. 457.
[R] Idem, lib. v, cap. 8, p. 470.

that by the Scriptural use of the term WINE the blood of Christ is figuratively indicated. Nothing therefore can be more evident than the meaning of TERTULLIAN, which is, that the bread and wine of the Eucharist, are the figure or symbol of Christ's real body and blood. And we can no more suppose, that he understood the words of Christ literally, than we can, that he understood, in their literal sense, the passages referred to in the Old Testament.

Besides, IRENÆUS, in reference to the Valentinians and Marcionites, says: "According to no opinion of the heretics, was the Word of God made flesh. For, if any one will examine their rules, he will find that the Word of God is represented by them all as without flesh, and impassible."[1] And TERTULLIAN says that "Marcion prefers to believe Christ to be a phantasm, altogether scorning the verity of his body."[s]

A phantasm is something that appears to be what it is not. As here used it indicates, that Marcion believed the human body of Christ to be not real, but only apparent.

Now had TERTULLIAN been a transubstantiationist, that part of his argument which relates to the Eucharist, would have been irrelevant; and Marcion might have replied to his confusion: "Hold, sir, your argument to prove the verity of Christ's body and blood from the eucharistic elements avails you not; for if your doctrine of this sacrament be true, then, so far from demonstrating Christ's body to be real, you rather prove, that the outward appearances of things are not certainly indicative of their interior nature, and, therefore, what appeared to be a real human body of Christ, might not have been

---

[1] Adv. Hæres., lib. iii, cap. 11, p. 219.
[s] De Anima liber, cap. xvii, p. 276.

such. We stand on common ground. You teach that what appears to the sight, touch, smell and taste, to be real bread and wine, is not real bread and wine; and I believe that what appeared to the sight and touch, to be a real human body, was not real, but only apparent."

5. CLEMENT of Alexandria, says: "The blood of Christ is two-fold; for, the one is his fleshly, by which we have been redeemed from corruption, but the other is his spiritual, that is, by which we have been anointed. And this is to drink the blood of Jesus, to partake of the Lord's incorruption. But the strength of the word is the spirit, as the blood is of the flesh. Analogously, therefore, wine is mingled with water, as the spirit is with man; and the mixture of wine and water feeds unto faith, but the spirit leads unto incorruption, and the mixture of both the drink and the word has been called the Eucharist, that is, a bestowal of distinguished thanks, of which they who partake by faith are made holy, body and soul, the Father's will together with the spirit and Word mystically mingling the divine mixture, man."[T]

In pursuing the subject of his discourse he afterwards remarks: "The Scythians, Celtæ, Iberians, and Thracians, all which are warlike nations, are especially addicted to drunkenness; and they consider it a pleasant and happy thing to exercise themselves in the pursuits of life. But we, a peaceful people, living together for enjoyment not for injury, drink sober draughts to one another, that our friendships may in reality be shown suitable to our name. How think ye the Lord drank when he was made man? So shamefully as we do? Did he not do it with urbanity and with becomingness? Did he not do it considerately? For know ye well,

[T] Pædagog. lib. ii, cap. 2. Oxon. 1715, pp. 177, 178.

he also partook of wine, for he also was a man. And he blessed the wine, saying, Take ye and drink; this is my blood, the blood of the vine. As to the word, 'shed for many for the remission of sins,' it allegorically signifies a holy stream of gladness. And, that it is necessary that he who drinks should do it temperately, he clearly showed by what he taught at the feast, for he taught not being drunken. But that what was blessed was wine, he again showed when he said to his disciples: 'Of this fruit of the wine I drink not, until I drink it with you in my Father's kingdom.' Moreover, that what was drank by the Lord was wine, he again says concerning himself when upbraiding the Jews' hardness of heart: 'For the Son of man, says he, came, and they say, Behold a man who is a glutton and a wine-bibber, a friend of publicans.' Let this be firmly fastened by us upon those called Encratites." [u]

In the chapter from which the above passages are selected, CLEMENT discourses upon the manner in which we are to conduct ourselves in the use of wine; *Pos to poto prosenekteon*—and argues that although "water is the natural, and, therefore, the sober drink for the thirsty," nevertheless the moderate use of wine has been sanctioned by the example of Christ and his Apostles. In proof of this, he refers to the miracle wrought at the marriage, in Cana of Galilee,[v] (John ii,) to the words of Christ, when he upbraided the Jews (Matt: ii, 19,) to the exhortation of the Apostle Paul to Timothy[w] (I Tim. v: 23,) and especially, to the employment of the "blood of the vine" at the institution of the Eucharist by Christ, which he proves to have been wine, after it was blessed, from the words, "Of this

---

[u] Idem Pædogog. lib. ii, cap. 2, p. 186.
[v] Ib. p. 184. [w] Ib. p. 177.

fruit of the vine I will not drink, until I drink it with you in the kingdom of my Father." Add to this, the pointed application of his whole argument to the Encratites, who held wine in such abhorrence, as to use mere water in the Lord's supper, and we have from this author, a most conclusive testimony against transubstantiation.

6. In opposition to the Marcionites, ORIGEN asks: "But if, as they say, Christ was destitute of flesh and blood, of what kind of flesh, or of what body, or of what kind of blood, did he give as images the bread and the cup, and command his disciples by these to make a remembrance of him?"[x]

In another place he undertakes to show, that Christ, our High Priest, abstained from wine when he approached the altar of his cross, in the same manner as did the high priest under the law, when about to go into the tabernacle of the congregation, (Levit. x: 9,) and observes: "The Saviour came into this world, that he might offer his flesh a sacrifice to God for our sins. Before he made this offering, whilst engaged in his dispensations, he drank wine. In fine, he was called a gluttonous man, and a wine-drinker, a friend of publicans and sinners. But when the time of his crucifixion drew near, and he was about to come to the altar, where he should immolate the sacrifice of his flesh, taking the cup, he blessed, and gave it to his disciples, saying: *Take ye and drink of this.* He said, do you drink who are not now about to come to the altar. But he, as it were about coming to the altar, says concerning himself: 'Verily, I say unto you, that I will not drink of the fruit of this vine until I drink it with you new in my Father's Kingdom.'"[y]

---

[x] Dialog de recta in Deum fide, Sect. iv, tom. i, p. 853, Paris, 1750.

[y] In Levit., Homil. vii, No. 1, tom. ii, p. 220.

From these remarks ORIGEN obviously believed that the Apostles drank WINE but not BLOOD in the Eucharist; otherwise the passage has no meaning. Indeed, he puts this beyond all controversy, by going on to show the propriety of Christ's abstaining then from *wine* "which makes glad the heart of man," inasmuch as he was affected with sadness for the sins of men.

Again, "If all that enters into the mouth goes into the belly, and is cast out into the draught, then even the food which is sanctified by the word of God and supplication, according to that which is material, goes into the belly, and is cast out into the draught: but, according to the prayer which is made over it, and the proportion of faith, it becomes profitable, and is the cause of that clear-sightedness of the mind which discerns unto profiting. And it is not the matter of the bread, but the word spoken over it, that profits him who eats worthy of the Lord. And thus much concerning his typical and symbolical body."[z]

Most certain, therefore, is it, that he did not consider that "which was sanctified by the word of God and prayer," to be the real body and blood of Christ. For, besides the irreconcilable disagreement between his words and such a belief, he elsewhere teaches, that Christ's body "after its resurrection, was, as it were, in a certain state, between that grossness of body which it had before its passion, and the manifestation of a soul destitute of such a body."[2] To say that such a heavenly and glorified body, enters the mouth, passes into the belly, and is cast out into the draught, would become a dementate better than a Christian philosopher.

[z] Com. in Matt. tom. xi, No. 14.
[2] Contra Celsum, lib. 2, p. 434, No. 62.

7. CYPRIAN, Bishop of Carthage, in a letter to Cæcilius, writes very decidedly against those heretical Aquarians who used water only in the Lord's Supper. A few passages from this epistle will suffice to show the author's views, respecting the nature of the element used in the Eucharist. He argues, with more zeal than wisdom perhaps, that water should be mingled with the wine, in order to represent the union between Christ and his people, the wine answering to the blood of Christ, and the water to believers. He says: "You know that we have been admonished, that in offering the cup, the tradition of the Lord should be preserved; neither should any thing be done by us different from what the Lord first did for us; so that the cup which is offered in his memory, should be offered mixed with wine. For when Christ says, 'I am the true vine,' the blood of Christ is not water assuredly, but wine. Nor can his blood, by which we have been redeemed and quickened, seem to be in the cup, when the wine is wanting in the cup, by which is represented the blood of Christ." He then speaks of Noah and Melchisedec as types of Christ, who drank and offered wine, and adds: "Who is more eminently a priest of the Most High God than our Lord Jesus Christ who offered a sacrifice to God the Father, and offered THIS SAME that Melchisedec offered, that is, BREAD and WINE, to wit, his BODY and BLOOD." . . . Again, "'I say unto you, that I will not henceforth drink of this creature of the vine, until on that day in which I will drink the new wine with you in my Father's kingdom.' In this place we find that the cup was mixed [?] which the Lord offered, and that it was WINE which he called his blood. Whence it appears, that the blood of Christ is not offered, if wine is wanting in the cup." . . . "And because Christ, who has borne our sins, has borne us all, we see by the water, that the people are understood,

but by the wine, the blood of Christ is shown forth. And when water is mixed with wine in the cup, the people are united to Christ, and the multitude of the faithful, are coupled and joined to him in whom they have believed.

This coupling and uniting of wine and water, is so mingled in the cup of the Lord, that this mixture cannot be separated. Whence, nothing can separate from Christ the Church, that is, the people in the Church, established in the faith, and firmly persevering in what they have believed, that love should not always draw them together and remain inseparable. Thus, in the sanctification of the Lord's cup, water alone cannot be offered, as neither wine alone can be; for if any one offer wine alone, the blood of Christ is without us; but if the water be alone, the people are without Christ." . . . "But the discipline of all religion and truth is subverted, unless that which is spiritually commanded, be faithfully preserved, if in the morning sacrifices any one fears, lest by the savor of the wine he smell of the blood of Christ."[A]

From all our sins may Christ's atoning blood cleanse you and
Your Brother,
E. O. P.

[A] Cyprian, Epist. lxiii, ad Cæcilium de Sacram. Dom. Calicis, tom. 1, pp. 146–150.

LETTER VIII.

VIEW OF THE POST-NICENE FATHERS RESPECTING THE BODY AND BLOOD OF CHRIST IN THE EUCHARIST.

DEAR BROTHER:—In my last, I examined in a manner somewhat circumstantial, the testimony of the most distinguished Fathers of the ante-Nicene Church, and found them, in letter, spirit and design, adverse to your modern doctrine of the Eucharist. In producing similar evidence from the later writings of the church, it will not therefore be necessary to quote in detail, or indulge in lengthened remark.

1. EUSEBIUS holds the following language: "He delivered to his disciples the symbols of the divine economy, commanding the image of his body to be made."[A] And, "They received a command, according to the institution of the new dispensation, to celebrate the remembrance of that sacrifice, by the symbols of his body and saving blood."[B]

2. MACARIUS of Egypt asks: "What are those things which eye hath not seen nor ear heard, neither have entered into the heart of man? Answer. At that time the great and just, and kings and prophets knew that the Redeemer would indeed come; but that he would suffer and be crucified, and his blood shed upon the cross, they neither knew nor had they heard; neither had it entered into their hearts, that there would be the baptism of fire and of the Holy Ghost; and, that in the

[A] Euseb. Demonstrat Evang., lib. viii, c. 1.
[B] Idem, Demonstr. Ev., lib. i, c. ult.

church there would be offered BREAD and WINE, the antitype of his flesh and blood, and that they who partake of the visible BREAD would spiritually eat the flesh of the Lord."[C]

3. CYRIL of Jerusalem exhorts: "Wherefore, with all assurance, let us partake of the body and blood of Christ; for in the type of bread his body is given thee, and in the type of wine his blood is given thee; so that, partaking of the body and blood of Christ, thou mayst be made. of the same body and blood with him."[D]

4. GREGORY NAZIANZEN, speaking of the Eucharist, says: "We shall now partake of the passover, typically indeed, yet more evident than the old; for the legal passover, I dare say, was a more obscure type of a type."[E]

5. AMBROSE, in his fourth book of the Sacraments, says: "Grant that this oblation, which is the figure of the body and blood of our Lord Jesus Christ, may be ascribed to us as reasonable and acceptable."[F]

6. JEROME teaches that "the flesh of Christ is understood in two ways; either it is that spiritual and divine flesh of which he says: *my flesh is meat indeed, and my blood is drink indeed;* and *except ye shall eat my flesh,* &c.; or that flesh which was crucified, and that blood which was shed by the spear of the soldier."[G] "It is indeed lawful to eat of this sacrifice which is admirably made in remembrance [of Christ,] but of that which Christ offered upon the altar of the cross, according to itself, it is permitted to no one to eat."[H] We are permitted

[C] Macar. Homil. xxvii.
[D] Catech. Mystagog. iv, § 1, Opera Lond. 1703, p. 29.
[E] Orat. ii in Pasch., tom. i, p. 692, Paris 1630.
[F] Lib. iv, cap. 5, de Sacram.
[G] Hieron. Com. in Ep. ad Ephes. i, tom. iii, p. 960.
[H] Dist. Can. de hac in Levit.

to eat of the one, but not the other. Why not, if the sacrifice and victim are the same? Because the former is typical, the latter was a real sacrifice of Christ, as he himself elsewhere says: "For a *type* of his blood, Christ offered, not water, but wine."[I]

7. AUGUSTINE, speaking of Christ's forbearance, says: "So great and so marvelous was the patience of our Lord, that bearing with Judas, though not ignorant of his purpose, he called him to the feast in which he commended and delivered to his disciples the FIGURE of his body and blood."[J] And, "The Lord did not hesitate to say, *This is my body*, when he gave the SIGN of his body."[K]

He urges the necessity of a spiritual participation of the body and blood of Christ, as follows: "This then shall be, that is, the body and blood of Christ shall be life to every one, if what is visibly taken in the sacrament, be in very truth eaten and drunk spiritually."[L]

8. FACUNDUS says: "The sacrament of adoption may be called adoption, just as the sacrament of the body and blood of Christ, which is in the consecrated bread and wine, we are wont to call his body and blood. Not indeed that the bread is *properly* his body, or that the wine is *properly* his blood, but because they contain in themselves THE MYSTERY of his body and blood. Hence it was that our Lord denominated the consecrated bread and wine which he delivered to his disciples, his own body and blood."[M]

I cannot conceive how words can be arranged so as to deny more explicitly the doctrine of a corporeal presence.

[I] Idem, lib. ii, adv. Jovinian.
[J] Aug. in Psal. iii.
[K] Idem, contra Adimant. cap. xii.
[L] Idem, Serm. cxxxi, vol. v, p. 924.
[M] Lib. ix, Defens. iii, cap. 5.

9. ISIDORE of Seville gives the following reasons for denominating bread and wine the body and blood of Christ: "Because bread strengthens the body, therefore it is called the body of Christ; but wine, because it operates blood in the flesh, is therefore referred to the blood of Christ. Now these two are visible, but being sanctified by the Holy Spirit, they pass into the sacrament of his divine body."[N]

The venerable BEDE says: "In the place of the flesh and blood of the lamb, Christ has substituted the sacrament of his flesh and blood, in the FIGURE of bread and wine."[O] "He gave to his disciples at the supper, the FIGURE of his most holy body and blood."[P]

I have now produced from the records of the ancient church a "cloud of witnesses" all bringing in the same testimony substantially in proof of my assertion, "that the fathers of the first six or seven centuries after Christ, speak of the eucharistic elements as the *figure* of Christ's broken body and shed blood." And in examining the Ante-Nicene Fathers, I showed from their language together with its scope and design, that they could not have believed the doctrine of Christ's bodily presence in the Eucharist, as now taught by the church of Rome. In order to place the testimony of the later ecclesiastical writers in the same impregnable position, I will cite a few other passages, in which they expressly teach:

II. *That the elements of bread and wine do not lose their proper nature in virtue of consecration.*

1. EPHREM of Antioch undertakes to prove the two natures of Christ from the words of St. John: *That which was from the beginning, which we have*

[N] De Eccles. Offic., lib. i, cap. 18.
[O] Com. in Levit. xxii.   [P] Idem, in Psal. iii.

seen and our hands have handled of the Word of life. He argues hence, that he was both palpable and impalpable, and affirms that "No man of sense can say that the nature of that which is palpable and that which is impalpable, of that which is visible and that which is invisible, is the same. In the same manner the body of Christ, which is taken by the faithful, DOES NOT DEPART FROM ITS SENSIBLE SUBSTANCE, and it remains inseparable from intelligible grace. And baptism, moreover, being made all spiritual, and being one, also preserves the propriety of its sensible substance, I speak of the water, and does not cease to be what it was."[Q]

In the same manner are we to understand FACUNDUS, the African bishop, in the passage cited above, p. 138, as teaching the persistence of the nature of the bread and wine after consecration, when he says, "that the bread and wine are not called the body and blood of Christ because they are properly such, but because they contain in themselves the mystery of his body and blood."

2. CHRYSOSTOM writes against the Apollinarians: "Christ is God and man; God on account of his impassibility, man on account of his passion. One Son, One Lord, the very same possessing, without doubt, one dominion, one power, in his united natures, although they exist not consubstantial; and each [nature] preserves the acknowledgment of its propriety unmixed, and because they are without confusion, I say they are two. For as before the bread is sanctified, we call it bread, but being sanctified by divine grace, through the medium of the priest, it is liberated from the appellation of bread and dignified with the name of the Lord's body, ALTHOUGH THE NATURE OF BREAD

[Q] Ephrem Theopolitani, in Photii Bibliotheca, Dis. 229 p. 794.

REMAIN IN IT and is declared to be not two bodies, but one body of the Son, so also here, the divine nature residing, that is, pervading his body, these both make one Son, one person."^R

"When this passage was first produced by PETER MARTYR," says Bingham, "it was looked upon as so unanswerable, that they of the Romish Church had no other way to evade the force of it, but to cry out, It was a forgery. PETER MARTYR left it in the Lambeth Library, but it was ravished thence in the reign of Queen Mary. BIGOTIUS, a learned French Papist, published the original, but the whole edition was suppressed. Yet, Le Moyne published it again in Latin among his *Varia Sacra*. And a learned Prelate, who now so deservedly holds the primacy in our own church, and whose indefatigable industry against Popery will never be forgotten, having procured the sheets which the Sorbon Doctors caused to be suppressed in BIGOTIUS' edition of Palladius, published it in our own tongue, with such of the Greek fragments as are now remaining. And in these monuments it will stand as the unanswerable testimony of ST. CHRYSOSTOM, and a key to explain all other passages of the Greek writers of that age, who were undoubtedly in the same sentiments, of the Bread and Wine still remaining unalterable in their substance."[1]

3. GELASIUS, chosen Bishop of Rome near the close of the fifth century, has left a treatise on the two natures of Christ against Nestorius and Eutyches, in which he uses the following language. "Certainly the sacraments of the body and blood of Christ which we take, are a divine thing; for which cause we also by the same, are made partakers

---

R Ep. ad Cesarium contr. Hæres. Apol.

[1] Bingham's Antiquities of the Christian Church, vol. i, book xv, chap. v, sec. 4, p. 791, Lond. 1727.

of the divine nature; nevertheless, THE SUBSTANCE OR NATURE OF THE BREAD AND WINE CEASE NOT TO EXIST; and truly, the image and similitude of the body and blood of Christ, are celebrated in the performance of the mysteries. Evidently, therefore, is it sufficiently shown by us, that this which we profess, celebrate, and take in his image, is to be thought in regard to Christ the Lord himself; so that as they [the bread and wine] pass into this, that is to say, into a divine substance by the efficacy of the Holy Spirit, their NATURE, nevertheless, remaining in its own propriety, so as to this principle mystery itself, [of the unity of Christ's two natures,] whose efficiency and virtue they, [the consecrated bread and wine,] truly represent to us, it is evident from their remaining properly such, that Christ is one, because he remains entire and true." s

4. THEODORET opposed the same heresy of Eutyches in the form of dialogue between Orthodoxus and Eranistes, the former being the advocate of the Catholic doctrine, the latter being the Eutychian representative. In Dialogue I, we read as follows:

"ORTHODOXUS.—Do you know that God called his body bread?

"ERANISTES.—I know it.

"O.—He elsewhere also calls his flesh wheat.

"E.—I know that also; *unless a grain of wheat fall into the earth, &c.*

"O.—But in the delivery of the mysteries, he called the bread, his body, and that which is mixed, his blood.

"E.—He did so call them.

"O.—But that which is his body by nature—*kata phusin to soma*—is also to be called his body, and his blood is to be called blood.

---

s De duabus Naturis in Christo.

"E.—It is confessed.

"O.—But our Saviour changed the names, and to his body he gave the name of the symbol, and to the symbol, the name of his body; and so having called himself a vine, he called the symbol, blood.

"E.—Very right. But I desire to know the reason of this change of names.

"O.—The scope is manifest to those that are initiated in divine things, for he would have those that partake of the divine mysteries, to attend, not to the nature of those things that are seen, but, upon the changing of the names, to believe the change made by grace. For he who called his body, which is so by nature, wheat and bread, and again termed himself a vine, has honored the visible symbols with the appellation of his body and blood, NOT CHANGING THEIR NATURE but adding grace to nature."[T]

Dialogue II.—

"O.—Pray tell me, of what are the mystical symbols offered to God by the priests, signs?

"E.—Of the body and blood of the Lord.

"O.—Of his body truly, or not truly such?

"E.—Of that which is truly [his body.]

"O.—Very well; For there must be an original of an image;—*tes eikonos archetupon*—for painters imitate nature, and draw the images of visible things.

"E.—True.

"O.—If then the divine mysteries are antitypes of a real body—*tou ontos somatos antitupa*—then the Lord's body is still a real body, not changed into the nature of the Deity, but filled with divine glory.

"E.—You have seasonably introduced the discourse of the divine mysteries; for thereby I will

[T] Dial I, Opera Paris, 1642, tom. iv, pp. 17, 18.

show that the body of the Lord is changed into another nature. Answer my question therefore.

"O.—I will.

"E.—What do you call the gift which is offered before the invocation of the priest?

"O.—I may not openly declare it, for perhaps some here present may not be initiated.

"E.—Answer enigmatically then.

"O.—I call it the food that is made of a certain grain.

"E.—How do you call the other symbol?

"O.—By a common name that signifies a kind of drink.

"E.—But how do you call it after consecration?

"O.—The body and blood of Christ.

"E.—And do you believe that you partake of Christ's body and blood?

"O.—Yes, I do believe it.

"E.—As then, the symbols of Christ's body and blood are one thing before the invocation of the priest, but after the invocation are changed and become something else; so, the body of the Lord, after his assumption, is changed into a divine essence.

"O.—You are caught in a net of your own weaving. For, after sanctification, the mystical symbols do not depart from their own nature; for THEY REMAIN STILL IN THEIR FORMER SUBSTANCE, AND FIGURE, AND FORM, and may be seen and touched such as they were before. But they are understoood to be what they are made and are believed and venerated, as being those things which they are believed to be."ᵘ

Here then we have the concurrent testimony of these distinguished Fathers of the Asiatic, European, and African churches, expressly teaching the

ᵘ Dial. II, pp. 84, 85.

non-departure of the substance of the bread in the Eucharist.

Should it be objected that the Fathers often mean by the terms *nature* and *substance* no more than the *qualities* of things, which we grant; nevertheless, we affirm the objection to be not well made; for the dispute with the Eutychians was not about the *qualities* of Christ's body, but about its *substance*, and therefore GELASIUS and THEODORET must have intended the substance of Christ's body. Otherwise their arguments were entirely inappropriate, and they failed to prove what they undertook to do.

The same remarks apply, essentially, to the error of the Apollinarians, and CHRYSOSTOM's reasoning against them; for the Eutychians were, after CHRYSOSTOM's time, condemned by the Council of Chalcedon for following the doctrine of APOLLINARIS; and this Council declared in opposition to these errors, "That one and the same Son, our Lord Jesus Christ, is to be acknowledged as being perfect in his Godhead, and perfect in his humanity, truly God and truly man, with a rational soul and a body;.... that the two natures were unconfounded, unchanged, undivided and inseparable; that the distinction of the two natures was not at all done away by the union; but rather that the peculiarity of each nature was preserved and concurred to one substance." (Act. v.) It was therefore the denial of these two distinct, substantial natures in the one person of Christ, by the ancient heretics, that called forth the language above cited; so that, when they undertake to prove this unchangeableness in the natures of Christ, by adducing as examples the bread and wine of the Eucharist, and the water of baptism, we are to understand them as teaching, that although a divine and spiritual grace is imparted to these elements, in virtue of consecration to a holy use, nevertheless, they preserve their former and proper substance, "unconfounded and unchanged."

Moreover, had these ancient Fathers believed the doctrine of a physical change in the bread and wine, it would have been easy and very natural for these heretics to reply to their assailants: "Honored Sirs, This illustration of yours rather strengthens our conviction of the truth of our doctrine. For you maintain, that, after the consecration of the bread and wine, these substances no longer remain in their proper nature, but are changed into the real body of Jesus Christ; in like manner do we believe that the human nature of Christ was, after his assumption, changed into the divine, being wholly absorbed by it." Now, had these keen-sighted defenders of the orthodox belief held such a doctrine, they would certainly have anticipated such an overwhelming reply; and common prudence would have restrained them from thus exposing themselves to be vanquished by their enemies. But that they did thus argue against the error of their enemies, and because no such reply was ever made, it follows, impliedly, that they did not believe any change of *substance* to be effected in the bread and wine of the Eucharist, in virtue of consecration.

III. Several of the ancient Christian writers compare the change wrought in the eucharistic elements with other like changes, in which, confessedly, no transmutation of substance takes place.

1. IRENÆUS, when speaking of the Eucharist in opposition to the errors of the Marcionites and Valentinians, says: "This oblation the pure Church alone offers to the Maker, offering of his creature to Him with thanksgiving. But the Jews do not now offer it, for their hands are full of blood; neither do they receive the Word through

whom it is offered to God. Neither do all the heretics; for some of them call another the Father besides the Maker; and, therefore, when they offer to him those things which, according to us, are his creatures, they represent him as greedy of what belongs to another.—But how shall it appear to them, that this bread, by which thanks are given, is the body of their Lord, and that cup his blood, if they deny him to be the Son of the Maker of the world, that is, his Word, by whom the tree bears its fruit, and fountains send forth their streams, and the earth gives, at first, the blade, afterward the ear, then the full grain upon the ear? But again, how say they that the flesh which is nourished by the body and blood of the Lord, passes to corruption and does not take life? Either, therefore, let them change their opinions, or abstain from offering those things which are commanded. But our opinion is agreeable to the Eucharist, and the Eucharist, on the other hand, confirms our opinion. For we offer to Him the things which are his, fitly declaring the communication and unity of the flesh and Spirit.

"For, as the bread which is of the earth, taking the invocation of God, is no longer common bread, but the Eucharist, consisting of two things, the earthly and the celestial; so also, our bodies taking the Eucharist are no longer corruptible, having hope of a resurrection."[v]

In order to be rightly understood, this passage requires some explanation. It appears from what IRENÆUS here and elsewhere says:

1. That the heretics against whom he writes, taught that God, the Father of our Lord Jesus Christ, is a being distinct from the Maker of the world, whom they denominated Demiurgus. Nev-

[v] Iren. Adv. Hæres, lib. iv, cap. 34, pp. 326, 327, Oxon. 1702.

ertheless, they continued to offer to God the Father, the sacrifice of the Eucharist, consisting of bread and wine, the creatures of Demiurgus, and thereby, as IRENÆUS declares, "offered the fruits of ignorance and passion and weakness, and sinned against the Father, reproaching him more than giving him thanks," inasmuch as they offered to him what belonged to Demiurgus by right of creation; and thus they represented the Father of Christ as requiring an offering to himself of that which belonged to another.

These errorists, therefore, were guilty of the grossest inconsistency, nay blasphemy; for while they professed to honor God the Father by the observance of the Eucharist, they dishonored him by representing him as covetous of what had been created by another, and to whom it properly belonged. Our author therefore, very pointedly rebukes them by exhorting either to change their opinion, or abstain from offering the sacrifice of the Eucharist to the Father of Christ.

Now had IRENÆUS held the doctrine of a physical change in the bread and wine, this rebuke of his would have been wholly irrelevant, and the accused heretic might have replied: "But, according to your own doctrine, these elements of bread and wine are transubstantiated into another and different substance, and therefore what is offered to God the Father does properly and emphatically belong to him, he being the author of this change or new creation; so that, we are consistent in our doctrine and practice." Such a reply would have completely silenced our orthodox objector, his whole argument being overthrown by his own doctrine.

(2) Equally would IRENÆUS have placed himself in the hands of his opponents, had he been a transubstantiationist, by demanding, "How it should appear to them, that the bread and cup are the body

and blood of their Lord, if they deny him to be the Son of the Maker of the world." As if he had asked, "How shall the creatures of Demiurgus appear to be the body and blood of the Son of another being, entirely distinct from this Maker of the world." Answer. "Being transubstantiated by God the Father's omnipotence, they are no longer the creatures of Demiurgus but of the Father." Thus would this learned Father of the church have been caught in his own net, and held at the mercy of his enemies.

(3) Again, these enemies of true Christianity, denied the body to be capable of a future resurrection to eternal life, being by nature corruptible. Our author undertakes to meet this error by stating their common doctrine, viz., that in the Eucharist our bodies are nourished by the bread and wine, to wit, the body and blood of Christ, which consists of two things, the one earthly, the other heavenly; and arguing hence that our bodies, being made the recipients of this gift and grace of God, have therefore, hope of a future resurrection to immortality. Thus, he in another place says, that "our bodies are not only *a* temple, but also *the* temple of Christ," and asks, "if it is not the part of the greatest blasphemy, to say that the temple of God in which dwells the Spirit of the Father, and the members of Christ, participate not of salvation, but are reduced to destruction."[1]

And in order to prove this precious doctrine of Christianity, he selects his argument from the doctrine of the Eucharist, as admitted by his very opposers, and affirms: "As the bread, which is of the earth, taking the invocation of God, is no longer common bread but the Eucharist consisting of two things, the earthly and the heavenly, so also, our

[1] Lib. v, cap. vi, p. 408.

bodies taking the Eucharist, are no longer corruptible, having hope of a resurrection."

His reasoning seems to be substantially as follows: "You admit that the bread and wine, which are by nature corruptible things, become, in virtue of God's benediction, the body and blood of Christ consisting of the earthly bread and wine, and the spiritual grace communicated by God; so do we affirm that our bodies, being made partakers of the Spirit of God, by a right participation of the Eucharist, are capable of the gift of God which is life eternal." Now the force of this illustrative comparison, depends upon the implied truth, and acknowledged belief of the persistence of the substance of the bread and wine of the Eucharist after consecration. Otherwise it would have been wholly inapposite; nay, it would have conduced greatly to strengthen the objection against the resurrection of the flesh, which was founded upon the supposition, that the substance of the flesh could not consist with the spirit in another life, and therefore that the former must be abolished. If therefore, they had believed a total abolition of the material bread and wine in the Eucharist to take place, then the heretics, not IRENÆUS, could say, "our opinion is agreeable to the Eucharist, and the Eucharist, on the other hand, confirms our opinion."

Moreover, IRENÆUS says: "When Christ had given thanks, taking the cup, he drank of it; and he promised to drink of the fruit of the vine with his disciples hereafter, proving both the earthly inheritance in which the new fruit of the vine should be drank, and the carnal resurrection of his disciples. For the flesh which rises again new, is the same as drinks the new cup. But he cannot be understood as drinking the fruit of the vine again, when constituted in his heavenly place with his disciples; neither, on the other hand, are they who drink it without flesh, for it is proper to flesh, not to spirit, to drink of the vine."¹

He evidently understands Christ to have taught his disciples, that the fruit of the vine which he would drink with them in his earthly kingdom after the resurrection, would be a NEW fruit, such, however, as would be adapted to their new resurrection flesh. If therefore, IRENÆUS be supposed to believe that Christ drank of his own real blood with his disciples at the last supper, then he must also have believed this most absurd consequence, that Christ's real blood would be *renewed* after the general resurrection! which is impossible. Hence he must have believed that Christ drank the proper fruit of the vine with his disciples, but not his own real and substantial blood.

2. CYRIL of Jerusalem says : "But ye are anointed with ointment, and are made the partakers and consorts of Christ. But see, lest you suppose that to be mere ointment; for as the bread of the Eucharist, after the invocation of the Holy Spirit, is no longer mere bread, but the body of Christ, so also this holy ointment is no longer mere ointment, nor, as one might say, common, after the invocation, but the chrism of Christ." ᵂ

Again: "For, *as* the bread and wine of the Eucharist before the holy invocation of the adorable Trinity, was mere bread and wine, but the invocation being made, the bread becomes the body of Christ, but the wine the blood of Christ, in the *same manner* the foods of this kind, of the pomp of Satan, being by their own nature mere foods, are defiled by the invocation of demons."² In another place he exhorts: "Come to baptism, not as to mere

---

¹ Lib. v, cap. 33, p. 453.
ᵂ Cateches. Mystag. iii, §3, p. 289. Ed. Oxon. 1703.
² Idem, Catech. Mystag. i, §.4, p. 281.

water, but to spiritual grace given with the water. For, *as* the simple offerings upon the altars are defiled by the invocation of idols; *so*, on the contrary, the simple water receives a power by the invocation of the Holy Spirit and of Christ, and acquires sanctity."[3]

By these several comparisons, he evidently ascribes a like change to the bread and wine of the Eucharist, the ointment of chrism, the water of baptism, and the foods offered to idols, in virtue of the invocations made over them respectively. But, confessedly, no other than a change of quality can be allowed to take place in the last three; therefore, no other than a change of quality can be allowed according to Cyril, to take place in the consecrated bread and wine of the Eucharist.

3. GREGORY of Nyssa, when speaking of the water of baptism, as the medium by which the body is cleansed, observes: "And the water that washes confers a blessing on the body that is baptized. Wherefore despise not the divine bath, nor lightly regard it as something common, because water is used. For that which operates is great, and wondrous effects arise from it. For this holy altar before which we stand, is by nature common stone, nothing differing from other flat stones which enter into the construction of our walls, and beautify our pavements, but when it has been consecrated to the service of God, and has received the benediction, it is a holy table, an immaculate altar, no longer being handled by all, but by the priests only, and they with feelings of veneration. Again, the bread is previously common bread, but when the mystery has devoted it to holy use, it is called, and is made the body of Christ. In the same manner, the mystical oil, and the wine, are things of little worth

---

[3] Idem, Catech. illuminat. iii, § 2, p. 34.

before the benediction, but after the sanctification which proceeds from the Spirit, each of these operates in an excellent manner. The same power of the word also makes a priest august and honorable, being separated from the community of the multitude, by the newness of the benediction. For, he was, until of late, one of the multitude and of the people, but is now suddenly set forth as a leader, a president, a teacher of piety, an instructor in the secret mysteries. And these things take place whilst he suffers no change of body or form, but he is in his appearance what he was, having, by some invisible power and grace, been changed in soul, for the better."[x]

Here GREGORY illustrates the change supposed to be wrought in the water of baptism, by like changes believed to be effected in the stone of an altar or table, the bread and wine of the Eucharist, the oil of chrism, and a priest, when consecrated for their respective places in the worship of God. And in regard to the cleric he expressly teaches, that no change either in his body or form was effected in virtue of consecration. This he undoubtedly believed to be true of all the other things mentioned in the category; otherwise, his illustrative comparison has no application, or force.

4. THEODOTUS says: "Both the bread and the oil are sanctified by the power of the name, nor are they the same as by their appearance they are taken to be, but they are changed by the power into a spiritual power. So also the water which is purified from evil and made baptism, not only contains the less, but also takes sanctification."[y] In

[x] Greg. Nyss. in Baptism. Christi, Opera tom. iii, pp. 369, 370. Paris, 1638.

[y] Theodot. Epitom. ad finem Operum Clement. Alexand., p. 800.

conclusion: From the foregoing communications, I trust I have fairly and clearly proved, that the early church knew nothing of the doctrine of transubstantiation, as now taught in your church. The Fathers of the first six or seven centuries speak of the eucharistic elements, as the *figure* of Christ's broken body and shed blood. In doing this I have not only cited their mere words, but have also shown from the scope and design of their writings, that they necessarily teach a persistence of the natural substance of the consecrated symbols. Very truly, therefore, did Cardinal Cusanus write, that "certain of the ancient Fathers are found of this mind, that the bread in the sacrament is not transubstantiated, nor changed in nature." [1]

God grant that you also may be enabled to understand and duly appreciate the numerous testimonies adduced.

To your careful and impartial consideration, therefore, the foregoing "cloud of witnesses" is submitted.

I remain yours,
E. O. P.

---

[1] Cusan. Exerc., lib. vi, cited by Breckinridge, Controv., No. 34, p. 283.

LETTER IX.

SECRET DISCIPLINE OF THE ANCIENT CHURCH.

DEAR BROTHER:—Your recent communication is a remarkable specimen of the expedients, to which men sometimes resort, in order to extricate themselves from the difficult position, into which they may have brought themselves, by their imprudence. Apparently full of confidence in the infallibility of the declarations of your church, and of the perfect truthfulness of whatever drops from the lips, or flows from the pen of your teachers, you make no scruple to deny *in toto*, that the Fathers speak of the eucharistic elements, as the *figure* of Christ's broken body and shed blood; but now, when stubborn facts press heavily upon you, the attempt is made to rid yourself of their burden, by feeble attempts at explanation, and by pressing into your service the "Secret Discipline" of the ancient church, thinking this may furnish you with a solution of all your difficulties. Nay, you seem to fancy that in this ancient usage you have found the key that interprets all the figures, symbols, and enigmas of the Fathers; a powerful telescope, that pierces the dark vista of many ages; and presents to your imagination a harmonious and charming system of Christian doctrine, in their too often fanciful and discordant productions. And, so completely are you dazzled by this discovery, that you beg me, "in the name of Jesus Christ, not to pass it lightly over; for a knowledge of it will fully and satisfactorily explain everything obscure and enigmatical in the writings of the Fathers, during the period that it was in force." And again you entreat me, as I value my immortal soul, to give this thing a particular and thorough investigation; and you assure me, that it will furnish "a full solution of all the apparent leanings of the Fathers toward Protestantism."

Why, my dear Brother, I have already given some attention to this ancient usage, and have formed some idea of its origin, nature and use; but it never occurred to me that my soul's salvation depends, in the least, upon a full and perfect understanding of the matter. And here permit me to say, that the representation which you have made of this subject, is altogether one-sided, and the conclusion which you have drawn from it, wholly unwarranted from the facts in the case.

For your entire argument proceeds upon the false assumption, that there was one grand secret observed by the ancient church, and no other. And this is more than intimated by you in the very statement of the subject, when you denominate it, "The Discipline of the Secret." That secret is no other, according to you, than transubstantiation, a doctrine so full of mystery, incomprehensibility, and divinity, that it could not with safety be divulged to the Christian novices, lest perchance they should be offended at it, and turn back to idolatry. This appears to be the substance of your reasoning.

As you have therefore treated this whole subject in a manner so partial and unsatisfactory, it devolves upon me to present it in its true light, and thereby show you the falsity of your deductions.

This topic I find ably and somewhat fully discussed by Bingham in his "Antiquities of the Christian Church:" I propose therefore to present you with this disquisition with such modifications as seem proper to its full comprehension, and appropriate to a fraternal correspondence.

THE SECRET DISCIPLINE. 157

I. He observes: "As to its original the learned ALBASPINÆUS (a bishop of the Romish church, who rejects the Secret Discipline of the ancient church as an insufficient proof of the doctrine of transubstantiation,) has rightly observed, 'that in the Apostolic age, and some time after, they were not so very strict in this discipline of concealing their sacred mysteries from the knowledge of the catechumens.' For he thus argues against the antiquity of the book called the *Apostolic Constitutions:* 'The last words,' says he, 'which forbid these eight books do plainly show that they were not written in the first age; for the Christians of the first age did never make any scruple of publishing their mysteries, as appears from the writings of JUSTIN Martyr.'[A]

"Mr. Albertine observes the same out of ATHENAGORAS and TATIAN.[1] And DAILLE joins in opinion with ALBASPINÆUS, and cites his authority with approbation.[2] And BASNAGE is so far from thinking that the Apostles concealed their mysteries from catechumens, that he supposes they administered the sacraments in their presence.[B]

"The beginning of this discipline seems to have been about the time of TERTULLIAN; for he is the first writer that makes any mention of it. He says, there was a 'secrecy and silence observed in all their mysteries.' And he blames the heretics of his own times for not regarding something of this discipline."[C]

II. Having learned something of the origin of this discipline, our next inquiry may very properly be: *What were the things concealed?*

[A] Albasp. Observat., lib i, cap. 13, p. 38.
[1] Albertin. de Eucharist, lib. ii, p. 709.
[2] Dalleus de Scriptis Ignatii, lib. i, cap. 22, p. 142.
[B] Basnag. Exercitat. in Baron., p. 419.
[C] Tertul. Apol., cap. 7.

1. The manner of administering baptism was one of them. This appears from a canon of the first Council of Orange, in which it was ordered that "Catechumens are never to be admitted to the baptistry."[D] And BASIL mentions the triple baptizing and the other rites of baptism, as things "which it was not lawful to the uninitiated to look upon."[E] AUGUSTINE asks: "What is that which is kept secret and not made public in the church? The sacrament of baptism, and the sacrament of the Eucharist. Even the pagans may see our good works, but the sacraments are concealed from them."[F] In like manner, GREGORY NAZIANZEN, speaking of baptism, says: "You have heard so much of the mystery as we are allowed to speak publicly in the ears of all; and the rest you shall hear privately, which you must retain secret within yourself, and keep under the seal of baptism."[G]

From which it appears, "that although the ancients acquainted the catechumens with the doctrine of baptism, so far as to make them understand the spiritual nature and design of it, yet they never admitted them to the sight of the outward ceremony, nor so much as to hear any plain discourse about the manner of its administration, till they were fitted and prepared for the actual reception of it."

2. The same discipline of secrecy was observed in reference to the unction of chrism, sometimes called confirmation. BASIL mentions it in connection with baptism and the Eucharist, all of which it was not deemed lawful for the catechumens to look upon.[H] And INNOCENT I, writing to another

[D] Concil. Arausicanum I, Can. 19.
[E] Basil. de Spiritu Sancto, cap. xxvii, p. 76. Bened. Edit Paris, 1839.
[F] Aug. Com. in Psal. ciii.
[G] Naz. Orat. xl, tom. 1, p. 672.
[H] Basil, Ubi Supra citat.

bishop about confirmation, and the form of words used in the administration of it, says: "I cannot speak the words lest I should rather seem to betray the mystery than answer the question proposed."[1]

3. "A third thing which they concealed from the catechumens was the ordination of priests. The Council of Laodicea has a canon to this purpose, 'that ordinations should not be performed in the presence of the hearers,' that is, the catechumens.[1] And CHRYSOSTOM, speaking of this office and the solemn prayers used at the consecration, delivers himself in an obscure and covert way, because of the catechumens 'He that ordains,' says he, 'invites the prayers of the church, and they join their suffrages, and echo forth what the initiated know; for it is not lawful to disclose all things before the uninitiated.'"[J]

4. "A fourth thing which they concealed from the catechumens, was the public Liturgy, or solemn prayers of the church; for one rank of the catechumens, the *audientes* or hearers, were permitted only to stay and hear the sermon, but not any prayers of the church. Another sort, called kneelers, or prostrators, had the prayers of the church particularly for themselves, but no others. And the Competentes stayed only to hear the prayers offered up for themselves and the Energumens,[2] and then were dismissed. They might not stay to hear so much as the prayers for the Penitents, much less the prayers for the church militant, or any others pre-

[1] Innocent, Epist. i, ad Decentium Eugubin, cap. 3.

[1] Concil. Laodicen, Can. 5, Binii Hist. Gen. Concil., tom. i, p. 242.

[J] Chrys. Hom. xviii, in 2 Cor. § 3, tom. x, p. 670. Paris, 1838.

[2] The Energumens were persons supposed to be troubled by evil spirits.

ceding the communion. But before all these, the usual word of command was given by the deacons, or sacred heralds of the church, *Ne quis audientum*, or *Ite, missa est.* Catechumens, depart.

"From this it is easy to collect farther, that the solemn office of the absolution of penitents was never performed in the presence of the catechumens. For the time of absolution was not till all others were dismissed, except the penitents themselves who were to be absolved, which was immediately before their going to the altar to begin the communion service, as seems to be clear from those words of OPTATUS;[1] where he speaks of it as the common custom, both in the church and among the Donatists, to give imposition of hands for absolution immediately before their going to say the Lord's Prayer at the altar. All these things therefore were kept secret from the catechumens; for they were never suffered to be hearers or spectators of any part of them."

According to the Apostolic constitutions the catechumens, energumens, and those about to be baptized, were all dismissed before the prayer for the penitents and their restoration to the blessing of the church.[2]

5. As the Eucharist was the great mystery in the Christian service, so the ancients were very careful to conceal the manner of its celebration from the catechumens. This is evident from those passages of AUGUSTINE and BASIL before quoted, and from CHRYSOSTOM, who says: "We shut the doors when we celebrate the mysteries and exclude the uninitiated."[k] "Moreover let the door be watched,

---

[1] Optat. contra Parmen, lib. ii, p. 57.
[2] See Apostolic Constitutions, book viii, chapters, 6, 7, 8 and 9. Edited by Irah Chase, D. D., 1848.
[k] Homil. xxiii al xxiv, in Matt. tom. vii, p. 327, § 3.

lest there come in any unbeliever, or one not yet initiated;[1] and let the Deacons stand at the doors of the men, and the Sub-Deacons at those of the women, that no one go out, nor a door be opened, although it be for one of the faithful, at the time of the oblation."[2]

Bingham tells us that CASAUBON makes the following observation upon this topic, which the learned ALBERTINE takes from him and defends strenuously: "That whereas there are three things in the Eucharist: 1. The symbols, or sacred elements of bread and wine, 2, The things signified by them, and 3, The rites of celebration; that which the ancients labored chiefly to conceal from the catechumens, was not the things signified, but only the symbols or outward signs, and the rites and manner of celebration. For they made no scruple to call the Eucharist by the name of Christ's body and blood before the catechumens, at the same time that they would not call it bread and wine, or speak particularly of the form and manner of administering it, as ALBERTINUS proves out of THEODORET and many others. Which shows, that the reason of concealing the mystery from the catechumens was not the belief of *transubstantiation*, as the Romanists pretend; for then they would have chosen rather to conceal the names of Christ's body and blood than the names of the outward symbols, and the mystical rites of celebration; the latter of which they studiously concealed, but not the former."

6. The ancients also concealed from the knowledge of the more imperfect catechumens, the more sublime doctrines of Christianity; such as the mystery of the Trinity and incarnation of Christ,

[1] Apostolic Constitutions, book ii, ch. 57.
[2] Idem, book viii, ch. 11, Chase's Edition. Vide et Epiphan. Hæres. 42, No. 3; Hieron. Com. in Gal. vi; et alios passim.

the creed of the church, and the Lord's prayer, which the catechumens did not learn till just before their baptism. Thus THEODORET says: "We do not teach this prayer to the uninitiated, but to the Mystagogi. For no one that is not baptized can presume to say: *Our father who art in heaven*, not yet having received the gift of adoption. But he that is made partaker of baptism may call God his father, as being adopted among the sons of grace."ᴸ Chrysostom also expresses himself very clearly on this point, saying: "He who calls God, father, confesses by one and the same epithet; the remission of sins, removal of punishment, righteousness, sanctification, redemption, adoption, the inheritance, brotherhood with the only-begotten and the abundant supply of the spirit. For it is not possible that he who has not obtained all these good things should call God, father."ᴹ "For that this prayer belongs to the faithful, both the laws of the church and the beginning of the prayer teach; because the uninitiated cannot call God, father."ᴺ

For such reasons they never taught the Lord's prayer to any of the catechumens, except the most advanced of them, the competentes, a few days before their baptism; as we learn from Augustine, who exhorts: "Learn therefore this prayer which ye are to repeat eight days hence when ye are to be baptized."⁴

SOSOMEN gives it as a reason why he did not insert the words of the Nicene Creed into his history, "that probably many uninitiated persons might read his book, who ought not to read or hear the

ᴸ Theodoret. Hæret. Fabul. lib. v, c. 28, tom. iv, p. 316.
ᴹ Chrys. Homil. xix al xx, in Matt. § 4, tom. vii, p. 284.
ᴺ Ibid. § 5, p. 287.
⁴ Aug. Homil. xlii, ex. 50, tom. x, p. 195.

Creed."[1] And Jerome says: "There is a custom amongst us of this kind, that we publicly teach for forty days the holy and adorable Trinity to those who are to be baptized."[2] "It is not lawful," says CLEMENT of Alexandria, "to relate to the profane the mysteries of the Word."[3]

III. What were the true reasons of this secret discipline of the ancient church?

1. "And the first is that the plainness and simplicity of the Christian rites might not be despised by the uninitiated, or give occasion to scandal to them before they were thoroughly instructed in regard to the nature of the mysteries. For both Jews and Gentiles, from whom Christian converts were made catechumens, were apt to deride the nakedness and simplicity of the Christian religion, as void of those pompous ceremonies and sacrifices, with which the pagan religions abounded. The Christian religion prescribed but one washing in water, and one oblation of bread and wine, instead of that multitude of bloody sacrifices, which the other religions commanded. Therefore, lest the plainness of these few ceremonies should offend the prejudiced minds of the catechumens, before they were well instructed about them, the Christian teachers usually adorned these mysteries with great and magnificent titles, such as would convey noble ideas to the minds of men concerning their spiritual effects, but concealing their other names, lest the simplicity of the things should offend them. When they spake of the Eucharist, they never mentioned bread and wine, but the sacrifice of the body and blood of Christ; and styled baptism, illumination and life,

---

[1] Sozomen, lib. 1, cap. 20, et Hieron. Epist. 61, ad Pammach, cap. 9.
[2] Hieron. Epist. 61, ad Pam. cap. 4.
[3] Clem. Alex. Stromut. lib. v, cap. 9, p. 680.

the sacrament of faith and remission of sins, saying little in the meantime of the outward elements of water. This was one plain reason why they denied catechumens the sight of their sacraments, and always spoke in mystical terms before them." In proof of the correctness of these remarks of the learned Bingham, the following ancient testimonies may be offered.

After quoting our Saviour's words, "Give not that which is holy to the dogs, nor cast your pearls before swine," CHRYSOSTOM observes: "They feign gentleness that they may learn [our secret mysteries;] but when they learn them, being different from other people, they turn them into ridicule, make a mock of them, and laugh at us as deceived.... Wherefore it is no small advantage that they remain in ignorance; for then they do not despise in the same manner. But if they learn, the injury is two-fold; for they do not thence bear fruit, but are injured the more; and to thee they furnish innumerable troubles. Let them hear, who shamelessly couple all things together and make things venerable to be despised. For when we celebrate the mysteries, we for this reason shut the doors and exclude the uninitiated; not that we find any infirmity in the mysteries, but because the multitude are yet too imperfectly disposed toward them."[o]

ATHANASIUS, writing in opposition to some who made a public display of the eucharistic sacrament, regards the practice as a violation of our Lord's command, "Give not that which is holy to the dogs, neither cast your pearls before swine," and adds: "We must not make a public display of the mysteries to the uninitiated, in order that the Greeks, being kept in ignorance, may not ridicule,

---

[o] Chrys. Hom. xxiii, al xxiv, in Matt. § 3, tom. vii, pp. 326, 327. Paris, 1836.

and that the catechumens may not be scandalized through curiosity."ᴾ

"These mysteries," says CYRIL of Jerusalem, "the church now relates to him who has changed from the catechumens. Nor is it a custom to relate them to the heathen; for we mention not the mysteries of the Father, and of the Son, and of the Holy Spirit, to a Gentile; neither do we speak clearly of the mysteries in the presence of the catechumens; but we often say many things covertly, that the faithful who know may understand, and that those who are ignorant may not be injured."ᵟ

"But if any one be a partaker [of the Eucharist] through ignorance," says the Apostolic Constitutions, "instruct him quickly, and initiate him, that he may not go out a despiser."

And the fourth Council of Toledo orders: "That henceforth no Jew should be obliged by force to believe." "But those who have some time since been compelled to come to Christianity,—as was done in the times of the most religious prince, Sisebut, because they have evidently been associated with the divine sacraments, have received the grace of baptism, have been anointed with chrism, and made partakers of the Lord's body and blood,—must be compelled to hold fast the faith which they have received, whether by force or necessity, that the name of the Lord be not blasphemed, and the faith which they have received be esteemed VILE and CONTEMPTIBLE."ᴿ

2. A second reason for this discipline was, that a greater veneration might be conciliated for the

ᴾ Athanasii Apolog. ad Imp. Constant, vol. i, p. 731. Paris. 1627.

ᵟ Cyril, Hierosol. Catech. Illum. vi, p. 60. Paris, 1631.

ᴿ Concil. Toletanum iv, Canon 56; Binii Histor. Gen. Conciliorum, tom. ii, part 2, p. 354.

mysteries in the minds of men on account of their ignorance of them, as we learn from BASIL, who says: "The Fathers knew well that the veneration of the mysteries was preserved by silence.—Moses, the great counsellor, did not make all parts of the sanctuary accessible to all, but kept the profane without the sacred enclosures,—well perceiving by his wisdom the real contempt had for what was trite and of itself apprehensible, but that the greatest regard was somehow naturally joined to what was most removed and rare. In the same manner, the Apostles and Fathers who from the beginning [?] enacted those things pertaining to the churches, preserved the veneration for the mysteries by secrecy and silence. For that which is exposed to the popular and vulgar ear, is no mystery at all. The reason of the delivery of these without writing is this, that the knowledge of the dogmas which appears very contemptible to the multitude, may not be despised on account of familiarity."[s]

And AUGUSTINE says: "You ought not to wonder, dear brethren, that in these mysteries we say nothing concerning the mysteries ; that we do not immediately interpret what we deliver. For in things so holy and divine, we observe the honor of silence."[1]

3. Another reason given by AUGUSTINE why the sacraments were not delivered to the catechumens was, that their curiosity might be excited, so that they should the more ardently desire them, and hasten to come to an experimental knowledge of them. He asks: "Why then could not the disciples bear aught of those things which were written

[s] Basil liber de Spiritu Sancto, cap. xxvii, vol. iii, pp. 76, 77, Paris, 1839.

[1] Aug. Sermo. i, inter. 40, Edit. a Sirmondo, tom. x.

after the ascension of the Lord, although the Holy Spirit was not yet sent to them, when now the catechumens may bear all things, the Holy Spirit not yet being received? Because, although the sacraments of the faithful are not delivered to these, it is not for this, that they cannot bear them, but that they may so much the more ardently desire them as they are the more honorably concealed from them."[T] Again: "The Jews see that the priesthood according to Aaron has now perished; and they acknowledge not the priesthood according to Melchisedec. To the faithful I speak; if the catechumens do not understand this, let them put away their slothfulness and hasten to a knowledge of it. There is no need therefore of disclosing the mysteries; the Scriptures intimate to you what is the priesthood according to the order of Melchisedec."[U]

4. From the passages cited from JEROME and CYRIL of Jerusalem, we may infer as a fourth reason of this ancient ecclesiastical usage, that the inexperienced minds of the Gentile converts, were not well qualified to receive the more profound doctrines of the Christian religion, such as the Trinity and the Incarnation.

5. Some of their sacred things were kept from the knowledge of the uninitiated, because the Christian teachers considered them inapproriate to the condition of those who had not yet been introduced into the church by baptism. Such were the Lord's Prayer and the Creed.

6. From the passages cited from CHRYSOSTOM, ATHANASIUS, CYRIL, and other authorities, we farther collect, that this secret discipline was observed by

[T] Aug. Expositio in Evang. Ioan., Tract. xcvii, tom. ix, p. 196, Paris, 1635.
[U] Enarratio in Psal. cix, tom. viii, p. 527.

the early Christians, both for the good of those who were excluded from the sight of their sacraments, and to save themselves the annoyance of the despising heathen.

Such, my Brother, was the origin, nature, and reasons of the secret discipline, as we gather from the records of the ancient church. In concluding the discussion of this subject, it only remains to us to determine, from these data, what bearing the *disciplina arcani* has upon the testimonies produced from the ancient Fathers, and briefly to consider the conclusion deduced from it by yourself.

1. We have seen that this discipline of secrecy cannot, according to the opinion of several learned men, both Romanist and Protestant, be traced beyond the age of TERTULLIAN, who flourished about two hundred years after the Christian era. JUSTIN Martyr, who preceded TERTULLIAN only about fifty years, in his Apology for the Christians to ANTONINUS PIUS, makes no scruple to describe very clearly to the Emperor the manner of celebrating the Eucharist, and the accompanying prayers, and even to repeat the description. Nay, he speaks of baptism with water and the incarnation of our Lord Jesus Christ. This quite spoils that fancied reasoning of yours, wherein you attempt to fasten this discipline of "utmost secrecy" upon the Apostles themselves.

2. We cannot urge the secret discipline of the ancient church, in proof of the Fathers speaking of the doctrine of the Eucharist in a manner obscure and enigmatical; for it was not so much the *doctrine* of this sacrament that was concealed as the *manner* of celebrating it, and the *nature* of the elements used. Besides, if we introduce this usage as an essential element in interpreting their descriptions of the Eucharist, then it is but fair to extend its application so as to use it in the exposition of

what they say in regard to all those other things which were secretly observed, such as the doctrine of the Trinity, the incarnation of Christ, baptism and the rest. Now if it be confessed as a general truth, that these ancient writers spoke in language "ambiguous and enigmatical" when they discoursed upon the Trinity, the incarnation of Christ, baptism, the ordination of the clergy, the Lord's Prayer, the Creed of the church, and those other kindred subjects which have been enumerated, then the darkness of uncertainty broods over the whole face of patristic literature; and it may be justly doubted whether we now have any correct knowledge of the faith of the ancient church. For if we must not take their language in its ordinary and proper sense, when they call the eucharistic bread and wine the *figure, symbols, image, type, antitype* and *signs* of Christ's body and blood, and further attribute to these emblems such qualities as pertain only to the earthly and corruptible, and even declare that they do not depart from their natural and proper substance; how shall it appear that they must be understood literally and properly, when they assert the consubstantiality of the three persons in the Godhead, the incarnation of Christ, or the baptism with water? If the language of the Fathers which I have cited, does not prove their belief of a figurative presence of Christ's flesh and blood in the Eucharist, then I affirm that their words prove just nothing, and therefore their testimony is unreliable and valueless on any point of controverted doctrine. For they affirm nothing in plainer terms than they do, that the eucharistic elements are the figure of Christ's broken body and shed blood. But, believing the Fathers to have been men of intelligence and moral honesty, I conclude that when they give a sober delineation of the Eucharist, or any other Christian doctrine, they used words in their common acceptation, and intended to be understood as meaning what they taught.

Again, were we to allow that the Fathers spoke in language obscure and unintelligible, when they addressed the unbaptized, this would by no means prove a general ambiguity in their words upon other occasions. Some of their lectures were originally addressed to the initiated, where no such ambiguousness was required, or would have been appropriate. Other parts of their productions were written in the form of commentary, where sound sense and sober description are especially called for: other works of theirs are elaborate defences of the Christian religion against the artfully subtle and malignant objections brought against it by its bitterest enemies: others also were written in the form of friendly and argumentative epistles to brother bishops and beloved churches. In such productions, intended for the instruction and use of all advanced Christians, the Fathers did doubtless intend to give, according to their respective ability, a truthful and intelligible representation of Christian doctrine. I do not mean to say, however, that they were always methodical in the arrangement of their thoughts, consistent and clear in their reasonings, or convincing in their conclusions; but I do insist, that on the subject of the Eucharist, they did not so depart from their usual style and mode of argumentation, as to form a general exception to their ordinary method of treating all the other leading doctrines of Christianity.

The representation which has now been made of the "Secret Discipline," might seem incomplete, were the passages quoted by you, and the conclusions deduced from them, to be unnoticed. Let us therefore consider those of them which relate to the

Sacrament of the Eucharist. 1. TERTULLIAN is cited, as saying of those who unjustly accused the early Christians of perpetrating horrible crimes in their secret assemblies: "Who are those who have made known to the world these pretended crimes? Are they those who are accused? But how could it be so, since it is the common law of all mysteries to keep them secret? If they themselves made no discoveries, it must have been made by strangers: but how could they have had any knowledge of them, since the profane are excluded from the SIGHT of the most holy mysteries, and those carefully selected who are permitted to be SPECTATORS."[1] And to a wife he says: "You would by marrying an infidel fall into this fault, that the pagans would come to the knowledge of our mysteries. Will not your husband know what you taste in secret before any other food; and if he PERCEIVES BREAD, will he not imagine that it is what is so much spoken of?"[2]

2. The Synod of Alexandria, held A. D. 340, in their synodical letter to the orthodox, say: "They (the Eusebians) are not ashamed to celebrate the mysteries BEFORE the catechumens and perhaps even BEFORE the pagans; forgetting that it is written, that we should hide the mystery of the king; and in contempt of the precept of our Lord, that we must not place holy things before dogs, nor pearls before swine. For it is not lawful TO SHOW THE MYSTERIES OPENLY to the uninitiated; less through ignorance, they scoff at them, and the catechumens be scandalized through indiscreet curiosity."[3]

3. ST. BASIL you quote as asking, "Which of the Saints has left us in writing, THE WORDS OF INVOCA-

---

[1] Tertul. Apol. cap. vii, p. 674, Paris, 1580.
[2] Idem, ad Uxorem. lib. ii, cap. 5, p. 430.
[3] Concil. Gen., tom. ii, p. 547.

TION in the consecration of the bread, and of the eucharistic cup?"[1]

4. And St. LENO, saying to the Christian women: "Know you not that the sacrifice of the unbeliever is public, but yours secret? That any one may freely approach his, whilst even for Christians, if they are not consecrated, it would be a sacrilege TO CONTEMPLATE yours?"[2]

5. Also, St. AUGUSTINE saying to the catechumen Honoratus, that, "When once he has been baptized, he will know WHERE, WHEN, AND HOW the great sacrament, the sacrifice of the new law is offered. Ask a catechumen if he eats the flesh of the Son of man and drinks his blood? he knows not what you mean. The catechumens know not WHAT the Christians receive; THE MANNER in which the flesh of our Lord is received is a thing concealed from them."[3]

6. And GAUDENTIUS discoursing, "We shall at present speak only of those which cannot be explained before the catechumens, but which notwithstanding it is necessary to disclose to the newly baptized.—This splendid Easter night requires our instruction to be adapted rather to the circumstances of the time, than to the lesson of the day, in order that the neophytes may, for the first time, be taught IN WHAT MANNER we partake of the paschal sacrifice."[4]

These are the only passages cited which appear to have a reference to the Sacrament of the Eucharist. You will perceive that I have taken the liberty to capitalize those words which seem to indicate the nature of the secrecy spoken of, which

[1] Basil de Spiritu Sancto, cap. 27, tom. iii, p. 55.
[2] De Continentia.
[3] Aug. Tract. xi, in Ioan., tom. ix, Paris, 1536.
[4] Gaudent. Explan. Exod. ad Neophyt.

most plainly consists of a concealment of the elements used, and of the rites and ceremonies employed in their consecration and administration; but not one word is said in them all of the incomprehensibility of the doctrine involved, or of the intellectual inability of the catechumens to understand them; which difficulties certainly should have been mentioned, had they been believed to exist. St. Augustine, however, settles this point when he says: "The sacraments of the faithful were not delivered to the catechumens, not because they could not bear them, but that they might so much the more ardently desire them, as they were the more honorably concealed from them."

I greatly wonder that such passages as you have quoted, should be produced, in order to account for the Fathers calling the eucharistic elements of bread and wine, the *figure* of Christ's broken body and shed blood; when not one of them ever thought of offering this secret usage as the reason of so denominating these emblems.

From the representation which has now been made, you cannot but perceive your utter failure at proof, in your attempt to account, from the secret discipline of the ancient church, for denominating the eucharistic elements the *figure* of Christ's broken body and shed blood.

For your whole argument proceeds upon the assumption, that there was but one thing kept within the veil of secrecy, and that one thing was the doctrine of the Eucharist; which was deemed too unintelligible and mysterious to be understood by the inexperienced catechumens. But your premises being proved untrue, your conclusion also must be false. You must therefore consent to interpret the Fathers as we do other ancient writers; by comparing one passage with another of the same writer, one author with another, and all of them with

15*

reference to the general scope and spirit of their productions. We must not select a few such passages only, as seem to favor our preconceived opinions, and neglect others of a different kind, if we wish to arrive at just results in our examinations; but we must take them together, and give them such an exposition as shall best accord with their general scope and design; otherwise, we shall fail to ascertain their true meaning, and be very likely to attribute to these ancient writers consequences false and contradictory.

Be your interpretation of the writings of antiquity what they may, let us ever have it in mind, that TRUTH is eternal, and therefore incapable of being changed, much less destroyed by the instrument through which it is viewed.

Your true Friend and Brother,

E. O. P.

LETTER X.

SEVERAL TERMS APPLIED TO THE EUCHARIST NOW USED BY ROMANISTS IN A SENSE DIFFERENT FROM THAT GIVEN THEM BY THE ANCIENT FATHERS.

DEAR BROTHER:—In the same communication in which you undertake to account from the secret discipline, for the Fathers' "use of enigmatical and ambiguous language, known and perfectly understood by the initiated, and at the same time, dark and mysterious to those who were not," you are pleased to inform me, that "in a certain sense, and so far as it does not affect or qualify the belief in a Real Presence, the Catholic may, with perfect consistency, apply the words, figure or symbol to the Eucharist, seeing that every sacrament as such, must be an outward sign, and consequently a figure or symbol."

But if the sacrament of the Eucharist "must be an outward sign, and consequently a figure or symbol," how do the Fathers speak "ambiguously and enigmatically" when they so denominate it? What need is there to introduce the secret discipline of the ancients to account for ambiguities and enigmas that have no existence? For if the sacrament of the Eucharist *must* be a figure or symbol, then it is properly such, and it is no ambiguity or impropriety so to call it. "And so far as it does not affect or qualify the belief in a Real Presence, the Catholic may, with perfect consistency, apply the words Figure or Symbol to the Eucharist." But suppose that it should so affect his belief in a Real Presence, that he can neither understand nor be made to believe that the Eucharistic elements are both the real body and blood of Christ, and, at the same time, a figure or symbol of them; must he, as your language intimates, cease to apply these words to them? Must he cease to call things by their proper names, if by so calling them his faith is endangered? And does your doctrine require the signification of things to be changed? By so doing, CLEMENT tells us that all true doctrine is overturned; and I fully believe it. Or do you mean that the signification of the terms *figure* and *symbol*, as applied to the Eucharist, depends upon the doctrine of the Real Presence? If so, you equally disturb the foundation of intelligible faith, and unsettle and overturn all true doctrine. For if language has no stable meaning independent of Christian doctrine, then I know of no way by which to arrive at any determinate knowledge of what is taught in the New Testament Scriptures.

But you do not claim the honor of being the original propounder of the evident incompatibility of denominating the Eucharistic elements the real body and blood of Christ, and, at the same time, a figure or symbol of that body and blood; for you quote the "clear words" of Pascal, which, you think, "cannot but be interesting to me, and will help to elucidate my objections." He says: "We believe that the substance of bread being changed into that of the body of our Lord Jesus Christ, he is really present in the Holy Sacrament. This is the Catholic faith which comprehends those two verities which seem opposed. The heresy of the present day, does not conceive that this sacrament contains altogether both the presence of Jesus Christ and his figure, and that he is both a sacrifice, and a commemoration of the sacrifice; it believes that we cannot admit the one of these verities without excluding the other. For this reason they strongly urge that this sacrament is figurative; and in this they are not heretic. They think that we exclude this verity, and thence it comes that they make us so many objections upon those passages of the Fathers which say thus. In fine, they deny the Real Presence, and in this they are heretics." These words, I admit, are "clear" enough; but they contain nothing but mere assertion, and serve not in the least to remove the "objections" alluded to. There is no need however of crossing the Atlantic to find a "clear" assertion of a reputedly able man.

Mr. John Hughes furnishes us with the same sort of argument, in his controversy with Mr. Breckenridge, when speaking of Protestants, he says: "They may say that the Fathers often applied the terms, *figure, sign, symbol, antitype, bread* and *wine*, to the Eucharist even after consecration. It is true they applied these terms to the exterior appearances—but this only proves that under these *signs, symbols*, &c., they believed the substantial existence of the thing signified, viz: the flesh and blood of Jesus Christ."

II. The application of these terms by the Fathers to the Eucharist after consecration being confessed, my task is limited to the consideration of the affirmation, "they applied these terms to the exterior appearances;" which necessarily implies that they did not apply the terms, *figure, symbol, type, antitype, image* and *sign*, to the substance of the elements.

In the first place I remark, that such an application of the terms under consideration is unsustained by any conventional and proper signification common to them all. I say, common to them all; for these several terms being indiscriminately applied to one and the same thing, are evidently employed in some sense in which they all agree.

Now the only signification which they all can possibly be allowed to bear as applied to the Eucharist, is evidently that of *symbolical,* or *typical* representation.

2. In this sense the Fathers use these same words when applied to other things besides the Eucharist. Thus, JUSTIN Martyr calls the paschal lamb a type of Christ; the offering of fine flour which was made for those who were cleansed of their leprosy, a type of the Eucharist; and the twelve bells upon the High Priest's garments, a symbol of the twelve Apostles.[A] CLEMENT of Alexandria tells us that "in Diospolis, a city of Egypt, there was delineated upon the temple called Pylon, a boy, which was a symbol of generation; an old man, which was a symbol of corruption; and a hawk, which was a symbol of God."[1] ORIGEN regards Joshua as the type of Christ,[2] and the body of Christ as a type of the Church.[3] And CYRIL of Alexandria calls Jonah a sign of Christ's resurrection.[4]

It is needless to multiply examples in a matter so plain. No one for a moment can suppose these respective authors intended to say that Christ existed under the appearance of a lamb; the Apostles under the appearance of tinkling bells; God under the appearance of a hawk; or the resurrection under the appearance or history of Jonah.

3. These terms the Fathers apply to the substance of the bread and wine, and not to their mere appearances, or accidents. TERTULLIAN says: "The bread which he took and distributed to his disciples,

[A] Justin Martyr, Dialog. cum Tryphone, pp. 218–220. Lond. 1732.
[1] Clement, Alex. Stromat, lib. v, cap. vii, p. 670. Oxon. 1715.
[2] Origen, Com. in Joan, tom. vi, No. 26.
[3] Idem, tom. x, No. 20.
[4] Cyril, Alex. Com. in Joan, lib. v, c. 4.

that he made his body, by saying, 'This is my body,' that is, a figure of my body."[1] According to Mr. Hughes, TERTULLIAN is made to say: "The bread which he took and distributed to his disciples, that he made his body, by saying, 'This is my body,' that is, an *exterior appearance* of my body;" which is futile and false. For TERTULLIAN is proving the reality of Christ's body against the error of Marcion, by showing that the real bread which he called his body, required that the thing symbolized by it should be real also. This is evident from what follows: "But it would not have been a figure, unless his body had been a true one." But Mr. Hughes' interpretation makes TERTULLIAN say: "But it would not have been an *exterior appearance* unless his body had been a true one." "Hold," says Marcion: "it would not have been an *exterior appearance* merely unless his body had been a *false* one—a mere phantasm." According to Mr. Hughes' version, therefore, nothing could have served better to confirm Marcion in his error than TERTULLIAN'S argument. For, like Marcion, the believer of a real presence rejects the external appearance as a certain indication of a corresponding substantial reality.

EUSEBIUS says: "He delivered to his disciples the SYMBOLS of the divine economy, commanding an IMAGE of his own body to be made."[2] According to Mr. Hughes, "He delivered to his disciples the *exterior appearances* of the divine economy, commanding an *exterior appearance* of his own body to be made!" How very *exterior* is this religion of ours, if it consists only of an external appearance. "Our Lord did not doubt to say, 'This is my body,' when he gave the SIGN of his body,"[3] says ST. AUGUS-

[1] Tertull. adv. Marcion., lib. iv, cap. 40.
[2] Euseb. Dem. Evang., lib. viii, cap. 1. [See above, p. 136.]
[3] Aug. contra Adimant, cap. 12. [See above, p. 138.]

TINE. "When he gave the *exterior appearance* of his body," says the transubstantiationist; who, after all, by his interpretation of the ancient Fathers, resolves Christ's body in the sacrament into a mere appearance. "In holy baptism," says THEODORET, " we see the TYPE of the resurrection, but we shall then see the resurrection itself; here we see the SYMBOLS of the Lord's body, we shall there see the Lord himself."[B] In this passage the terms TYPE and SYMBOLS have a corresponding meaning, both signifying *a typical representation.* The distinction between the symbolical and real presence of Christ is very marked. On the words of Jeremiah, "They shall flow unto the goodness of the Lord, for wheat, and wine, and oil," ch. xxxi, v. 12, JEROME remarks: "Of which the BREAD of the Lord is made, and the TYPE of his blood is filled, and the blessing of sanctification shown forth."[C]

MACARIUS of Egypt says: "In the church is offered BREAD and WINE, the ANTITYPE of Christ's flesh and blood, and they that eat the visible BREAD do eat the flesh of the Lord spiritually."[1]

THEODORET remarks: "If the Lord's flesh be changed into the nature of the divinity, wherefore do they partake of the ANTITYPES of his body; for when the truth is taken away the TYPE is superfluous."[2]

CYPRIAN says: "Our Lord, at the table where he participated in the last feast with his disciples, gave, with his own hands, BREAD and WINE; but upon the cross he delivered his body into the hands of the soldiers to be wounded, that sincere truth and true sincerity, being more deeply impressed upon the Apostles, might make known to the Gen-

[B] Theodoret Com. in I Cor., xiii.   [C] Tom. ii, p. 648.
[1] Macar. Homil. xxvii. [See above, p. 136-7.]
[2] Recapit. in fine Dialog. iii.

tiles how BREAD and WINE became his flesh and blood, and in what manner causes agree with their effects, and the names or species of things diverse are referred to one essence, and the things signifying and those signified are understood by the same terms."[D] "And he offered the same that Melchisedec offered, that is, *bread* and *wine*, to wit, his body and blood." "Nor can his blood by which we have been redeemed and quickened, seem to be in the cup when *wine* is wanting in the cup."[1] "Neither did he reject *bread* by which he represents his own body,"[2] says TERTULLIAN.

ST. AUGUSTINE asks: "How is the bread his body, and the cup, or what the cup contains, his blood? These things, my brethren, are therefore called sacraments, because in them one thing is seen, another is understood."[3] And, "the sacrament of the body and blood of Christ which is in the consecrated *bread* and *wine*, we are wont to call his body and blood. Not indeed that the *bread* is *properly* called his body, and the *cup* his blood; but because they contain in themselves the mystery of his body and blood."

These passages suffice to show that when the Fathers apply the terms *figure, image, sign, symbol, type, antitype, bread* and *wine*, to the consecrated elements, they employ them with reference to the substance of those elements, and not to their mere external qualities, or accidents. Their plain meaning therefore is, that these elements are the symbolical representatives of Christ's real flesh and blood; for that interpretation which refers these

[D] Opera, p. 473.   [1] Cyprian, Epist. lxiii, ad Cæcilium.
[2] Adv. Marcion, lib. i, cap. 14.
[3] Aug. Serm. ad recent Baptizat.
[4] Facund. Defens. Concil. Chalced., lib. ix, cap. 5. (Vid. p. 138.)

terms to the exterior appearance only, makes the Fathers chargeable with the most frivolous nonsense and self-contradiction.

4. Not only do the Fathers make a distinction between the image, figure and type of a thing constructively, but they also do the same definitively, as we conclude from the following: "The image will not in every respect be equal to the truth; for it is one thing to be according to truth, and another to be the truth itself."[E] "For no one is an image of himself."[F] And, "No one can be an image of himself."[G] Because "It would be no longer an image if it were altogether the same as that of which it is an image."[H] Nay, "What more absurd than to be called an image with respect to one's self."[I] "Nor is a figure the truth, but an imitation of the truth."[J] "A type is not the truth, but rather introduces the likeness of the truth."[K] And, "A pledge and image belong to something else, that is, they look not to themselves but to something else."[l]

They make a *type, sign, image,* and *symbol* inferior to that of which it is a type; and a symbolical representation of what is absent from the sign.

CHRYSOSTOM observes: "Well did the Apostle say, 'In righteousness and true holiness,' Eph. iv : 24. There was once a righteousness and holiness amongst the Jews; but that was not true but typical right-

[E] Tertull. contra Marcion, lib. ii, cap. 9.
[F] Hilarius de Synodis.
[G] Ambros. de fide, lib. i, c. 4.
[H] Greg. Nyssen, de Anima et Resurrectione.
[I] Aug. de Trinit., lib. vii, c. 1.
[J] Gaudent. Tract. ii, in Exod.
[K] Cyril. Alex. in Amos vi.
[L] Bertram. de Corp. et Sang. Dom.

eousness. For the being pure in body was a type of purification; it was a type of righteousness, not true righteousness."[M]

"It is as much inferior to it as a sign is of the thing of which it is a sign."[N] "Here is the shadow, here the image, there the truth. The shadow was in the law, the image is in the gospel, the truth is in the heavens."[O] "Therefore ascend, O man! into heaven, and you shall see those things of which the shadow and image were here."[P]

"For after his coming there will no longer be any need of the symbols of his body, his body then appearing."[Q] And Maximus, the interpreter, of the spurious Dionysius, speaking of bread and wine which he calls "holy gifts," says: "They are the symbols of things above that are more true."[R] "For the things of the old dispensation were a shadow, those of the new, an image, but the condition of things to come is the truth."[S]

III. Again: Your church employs the term *species* to designate the exterior appearances of bread and wine in the Eucharist, to the exclusion of their substance.[1]

The Fathers apply the term to the *substance* of these elements. When speaking of the bread in the sacrament, AUGUSTINE says: "When by the hands of men it is brought to that visible *species*, it is not sanctified that it should become so great a

[M] Chrysost. Hom. xiii, in Ep. ad Ephes.
[N] Idem, Hom. viii, in Ep. ad Rom.
[P] Idem, in Psal. xxxviii.
[O] Ambros. de Offic., lib. i, cap. 48.
[Q] Theodoret in I Cor. xi. 26.
[R] Hierarch. Eccles. c. 1.
[S] Idem, c. 3.
[1] See Council of Trent, Sess. xiii, canon 2. (Cited above, p. 22.)

sacrament except by the invisible operation of the Spirit of God."ᵀ

Also, speaking of the Jews, he says: "Behold the signs are varied, faith remaining the same. There, the rock was Christ; to us, that which is placed upon the altar of God is Christ; they drank the water flowing from the rock for a great sacrament of the same Christ. What we drink the faithful know. If you regard the visible *species*, it was another thing, if the intelligible signification, they drink the same spiritual drink."ᵁ

GAUDENTIUS says: "By the species of wine his blood is rightly expressed; for when he says in the gospel, *I am the true vine*, he fully declares that all the wine which is offered in a figure of his passion, is his blood."ⱽ Here *the species of wine* in the first clause is equivalent to *all the wine* in the latter.

RUPERTUS ABBAS teaches, that "nothing of the sacrifice enters into him who is destitute of faith, except the visible *species* of bread and wine."ᵂ

WALFRIDUS STRABO says, that "Christ delivered to his disciples the sacraments of his body and blood, in the *substance* of bread and wine." And adds; "that nothing could be found more suitable than these *species*, to signify the unity of the head and members."ˣ

IV. The Catechism of the Council of Trent has the following language, in reference to the bread and wine of the Eucharist: "The accidents which present themselves to the eyes, or other senses, exist in a wonderful and ineffable manner without

ᵀ Aug. de Trinit. lib. iii, c. 4.
ᵁ Idem. in Joan. Tract, xlv.
ⱽ Gaudent. Tract. ii in Exod.
ᵂ Rupert. de Offic., lib. ii, cap. 9.
ˣ De Rebus Eccles., cap. 16.

a subject. The accidents of bread and wine we see; but they inhere in no substance, and exist independently of any. The substance of bread and wine is so changed into the body and blood of our Lord, that they altogether cease to be the substance of bread and wine."[1] The eucharistic elements are, therefore, made an exception to the general laws of matter, inasmuch as the properties of bread and wine are affirmed to subsist without the presence of these substances.

On the contrary, the Fathers affirm the inseparability of substances from their accidents, not excepting the Eucharist, as a few examples will show. Thus, "Water cannot be understood without moisture, nor fire without heat, nor a stone without hardness. For these are united to one another: the one cannot be separated from the other, BUT THEY ALWAYS COEXIST."[y] "Every quality is in a substance."[z] "There being no substance quality is annihilated."[a] And, "Quality cannot be separated in its hypostasis from matter."[b] "But if by your reasoning you distinguish figure from a body, nature admits not the distinction, but the one is understood in conjunction with the other."[c] "As that is not a body which has not color and figure, solidity, space and weight, and other properties; so, where these which have been mentioned do concur, they produce a bodily subsistence."[d]

GREGORY NAZIANZEN, when arguing the personality and divinity of the Holy Spirit, says: "He is

[1] Roman Catechism, p. 207, cited by Elliott, vol. 1, p. 247.
[y] Iren. adv. Hæres. l. ii, c. 14.
[z] Athanas. Orat. iv, contra Arianos.
[a] Isidor. Pelusiot. lib. ii, Epist. 72.
[b] Methodius apud Photium, codic. 232.
[c] Basil. Epist. xliii.
[d] Greg. Nyssen. de Opificio Hom. cap. 24.

to be supposed to belong either to those things which subsist by themselves, or to those which are observed in something else; the former of which, those skilled in those things, call substance, the latter, accident. If, then he be an accident, this would be the power of God."[e] He assumes that accidents must have some subject to which they belong. "It is monstrous and the farthest from truth," says St. Augustine, "that that which would not be unless it were in a subject, would be able to exist when that subject, should cease to be."[f] "When the subject is changed, every thing in the subject is necessarily changed."[g] And, "Take away bodies from their qualities, and there will be nothing where [these qualities] should be, and therefore they will necessarily cease to exist."[h] Cyril of Alexandria teaches the same. In his dialogue concerning the Trinity, he asks, "Do you suppose that black and white can subsist by themselves? By No Means."[i] He calls it madness to affirm that the essence of the Son consists in subjection to the Father. For, he asks: "How can subjection be conceived to subsist by itself without existing in any thing real?" And afterward: "If there be no subject, and nothing pre-exists in which those things are wont to be done, how can those things exist by themselves which are understood and defined in the order of accidents?"[1] And in another place when arguing that the Son, though proceeding from the Father, is inseparable from him, he illustrates by the inseparability of accidents from their subjects, as follows: "We see heat in separably proceeding from fire, but it is the fruit

[e] Greg. Naz. Orat. xxxvii.
[f] Aug. Soliloq. lib. ii, c. 12.
[g] Idem, de Immortalitate Animæ, cap v.
[h] Idem, Epist. lvii, ad Dardanum.
[i] De Trinitat. Dial. ii.   [1] In Joan, lib. 4, cap. i.

of the very essence of fire, proceeding inseparably from it; as also splendor is the fruit of light. For light cannot subsist without splendor, nor fire without heat; for what is begotten of them does always adhere to such substances."[j]

Thus did the ancient Fathers undertake to prove the personality of the Holy Spirit, and the eternity of the Son of God from the inseparability of accidents from their subjects. One of them goes so far as to say, that if God himself had accidents they would exist in his substance.[1] It appears therefore, if their reasoning be correct, that the doctrine of the Trinity and the dogma of Transubstantiation are defended by arguments based upon evidence quite contradictory; so that we are in little danger of making shipwreck of the former, by rejecting the latter. From the evidence collected under this head, we may fairly conclude, that the ancient defenders of the Christian faith would never have used such arguments in proof of the Trinity, had one of their principal doctrines required for its very existence, evidence of a perfectly opposite character. I believe they were men of too much common sense, thus to array the evidences of the truth of Christianity in fatal conflict, the one against the other.

V. Your church differs from the ancient Fathers, in ascribing to the eucharistic elements properties and mode of being which they deny all bodies, not excepting the Lord's glorified body.

The Council of Trent says: "If any one shall deny that in the venerable sacrament of the Eucharist, whole Christ is contained under each species, and under every part of each species when a separation is made; let him be anathema."[2]

---

[j] Idem, Thesaur. Assert. 16.
[1] Vide Athanas. Orat. iv, contra Arianos.
[2] Sess. xiii, Can. 8. (See above p. 22.]

The believer of transubstantiation is therefore compelled to admit,

1. That a body can exist in more places than one at the same time: for, according to his theory, the same body of Christ is in every place where the consecrated elements exist.

2. That such a body exists within itself and contains itself; otherwise we cannot well account for the alleged fact, that when a separation is made, the whole body of Christ is contained in every fragment, however minute.

3. That his body exists in an invisible and impalpable manner, like a spirit, although it be present before us.

1. AUGUSTINE says: "You must not doubt that Christ entire is everywhere present as God, and is in the same temple of God as an inhabiting Deity, and is in a certain place of heaven by reason of the measure of his true body."[k] "Our Lord is above; but truth, the Lord, is also here. For the body of the Lord in which he arose, must be in a place; his truth is everywhere diffused."[l] "According to his bodily presence, he cannot be at the same time in the sun, in the moon, and upon the cross."[m]

THEODORET says of Christ's body after his resurrection: "It is nevertheless a body having its former circumscription."[n]

"Man, or any thing else like him," says HILARY, "when he is anywhere, is not then elsewhere; because that which is there, is contained where it is; so that he that is placed any where cannot be every where, on account of the infirmity of his nature."[o]

[k] Aug. Ep. lvi, ad Dardanum.
[l] Idem, Tract. xxx, in Joan.
[m] Idem, contra Faustum, lib. xx, c. 11.
[n] Theodoret, Dialog. ii.
[o] Hilarii, lib. viii, de Trinitate.

From the foregoing, these writers evidently considered Christ's human body as subject to the same absolute conditions of being, as all other bodies, notwithstanding its resurrection from the dead to a state of incorruption and glory.

2. The Bishop of Hippo also teaches, that " God entire is in heaven and entire on earth, not in alternate times, but both at the same time, which no corporal body is capable of."[p] Consequently, the body of Christ cannot be, at the same time, both in heaven and on earth in the sacrament. And, "However great or small a body may be, it occupies a space of place, and so fills that same place, that its whole is in no part of it."[q] And again, "There can be no body, either celestial or terrestrial, aerial or humid, which is not less in its part than in its whole; nor can it in any manner have another part in the place of this part."[r]

Nazianzen asserts, that "a vessel of the capacity of one measure will not contain two measures, nor will the space of one body contain two or more bodies."[s] This he says when proving the two perfect natures of Christ, and thereby admits that if Christ's two natures were both corporeal, that he could not contain two perfect natures.

Cyril of Alexandria repeatedly says that "nothing contains itself."[t]

"He that dwells in the tabernacle," says the "golden-mounted" orator of Constantinople, "and the tabernacle itself, are not the same; but one thing dwells in another—for nothing dwells in itself."[u]

[p] Aug. de Civitate Dei, lib. xxii, c. 29.
[q] Idem, Epist. iii, ad Volusian.
[r] Idem, contra Epist. Manichæi, c. 16.
[s] Greg. Naz. Orat. li, tom. i, p. 741.
[t] Cyril, Alex. Dial. vi. Vide et Dial. v, et vii.
[u] Homil. x, in Joan, citat. a Theodoret, Dial. ii. Vide et Irenæi adv. Hæres. lib. ii, c. 1.—Tertull. contra Marcion, lib. i, c. 15—et Epiphan, Hæres. xlii, sec. 7.

3. Tertullian says: "I understand nothing else to be the body of a man except what is seen and apprehended."[v] "God is incorporeal and therefore invisible,"[w] says Methodius.

Gregory Nazianzen asks, "Whether God is a body, and how is it immense, unbounded, without shape, impalpable and invisible? This is not the nature of bodies,"[x] he replies.

Gregory of Nyssen,—"That is not a body in which do not exist color, figure, solidity, space, weight, and the rest of its properties."[y]

Augustine, speaking of our Lord, says: "He is always with us by his divinity, but were he not corporeally absent from us, we should always carnally see his body."[z]

Fulgentius makes use of the following remarkable language: "Every thing so remains as it has received of God that it should be, one thing in this manner, and another in that. For it has not been so given to bodies that they should exist as spirits have received."[a]

From the passages cited in this communication it appears that the Fathers regarded all bodies, whether celestial or terrestrial, as subject to the following general laws: They occupy a certain space of place—are greater than their parts—cannot be contained in themselves—have necessarily certain sensible properties—and are limited to a single place at one time; all which directly overthrows that most strange doctrine of transubstantiation, which is contrary to the fundamental prin-

[v] Tertull. de Resurrec., c. 35.
[w] Method. apud Photium, Cod. 234.
[x] Orat. xxxiv, tom. i, p. 540.
[y] Cry. Nyssen. de Opificio, Hom. c. 24.
[z] Aug. de Verbo Domini, Serm. lx.
[a] Fulgent. de Fide ad Petr., c. 3.

ciples of knowledge and repugnant to the common judgment of mankind.

With the cordial regards of

Yours sincerely,

E. O. P.

LETTER XI.

THE TERMS BODY AND BLOOD OF CHRIST, AND THE EXPRESSION, MAKING THE BODY AND BLOOD OF CHRIST, NOW USED IN A SENSE DIFFERENT FROM THAT GIVEN THEM BY THE ANCIENT CHURCH.

DEAR BROTHER:—When speaking of the eucharistic elements, it was usual with the ancients, to call them the *body* and *blood* of Christ. "Almost all," says ST. AUGUSTINE, "do indeed call the sacrament his body."[A] It is this undisputed usage upon which you seize, and which you press into your service as if decisive of your doctrine. But before you conclude from this kind of expression, a physical change to have been believed, you ought to show in what sense these words were used. As you have neglected to do this, it devolves upon me to make such suggestions in relation to this phraseology, as shall enable us to form a right estimate of its true import. What then do the Fathers mean, when they call the sacramental elements the *body* and *blood* of Christ? You profess to believe, that nothing less than his real flesh and blood are intended; I, on the contrary, suppose them to intend no more than the sacrament of that real body and blood, to wit, bread and wine in their proper substance, but sanctified by the invisible operation of the Holy Spirit, and thereby made the vehicles of spiritual grace to the worthy recipient. For the correctness of this view I offer you the following considerations:

[A] Aug. de Verb. Dom. Serm. liii.

1. When the Fathers call the consecrated Eucharist the body of Christ, they sometimes use certain restrictive terms, which indicate that they did not intend to call it his real and proper body.

"But we," says ORIGEN, "giving thanks to the Maker of the universe, with prayer and thanksgiving for his gifts, eat the BREAD which is offered, and which by prayer is made a CERTAIN HOLY BODY, and sanctifies those that use it with good proposal."[B] Here the term CERTAIN plainly intimates that he does not use the word BODY in its proper sense, but with an accommodated or figurative signification. For, as no one would call pure gold, a certain gold, or pure silver, a certain kind of silver, so ORIGEN is not to be supposed to designate the real and proper body of Christ by the expression, "a certain holy body."

ST. AUGUSTINE makes use of the qualifying term. "Christ took in his hands what the faithful know, and in a CERTAIN MANNER carried himself when he said, 'This is my body.'"[C] And, "After a CERTAIN MANNER the sacrament of the body of Christ, is the body of Christ, and the sacrament of the blood of Christ, is the blood of Christ."[D]

The venerable BEDE also uses the same expression. "Christ, in a CERTAIN MANNER," says he, "was carried in his own hands."[E]

The expression already cited from ST. AUGUSTINE, "almost all do indeed call the sacrament the body of Christ," also shows these terms to be used in a catachrestic sense. For who would say that almost all call *men, men,* or a *lion, lion?* Do not all call them so? Most certainly; and that too

[B] Origen, contra Celsum, lib. viii, No. 33.
[C] Aug. in Psal. xxxiii.
[D] Aug. ad Bonifac. Epist. xxiii.
[E] Bæda in Psal. xxxiii.

because such are their proper names. But to say that almost all call rulers, gods, is equivalent to saying, that for certain reasons rulers are so called, but not because they are properly such.

2. The Fathers well knowing the Eucharist to be, not the real and proper body of Christ, give several reasons for calling it his body.

From its similitude, in some sense, to those things of which it is a sacrament. ST. AUGUSTINE says: "If the sacraments had not some similitude of those things of which they are sacraments, they would not be sacraments at all; but from this likeness they also take, for the most part, the names of the things themselves."[F]

The author of the Book of Sacraments under the name of AMBROSE, remarks: "Perhaps thou sayest, I do not see the species of blood. But it has its similitude. For as thou hast received the likeness of his death, so thou drinkest the likeness of his precious blood."[G]

ISIDORE of Seville says: "Because bread strengthens the body, it is therefore called the body of Christ; but the wine, because it operates blood in the flesh, is therefore referred to as the blood of Christ."[H]

They called the Eucharist the body and blood of Christ, because it was considered as the symbolical representation of Christ.

"Wherefore with all assurance," exhorts CYRIL, "let us partake of the body and blood of Christ; for in the type of bread his body is given thee, and in the type of wine his blood is given thee."[1] "When the Lord said, 'this is my body, and this

---

[F] Aug. Epist. xxiii. Vide et Bædam, in Epist. ad Rom., cap. vi.

[G] Ambros. de Sacram., lib. iv, c. 4.

[H] Isidor. de Offic. Eccles., lib. i, c. 18.

[1] Cyril, Ierosol. Catech. Mystag. iv.

is my blood,' it was fit that they who set forth the bread, should after the giving of thanks, reckon it to be his body and partake of it; and account the cup to be *in the place of his blood.*"[1]

The author of the Commentaries attributed to JEROME, says "Christ left to us his last remembrance, or memorial; just as if some one going a journey, should leave some pledge to one whom he loved, that as often as he should see it he might call to mind his favors and friendships."[1]

And in general terms, AUGUSTINE says: "All things signifying seem in some manner to take the persons of those things which they signify, as it is said by the Apostle: *The rock was Christ,* because that rock of which this is spoken then signified Christ."[2] In this manner do the Fathers give us their *reasons* for designating the consecrated elements, the *body* and *blood* of Christ; which shows that they did not consider them his natural and proper, but his representative body and blood. For it is not required to give reasons for calling things by their proper names. Who would think of giving a reason for calling iron, iron, wood by the name of wood, or water by the name of water? Whenever their respective names are pronounced, no one thinks of giving a reason for thus calling them; because they are understood to be properly what they are denominated. If therefore the ancients had, by universal consent, understood the consecrated elements to be the very substantial body and blood of Christ, it is difficult to account for their giving their reasons for so calling them.

3. When speaking of the sacramental body and blood of Christ, the Fathers, in their very language, point at something different from his proper blood.

[1] Victor Antioch, in Marc xiv.
[1] Com. in I Cor. xi.
[2] Aug. de Civitate Dei, lib. xviii, c. 48.

Having formerly cited several passages to this effect,[1] I shall add but a few more.

CHRYSOSTOM inquires, "What is the bread? The body of Christ. What do they who partake become? The body of Christ. Not many bodies but one body."[J]

"The *bread* being taken, and afterward the cup of *wine*, he testified that they were his BODY and BLOOD,"[K] says TATIAN the Syrian. "Who is more a priest of the Most High God than our Lord Jesus Christ? Who offered this SAME that Melchisedec offered, that is *bread* and *wine*, to wit, his *body* and *blood*." And "we find that the cup was mixed which the Lord offered, and that what he called his *blood* was *wine*."[2] "When our Lord reached the consecrated BREAD and WINE to his disciples, he thus said, 'THIS IS MY BODY.'"[L] And JEROME says: "Let us hear that that BREAD which our Lord broke and gave to his disciples, is the BODY of our Saviour."[M]

Again, when speaking of those virgins who were reproved for drinking wine to excess; "they made this excuse, joining sacrilege to drunkenness, and said, far be it that I should abstain from the blood of Christ."[N] So common was it, in that age, to call wine the blood of the Redeemer.

LEO the Great speaking of the Manichees, who through fear of the laws came to the communion of the Catholics, gives the following as a direction how to discover them. "They so conduct themselves in the communion of the sacraments, that they may

---

[1] See Letters vii and viii.
[J] Chrysost. Homil. xxiv, in I Cor.
[K] Tatian Syrus. Harmon. in Biblioth. Patrum, tom. vii.
[2] Cyprian, Ep. lxiii, ad Caecilium. (See above pp. 134-5.)
[L] Gaudent. Tract. ii, in Exod.
[M] Hieron. Ep. ad Hedibiam.
[N] Idem, Ep. ad Eustach.

sometime be more safely concealed. With an unworthy mouth they take the body of Christ, but altogether refuse to drink the blood of our redemption."[o] The reason why they would not partake of the cup was that the use of wine was altogether forbidden by them; as ST. AUGUSTINE says:[1] "They drink no wine, saying, it is the gall of the princes of darkness." FACUNDUS says: "Our Lord himself called the blessed BREAD and CUP which he delivered to his disciples, his BODY and BLOOD."[p] "This is my body, that is, in a sacrament," says DRUTHMARUS.[q] And the Ethiopic churches are said to use this phrase. "This BREAD is my BODY."[r] The Council of Carthage decreed against the Armenians, that "nothing but the body and blood of the Lord should be offered, as the Lord himself delivered, that is, *bread, and wine mixed with water.*"[s]

4. The Fathers also speak of Christ's body in the Eucharist as being *sanctified* by the Spirit of God.

ISIDORE of Seville, "By his command we call this the body and blood of Christ, which being made of the fruits of the earth, is *sanctified* and made a sacrament by the invisible operation of the Spirit of God."[t]

What they mean by the term sanctification, may be seen from the following: "To sanctify any thing, this is to vow it to God."[u] "That which is said to be sanctified does not partake of all holiness, but it rather signifies that which is devoted to God

[o] Leo Mag. Serm. iv, de Quadrag.
[1] De Hæres, 46.
[p] Facund. Defens. iii, lib. ix, cap. ult.
[q] Com. in Matt. xxvi.
[r] Ludolph. Æthiop. Hist. lib. iii, c. 5, n. 56.
[s] Pandect. Canon, p. 565.
[t] Isidor. Originum, lib. vi, c. 19.
[u] Origen, in Levit. Hom. xi.

unto his glory."[v] Would it not be impiety to say that the glorified body of our Lord which is united to his divine nature, does not partake of all holiness? Again: "We say that a place, or bread, or wine is sanctified, which is set apart for God, and put to no common use."[w] And, "That which is sanctified and offered is sanctified because it is offered: therefore it was not holy before."[x] This cannot be true of the proper body of Christ which was always holy; but only of the typical bread, which before consecration was common, or unsanctified bread. When therefore we hear St. Augustine saying: "That which is upon the table of the Lord—is *blessed* and *sanctified*,"[y] we must not understand him as meaning, "that Holy Thing' [Luke i, 35,] which was born of Mary, and is now in heaven, but the consecrated symbol of that holy and glorified body." For the sanctification here spoken of is *actual*—it is that which takes place through the agency of the creature, and not that which consists simply of a holiness as existing above and independently of us.

The language of these Fathers very illy applies to the doctrine of transubstantiation. For it is certain that the "glorified body of the cross" does not depend for its sanctification upon being offered by us. Nor can it be true of this, that it was not holy before being offered. But with the Protestant view of this sacrament the language of these Fathers perfectly harmonizes.

5. The Council of Trent teaches that Christ entire is contained under every part of each species; consequently, there is no such thing as breaking

---

[v] Cyril Alex. Com. in Esaiam, lib. 1, Orat. vi, p. 178.
[w] Jobius, apud Photium, Cod. 222.
[x] Hesych. in Levit. lib. vii.
[y] Aug. Ep. lix, ad Paulum.

the body of Christ in the sacrament, or taking a portion of it; because, however small the particle may be, it is said to contain whole Christ. This also disagrees with the teaching of antiquity.

ORIGEN says: "When ye take the body of the Lord, ye preserve it with all care and veneration, lest any little of it fall, lest any thing of the consecrated gift should slip down [to the ground.]z

Here the phrase *any little of it*, referring to the *body of the Lord*, plainly implies that the Lord's body in the sacrament may be divided into parts, otherwise no *part of it* could fall to the ground.

And ST. AUGUSTINE speaking of that which, upon the Lord's table, is blessed and sanctified, says: "It is broken into small parts to be distributed."a And elsewhere his expression is: "To take a part of the body of the immaculate lamb."b This cannot be true of the real body of Christ, as the Tridentine doctors very well knew.

The foregoing representation sufficiently shows, that the ancients used the terms *body* and *blood* of Christ, when speaking of the Eucharist, in a sense entirely different from that in which your church employs them at the present day. It is therefore unnecessary to enter upon any particular reply to those passages cited by you, in which this kind of expression is used. In regard to the words used there is no dispute. Our business is, therefore, to ascertain the sense given them by their authors. But the sense given them by you leads directly to insurmountable difficulties, and makes them entirely nugatory. And the only meaning which can possibly be attached to the phraseology under consideration, is that which contemplates the eu-

z Origen, Hom. xiii, in Exod. n. 3.
a Aug. Ep. lix, ad Paulum.
b Idem, Ep. lxxxvi, ad Casul.

charistic elements as the symbols of Christ's real body and blood.

II. Let us also consider that other kind of expression in which the Eucharist is said to be *made* the body and blood of Christ; and if we succeed in proving their use to be contrary to that assigned them by your church, we shall as conclusively establish the opposite or Protestant sense.

When theologians of your communion speak of *making* Christ's body in the Eucharist, they are to be understood as meaning that same body that appeared upon the earth and was crucified.

Cardinal BIEL says: "He who created me, has, if it be lawful to speak it, given to me to create himself, and he who created me without me is created by my mediation."[c]

And in the same lecture he makes a comparison between the Virgin and the priests: "She by saying *eight* words, conceived the Son of God and Redeemer of the world; they that are consecrated by the Lord, by *five* words daily call the Son of God and the Virgin bodily before them." And he then cries out, "Consider O ye priests in what rank and dignity ye are placed."[d] To the same purpose we may quote that famous declaration of RABANUS MAURUS, archbishop of Mentz, who in the ninth century opposed the newly taught doctrine of a corporeal change. "Some persons of late," says he, "not entertaining a sound opinion respecting the sacrament of the body and blood of our Lord, have actually ventured to declare that this is the identical body and blood of our Lord Jesus Christ; the identical body, to wit, which was born of the Virgin Mary, in which Christ suffered on the cross, and in which he arose from the dead."[1] From

[c] In Canon. Missæ, Lect. iv.   [d] Ibid.
[1] Ep. ad Heribald, cap. 33.

which it appears, that when they speak of creating, or making Christ's body, they mean that same body which had a prior existence. The Fathers teach the contrary, as a few passages from their writings will show.

"That which already has a being is not made, but that which has not an existence."[e] "Nothing which has a *fieri* is without a beginning, but its beginning takes place when its *fieri* begins."[f] "Everything that is made, was not before it was made."[g] "What is made begins to be."[h] "For to make is true of that which was not at all."[i] "To be made is wont to be the property of him who never subsisted before."[j] "For that which already exists, cannot certainly be brought into being, but that which does not exist."[k] And, "those things which have already sprung up, cannot return again into that state that they should be generated by a new creation."[l]

Such being the sense in which the Fathers use the expression *to make*, we have the means at hand of solving all those passages in which they speak of *making* the Lord's body in the Eucharist. Let us examine their phraseology by their own general principles.

GREGORY of Nyssen's Rule is: "If he made it, he made that which was not at all."[m] Application: "It was common bread before, but when the

[e] Athenag. de Resurrect.
[f] Tertull. lib. contra Hermog., c. 19.
[g] Hilar. de Trinit., lib. xii.
[h] Ambros. de Incarn., lib. iii.
[i] Aug. de Moribus Manich, cap. vii.
[j] Vigil., lib. iii, contra Eutych.
[k] Cyril. Alex. Thesaur., Assert. 20.
[l] Cassian de Incarn., lib. vii, c. 2.
[m] Greg. Nysseni contra Eunom., lib. iii.

mystery has consecrated it, it is called and is MADE the body of Christ."[n]

In the first passage he tells us that TO MAKE is to produce or bring into being a new existence; but in the latter, he says the bread after its consecration is made the body of Christ. But the proper and real body of Christ had an existence before the consecration of the Eucharist. How then was it made the body of Christ? Not substantially, because, as we have just said, his real body has a real existence previously to the consecration of the bread. Plainly therefore, GREGORY must have meant the making it not a substantial, but a symbolical body; for this it had not before, as common bread, but was made such by consecration. And here, without departing from this general rule of GREGORY, there may be a successive and continual making of Christ's symbolical body; for it is according to the nature of a symbol to be brought into existence at the will of the operator, and to cease to continue such, when the purposes for which it was made have been accomplished.

Again, our author says a little after: "We submit to the Holy Spirit that we may be made that which he is and is called."[o] That is, that we be made morally pure and holy like the Holy Spirit, be created anew in righteousness and true holiness, but not made what the Holy Spirit is in substance; for the Holy Spirit most certainly has a substantial being before we submit to him; and therefore, according to GREGORY's rule, we cannot be made what he is in substance, because this would be equivalent to a new creation, or making of the Holy Spirit.

TERTULLIAN also gives it as a general rule, that, "*What is made has its beginning when it is made.*"

[n] Idem, de Baptismate Christi, tom. iii, p. 370.
[o] Page 372.

He makes the *fieri* and the *esse* co-existent. Elsewhere he says: "The bread which was taken and distributed to his disciples, that he MADE his body."[1]

AUGUSTINE says: "To make is true of that which was not at all." Again, "Not all bread, but that which receives the benediction of Christ is MADE his body."[p] And, "Our bread and cup are MADE mystical to us by a sure consecration, and do not grow so."[2]

In the same manner are we to understand like expressions, to be found in the writings of others of the ancients; thus, "when the invocation is made, the bread is MADE the body of Christ, and the wine the blood of Christ."[q] And AMBROSE says: "This body which we make is of the Virgin;" which he explains by another accompanying expression: "It was the true flesh of Christ that was crucified and buried: it is therefore truly the sacrament of his flesh."[r] He makes a very marked distinction between Christ's true or natural flesh and that which is sacramental. The same distinction he elsewhere makes, as do others of the Fathers; but the passages quoted are sufficient to show in what sense we are to understand the phraseology considered.

In the above citations, which have been made as containing a general principle, there is, however, one idea implied which it is proper to notice, before taking leave of this topic. It is this: That no one and the same thing exists manifold at the same time. For very truly and philosophically do the Fathers teach, that when any thing is MADE, it then BEGINS TO EXIST. But as one thing can have but *one*

---

[1] Tertull. adv. Marcion, lib. iv. c. 40. [See above, page 127.]
[p] Aug. Serm. lxxxvii, de Diversis.
[2] Idem, contra Faustum, lib. xx, c. 13.
[q] Cyril, Ierosol. Catech. Mystag i, § 4.
[r] Ambros., lib. de iis qui initiant., c. 9.

creation, so it can have but *one existence*. Observe also: this is laid down as a universal law; and from this law you may not except the mystery of the Eucharist, without first showing that the Fathers make such exception. But they no where do so; consequently they utterly condemn that doctrine, which teaches that the same real body and blood of Christ existed in a myriad of places, under as many forms, at one and the same time.

Accept these considerations with assurances of the continued friendship of

Your Brother,

E. O. P.

LETTER XII.

SEVERAL OTHER POINTS RELATING TO THE EUCHARIST IN WHICH THE ANCIENT CATHOLIC AND THE PRESENT ROMAN CHURCHES DIFFER.

DEAR BROTHER:—In my last I discussed those kinds of expression in which the consecrated elements are said to be, and to be made the body and blood of Christ. Closely allied to the latter of these is that other kind of phraseology, wherein these elements are said to be CHANGED into the body and blood of Christ. These also you cite as proving, that in the mind of antiquity, a physical change was intended. The nature of this change, as taught in your church, is expressed in the second canon of thirteenth session of the Council of Trent, as follows:

"If any one shall say that in the most holy sacrament of the Eucharist the substance of the bread and wine remains, together with the body and blood of our Lord Jesus Christ, and shall deny that wonderful and singular conversion of the whole substance of the bread into his body, and the whole substance of the wine into his blood, the species of bread and wine only remaining, which conversion the Catholic Church most fitly terms transubstantiation; let him be anathema."[1]

Very fitly did the doctors of Trent call this affirmed change *wonderful* and *singular;* for it is plainly no other than a destruction or annihilation of the substance of the bread and wine and the crea-

---

[1] See above, Letter ii, p. 22.

tion of another substance of an entirely different nature. That the ancient Fathers of the church had no idea of any such change in the consecrated elements is evident from the following:

1. They distinguish the *change* or *conversion* of a thing from the abolition of its substance.

TERTULLIAN urges it as a great absurdity against certain errorists, that, according to them, "to be changed is to perish wholly from what it was before."[1] They denied the rising again of these same bodies at the resurrection; to which he urges the language of the Apostle Paul [I Cor. xv,] to prove that there will be a change, but not a destruction of our flesh. He affirms: "A change is one thing, destruction another. But the flesh will perish when changed if it shall not remain the same in the change as shall be exhibited in the resurrection..... As therefore, that which is destroyed is not changed, so that which is changed is not destroyed. For to perish is altogether not to be what it had been; but to be changed is to be otherwise than what it was.

Moreover whilst it exists otherwise it can still exist, for it has a being which does not perish, for it suffered a change, but not destruction."[A]

When controverting the error of the Eutychians, who thought the human nature of Christ was converted into his divinity, so that nothing of its substance remained after its assumption, GELASIUS says: "By a union with the Deity, our condition would not seem to be glorified, but rather consumed, if in glory it does not subsist the same, but the Deity existing alone, the humanity now ceases to be there:... in this manner, it will not be found to be sublimated, but rather abolished."[B]

---

[1] Quasi demutari, sit in totum et de pristino perire. Tertull. de Resurrec. Carnis, c. 55.

[A] Ibid.   [B] Gelas. de Duabus Naturis.

TERTULLIAN says to Marcion: "If thou defendest a transfiguration and conversion of any substance whatever, in its transition, then Saul also, when changed into another man, went out of his body. So it is possible, in the event of the resurrection, that with the preservation of the substance, there should be change, conversion and reformation."[C] They lay down as general rules: "To be made does not signify a change of nature entirely."[D] "Whatsoever the Holy Spirit touches, that is sanctified and changed."[E] And, "By the fire of the Holy Spirit, all things that we think, speak and do, are changed into a spiritual substance."[F] "For such as is that by nature which is received, into this it is necessary that the partaker should be changed.

Plainly and philosophically therefore does antiquity teach that change is not a destruction of substance; but it is such a modification of that substance, by the accession of new qualities, that it passes into another condition, or mode of existence. Not even when they speak of a change of substance, that is, a change which affects the substance, are we to understand them as teaching an abolition of that substance essentially, and the creation of something else. This is that *wonderful* and *singular* conversion called transubstantiation, a something unique in the known universe of things created; perfectly isolated; and refusing any community with all the rest of God's wonderful works! It is the annihilation of one substance and the creation of another already having an existence, but pre-

[C] Tertull. de Resurr. Carn. c. 55.
[D] Cyril, Alex. Thesaur. Assert. 20.
[E] Cyril, Ierosol. Catech. Mystag. v.
[F] Hieron. in Ezekiel xliii.
[G] Greg. Nyss. Homil. viii, in Ecclesiast. tom. i, p. 456.

serving the same dimensions and weight, the same chemical and physical properties as the thing destroyed! Indeed, so entirely different is transubstantiation from any known transmutation, that Scotus says: "Properly speaking, I say that transubstantiation is not a change."[H]

2. The Fathers make use of the same terms, expressive of change and conversion, when speaking of other things in which, confessedly, there is no change of substance, as they do when treating of the Eucharist.

"Let them learn," says Ambrose, "that nature can be changed when the rock flowed with water, and the iron swam above the water."[I] And when speaking of the waters of the Red Sea and the river Jordan standing in heaps, he says: "Is it not clear that the nature of the waves of the sea and of the course of the water was changed?"[J] "The hand of Moses was changed into snow,"[K] says Epiphanius. And Chrysostom speaking of the Babylonian furnace, says: "The elements unmindful of their proper nature were changed into what was more profitable to them; and the beasts were no longer beasts, nor the furnace a furnace."[L] And St. Augustine is bold to say, "By sin man fell from the substance in which he was made."[M]

When speaking of regeneration the Fathers use language equally strong, representing it as capable of "changing us into the Son of God."[N]

[H] Dist. iv, Art. xi, Sec. 1.
[I] Ambros. in Hexæm., lib. iii, c. 2.
[J] Idem, lib. de iis qui initiat. c. 9.
[K] Epiphan. Hæres. lxiv.
[L] Chrysost. in Psal. x.
[M] Enarrat. in Psal. lxviii, Serm. i, § 5.
[N] Cyril, Alex. Dial. iii, de Trinit.

"Our souls" says MACARIUS, "must be altered and changed from their present condition into another and divine nature."[o]

GREGORY of Nyssen says: "They are no longer men who are introduced into the mysteries of this book, [Song of Songs;] but are changed in nature, through the discipline of Christ, into something more divine."[p] As already stated, he lays it down as a general principle, that the partaker is changed into that of which he partakes; which he illustrates as follows: "For he who loves good, will himself become good, the goodness of that which exists in itself changing him who receives it into itself. For this cause he who always is, has offered himself to us to be eaten, that we receiving him into ourselves may be made that which he is. For he says, 'my flesh is meat indeed, and my blood is drink indeed.'"[1] Again, "Paul did so manifestly imitate Christ, that in his own soul he showed his governing principle to have been changed, the very form of his soul being changed into the prototype, [Christ,] by the most exact imitation; so that he no longer seemed to be that Paul who lived and spoke."[2] According to this, the imitators of Christ are changed into himself, being made partakers of the divine nature; so that a Christian may as well be called Christ whole and entire, as the consecrated Eucharist.

When the ancient writers speak of our resurrection bodies and the incarnation of Christ, they deliver themselves in like terms.

When speaking of the resurrection, TERTULLIAN says: "We shall be changed, in a moment, into an

[o] Macarii, Homil. xliv.
[p] Greg. Nyss. in Cant. Hom. i.
[1] Idem, in Ecclesiast. Hom. viii.
[2] Idem, de Perf. Christi, tom. iii, p. 276.

angelic substance."ᵠ He does not mean that the proper substance of our bodies will disappear, but only changed in its qualities so as to be like angels.

HILARY expresses the same modification, as a "change of terrene bodies into a spiritual and ethereal nature."ᴿ

MACARIUS speaking of the Saints says: "They are all changed into a divine nature."ˢ "Let him come, let him come," says CHRYSOLOGUS, speaking of Christ, "that he may repair our flesh, make our soul new, and change its very nature into a celestial substance."ᵀ Because at the resurrection there will be "Another form of this life, even a change of our nature."ᵁ "When our flesh is converted into the body of an angel."ⱽ And "When it shall put on incorruption and immortality, it will no longer be flesh and blood, but will be changed into a celestial body."ᵂ So of Christ, GREGORY of Nyssen says: "After his resurrection he took a body transelemented into incorruption."ˣ And CHRYSOLOGUS, speaking of his incarnation, says: "God is changed into man."ʸ

To the water of baptism the ancients attributed the same change and efficacy, as they did to the bread and wine of the Eucharist.

"The Red Sea signified the baptism of Christ. Whence does the baptism of Christ look red unless

[Q] Tertull. contra Marcion, lib. iii, c. ult.
[R] Hilar. in Psal. cxxxviii.
[S] Macar. Hom. xxxiv.
[T] Chrysol. Serm. xlv.
[U] Cyril, Alex. Orat. in Resur. Christi.
[V] Aug. Serm. xii, Edit. Sirmondo.
[W] Aug. contra Adimant. c. 12.
[X] Greg. Nyssen, in Cant. Canticorum, Hom. i.
[Y] Chrysolog. Serm. xlv.

consecrated by the blood of Christ."ᶻ "Through the energy of the Spirit, the sensible water is transelemented into a certain divine and unspeakable power."ᵃ

Speaking of the Ethiopian eunuch, JEROME says: "Immediately he was baptized in the blood of the Lamb, about whom he was reading. The man deserved to be called an apostle; and was sent [as such] to the Ethiopians."ᵇ LAURENTIUS NOVARENSIS exclaims: "Thou shalt sprinkle me with water mixed with the sacred blood of thy Son."ᶜ And the writer, under the name of Cæsarius, says: "The soul goes into the living waters as if consecrated red by the blood of Christ."ᵈ

These passages show that, in the mind of these writers, the water of baptism is changed into the blood of Christ; that is, his *efficacious* blood, as will further appear from the following: "I am changed into Christ by baptism."ᵉ "He that is received by Christ and receives Christ, is not the same after baptism as he was before it; but the body of the regenerate becomes the flesh of him who was crucified: this change is by the right hand of the Most High."ᶠ

"The sensible water," says CYRIL, as just quoted, "is transelemented into a certain divine and unspeakable power, and furthermore, sanctifies those upon whom it comes."ᵍ

ᶻ Aug. Tract. xi, in Joan.

ᵃ Cyril, Alex. Com. in Joan. iii, v. 5.

ᵇ Hieron. Com. in Esaiam, liii, v. 7.

ᶜ Laurent. Novar. Hom. i, de Pœnitentia, Bibl. Patrum, tom. ii, p. 127.

ᵈ Homil. v.

ᵉ Greg. Nazianz. Orat. xl.

ᶠ Leo. Mag. de Passione Dom., Serm. xiv.

ᵍ Com. in Joan. iii, v. 5.

"The water differs from the spirit only in our conception, for it is the same in energy," says AMOMIUS.[h]

And LENO VERONENSIS says: "Our water receives the dead and vomits them forth alive, they being made true men of animals, and shall pass from men into angels."[i]

If this account be insufficient we may cite the rhetorical descriptions of ST. JOHN CHRYSOSTOM, who exclaims: "They who are baptized put on a royal garment, a purple dipped in the blood of the Lord."[1] Nay, "He who is baptized immediately embraces the Lord himself, is united to his body, and incorporated with that body which is seated above, whither the devil can have no access."[2]

The correspondent efficiency ascribed to the two Christian sacraments by the ancients, will very clearly appear, if we compare these passages with what they say of the effects of the Eucharist.

GREGORY of Nyssen: "As a little leaven, according to the Apostles, likens the whole mass to itself, so the body put to death by God, coming into our body, converts and changes the whole into itself." And, "His immortal body being in him that receives it, changes the whole into its own nature."[3] "He that receives me by a participation of my flesh," says CYRIL, "shall have life in himself, being wholly transelemented into me."[j]

LEO the Great teaches that "we are the flesh of Christ taken from the womb of the Virgin,"[k]

[h] Amomius Catena, in Joan. iii, v.
[i] Zeno. Ver. Serm. ii, ad Neoph. post Baptism.
[1] Chrysost. Hom. lx, ad Illuminandos.
[2] Idem, Hom. vi, in Coloss.
[3] Greg. Nysseni, Orat. Catech., cxxxvii.
[j] Cyril, Alex. in Joan., lib. iv, c. 3.
[k] Leo. Mag. Serm. x, de Natur. Dom.

Also, "The participation of the body and blood of Christ intends no other, than that we should pass into that which we take."¹ And, "In that mystical distribution of spiritual food, this is imparted; this is taken; that receiving the virtue of the celestial food, we should pass into the flesh of him who was made our flesh."¹

And FULGENTIUS says: "No one of the faithful ought to be troubled about those who, with sound mind, are lawfully baptized,—although death overtake them before they are permitted to eat the flesh and drink the blood of the Lord—by reason of that declaration of our Saviour where he says: 'Except ye eat the flesh of the Son of man,' &c.—For whosoever shall consider the truth of the mystery, will see that this is done in the baptism of holy regeneration." ᵐ

I have now shown from the *usus loquendi* of the ancients, that the terms *change, conversion* and their equivalents, do not signify, in their writings, any such transubstantiation of the eucharistic elements, as that now believed by Romanists to take place. All the change that was, in the early ages of the church, believed to be effected, was such a change of quality as was understood to take place in the water of baptism, the oil of chrism, and the like. Call this what we will, it was not considered as a change or destruction of the bread and wine, but only such a conversion, as was believed to be produced by the descent of the Holy Spirit upon them, and so entering them and sanctifying them that they became the symbolical body and blood of Christ, and the vehicles of spiritual grace to the faithful.

---

¹ Idem, Serm. xiv, de Passione Christi.

¹ Idem, Epist. xxiii. See also a passage cited from Theodotus, above, p. 153.

ᵐ Fulgent. de Baptism Ethiop., cap. xi, p. 611.

The above discussion of this phraseology of the Fathers is a sufficient reply to all those passages brought by you from the ancient Liturgies, in which this mode of speaking is of frequent occurrence. The Fathers undoubtedly taught, in their public Liturgies, the same doctrine in regard to the Eucharist that they taught in their individual writings; therefore, the remarks which have been made in this communication, upon the use of certain modes of expression, are applicable to those passages in the Liturgies, in which the same phraseology occurs.

II. There are other considerations which may be offered in this connection, as confirmatory of the interpretation which has been given of the language of the ancient Fathers.

1. Contrary to the express declarations of these writers, the advocates of transubstantiation teach, as a necessary consequence of this doctrine, that the wicked, equally with the good, eat the real body of Christ in the Eucharist.

DOMINO SOTO says: "It is undoubtedly to be held that the body of Christ descends into the stomach, although it is taken by a wicked man."

AQUINAS teaches that "since the body of Christ always remains in the sacrament, until the sacramental species are corrupted, it follows also that wicked men eat Christ's body."[2]

ALEUSIS also, noticing the opinion of some who thought that, as soon as the body of Christ was touched by a sinner's lips, it withdrew itself, says:

---

[1] Est indubiò tenendum quod corpus [Christi] descendit in stomachum, etiamsi ab iniquo sumatur. Dom. Soto in Dist. iv, quest. 12, art. 1, No. 3.

[2] Cum corpus Christi in sacramento semper permaneat, donec species sacramentales corrumpantur, etiam injustos homines Christi corpus manducare consequitur. Aquin., Part. iii, quæst. 80, art. 3.

"This opinion is erroneous, and manifestly contrary to the holy [doctors;] and therefore it is commonly held, that in this there is no difference between the just and the unjust, since both take that true body of Christ in the sacrament." And a little after he adds: "Whence it is to be granted, that the wicked take the thing of the sacrament which is the true body of Christ, which was born of the Virgin."[1]

So also they legitimately teach, that if "a dog, hog, or mouse eat the consecrated host, the substance of Christ's body does not cease to exist under the species, so long as these species remain."[2]

2. It follows also from this doctrine that the *real* eating of Christ's body in the Eucharist is inseparable from the *sacramental* eating, but distinct from the *spiritual.* This is evident from the decree of the Trent doctors, who pronounce that:

"If any one shall affirm that Christ, as exhibited in the Eucharist, is eaten in a SPIRITUAL manner only, and not also SACRAMENTALLY and REALLY; let him be anathema."[3] All this is plainly different from the teaching of the Fathers.

[1] Illud sentire erroneum est et manifeste contra sanctos; et ideo communiter tenetur quod in hoc non est differentia inter justum et injustum, quia uterque ipsum verum corpus Christi sumit in sacramento—Unde concedendum, quod mali sumunt rem sacramenti, quod est corpus Christi verum, quod natum est de virgine. Aleusis, Part. iv, qu. 11, memb. 2, art. 2, sec. 2.

[2] Dicendum, quod etiamsi mus vel canis hostiam consecratam manducet, substantia corporis Christi non desinit esse sub speciebus, quamdiu species illæ manent. Aquinas, Part iii, quæst. 80, art. 3. Si canis vel porcus deglutinat hostiam consecratam integram, non video quare vel quomodo corpus Domini non simul cum specie trajiceretur in ventrem canis vel porci. Aleusis in loco cit. sec. 1. See also the Roman Missal.

[3] Si quis dixerit, Christum in Eucharistia exhibitum, spiritualiter tantum manducari, et non etiam sacramentaliter ac realiter; anathema sit. Sess. xiii, can. 8.

ORIGEN, after speaking at some length of the partaking of the typical and symbolical body of the Lord, adds: "And much might be said concerning that Word who was made flesh, and that true meat which he that eateth shall live forever, no vile person being able to eat this; for if it were possible that he who still continues wicked should eat him who was made flesh, who is the Word and living bread, it would not have been written, that whosoever eateth this bread shall live forever."[n]

Speaking of those who love pleasure more than God, JEROME says: "Whilst they are not holy in body and spirit, they neither eat the flesh of Jesus, nor drink his blood, concerning which he says: 'He that eateth my flesh and drinketh my blood hath eternal life.'"[o]

ST. AUGUSTINE says: "Of that bread both Judas and Peter took part from the very hand of the Lord."[p] He means the sacramental bread without doubt; for he elsewhere teaches that the disciples "ate the bread which is the Lord, but Judas the bread OF the Lord, in opposition to the Lord; they ate life, but he punishment."[q] Again he says: "The sacrament of this thing, that is, of the unity of the body and blood of Christ, is prepared upon the Lord's table, and is taken from the Lord's table, by some to life, by others to destruction. But the thing itself of which it is a sacrament, is for life to every man; to no one whatever that partakes of it, shall it be for destruction."[r] Another passage cited by his disciple, PROSPER, who gathered up the sentences of his master, is to the point: "He receives

---

[n] Origen, Com. in Matt., tom. xi, No. 14.
[o] Hieron. Com. in Esaiam lxvi, v. 17.
[p] Aug. contra Donatist. cap. vi.
[q] Idem, Tract. lix, in Joan.
[r] Tract. xxvi, in Joan. vi.

the food of life, and drinks the cup of eternity, who abides in Christ, and whose inhabitant is Christ. For he who disagrees with Christ, neither eats his flesh nor drinks his blood, although he daily take with indifference the sacrament of so great a thing, to the condemnation of his presumption."[s]

Accordingly, the *res sacramenti* is received by the good only; which flatly contradicts the language of transubstantiation. Indeed, the doctrine of antiquity is, that "the flesh of the Lord is the food of believers."[t]—"The meat of the saints."[u]—And "the bread of life."[v] For "he that receives this food is above death."[w]

A passage or two from St. Augustine will further show, if need be, the distinction made by him between the sacramental and the real, or spiritual eating of Christ. "I have commended a certain sacrament unto you; spiritually understood it shall quicken you. Although this must be celebrated visibly, nevertheless it must be understood invisibly."[x]

Having spoken of the healthful repast received, by a participation of the body and blood of Christ, he concludes: "But then, this shall be [the sum,] that is, the body and blood of Christ shall be life to every one, if what is visibly taken in the sacrament, be in very truth eaten and drank spiritually."[y] Again, "When Christ says 'He that eateth my flesh, and drinketh my blood, dwelleth in me and I in him,' he shows what it is, not in sacrament

---

[s] Lib. Sentent. ex Aug., sent. 341, vel. 339.
[t] Hieron. in Oseam viii.
[u] Isidor. Sevill., in Gen. xxxi.
[v] Ambros. in Psal. cxviii.
[w] Chrysost. in Joan vi, v. 49.
[x] Aug. Enarrat. in Psal. xcviii, § 9.
[y] Aug. Serm. cxxxi, tom. v, p. 924.

only, but really to eat the body and drink the blood of Christ."[z] And this he makes equivalent to Christ's saying, "he that does not abide in me and I in him, should neither say nor think, that he eats my body and drinks my blood."

They also distingush the bodily from the sacramental presence. "The flesh and blood of this sacrifice, before the advent of Christ, was promised by victims of resemblance; in the passion of Christ it was made by the truth itself; since the ascension of Christ, it is celebrated by the sacrament of memory."[a]

The author of the Comment. on the Epistles of Paul, in the works of JEROME, remarks upon these words; *He took bread, and after he had given thanks he brake it;* "That is, blessing us even when about to suffer, he left to us his last remembrance or memorial. As if any one going into a foreign country, should leave some pledge with him whom he loved, that as often as he should look upon it, he might call to mind his favors and friendships; which he, if he loved him perfectly, could not behold without great affection and weeping."[b]

BEDE says: "As Moses bears witness of the tree of life being placed in the midst of Paradise, so by the wisdom of God, to wit, of Christ, the Church is quickened, of whom, even now in the sacraments of his flesh and blood, she receives the pledge of life; and will hereafter be blessed with the sight of his presence."[1]

3. The ancients teach that Christ is corporeally absent from the earth. "Ascend with us," says

---

[z] Idem, de Civitate Dei, lib. xxi, c. 25.

[a] Idem, contra Faust. lib. xx, c. 21.

[b] Hieron. Com. in I Cor. xi.

[1] Beda in Prov. lib. i, c. 3. Vide et Primasius in I Cor. xi, et Chrysost. in I Cor. xi.

AMBROSE, "that we may, with our minds, follow thee whom we cannot see with our eyes. St. Paul has taught us how we should follow thee, and where we may find thee. 'Seek those things which are above where Christ sitteth,' &c. Therefore we ought not to seek thee upon the earth, nor in the earth, nor according to the flesh, if we would find thee..... Mary could not touch him because she sought him on the earth; Stephen touched him because he sought him in heaven; Stephen among the Jews saw him absent."[1] AUGUSTINE assures us that "Our Lord absented himself in body from the whole church, and ascended into heaven that faith might be edified; for if thou didst know nothing except what thou seest, where is faith."[2] "We believe in him who now sits at the right hand of the Father; nevertheless, whilst we are in the body we are journeying in a strange country from him; nor can we show him to those who doubt, or deny him, and say, where is thy God?"[3] "This," says VIRGILIUS, "was to go to the Father and recede from us, to bear away from the world the nature which he took from us."[4] "When he was upon earth he was not in heaven; and now because he is in heaven, he surely is not upon the earth;—and because the Word is everywhere, *but his flesh is not everywhere*, it appears that one and the same Christ is of both natures, and that he is everywhere according to the nature of his divinity, and is contained in place, according to the nature of his humanity.—This is the Catholic faith and confession which the Apostles delivered, the martyrs confirmed, and the faithful guard even now."[5] "When Christ was raised into heaven in

[1] Ambros. Com. in Luc. xxiv.
[2] Aug. de Tempore, Serm. cxl.
[3] Idem, Serm. lxxiv, de Diversis.
[4] Vigil. Taps. contra Eutych. lib. 1.   [5] Idem, lib. 4.

the presence of his disciples, he made an end of his bodily presence."[c] For "Christ ascending to his Father as a conqueror after his resurrection, corporeally left the church, which he has nevertheless never left destitute of the aid of his divine presence, always remaining in it, even to the consummation of the world."[d] Nay more, "How did he bodily ascend into heaven and still be said to be in his faithful ones upon the earth, unless the immensity of the divinity which can fill heaven and earth is in him?"[1] "Though Christ be out of the world in the flesh, nevertheless, he is present with those who are in him; and his divine and unspeakable nature knows the universe, being absent from no creature, nor leaving any one, but is every where present to all, and fills all."[2]

If, according to these testimonies, Christ is both in heaven and on earth at the same time, only because he is divine, how shall his body be present both in heaven and in the sacrament on earth, at the same moment, unless this also be divine?

Your Brother,

E. O. P.

---

[c] Leo Mag. Serm. ii, de Ascension Domini.
[d] Beda, Com. in Marc xiii.
[1] Fulgent. ad Trasimund, lib. ii, c. 18.
[2] Cyril, Alex. in Joan ix, v. 5.

LETTER XIII.

EVIDENCE OF THE SENSES PATRISTICALLY CONSIDERED.

DEAR BROTHER:—By your quoting that passage of CYRIL of Jerusalem where he says: "That which seems to be bread is not bread, although perceptible to the taste, but the body of Christ; and that which seems to be wine is not wine although to the taste it appear such, but the blood of Christ,"[1] you confess the doctrine of transubstantiation to require the rejection of the evidence, which the senses bear to the nature of the eucharistic elements. So the Roman Catechism admonishes: "The pastor will, first of all, impress on the minds of the faithful the necessity of detaching, as much as possible, their minds and understandings from the dominion of the senses; for were they, with regard to this sublime mystery, to constitute the senses the only tribunal to which they are to appeal, the awful consequences must be their precipitation into the extreme of impiety. Consulting the sight, the touch, the smell, the taste, and finding nothing but the appearances of bread and wine, the senses must naturally lead them to think that this sacrament contains nothing more than bread and wine. Their minds, therefore, are as much as possible to be withdrawn from subjection to the senses, and excited to the contemplation of the stupendous power of God."[2]

---

[1] Cyril. Ierosol. Catech. Mystagog. iv, cap. 3.
[2] Roman Catechism, p. 206, cited by Elliott on Romanism, vol. i, p. 247.

Having, in my sixth letter, made some general remarks on the testimony of the senses, and its importance in settling the foundations of the Christian religion, I shall not here repeat what has been said, but will confine myself within the limits of such evidence as may be gathered from antiquity; especially, since you bring your appeal before the tribunal of the "Holy Fathers," and seem to prefer their judgment, before the decisions of reason and sense.

And now I am bold to affirm, that the ancient Christian Fathers, rightly understood, do not reject the evidence which the senses bear, in regard to the physical properties of the eucharistic elements.

In proof of this statement I offer you the following:

1. They appeal to these senses when they argue for the reality of Christ's human body in opposition to the error of the Marcionites, Valentinians and other false teachers, who said that our Saviour existed only in appearance, as a phantasm.

IRENÆUS says: "These things were not done in appearance only, but in the reality of truth; for if he appeared to be a man when he was not, he neither remained the Spirit of God, which he was in truth, since a spirit is invisible, nor was there any truth in him; for those things were not what they appeared to be."[A] So certain does he consider the evidence of the senses, that he does not hesitate to try the *truthfulness* of the Son of God by their testimony; and he thereby shows a willingness for the whole cause of Christianity to stand or fall with such evidence; which would be the height of temerity, were such testimony to be regarded other than infallible. Again; "As Christ therefore rose again in the substance of flesh, and showed

[A] Iren. adv. Hæres. lib. v. c. 1.

to his disciples the print of the nails and the opening of his side, but these are indications of his flesh which rose again from the dead, so also, he says, he will raise us by his power."[1] For the truth of the resurrection of Christ's flesh, the senses of his disciples are here produced as the witnesses; and our certainty of a future resurrection of our bodies, is measured by the certainty of their testimony.

TERTULLIAN adopting Marcion's interpretation of the words of our Saviour to his disciples, "Behold it is I myself; for a spirit hath not flesh and bones as ye see me have," says, "Behold he cheats and deceives and circumvents the eyes, the senses, the approaches and touches of all men. Thou therefore shouldst not have brought Christ down from heaven, but from some company of jugglers."[B] "It is sufficient for me to define that which is agreeable to God, to wit, the truth of that thing which he has made an object of the three senses that bear testimony to it, namely, sight, hearing, and touch."[C] Afterward he adds: "Now thou honorest thy God with the title of fallaciousness, if he knew himself to be something else than what he made men think he was."[D] Because he deceived their senses, which were their only medium of arriving at a knowledge of the reality of his body. Equally do Romanists, in rejecting the evidence of the senses, attribute "the title of fallaciousness" to God the author of nature, who has made these external senses the instruments by which we obtain a knowledge of the external world.

And, "why does Christ offer to their inspection his hands and his feet, which members consist of

---

[1] Idem, c. 7.
[B] Tertull. de Carne Christi, c. 5.
[C] Idem, adv. Marcion, lib. iii, c. 10.
[D] Idem, c. 11.

bones, if he had no bones? Why did he add, 'And know that it is I myself,' whom they had before known to be corporeal?"[E] May we not with equal propriety ask: Why does he offer to our inspection the accidents of bread and wine, if there be no bread and wine remaining there; especially, since we have before known them to be bread and wine?

AUGUSTINE uses the following language: "Our eyes themselves do not deceive us; for they can report to the mind their own affection only. If any one think that an oar is broken in the water, and when removed thence, made whole again, he has not a bad reporter, but he is a bad judge. For the eye could not, according to its nature, perceive it otherwise in the water neither ought it: for if the air is different from water, it is just that it should be perceived in the air otherwise than in the water. Wherefore the eye sees rightly, for it was made only to see; but the mind judges wrongly."[F] Again he says: "There is no cause to doubt of Christ's resurrection, whose presence the eye recognizes, the hand handles, and the finger examines..... If, perchance, we should say that the eyes of Thomas were deceived, we could not say that his hands were. For in the manifestation of his resurrection, there might be uncertainty from the sight, but no doubt could arise from the touch."[G] Moreover, "This which is like magic, ye are said to assert, that his passion and death were only in appearance, and in a deceitful shadow, so that he seemed to die who did not die. From which it follows that you say, that his resurrection also was shadowy, imaginary and fallacious; for there can

[E] Idem, adv. Marcion, lib. iv, c. 43.
[F] Aug. de Vera Religione, cap. xxxiii.
[G] Idem, de Temp. Sermo. clxi.

be no true resurrection of him who has not truly died: So it would follow that he also showed false scars to his doubting disciples; nor did Thomas exclaim, 'My Lord and my God' because he was confirmed by the truth, but deceived by a fallacy."[H] And, "Who except demons that are the friends of cozenage, would persuade them that Christ suffered fallaciously, died fallaciously and showed his scars fallaciously?"[I]

CHRYSOSTOM represents Christ as saying: "It does not belong to me to deceive mine with a phantasm; if the sight is afraid of a vain image, let the hands and fingers prove the truth of my body. Some mist may possibly deceive the eyes, but a corporeal touch knows a true body."[J]

HILARY says: "He takes away the foolish rashness of those who contend that our Lord was seen in the flesh in a deceitful and false body; that the Father, by giving the lie to the truth, showed him in the habit of false flesh, [as Romanists profess now to show his body in the habit of false bread,] not remembering that after the resurrection of his body, it was said to the Apostles, who believed they saw a spirit; 'Why are ye troubled,' &c. 'Behold my hands and my feet, that it is I myself, touch me and see, for a spirit hath not flesh and bones as ye see me have.'"[K]

EPIPHANIUS very largely argues the truth of Christ's body from what was sensibly done to it. His inquiry is: "How was he apprehended and crucified, who, according to thy saying, could not be touched? For thou canst not define him to be

[H] Idem, contra Faustum, lib. xxix, c. 2.
[I] Idem, lib. xiv, c. 10.
[J] Chrysost. de Resurrec. Hom. ix.
[K] Hilar. in Psal. cxxxvii.

a phantasy who fell under the touch."[L] From the expression: "He was known to them in the breaking of bread," he asks Marcion, "Whence was this breaking of bread? Was it by a phantom or by a body bulky and truly acting?"[M] By a body truly acting as their senses could testify. In like manner may we affirm the eucharistic elements to be bread and wine but not flesh and blood.

The general inference to be made from the foregoing testimonies is, that these Fathers could not have held and taught a doctrine which required them to reject the evidence of their senses; for if they had, the errorists against whom they wrote would have replied to their discomfiture: "But you are not consistent; you tell us not to trust to our senses when we approach the sacramental table of the Lord, assuring us, that although the consecrated elements appear to be bread and wine still, nevertheless they are so changed into another substance, that the nature of the bread and wine is entirely lost. If therefore our senses may be deceived in a matter so common, and subject to the cognizance of thousands daily, through successive ages, as all believe, why are we charged with heresy for believing that Christ came not into the world with real flesh and bones like ourselves, but only so in appearance? You also teach the insecurity and danger of trusting to what the senses report; we therefore, no more than yourselves, are guilty of the severe charge of absurdity, impiety and blasphemy."

But since no such objection was ever made by those most acute and subtle opposers of the Christian faith, it is morally certain that the doctrine of transubstantiation was unknown to the ancient church.

[L] Epiphan. Hæres. xlii, Refert. 4.
[M] Idem, Ref. 77.

2. Nevertheless, it is objected, that some of the Fathers exhort to disregard the evidence of the senses, when we contemplate the mystery of the Eucharist. Thus CYRIL of Jerusalem says: "That which seems to be bread is not bread, although perceptible to the taste, but the body of Christ; and that which seems to be wine is not wine, although to the taste it appears such, but the blood of Christ."[1]

CHRYSOSTOM says: "The Word of God is superior to sight; and so should we do in the mysteries, not looking only upon those things which lie before us, but holding fast his words. For his word does not deceive, but our sense is easily led astray."[2]

As these passages appear contradictory of those just produced, and seem to present an objection against the trust-worthiness of our bodily senses, in the testimony which they bear to the nature of the eucharistic symbols, it is important to give them a careful examination.

In the first place, it may be remarked, that *signs* are of two kinds. The first kind has a conformity of lineament with the prototype, as the portrait of a man. The other has not this sensible conformity. Thus, the rain-bow is a *sign* that the earth shall no more perish by a flood. The former is significant, in proportion to the fitness and perfection of the visible representation, and is a proper object of sense; the latter takes its significance from the will of the institutor; and is not simply an object of mere sense. The first we judge by sense, the second we judge not by sense, but by that faith which we are enabled to exercise in the authority of the institutor. To this latter class, belong the eucharistic symbols. They have not the visible exterior lineament and shape of the being

---

[1] Ubi Sup. citat.   [2] Chrysost. in Matt., Hom. 82 al 83, § 4.

represented, but they are signs of that being, because they have been constituted such by our Lord Jesus Christ. St. Augustine says: "These things, my brethren, are therefore called sacraments, because in them one thing is seen, another is understood."¹ And, "Because the sacraments are signs of things, they are one thing in their [visible] existence, another in their signification."ᴺ In giving a general rule in this case, he says: "I say this, treating of signs, let no one attend to what they are in themselves, but rather to what they are signs of, that is, what they signify."²

It was this invisible signification and supposed efficacy of the Eucharist which the ancients contemplated by faith, not by sense; but they never deny the testimony of the sight, so far as it regards the external symbols of bread and wine.

Chrysostom bears a lucid testimony to this effect. "It is called a mystery, because we contemplate not what we see; but we contemplate one thing, and believe another. For such is the nature of our mysteries. In regard to them, therefore, we are affected differently, I in one way, the unbeliever in another. When he hears of baptism, he thinks of the water simply, but I do not simply look at what is seen, but also to the cleansing of the soul by the Holy Spirit; he thinks that my body only is washed, but I believe that the soul is made pure and holy; and I consider the burial, resurrection, sanctification, righteousness, redemption, adoption, the inheritance, the kingdom of heaven and the gift of the Spirit. For I do not judge of the things which are indicated, by sight, but with the eyes of the mind. I hear, 'the body of Christ,' and I under-

---

¹ Serm. ad recent Bap. apud Bedam et alios.
ᴺ Contra Maxim. lib. iii, c. 22.
² De Doctr. Christi, lib. ii, c. 1.

stand what is said in one way, the unbeliever in another." This he admirably illustrates still farther, as follows: "And, as children looking upon books, know not the power of the letters, nor understand what they see; nay, even though he be a man unskilled in letters, the same thing will happen to him; but the man of skill will discover much hidden power laid up therein, complete lives and histories. And when an unskillful man receives a letter, he supposes it to be paper and ink only; but he that has skill hears a voice and converses with him who is absent, and replies again by letters whenever he wishes. So also it is in a mystery; the unbelievers, although they hear, yet seem not to hear, but the believers having skill by the Spirit, see its hidden power."[1]

It appears, therefore, that in the sacrament of the Eucharist two things were considered, namely, the visible symbols of bread and wine, and their sacramental reason, or signification, which is acquired by consecration. It is this latter element of the Eucharist to which both CYRIL and CHRYSOSTOM refer when they teach that the sense is not to be credited when we look upon the elements, as will further appear.

3. From the fact that the Fathers use similar language when speaking of the water of baptism, and other things, in regard to which, no one doubts the correctness of the information obtained through the senses.

GELASIUS CYZICENUS says: "Our baptism is not to be contemplated with the eyes of sense, but with those of the mind."[o]

"You ought not," remarks AUGUSTINE, "to estimate these waters with your eyes, but with your mind."[p]

[1] Chrysost. in I Cor. Homil. vii, § 1.
[o] Gelas. Cyzicen. in Diatyposi, cap. 4.
[p] Aug. Serm. xl, a Sirmondo Edit.

AMBROSE observes: "As to what you have seen, to wit, the waters, and not those alone, but the Levites there ministering, and the bishops asking questions and consecrating; first of all the Apostle has taught thee, not to contemplate those things which are seen by us, but those that are not seen; because those that are seen are temporal, but those that are not seen are eternal..... Do not therefore believe thy bodily eyes alone. That is rather seen which is not seen, because that is temporal, but this is looked upon as eternal, which is not comprehended by our eyes, but is seen by our mind and understanding."[Q]

So also the author of the Book of Sacraments in AMBROSE speaks: "What you have seen you could behold with your bodily eyes, and with human sight; but you saw not those things which are operated, and are not seen. Much greater are those which are not seen, than those which are seen; because those that are seen, are temporal, but those not seen, are eternal."[R]

CYRIL of Jerusalem says: "Come not to baptism as to mere water, but as to spiritual grace given with the water.—The water indeed purifies the body, but the Spirit seals the soul.—Therefore, do not attend to the simple element of water."[S] Also, when speaking of chrism, he says: "But see that you do not consider that to be mere ointment.—This holy ointment is not mere, nor, so to speak, common ointment, after the invocation, but the grace of Christ and the Holy Spirit."[1]

CHRYSOSTOM, when speaking of baptism, also says: "Let us believe the declaration of God, for this is

[Q] Ambros. de his qui initiant., c. 3.
[R] Lib. i, cap. 3.
[S] Cyril, Ierosol. Catech. Illuminat. iii, § 2.
[1] Idem, Catech. Mystagog. iii, § 3.

more credible than sight; for the sight is often deceived, but that cannot possibly fail."ᵀ This kind of expression is frequent with this writer. In one place he exhorts to give alms to the poor, "as if we were giving them to Christ; for his words are more credible than sight." And when a poor man is seen, he bids us "remember the words whereby Christ signified that he himself is fed. For although what is seen is not Christ, yet, under this form, he asks and receives alms."ᵁ The meaning of which is: "When you see a man apparently needy, give him alms, though you cannot, by his simple appearance, determine whether he is actually an object of charity; for, in so doing, you will be certain to act according to the command of Christ, which is so plainly revealed, that it cannot be mistaken, though you may sometimes err in the selection of the object of your beneficence." In this sense he is doubtless right when he says, the word of God is more to be believed than our sight.

In the same way are we to understand the Fathers, when they tell us not to believe our sight, in the matter of the sacraments. They mean, that we are not to form our judgment of their sanctification and efficacy from their visible appearance; for the effect of the believed operation of the Holy Spirit upon them, was considered as something beyond the province of sense. The mind only, they considered capable of contemplating the wonderful moving of the Spirit, in and by the symbols of the bread and wine of the Eucharist, of the water of baptism, and of the ointment of chrism. They did not, therefore, reject the evidence of the senses in matters properly cognizable by our corporeal or-

---

ᵀ Chrysost. in Joan., Homil. xxiv.
ᵁ Idem, in Matt., Homil. lxxxix.

gans; for this they deny, both in their reasoning with their opponents, as we have already seen.

4. In direct terms, when they unequivocally tell us, that the senses are faithful and infallible guides to the truth. Thus, CHRYSOSTOM defines deception to consist in a thing "not appearing to be what it is, but in appearing to be what it is not."[v] And in another place he declares, that "through these senses we learn all things accurately, and we consider them instructors worthy of belief in what we see or hear, seeing that they neither feign nor speak falsely."[w] Agreeably to the foregoing, another writer affirms, that "we know the whole world by the apprehension of sense; and through that energy, which is according to our sense, we are led unto the conception of the thing and idea which is beyond the sense; and the eye is made to us the interpreter of the wisdom of the Almighty, which is everywhere seen, indicating through itself Him who embraces all things."[x] "For what in our members is deserving of more honor than the eyes? Through these we apprehend the light; by them we recognize those who are our friends and who our enemies; and distinguish what is our own from what belongs to another: they are the guides and teachers of every work, and the natural and inseparable conductors of an unerring journey."[y]

How comprehensive is this language; no less than the whole world is the field of our sensible apprehension; nothing less is our eye than the interpreter of the wisdom of God, the guide and teacher of every work, and the conductor of the way, without error. But false, utterly false is all

[v] Chrys. in Ep. ad Eph., Hom. xiii.
[w] Idem, in Joan., Homil. xxx al xxix, § 1.
[x] Gregor. Nyssen, de Anima et Resurrec., tom. iii, p. 188.
[y] Idem, Hom. vii, in Cantic. Canticorum, tom. i, p. 577.

this, if the eye, together with the other senses, is not to be credited in the interpretation which it gives of the nature of the eucharistic symbols.

Should we travel back to a still earlier age of the Christian church, and visit that famous School of Alexandria, in Egypt, we might hear its learned master speaking as follows, when instructing his pupils about the nature of syllogistic reasoning, a notable method of ratiocination in the times of classic antiquity. "Either all things need to be demonstrated, or some are credible of themselves. But, if the former be true, we shall proceed to infinity in seeking a demonstration of each demonstration, and thus the demonstration will be destroyed; but if the latter be true, then those very things which are of themselves credible, will constitute, the beginnings of the demonstrations. Now philosophers confess the beginnings of all things to be indemonstrable; so that, if there be a demonstration, there is every necessity that, in the first place, there be something credible of itself, which is called prime, and indemonstrable. Every demonstration then, is reduced to an indemonstrable source of belief. But there are also other beginnings of demonstrations besides the fountain of belief, namely, those things which appear evident to *sense* and mental perception. For those that meet the *sense* are simple and incapable of analysis; and those that appear to the mental perception, are simple, logical and prime." And he concludes by saying: "If any one begins with these things which are clear to *sense* and mental perception, and then brings a fit conclusion, he truly demonstrates."[z]

A little after when he treats of the analysis of the demonstration, he says; "Each of those things demonstrated, is demonstrated by certain other

[z] Clement. Alex. Stromat. lib. viii, c. 3.

demonstrations, and these previously demonstrated by others, until we run back to things of themselves credible, or to those evident to *sense* and mental perception."[a] By "those things of themselves credible" he means the axioms, or first principles of knowledge, which lie at the very foundation of science, such as, the whole is greater than its part; two things which are equal to a third, are equal the one to the other, and the like. And by his classing our perceptions by the senses with these elementary truths, and laying them at the bottom of all reasoning, he shows, like a true philosopher, the credibility of our external senses; nay, their absolute certainty of the things to which they bear testimony.

Contemporary with CLEMENS ALEXANDRINUS, flourished TERTULLIAN in the Latin Church, well known as an eloquent and zealous defender of the Christian doctrines. In his book, "On the Soul," he makes a bold attack upon the Academicians who condemned the testimony of the five senses, because the ideas obtained through them, are sometimes found to disagree with the truth. They argued, that "to the sight, an oar partly under the water, appears bent or broken; to the touch, the pavements appear less rough to the feet than to the hands; to the hearing, thunder may be mistaken for a common vehicle, and *vice versa;* to the smell and taste, the same ointments and wines by subsequent use, appeared depreciated. Therefore they said; 'Thus are we deceived by the senses until we change our opinions.'" In reply, our author considers the deception attributable, neither to the things themselves, nor to the senses, but to certain intervening conditions.

"For," says he, "though in the water the oar appears bent or broken, the water is the cause of

[a] Ibid.

the deception. In short, without the water the oar is to the sight whole;—In this manner, therefore, no mistake of the senses will be without its cause. Since, if the causes deceive the senses, and through the senses the opinions, the fallacy is to be attributed neither to the senses which follow the causes, nor to the opinions which are directed by the senses, following the causes. They are insane who see beings of one kind in those of another, as Orestes mistook his sister for his mother, and Ajax a flock of sheep for Ulysses, as Athamas and Agave, their children, for wild beasts. Will you reproach the eyes, or the Furies, with this deception?" He goes on to exculpate the causes from blame and adds: "If, therefore, even the very causes are acquitted of dishonor, how much more the senses which are preceded by the causes; seeing that the verity, credibility, and integrity of the senses, are hence most effectually vindicated; since they do not report otherwise than what that condition demands, which causes something to be reported by the senses otherwise than it exists in the things. What doest thou, O most malapert Academy? Thou overturnest the whole state of life, thou disturbest all the order of nature, thou darkenest the providence of God, who [according to thee] has placed the senses, deceitful and false masters, over all his works, in order to understand, inhabit, dispense and enjoy them. By these is not every condition served? Through these does not favorable instruction also come to the world? So many arts, so many devices, so many sciences, business, offices, commerce, remedies, counsels, solaces, provisions, dress, ornament and all things? They season all the enjoyment of life; so that through these senses man alone of all animals is distinguished as rational, capable of intelligence and learning in science." He after this breaks out: "It is not lawful, it is not lawful to us to call into doubt these senses, lest also a question arise concerning their credit in Christ, lest perchance it be said that he falsely beheld Satan cast down from heaven, or falsely heard the voice of his Father testifying of him, or was deceived when he touched the mother of Peter's wife, or afterward perceived another odor of the ointment which he accepted for his burial, and afterward perceived another taste of the wine which he consecrated in memory of his blood. For so does Marcion prefer to believe him a phantasm, scorning the verity of an entire body in him. But it was not his nature to play the mock upon the Apostles. Faithful was their sight and hearing upon the Mount; faithful the taste of that wine at the marriage of Galilee, although water before; faithful was the touch of Thomas,[1] who thenceforth believed. Recite the testimony of John: 'What we have seen,' says he, 'what we have heard, and seen with our eyes, and our hands have handled of the word of life.' FALSE THEREFORE IS HIS TESTIMONY, IF THE SENSE OF SIGHT, HEARING AND TOUCH GIVES THE LIE TO NATURE."[b]

Comment upon language so plain and decisive is needless. I will produce another short passage only from this author, who, upon the words "*Wo unto them that make sweet, bitter, and put darkness for light*," thus remarks: "The prophet doubtless designates those that do not preserve these words in their proper light; that the soul is nothing else than what it is called, and flesh nothing else than what is seen, and God no other than he is declared

---

[1] Origen, when writing against the infidel Celsus, argues the touch of Thomas, as proving that Christ suffered real wounds, and assumes the infallibility of the senses throughout. Vid. Orig. contra Celsum, lib. ii, § 60, et seq.

[b] Tertull. lib. de Animæ, c. 17.

to be."ᶜ   He makes the sight the judge of what is flesh, and by consequence of what is not flesh, for it would be absurd to say that the sight is competent to determine what any one thing is, while it is incapable of distinguishing that given thing from other objects. So diametrically opposed to the dogma of Rome are the ancient Christian Fathers. Well may we conclude, that the unphilosophical doctrine of transubstantiation was altogether unknown, during the early ages of Christianity.

5. I will close my citations from the Fathers with a passage from St. AUGUSTINE, together with the remarks which the learned Bingham makes upon it. He says; "St. AUSTIN uses the same argument with TERTULLIAN in one of his homilies to the newly baptized; which, though it be not now among St. AUSTIN's works, yet it is preserved by FULGENTIUS—de Bapt. Æthiop. c. xi,—BEDE, in I Cor. x,—and BERTRAM, de Corp. et Sang. Dom. Here instructing them about the sacrament he tells them; 'This which you see upon the altar of God, you also saw last night; but what it is, what it means, and of how great a thing it contains a sacrament, you have not yet heard. What you see therefore is bread and the cup, which your own eyes report to you. But that about which your faith requires to be instructed, is that the bread is the body of Christ. But such a thought as this will presently arise in your hearts: Christ took his body into heaven, whence he shall come to judge the quick and the dead; and there he now sits at the right hand of the Father. How then is bread his body? Or how is the cup, or what is contained in the cup his blood? These things, my brethren, are therefore called sacraments because in them one thing is seen, and another is understood. That

---

ᶜ Tertull. de Carne. Christi, c. 24.

which is seen has a corporal species, that which is understood has a spiritual fruit. If therefore you would understand the body of Christ, hear what the Apostle says to the faithful; *Ye are the body of Christ and his members.* If, therefore, ye be the body and members of Christ, your mystery or sacrament is laid upon the Lord's table; ye receive the sacrament of the Lord. Ye answer, *amen*, to what ye are, and by your answer subscribe to the truth of it. Thou hearest the minister say to thee, 'The body of Christ,' and thou answerest, *amen*. Be thou a member of the body of Christ that thy *amen* may be true.

"But why then is this mystery in BREAD? Let us here bring nothing of our own, but hear the Apostle speak again. When therefore he speaks of this sacrament, he says, *We being many are one Bread, and one Body.* Understand and rejoice. We being many are unity, piety, truth and charity, one Bread and one Body. Recollect and consider that the bread is not made of one grain, but of many. When ye were exorcised, ye were then, as it were, ground; when ye were baptized, ye were, as it were, sprinkled, or mixed and wet together into one mass; when ye received the fire of the Holy Ghost, ye were, as it were, baked. Be ye therefore what ye see, and receive what ye are."[d]

Upon this passage Bingham makes the following appropriate remarks: "Here ST. AUSTIN first says plainly, that it was bread and wine that was upon the altar, for which he appeals to the testimony of the senses. 2. That this very bread and wine is the body and blood of Christ. Consequently it could not be his natural body in the substance, but only sacramentally. 3. He says, the natural body of

---

[d] Aug. Serm. ad recent. Baptizat. apud Fulgent., Bedam et Bertram.

Christ is only in heaven; but the sacrament has the name of his body, because, though in outward, visible and corporeal appearance, it is only bread, yet it is attended with a spiritual fruit. 4. Lastly, he says that the sacrament is not only a representation of the natural body of Christ, but also of the mystical body, the Church; and that as a symbol of the church's unity, it is called the body of Christ in this sense, as well as the other. So that if there were any real transubstantiation, the bread must be changed into the mystical body of Christ, that is, his Church, as well as into the body natural."

6. We have now seen that the Fathers regarded the evidence of the senses as infallible in all matters properly cognizable by them, and that when speaking of the sacraments, they exhort to discredit these senses, they have reference to their sacramental reason, but not to their material qualities. In order to render our discussion of this subject more complete, it seems highly proper to glance again briefly at those passages of CYRIL and CHRYSOSTOM, which the abettors of transubstantiation produce to disprove the testimony which the senses bear to the nature of the eucharistic elements. For I suppose that any given passage of an author is to be interpreted according to the evident scope and design, not only of all his written productions, but also of the context in which it is found, not by seizing upon isolated expressions and judging of them by their literal meaning, irrespective of what precedes or follows. A few passages from the Mystagogical lecture of CYRIL, will enable us to see its general scope and design. He observes: "And this teaching of the blessed Paul, is sufficient to assure you concerning the divine mysteries; being made worthy of which, ye were made the same body and blood with Christ. For he of late exclaimed, that 'in that night in which our Lord Jesus Christ was be-

trayed, having taken bread and given thanks, he broke and gave to his disciples, saying, Take eat, this is my body. And having taken the cup and given thanks, he said: Take drink, this is my blood.... for in the type of bread his body is given thee, and in the type of wine his blood is given thee; so that, partaking of the body and blood of Christ thou mayst be made the same body and blood with him. For so we are made Christ-bearers when his body and blood are imparted into our members, so that, according to blessed Peter, we are made partakers of the divine nature.' When Christ formerly addressed the Jews, he said: 'Except ye eat my flesh and drink my blood ye have not life in yourselves.' But they not understanding those things spiritually spoken, and being scandalized, went back, SUPPOSING THEY WERE EXHORTED TO THE EATING OF HIS FLESH. There was under the Old dispensation the shew-bread, but this has come to an end. But in the New dispensation, there are the heavenly bread and the cup of salvation which sanctify the soul and body. As bread is adapted to the body, so the Word is suited to the soul. Therefore consider them not as MERE BREAD and MERE WINE. For they are, according to the word of the Lord, the body and blood of Christ. Although the sense suggest this to thee, nevertheless let faith confirm thee. Nor shouldst thou judge the thing by the taste, but by a faith assured beyond a doubt, being accounted worthy the body and blood of Christ. And David explains to thee the force of this, when he says: 'Thou preparedst a table before me in the presence of mine enemies.' What he says is something like this: Before thy advent demons prepared a table for men, which was polluted and defiled, and full of diabolical power; but after thy advent, O Lord, thou didst prepare a table before me. When man says to God: 'Thou hast prepared a table before me,' what else does he mean but that *mystical* and *spiritual* table which God has prepared for us in opposition and instead of that prepared by demons? And very fitly so, for that had communion of devils, but this communion of God.... 'And thy cup which intoxicates me, how excellent.' You see here the cup is spoken of which Jesus took in his hands, and giving thanks, said: 'This is my blood which is shed for many for the remission of sins.' Therefore Solomon, obscurely denoting this grace, says in Ecclesiastes: 'Come, eat thy bread with joy,' that is, *spiritual bread*. Come, make a healthful and blessed invocation. 'And drink thy wine with a good heart,' that is, *spiritual wine*..... Having learned this, and having been assured that that which seems to be bread is not [mere] bread, although perceptible to the taste, but the body of Christ, and that that which seems to be wine is not [mere] wine, although to the taste it appear such, but the blood of Christ; and that David of old time, spake in the Psalm concerning this: 'And bread strengthenth the heart of man, and with oil his face is gladdened;' do thou, partaking of this [bread] as *spiritual*, strengthen thy heart, and gladden the face of thy soul."[1]

Such is the language of more than half of this short lecture of CYRIL; and yet a single passage is selected from it, without regard to its general scope, to prove that our senses are not to be believed, in the testimony which they bear to the nature of the eucharistic elements; whereas, nothing can be more evident than the fact, that throughout this lecture, the author discourses of the spiritual manducation of Christ's body in the Eucharist, whose presence is not to be "judged by the taste, but by a faith assured beyond a doubt." I wonder that men of

[1] Cyril, Ierosol. Catech. Mystagog. lv.

honest sincerity can make such a garbled use of the writings of the ancient dead. It must be a bad cause that requires such a perversion of their plain meaning.

Let us pass to the golden-mouthed orator of Constantinople. "We believe God everywhere and contradict nothing, although what is said seem opposed to our reasonings and sight; but let his word be superior to our reasonings and sight; and so should we do in the mysteries not looking only upon those things which lie before us, but holding fast his words. For his word does not deceive, but our sense is easily led astray. That has never failed, this is often deceived. Since therefore the word says, 'This is my body,' let us be persuaded and believe, and CONTEMPLATE IT WITH SPIRITUAL EYES. For Christ has delivered to us nothing [merely] sensible, but by things sensible he has delivered all things spiritual. For thus also in baptism, by a sensible thing, the gift of water is made; but that which is wrought is spiritual, the birth and regeneration, or renovation. For if thou wert incorporeal he had delivered these gifts naked and incorporeal; but since the soul is connected with a body, he has delivered to thee the spiritual in the sensible. How many now say, I would see his form, his figure, his garments and sandals?

"Behold thou seest him, thou touchest him, thou eatest him. And thou desirest to see his garments: but he gives himself to thee not to see only, but also to touch, and to eat and take within."[E]

This passage needs no explanation. Whoever reads may understand that CHRYSOSTOM speaks of the spiritual, but not the sensible part of the Eucharist, when he says, "let his word be superior to our reasonings and sight." The explanation which

---

[E] Chrysost. in Matt, Hom. lxxxii al lxxxiii, § 4.

has been given above of the language of the Fathers is, therefore, fully confirmed by an impartial and candid examination of the context.

I have dwelt upon this subject of the testimony of the senses, because of its importance; and I have preferred to allow the Fathers to discuss it in their own language; not because they speak more truly or more authoritatively than the true and Protestant Church of God now utters her caution against that fatal delusion, which requires the rejection of the evidence of the senses, in a matter as properly an object of their observation as any other, and in regard to which, their testimony is as reliable as it is respecting any thing else in nature. Indeed, no less do the principles involved in transubstantiation, than those of the ancient school-men, "overturn the whole state of life, disturb all the order of nature, and darken the providence of God." And we may add, sap the very foundation of all revealed religion, by destroying the credibility of the testimony of those who heard the words of the Lord, and testified to the signs and wonders wrought in confirmation of their divine origin.

Should it however be objected that "the senses cannot determine the composite nature of things, but only their tactual and apparent qualities;" we answer; this only is their proper sphere of observation. It is not necessary to the credibility of the senses, that they be able to determine the chemical elements, or ultimate atoms of bodies: it is enough that they confine themselves to those properties usually denominated *natural.* Otherwise we should be led into very strange and even absurd speculations respecting the general experience of mankind. If it be allowed that the senses are incompetent judges of things, because they cannot ascertain the nature of the ultimate particles of bodies, then it will follow, that for the thousands of years preceding the revelations of modern science, the whole world has been unable to determine whether iron were gold, whether wood were stone, whether bread were flesh, or water were fire, or something else. Besides, if the senses must be rejected because of this inability to scan the secret recesses of nature's laboratory, then there is a necessity of putting to the test of scientific analysis, every article of merchandise before the buyer can be absolutely certain that he is not deceived in the object of his purchase. Nay, he can never arrive at such certainty because the analysis cannot be made without their aid. But the general sentiment of mankind is not yet prepared to adopt a principle so repugnant to universal experience.

It is with the natural philosophy of bodies that the bodily senses are concerned; and within this, their appropriate circle, they serve to discriminate and determine with a certainty that knows no superior within the created universe.

Believe me yours truly,

E. O. P.

LETTER XIV.

HALF-COMMUNION.

DEAR BROTHER:—Having examined the testimony of antiquity in proof of a figurative presence of Christ's flesh and blood in the Eucharist, I pass to the consideration of several usages connected with the celebration of this sacrament, wherein the ancient Christians differ from the present practices of the Papal church. The Council of Trent teaches very consistently with the doctrine of transubstantiation, and what appears to be a legitimate consequence of it, that "Christ entire is contained under every part of each species when a separation is made." If this be true, it is impossible to human reason to assign any sufficient cause, why communion in both species should ever have been commanded or practiced. The practice of your church of communicating the laity in one kind only, if not the direct and natural consequence of the doctrine in question, is certainly in perfect keeping with it, as the most common mind cannot fail to perceive. For if Christ entire is received under every part of each species, he cannot certainly be more perfectly received under both.

But this usage is opposed to the express and plain command of our Saviour, and to the practice of the ancient church.

On this latter point I offer you a few testimonies.

IGNATIUS exhorts the Philadelphians "to use one faith, one preaching, and one Eucharist; for the flesh of the Lord is one, and his blood which has been shed for us is one; and one bread is broken to all and one cup distributed to all."ᴬ In this passage there is no such confusion of the body and blood of Christ under a single kind, as is taught by the doctors of Trent. The bread and the cup are mentioned separately as being the separate and distinct representatives of Christ's flesh and blood. And I know not of a single passage to be found in all the writings of antiquity, in which the sacramental flesh and blood of Christ are said to exist under a single species.

In his Apology for the Christians to the Emperor, JUSTIN the Martyr says: "When the president has given thanks, and all the people responded, those called by us deacons give to each of those present to partake of the bread, and wine and water of the Eucharist; and to those not present they carry them." And a little after he repeats substantially the same thing, and assures us that "the impartation and reception of those things blessed, is made to each one; and to those not present they are sent by the deacons."[1]

IRENÆUS says that our flesh is fed by the body and blood of Christ, so that it is increased by them and consists of them. He argues the resurrection of our bodies to immortality, from their having been made the recipients of the sacrament of Christ's quickening body and blood.[2] But no one ever supposed, that IRENÆUS intended to argue for the resurrection of the priests only. If he did not thus argue, he must certainly have considered the body and blood to belong to the laity equally with the clergy.

When writing upon the "resurrection of the flesh," TERTULLIAN makes use of the same language:

ᴬ Ignat. Epist. ad Philadelph.
[1] Apol. i. (See above, p. 123.)
[2] Iren. adv. Hæreses, lib. v, c. 2; et lib. iv, c. 34.

"Our flesh is fed with the body and blood of Christ."[1] And in his book to his wife he speaks twice of her taking the cup, which confessedly refers to the Eucharist.[2]

Cyprian says, "We do not leave unarmed and naked those that we urge and exhort to the contest [of martyrdom] but we fortify them with the protection of Christ's body and blood..... For in what manner shall we teach or incite them to pour out their own blood in the confession of his name, if we deny the blood of Christ to those about to engage in the contest? Or how shall we make them fit for the cup of martyrdom, if we do not first admit them to drink, in the church, the cup of the Lord by right of communication?"[3] And in the Epistle to the people of Thibaris, which passes under his name, the author remarks: "Now the contest harder and fiercer threatens, for which the soldiers of Christ ought to prepare themselves by an incorrupt faith and strong valor; considering that for this reason they daily drink the cup of Christ's blood, that they may be able to pour out their blood for Christ. For this is to will to be found with Christ, to imitate what Christ taught and did."

[1] Caro corpore et sanguine Christi vescitur. Tertul. de Resurrec. Carnis, lib. c. 7, p. 330.

[2] Idem, ad Uxorem.

[3] Quos excitamus et hortamur ad prœlium, non inermes et nudos relinquamus, sed protectione sanguinis et corporis Christi muniamus..... Num quomodo docemus aut provocamus eos in confessione nominis sanguinem suum fundere, si eis militaturis Christi sanguinem denegamus? Aut quomodo ad martyri poculum idoneos facimus, si non eos prius ad bibendum in Ecclesiâ poculum Domini jure communicationis admittimus? Cyprian, Ep. liv, ad Cornelium.

[4] Considerantes idcirco se quotidie calicem sanguinis Christi bibere, ut possint et ipsi propter Christum sanguinem fundere, etc. Idem, Ep. lvi, de Exhort. Martyr. ad Thibaritanos.

CHRYSOSTOM says: "There are some things wherein there is no difference between the priest and the people; as, when they are to partake of the tremendous mysteries; for we are all alike admitted to them. Not as in the times of the Old dispensation, when the priests ate one thing and the people another, and it was not lawful for the people to partake of what the priest did. It is not so now, but there is one body and one cup proposed to all."[B]

AUGUSTINE tells the newly baptized, "That when they should prove themselves, then they should eat of the Lord's table and drink of the cup."[1] And JEROME his contemporary says, "The priests serve the Eucharist and divide the Lord's blood to his people."[2]

2. These testimonies are sufficient to prove the antiquity of a usage which is so clearly delivered, that you are not disposed to call it in question. Nevertheless, to acquit your church of the guilt of heresy and the crime of perverting any part of the Christian doctrine, you are pleased to dignify this ancient practice—which is no other than the obedient performance of the divine, and almost dying command of our Lord and Saviour, "DRINK YE ALL OF IT,"—with a place among those "forms or methods" which "are mere matters of discipline that may be changed or altered, as often as the wisdom of the church thinks necessary."

Whatever Jesus Christ has taught us to believe and practice, I have always regarded as doctrine; but the *manner* in which we perform his sacred injunctions, I suppose may be regarded as belonging to

[B] Chrysost. Hom. xviii, in II Cor. § 3. Opera Paris, 1838, tom x, p. 670.

[1] Ut cùm scipsos probaverint, tunc de mensa Domini manducent, et de calice bibant. Aug. de Fide et Operibus.

[2] Sacerdotes Eucharistiæ Serviunt, et sanguinem Domini populis ejus dividunt. Hieron. in Sophon. cap. 2.

what is commonly termed discipline. And your learned Mr. Hughes repeatedly says, in his controversy with Mr. Breckenridge, that Jesus Christ taught no opinions, but all his instructions were doctrines. How then comes it to pass, that our Lord's plain and positive injunction to drink of the cup, is only a mere matter of discipline that must bow to the will or caprice of men's changing opinions? Will you, when you wish to insult the better informed judgment of your neighbors, tell them that their faith is but a system of opinions, and that Jesus Christ delivered no opinions, but all doctrines; and when you wish to excuse your abrogation of Christ's plain command, tell us that his divine injunction is no better than a mere "mode or method," which may be changed as circumstances dictate? Is this worthy men of intelligence? If there be any thing in the Gospel of God our Saviour that may be called a doctrine, it is that command of his to his Church, to drink of that cup which he instituted in memory of his bloody passion upon the cross. And if it be possible to fallen and rebellious creatures to disobey such command, and sacrilegiously pervert any divine institution, then has the church of Rome done thus in regard to the use of the cup in the Eucharist. As proof of this, I will offer you the testimony of several of the ancients, including some of those by you denominated Popes of the church.

ST. CYPRIAN, writing to Cæcilius in condemnation of the practice of the Aquarians who used no wine, but water only, in the Eucharist, says: "Wherefore, if Christ alone is to be heard, we ought not to heed what another before us may have supposed should be done, but what Christ who is before all, first did; for it is not meet to follow the custom of man, but the truth of God..... If it is not lawful to break the least of the Lord's commandments, how much more is it not right to infringe commands so great, so grand, and so much pertaining to the very sacrament of the Lord's passion, and our redemption; or by human tradition to change it into something different from that which has been divinely instituted."[1] Upon this passage we may observe, that our author regards the full and proper exhibition of the cup as essential to the full and proper celebration of this sacrament; that the command to do this occupies a high position amongst the divine precepts of our Saviour, and, consequently, cannot be classed with those disciplinary regulations, which may be changed according to circumstances; and that the example and command of Christ in this matter, are superior to any human authority; so that, notwithstanding the opinions and traditions of men, God's truth as contained in his word, is constantly to be followed. If then it be a culpable infringement of Christ's precept and example, to substitute water for wine, in the exhibition of the cup, much more is it a gross violation of his divine command, to deny the people the cup altogether. Especially does this appear when we consider, that the universal participation of the cup is more expressly enjoined, than the use of the other species.

"It is an indignity to the Lord," says AMBROSE, "to celebrate the mystery otherwise than it was delivered by him. For he cannot be devout who

---

[1] Quare si solus Christus audiendus est, non debemus attendere, quid alius ante nos faciendum putaverit, sed quid, qui ante omnes est, Christus, prior fecerit. Neque enim hominis consuetudinem sequi oportet, sed Dei veritatem..... Quod si nec minima de mandatis dominicis licet solvere; quanto magis tam magna, tam grandia, tam ad ipsum dominicæ passionis et nostræ redemptionis sacramentum pertinentia, fas non est infringere, aut in aliud, quàm quod divinitus institutum sit, humanâ traditione mutare? Cyprian, Ep. lxiii, ad Cæcilium de Sacram. Domini calicis.

presumes to give it in any other way than it was given by its author."[c]

Pope JULIUS, elected to the See of Rome, A. D. 337, says: "We have heard of some who, kept back by a schismatic disposition, have consecrated milk instead of wine in the divine sacrifices, contrary to the divine laws and apostolic institutions; and others also, who extend to the people the Eucharist dipped instead of the full communion. . . . . How contrary this is to the Evangelic and Apostolic DOCTRINE, and adverse to the custom of the Church, it is not difficult to prove from the very fountain of truth, from which proceeded these mysteries of the sacraments which have been ordained."[1]

Pope LEO the Great, elected A. D. 440, speaks of those who "with unworthy mouth take the body of Christ but altogether refuse to drink the blood of our redemption; . . . . Whose sacrilegious dissembling should be laid hold of, and themselves noted and prohibited from the company of the saints, should be expelled by sacerdotal authority."[2]

Pope GELASIUS, elected A. D. 492, also says: "We find that some, a portion of the sacred body

[c] Ambros. in I Cor. xi.

[1] Audivimus quosdam scismatica ambitione detentos, contra Divinos ordines, et Apostolicas Institutiones, lac pro vino in divinis sacrificiis dedicare: alios quoque intinctam eucharistiam populis pro complemento communionis porrigere . . . Quod quàm sit Evangelicæ et Apostolicæ doctrinæ contrarium, et consuetudini ecclesiasticæ adversum, non difficile ab ipso fonte veritatis probabitur, a quo ordinata ipsa sacramentorum mysteria processerunt. Julii Epist. ad Episc. Ægypt. apud Gratian. de Consecr., dist. 2, c. 7. Cited by Bingham, bk. xv, ch. v, sec. 1.

[2] Ore indigno corpus Christi accipiunt, sanguinem autem redemptionis nostræ haurire omnino declinant. . . . . Quorum deprehansa fuerit sacrilega simulatio, notati et prohibiti a sanctorum societate sacerdotali auctoritate pellantur. Leo, Serm. iv, de Quadragesima. Cited by Bingham.

being received only, abstain from the cup of the holy blood; who doubtless, (because they are taught to be bound by what superstition I know not,) should either receive the sacraments entire or be kept wholly from them; BECAUSE THE DIVISION OF ONE AND THE SAME MYSTERY CANNOT TAKE PLACE WITHOUT GREAT SACRILEGE."[1]

So unqualifiedly do these ancient writers refute and condemn this modern and heretical notion of yours, which makes the communion of the cup a matter of mere discipline, and so little important that it may be indulged or forbidden by the church whenever she thinks proper. I dare say these ancient Popes would expel you all "by sacerdotal authority," were they in a position so to do, unless you should speedily repent, and return to the ancient doctrine and practice of the Church.

3. But the practice of communicating in both kinds, was not limited to the first five centuries after Christ. It has continued in the purer churches of the East until the present, and did not, in the Latin Church, go into general disuse during the period of more than a thousand years after Christ.

PASCHASIUS, A. D. 831, who is considered to be the father of transubstantiation, teaches the practice and necessity of receiving both species in the following language: "But the priest, because he seems to act between God and the people instead of Christ, offers their vows and gifts to God by the hands of the angel, and renders back by the body and blood what is obtained, and distributes to every

---

[1] Comperimus quod quidam sumpta tantummodo corporis sacri portione, à calice sacri cruoris abstineant. Qui proculdubio (quia nescio qua superstitione docentur abstringi,) aut integra sacramenta percipiant, aut integris arceantur: quia divisio unius ejusdemque mysterii sine grandi sacrilegio non potest provenire. Gelas. apud Gratian de Consecr., dist. 2, c. 12. Cited by Bingham.

one."[1] Again he says: "And therefore, it is he alone that breaks this bread, and, by the hands of his ministers, distributes to the faithful, saying, Take and drink ye all of this, as well ministers as the rest of the faithful, this is the cup of my blood of the New and eternal Testament."[2] And, "It is manifest and clear to all, that in this mortal life we cannot live without food and drink; so therefore we cannot come to life eternal, unless we are nourished to immortality by both these."[3]

ALGERUS, a zealous defender of the doctrine of PASCHASIUS, fully agrees with him, some three centuries afterward, in the necessity of communicating in both kinds. "Because," says he "we so live by food and drink that we can be deprived of neither one nor the other, he would [therefore] that both should be in his sacrament."[4] Again, he argues that "Christ has redeemed our lost body and soul by his body and soul, and his body and blood are taken by the faithful, that by the body and soul of Christ our whole man may be quickened."[5] He

---

[1] Cæterum sacerdos quia vices Christi visibili specie inter Deum et populum agere videtur, infert per manus Angeli vota populi ad Deum et refert: Vota quidem offert et munera, refert autem impetrata per corpus et sanguinem, et distribuit singulis. Paschas. Ratbert. de Corp. et Sang. Dom., cap. xii.

[2] Et ideo hic solus est qui frangit hunc panem, et per manus ministrorum distribuit credentibus, dicens, Accipite et bibite ex hoc omnes, tam ministri quam et reliqui credentes, hic est calix sanguinis mei novi et æterni testamenti. Idem, cap. xv.

[3] Constat igitur et liquet omnibus, quod in hac mortali vita sine cibo et potu non vivitur, sic itaque ad illam æternam non pervenitur, nisi duobus istis ad immortalitatem nutriatur. Idem, cap. xix.

[4] Quia potu et cibo ita vivimus ut alterutro carere nequeamus, utrumque in sacramento suo esse voluit. Algerus de Sacram., lib. ii, cap. v.

[5] Nos qui corpore et anima perieramus, corpus per corpus, et animam per animam Christus redimens, ... simul corpus

also quotes Augustine as teaching that "neither the flesh without the blood nor the blood without the flesh is rightly communicated;" and that passage of Pope Gelasius, which has just been cited.

Gratian, A. D. 1170, says: If, whenever Christ's blood is poured out, it is poured out for the remission of sins, I ought always to receive it that my sins may always be forgiven me."[1]

Aquinas, A. D. 1260, not so well instructed in transubstantiation as his successors, teaches that "Christ's body is not sacramentally under the species of wine, nor his blood sacramentally under the species of bread; therefore, that Christ may be sacramentally taken, it is necessary that he be received under both species."[D]

Again he says: "According to the ancient custom of the church, all men as they communicated in the body so they communicated in the blood; which also to this day is kept in some churches."[2] About the same time, A. D. 1265 or 1266, we are told that one Decanus, with some associate monks, gave the body and blood of Christ to the army of Charles, King of Sicily, as they were about to go to battle against Manfred.[3]

4. Communion in both kinds may be further proved from several practices formerly observed by Christians.

et sanguis sumitur, a fidelibus .... ut sumpto corpore et anima Christi totus homo vivificetur. Idem, cap. viii. Vide et Hugo de S. Victore, tom. v, cap. 6.

[1] Si quotiescunque effunditur sanguis Christi in remissionem peccatorum effunditur, debeo illum semper sumere, ut semper peccata mihi dimittentur. Gratian. de Consecrat. dist. 2.

[D] Aquinat, part iii, q. 76, art. 2.

[2] Idem, Com. in Joan. vi, sec. 7.

[3] Cum exercitu esset in procinctu, Decanus Meldensem, associatis sibi Monachis, corpus et sanguinem Christi regiis

The consecrated elements were held in great veneration by the ancients; and they took great care that no disrespect should befall them.

In the time of JULIUS some were accustomed to dip the bread in the wine and give it. Both Pope and the Council of Braga, some centuries after, forbade this practice in nearly the same words. Subsequently the Council of Clermont, taking notice of this same practice, decreed "that no one should communicate from the altar unless he took the body separately, and in like manner the blood, except through necessity and with care."[1] This intinction was, however, generally forbidden except in some extraordinary cases. Thus the Council of Tours orders the sacrament to be administered to the sick dipped, "that the presbyter may in truth say to the sick man, the body and blood of the Lord be profitable to thee."[2]

This practice is still observed by the Greek, Syrian and Armenian churches of the East, some of them giving the elements mixed in a spoon, others dipping the bread into the wine.[3]

About the time of BERENGARIUS, it was the practice to suck the wine from the cup through quills to prevent it from being spilt. This appears in the order of celebrating Mass by the Pope, taken from several books of the *Ordo Romanus*, in the Liturgies of Cassander, in which the arch-deacon is said "to receive a pugillaris from the regionary sub-deacon,

---

militibus dedisse. Apud du Chesne, Hist. Franc. tom. v, p. 840, cit. Dalleo de Cult. Lat. lib. v, cap. 12.

[1] Ne quis communicet de altari, nisi corpus separatim et sanguinem similiter sumit, nisi per necessitatem et per cautelam. Apud Baron. Concil. Claramont, Can. 28.

[2] Quæ sacra oblatio intincta esse debet in sanguine Christi ut veraciter presbyter possit dicere infirmo, Corpus et sanguis Domini proficiat tibi. Apud Burchard, lib. v, cap. 9.

[3] Southgate's Visit to the Syrian Church, 1841, p. 210.

with which he confirms the people."[1] And in his note on the word *pugillaris*, Cassander says, they were *pipes* or *canes* with which the blood was sucked from the cup of the Lord."[2] Again, "When the Pontiff has taken the body of Christ, the cardinal bishop reaches to him a pipe, which the Pope puts into the cup which is in the hands of the deacon, and sucks a part of the blood."[E]

We may smile at this little superstition of the dark ages; nevertheless, it shows that the people were accustomed to receive, in some way, that part of the Eucharist of which the laity of Rome now quietly allow themselves to be deprived.

As further proof of communion in both kinds we might, if necessary, produce the ancient practice of some errorists, as noticed by CYPRIAN and JULIUS, who, by using milk instead of wine, plainly confessed the importance of two species to the perfection of this sacrament.

Indeed, I know of no others, except the present Papal church and the ancient Manicheans, that ever communicated in one species only; so that Rome can, in this respect, boast of standing side by side with those olden and notorious heretics.

5. Having sufficiently proved from antiquity the practice and necessity of communicating in both species, we may briefly notice the introduction of the contrary usage in the Latin communion, which, Elliott says was done by the Council of Constance. "But properly it was Innocent III, who made it a law; for the Council of Constance did not even act upon the decrees drawn up by the Pope; and

---

[1] Archidiaconus accepto a subdiacono regionario pugillari, cum quo confirmat populum. Cassand. Liturg in Ordine Celebrat. Missæ per Roman. Pontificem.

Fistulæ seu cannæ, quibus sanguis e Dominico calice exugebatur. Ibid.

[E] Idem, Sacrar. Cerimon. l. 2.

this candid Roman Catholics acknowledge, though some of them may deny it, and others are ignorant of the fact. Afterward the Council of Trent decreed in favor of half-communion. The Pope's faction was so powerful at that Council, that, contrary to the institution of our Lord, they carried the measure which the Council of Constance had introduced."[1] The decree of the Council of Constance by which communion in one kind was established, reads as follows:

"Whereas, in several parts of the world, some have rashly presumed to assert that all Christians ought to receive the holy sacrament of the Eucharist under both species of bread and wine, and that also after supper, or not fasting, contrary to the laudable custom of the church, justly approved of, which they damnably endeavor to reprobate as sacrilegious; hence it is that this holy general Council of Constance, assembled by the Holy Ghost to provide for the salvation of the faithful against *this error*, declares, decrees and defines, that although Christ did after supper institute this holy sacrament, and administer it to his disciples in both kinds, of bread and wine, yet, notwithstanding this, the laudable authority of the sacred canons, and the approved custom of the church, hath fixed and doth fix that this sacrament ought not to be made after supper, nor received by the faithful not fasting. And as this custom has been reasonably introduced in order to avoid certain dangers and scandals, seeing that, although in the primitive church this sacrament was received by the faithful under both species, it was afterward received by the celebrants under each species, and by the laity under the species of bread only; and since it is most certainly to be believed, and in no wise to be doubted, that

---

[1] Elliott on Romanism, vol. 1, p. 294.

the entire body and blood of Christ are truly contained as well under the species of bread as under the species of wine, [this custom] therefore being approved, is now to be held for a law. Also, in regard to this matter, this holy synod decrees and declares to the reverend fathers in Christ, patriarchs and lords, that they effectually punish the transgressors of this decree who exhort the people to communicate under both species of bread and wine."[F]

The Council of Trent declares that, "Although Christ the Lord did, at the last supper, institute this venerable sacrament and deliver it to the Apostles in the species of bread and wine, nevertheless it does not follow from this institution and delivery, that all the faithful of Christ are bound by the statute of the Lord to receive both species."[1]

"Moreover the Council declares that, although our Redeemer, as before said, did at that last supper, institute and deliver to the Apostles this sacrament in two species, it must, nevertheless, be confessed that Christ, whole and entire, and a true sacrament, is taken under either species."[2]

The Council also enacted the following at its 21st session:

Can. 1. "If any one shall say that all and every one of the faithful of Christ ought by divine pre-

[F] Concil. Constant. Sess. xiii, A. D. 1414.

[1] Etsi Christus Dominus in ultima cœna venerabile hoc sacramentum in panis et vini speciebus instituit, et Apostolis tradidit; non tamen illa institutio et traditio eo tendunt, ut omnes Christi fideles statuto Domini ad utramque speciem accipiendam astringantur. Conc. Trident. Sess. xxii, c. 1, A. D. 1562.

[2] Insuper declarat, quamvis Redemptor noster, ut antea dictum est, in suprema illa cœna hoc sacramentum in duabus speciebus instituerit, et Apostolis tradiderat; tamen fatendum esse, etiam sub altera tantum specie totum atque integrum Christum, verumque sacramentum sumi. Idem, cap. 3.

cept, or, as necessary to salvation, to take both species of the most holy sacrament of the Eucharist; let him be anathema."

Can. 2. "If any one shall say that the Holy Catholic Church had not just and reasonable causes to communicate the laity and even the non-celebrating clergy under the species of bread only, or that she has erred therein; let him be anathema."

Can. 3. "If any man shall deny that Christ, the fountain and author of all graces, is taken whole and entire under the one species of bread, because, as some falsely assert, he is not taken according to Christ's institution under each species; let him be be anathema."[1]

Plainly, therefore, do these Councils confess, 1. that Christ instituted this sacrament and delivered it to the primitive church in both kinds; 2. that the Church of Rome has, for certain reasons, changed what Christ originally ordained and commanded to be done in memory of him, so that now she "decrees and declares effectual punishment" to be inflicted upon the transgressors of her law, and pronounces her dreadful curse upon all who dare oppose her assumptions and appeal to the authority of Jesus Christ, the divine author of the Christian religion. This assumption of more than divine exaltation is

---

[1] Can. 1. Si quis dixerit, ex Dei præcepto, vel necessitate salutis, omnes et singulos Christi fideles utramque speciem sanctissimi Eucharistiæ sacramentis sumere debere; anathema sit.

Can. 2. Si quis dixerit, sanctam Ecclesiam Catholicam non justis causis et rationibus adductam fuisse, ut laicos, atque etiam clericos, non conficientes, sub panis tantummodo specie communicaret, aut in eo errasse, anathema sit.

Can. 3. Si quis negaverit, totum, et integrum Christum omnium gratiarum fontem et auctorem sub una panis specie sumi, quia ut quidam falsò aeserunt, non secundum ipsius Christi institutionem sub utraque specie sumatur; anathema sit. Concil. Trident. Sess. xxi.

a prominent mark of the "man" whose character the inspired penman most graphically describes in II Thess. ii. READ IT.

From the evidence which has now been produced, it is certain that all Christian churches communicated in both species for more than a thousand years after Christ. It was about the beginning of the twelfth century that communion in one kind began to be practiced in some of the Latin churches, as we gather from the passage cited from ST. THOMAS AQUINAS, and from the testimony of BONA, a Romish author of the seventeenth age, who says: "It is certain that all, everywhere, both the clergy and laity, men and women, anciently took the sacred mysteries under each species when they were present at their solemn celebration; and they made their offerings and participated of those things which were offered. But without a sacrifice, and without the church, communion was always and everywhere in use under one species. To the first part of this assertion all, as well Catholics as sectaries, agree; nor can he, who is imbued with the least knowledge of ecclesiastical affairs, deny it. For always and everywhere from the beginning of the church even to the twelfth age the faithful communicated under the species of bread and wine. In the beginning of this age the use of the cup began, by little and little, to pass out of use, the bishops for the most part forbidding it to the people on account of the danger of irreverence and of effusion."[1]

[1] Certum est omnes passim clericos et laicos, viros et mulieres sub utraque specie sacra mysteria antiquitus sumpsisse, cùm solemni eorum celebrationi aderant, et offerebant et de oblatis participabant. Extra sacrificium verò, et extra Ecclesiam semper et ubique communio sub unâ specie in usu fuit. Primæ parti assertionis consentiunt omnes, tam Catholici, quam sectarii; nec eam negare potest, qui vel levissima rerum

HALF—COMMUNION.

6. The advocates of the innovation do, however, offer their arguments and reasons for communicating the people under one species only.

"They say," says Elliott, "that the Apostles were commanded to take of the cup as well as the bread because they were clergymen; To this we answer, that it was to the Apostles only he gave the bread also; therefore the laity should have neither bread nor cup, if the objection be true. Besides, the Apostles though not officiating, received the cup; hence the non-officiating clergy are to have the cup also. Thus their doctrine has no support from the foregoing argument of theirs. But they have a strange quibble which they introduce in this place. They grant, indeed, that the Apostles were laymen, and represented the whole body of Christians, when they received the bread; but when our Saviour said these words, *Hoc facite*—*Do this*, by these words he ordained them priests; and these words were spoken before he gave them the cup. So that when he came to dispense the other part of the sacrament to them, that is, the the wine, they then did not receive as laymen, and the representatives of the people, but as clergymen. It appears the Council of Trent had reference to this quibbling sophism when they made the following canon: 'If any one shall say, that by these words, *Do this in remembrance of me*, Christ did not institute his Apostles priests, or did not ordain, that they and other priests should offer his body and blood; let him be accursed!'[1]

Ecclesiasticarum notitia imbutus sit. Semper enim et ubique ab Ecclesiæ primordiis usque ad sæculum duodecimum sub specie panis et vini communicarunt fideles; cœpit paulatim ejus sæculi initio usus calicis obsolescere, plerisque Episcopis eum populo interdicentibus ob periculum irreverentiæ et effusionis. Bona Rer. Liturg, lib. ii, cap. 18, No. 1.

[1] Si quis dixerit, illis verbis, Hoc facite in meam commemorationem, Christum non instituisse apostolos sacerdotes; aut

'But,' it is said, 'our Saviour himself, after his resurrection, administered the sacrament in one kind. For St. Luke says, that sitting down with his two disciples at Emmaus, he took bread and blessed it, and brake, and gave to them." But this was not administering the sacrament at all. It was a thanksgiving to God, as was usual at every meal, and as he did when he fed the multitudes with the loaves and fishes, according to the maner of the Jews, both at that time and since.

They also argue, that in the Acts of the Apostles it is said 'that the disciples met together to break bread on the first day of the week.' (Acts ii: 42.) 'This,' say they, 'refers to the Eucharist, and the cup is not once mentioned as given.' But it is not certain that this refers at all to the sacrament. And supposing it does; as in Scripture language common feasts are expressed by the single phrase of eating bread, which certainly does not prove that the guests drank nothing; so neither does it prove, by a religious feast being expressed in the same manner, that the guests drank nothing. Besides, if there is no mention of the laity receiving the cup, there is none of the priests receiving it. Yet they think this absolutely necessary; and if one may be taken for granted without being particularly mentioned, so may the other also. Add to all this, that where St. Paul speaks in form of this sacrament, he mentions the cup as a necessary part thereof.

They also plead, 'that the laity, by receiving the body of Christ, receive his blood also; for the blood is contained in the body.' But they ought to consider that the wine was intended to be a memorial of the blood *shed* out of the body; and therefore

non ordinasse, ut ipsi, aliique sacerdotes offerrent corpus et sanguinem suum; anathema sit. De Sacrificio Missæ, can. 2.

they who do not receive the cup, do not make this memorial which Christ commanded. Besides, why did Christ institute the cup? If his disciples, in receiving the bread, had received both the body and blood, what need was there afterward in giving them the cup, and calling it the New Testament in his blood? Again, if partaking of the bread be the communion both of the body and blood of Christ, why did Paul make such a distinction between the bread and the cup, calling one the communion of the body of Christ, and the other the communion of his blood? Lastly, if both the body and blood are received in the bread, what does the priest who administers receive when he takes the cup?

They also urge, 'If any man eat of this bread he shall live forever,' (John vi: 51.) But they must first show that this verse, and indeed the context at large, relates to the Lord's Supper. And this they cannot do according to the principles of their church, which require that they 'receive and interpret Scripture not otherwise than according to the unanimous consent of the Fathers.' Now the Council of Trent (Sess. 21, c. 1,) acknowledge that the Fathers and Doctors gave *various interpretations* (varias interpretationes) of this portion of the sixth of John. We also insist that bishops of Rome, cardinals, bishops, and other doctors of their church, upward of thirty in number, deny that their doctrine, with respect to the Eucharist, is to be collected from this chapter.

From the phrase, *as often as ye drink it*, they argue that the cup in the Eucharist may sometimes be omitted. But it should be remembered that the same phrase, *as often as*, is applied to the bread as well as to the cup.

From the passage, 'Whosoever shall eat this bread AND drink this cup unworthily,' (I Cor. xi:

27,) Roman Catholics complain that the Protestants have corrupted the text, as both the Greek and Vulgate, instead of καὶ, and *et*, AND, have ἢ, and *vel*, OR: 'Whosoever shall eat this bread OR drink this cup unworthily.' To this we reply, 1. This criticism gives no countenance to communion in one kind, because their own Greek, Latin, and English Testaments (I Cor. xi : 26, 28, 29; x : 16, 17,) no less than five tims use καὶ, AND, in joining the bread and cup together, to be both received in remembrance of Christ. Therefore, to say the cup is not necessary, is to make the Apostle contradict himself, as well as our Lord's institution. 2. That καὶ, *and*, is the true reading, and not ἢ, *or*, both MSS. and versions sufficiently prove; and that *et*, not *vel*, is the proper reading of the Vulgate, original editions formed by Roman Catholics themselves prove. See these points established by Dr. A. Clarke on I Cor. xi : 27, at the end of the chapter. 3. Besides, whatever may be the true reading, the doctrine of half-communion gains nothing; because the Apostle plainly teaches that EITHER to eat OR drink unworthily was wrong. And that the Corinthians *did drink* of the cup, and that some of them did drink *unworthily*, or in an irreverent manner, is plainly declared in the context."[1]

7. Various *reasons* for this change are given, the principal of which are contained in the following passages from the Roman Catechism: "The church, no doubt, was influenced by numerous and cogent reasons, not only to approve, but confirm by solemn decree, the general practice of communicating under one species. In the first place, the greater caution was necessary to avoid accident or indignity, which must become almost inevitable if the chalice were administered in a crowded assemblage.

[1] Elliott, vol. i, pp. 291, 292.

In the next place, the holy Eucharist should be at all times in readiness for the sick; and if the species of wine remained long unconsumed, it were to be apprehended that it might become vapid. Besides, there are many who cannot bear the taste or smell of wine; lest, therefore, what is intended for the nutriment of the soul should prove noxious to the health of the body, the church, in her wisdom, has sanctioned its administration under the species of bread alone. We may also observe, that in many places wine is extremely scarce, nor can it be brought from distant countries without incurring very heavy expense, and encountering very tedious and difficult journeys. Finally, a circumstance which principally influenced the church in establishing this practice, means were to be devised to crush the heresy which denied that CHRIST, WHOLE AND ENTIRE, IS CONTAINED UNDER THE SPECIES OF BREAD WITHOUT THE BLOOD, AND THE BLOOD UNDER THE SPECIES OF WINE WITHOUT THE BODY. This object was attained by communion under the species of bread alone; which places, as it were, sensibly before our eyes, the truth of the Catholic faith."[1] The capitalizing is ours of course.

Such are the avowed *reasons* for half-communion. And the principal of these has its cause in the determination to "crush" forever the belief,—which is based upon our Saviour's words at the institution, and which prevailed for some twelve centuries after, even to the time of Aquinas,—that the species of bread answers only to the body of Christ, and the species of wine to his blood. Thus has Rome corrupted the doctrine of our Saviour; and then, to support and protect that corruption, she has perverted a plain and positive institution, and uttered her curse against those who dare renounce

[1] Catechism, p. 228, cited by Elliott, vol. i, p. 295.

her novelties and embrace the pure gospel of Christ.

8. There are, without doubt, some things pertaining to the Eucharist which are only circumstantial, and others which must be regarded as essential. The former are such as the place of celebrating, the time, the posture of the participants, and their number. For no one supposes it necessary to the being of the sacrament that it be made in an upper chamber, in the evening, reclining according to the ancient practice at an ordinary meal, or that there be just twelve to partake at a time. These are but accidental circumstances, and in no manner affect the essence of the sacrament.

But it is necessary to the right and proper performance of this commemorative sacrament, that its spirit and design be maintained. Now its design evidently is, to perpetuate in the minds of men the sacrificial death of Christ upon the cross, by means of those sensible symbols of bread and wine which he did himself select, as the typical representations of his broken body and shed blood. It seems, therefore, necessary to the right observance of this sacrament, that the suitable matter, or material be employed, that there be something present which will answer to what was used by the Lord at its institution, and shall fitly point out the thing to be signified. And as this something derives its fitness and significance from the will of the institutor alone, it is evident that the emblems chosen and employed by him, are the only things that can be fitly employed by us. And as no human authority can substitute anything essentially different from what Christ used, so also it can neither increase nor diminish their number. I conclude, hence, that they who do not receive the essential matter of this sacrament as instituted by our Lord, and designed by him to be observed and perpetuated, do not receive a full and proper sacrament. Such is the condition of the whole Romish laity. They do not receive the Eucharist properly and fully, and therefore, do they fail to show forth the bloody passion of him who shed his blood for our redemption and salvation.

The views of Dr. Adam Clarke are so forcible and pertinent to this point, that I will close this topic with an extract from his "Discourse on the Nature and Design of the Eucharist." He observes: "With respect to the *bread*, he had before simply said, *Take, eat, this is my body;* but concerning the *cup* he says, *Drink ye all of this;* for as this pointed out the very *essence* of the institution, namely, the blood of atonement, it was necessary that each should have a particular application of it; therefore he says, *Drink* ye ALL OF THIS. By this we are taught that the *cup* is essential to the sacrament of the Lord's Supper; so that they who deny the *cup* to the people, sin against God's institution; and they who receive not the cup, are not partakers of the body and blood of Christ. If either could, without mortal prejudice, be omitted, it might be the bread; but the cup, as pointing out the blood poured out, that is, the life, by which alone the great sacrificial act is performed, and remission of sins procured, is absolutely indispensable. On this ground it is demonstrable, that there is not a Popish priest under heaven who denies the cup to the people (and they all do this) that can be said to celebrate the Lord's Supper at all; nor is there one of their votaries that ever received the holy sacrament! All pretension to this is an absolute farce, so long as the cup, the emblem of the atoning blood, is denied. How strange it is that the very men who plead so much for the bare literal meaning of, *This is my body*, in the preceding verse, should deny all meaning to, *Drink ye all of this cup*, in this verse! And though Christ has in the most positive manner enjoined it, they will not permit one of the laity to taste it! O what a thing is man! a constant contradiction to reason and to himself. The conclusion, therefore, is unavoidable. The sacrament of the Lord's Supper is not celebrated in the Church of Rome. Should not this be made known to the miserable deluded Catholics over the face of the earth?"

Yours, with a whole Christianity,

E. O. P.

LETTER XV.

SACRIFICE OF THE MASS.

DEAR BROTHER:—Closely allied to transubstantiation, is the modern doctrine of the sacrifice of the Mass, which you tell me was taught by the Fathers. For this piece of information, I presume you are indebted more to the doctors of your church, than to the ancient Fathers. For you seem to content yourself with the bare affirmation, without even an attempt at proof. In reply I might simply repeat the words of the learned CHAMIERE, that "neither the name nor the thing was known for the first three hundred years." But you might justly accuse me of a want of Christian courtesy and moral courage, were I to adopt, without proof, a proposition, at once so general and opposed to the opinions and practice of your church. I shall, therefore, add some considerations to those already suggested in a former communication on the Sacrifice of the Mass. [pp. 101–105.] In order, however, to have the doctrine in question more fully before our mind, we may premise the canons of the Council of Trent on this subject, which, together with the citations made before, [p. 100, et seq.] will afford a view of the doctrine sufficiently comprehensive for our present purpose.

Canon 1. If any one shall say, that a true and proper sacrifice is not offered to God in the Mass; or that what is offered is no other than giving us Christ to eat; let him be anathema.

Canon 2. If any one shall say that by these words, "Do this for a commemoration of me,"

Christ did not appoint his Apostles priests, or did not ordain that they and other priests should offer his body and blood; let him be anathema.

Canon 3. If any one shall say that the sacrifice of the Mass is one of praise and thanksgiving only, or a bare commemoration of the sacrifice made on the cross, but not propitiatory, or that it is profitable to him only who takes it, and ought not to be offered for the living and the dead, for sins, punishments, satisfactions, and other necessities; let him be anathema.

Canon 4. If any one shall say, that the most holy sacrifice of Christ, made on the cross, is blasphemed by the sacrifice of the Mass; or that the latter derogates from the glory of the former; let him be anathema.

Canon 5. If any one shall say, that to celebrate Masses in honor of the saints, and in order to obtain their intercession with God, as the church intends, is an imposture; let him be anathema.

Canon 6. If any one shall say, that the canon of the mass contains errors, and ought therefore to be abolished; let him be anathema.

Canon 7. If any one shall say, that the ceremonies, vestments and external signs which the Catholic Church uses in the celebration of masses, are incitements to impiety more than helps to religion; let him be anathema.

Canon 8. If any one shall say, that the masses in which the priest alone communicates sacramentally are unlawful and ought therefore to be abolished; let him be anathema.

Canon 9. If any one shall say, that the rite of the Roman Church, by which a part of the canon and the words of consecration are uttered with a low voice is to be condemned; or that mass ought to be celebrated in the common tongue only; or that water is not to be mixed with the wine in offering the cup, because it is contrary to Christ's institution; let him be anathema.[1]

Such is the doctrine you are required to believe or submit to the manifold CURSE of "Holy Mother." Was it a doctrine of the early Church of Christ?

I do not deny that the ancient writers often speak of the Eucharist as a sacrifice; and indeed, we Protestants agree with the Fathers in denominat-

[1] Canon 1. Si quis dixerit, in missa non offerri Deo verum et proprium sacrificium, aut quod offerri non sit aliud, quam nobis Christum ad manducandum dari; anathema sit.

Canon 2. Si quis dixerit, illis verbis, Hoc facite in meam commemorationem, Christum non instituisse apostolos sacerdotes; aut non ordinasse, ut ipsi, aliique sacerdotes offerrent corpus et sanguinem suum; anathema sit.

Canon 3. Si quis dixerit, missæ sacrificium tantùm esse landis et gratiarum actionis, aut nudam commemorationem sacrificii in cruce peracti non autem propitiatorium; vel soli prodesse sumenti; neque pro vivis et defunctis, pro peccatis, pœnis, satisfactionibus et aliis necessitatibus offerri debere; anathema sit.

Canon 4. Si quis dixerit, blasphemiam irrogari sanctissimo Christi sacrificio in cruce peracto, per missæ sacrificium, aut illi per hoc derogari; anathema sit.

Canon 5. Si quis dixerit, imposturam esse, missas celebrare in honorem sanctorum, et pro illorum intercessione apud Deum obtinenda, sicut ecclesia intendit; anathema sit.

Canon 6. Si quis dixerit, canonem missæ errores continere, ideoque abrogandum; anathema sit.

Canon 7. Si quis dixerit, ceremonias, vestes et externa signa, quibus in missarum celebratione Ecclesia Catholica utitur irritabula esse magis, quam officia pietatis; anathema sit.

Canon 8. Si quis dixerit, missas in quibus solus sacerdos sacramentaliter communicat, illicitas esse ideoque abrogandas; anathema sit.

Canon 9. Si quis dixerit, Ecclesiæ Romanæ ritum, quo summissa voce pars canonis et verba consecrationis proferuntur, damnandum esse; aut lingua tantum vulgari missam celebrari debere: aut aquam non miscendam esse vino in calice offerendo, eo quod sit contra Christi institutionem; anathema sit. Concil Trident. Sess. xxii de Sacrificio Missæ.

ing this sacrament a sacrifice; for the term sacrifice and oblation is used, as well in Scripture as in antiquity, in a general and improper or metaphorical sense. In this manner it is applied to the internal emotions of the mind, such as penitence and sorrow for sin. "The sacrifices of God are a broken spirit, a broken and contrite heart, O God thou wilt not despise." (Ps. li: 17.) Also the more external expressions of worship are designated in a like manner. "We render unto the Lord the calves of our lips," (Hos. xiv: 2,) and "offer unto God thanksgiving;" (Ps. l: 14,) which the Apostle more fully expresses when he exhorts to "offer the sacrifice of praise to God continually, that is, the fruit of our lips, giving thanks to his name." (Heb. xiii: 15.) Here the metaphor is kept up by a variety of phraseology; and, in the next verse, it is applied to works of mercy and charity towards others. "But to do good and to communicate forget not, for with such sacrifices God is well pleased." Elsewhere he calls the charity of the Philippians "an odor of a sweet smell, a sacrifice acceptable, well pleasing to God." (Phil. iv: 15.) He also calls their faith in Christ a sacrifice and service, λειτουργία, (Ch. ii: 17,) which latter term your advocates of mass-worship would have to signify *sacrifice* as they use the word. But this term gives them no support, for the Apostle makes the preacher of the gospel a λειτουργόν, and the conversion of the Gentiles an *offering acceptable to God*. (Rom. xv: 16.) And a little after he tells the converted Romans that they ought to minister λειτουργῆσαι,—not sacrifice—their carnal things to the poor saints in Jerusalem. (v. 27.) And in the same epistle he denominates the civil rulers ministers, λειτουργοί, (xiii: 6,) not sacrificing priests surely.

St. Peter not only makes works of piety, 'spiritual sacrifices acceptable to God through Jesus Christ,' but he also ascribes a holy priesthood to all Christians to offer them. (I Pet. ii : 5.) So also St. John calls Christians "priests unto God." (Rev. i : 6.)

As the Holy Scriptures use this accommodated mode of expression, so also did the ancient writers of the church apply terms denoting sacrifice and offering to all parts of religious worship, and more especially to the Eucharist, which was considered one of the most solemn and impressive of all our devotions. So that it avails nothing, to produce a long list of places where the Eucharist is called a sacrifice and oblation, unless at the same time it be proved, that they use these terms in their full and proper sense. But that the Fathers do not apply these terms to this sacrament, in their full and proper signification, I deduce from the following considerations:

I. When the primitive Christians presented themselves for communion, it was their practice to bring with them their offerings of bread and wine, and other appropriate things, a part of which was consecrated for the Eucharist; and the rest was used for a common feast of love and religious entertainment, or for the maintenance of the clergy and the poor, to whom they were afterward distributed. In his first Epistle to the Corinthians (ch. xi,) the Apostle alludes to these primitive *Love-feasts* which, at an early age of the church, were allowed to go into desuetude on account of some abuses connected with them.

CLEMENT of Rome makes mention of the Christian practice of performing these oblations at the times appointed; speaks of them as offerings and service;[1] and commends those that make them, by pronouncing them acceptable and blessed.[A]

[1] Clem. Rom. Ep. 1, ad Corinth. p. 85. Edit. Oxon.
[A] Idem, p. 86.

IGNATIUS also speaks of offering and bringing a sacrifice, which he will have no one do without the good pleasure of the bishop of his church, according to the good pleasure of God.[1] The third of those canons called Apostolical, forbids a bishop or presbyter to offer at the altar of God any thing contrary to the command of the Lord, such as honey, milk, or beer instead of wine, or birds, or any kind of animals or pulse;[2] which pretty strongly implies that the communicants were accustomed to bring together such articles of food as an *offering*, for the purposes already mentioned. And in order to guard against any innovation in the Eucharist, it seems to have been considered expedient to frame an express rule, and attach deposition from clerical standing as the penalty of transgression. Hence the importance of preserving the *matter* of the Eucharist unchanged.

"We worship the Maker of the Universe," says JUSTIN, "who needs not blood and libations and incense, speaking, as we have been taught, with the word of prayer and thanksgiving for all those things we offer, singing his praise as much as we are able, reputing this the only honor worthy of Him, not consuming with fire the things made by him for food, but *offering* them for ourselves and those in need."[B]

IRENÆUS says: "The Church offers to God, who furnishes us food, the first fruits of his gifts—the first fruits of his creatures; not as if he needed them; but that we may be neither unfruitful nor ungrateful."[C] That this author had no idea of offering up Christ, body, soul and divinity in the Eucharist, is very evident from his calling the

[1] Ignat. Ep. ad Smyrn.
[2] Can. 3.
[B] Apol. ad Ant.
[C] Iren. adv. Hæres. lib. iv, cap. 32.

things offered by the church, "the first fruits of his creatures;" which idea he expresses repeatedly in various forms,[1] and proves against the Marcionites, that the Father of Christ is the Maker of the world, because his creatures are offered in the Eucharist. "How," says he, "shall it clearly appear to them that this bread, by which thanks are given, is the body of their Lord, and the cup his blood, if they say that he is not the son of the Maker of the world, that is, his Word, by whom the tree bears its fruit and the fountains send forth their streams, and the earth gives at first the blade, afterward the ear, and then the full grain upon the ear."[2] I suppose it would not be considered quite orthodox to call the divinity of Christ the creature of God, nor in very good taste to associate so closely, the glorified and incorruptible body and soul of Christ with the growing of grapes and wheat, as IRENÆUS here does the eucharistic offerings made in his time by the church. Indeed, he must be something more than a sound scholar who can distinguish THIS OBLATION—hanc oblationem—THIS BREAD—eum panem,—and the CUP—calicem—from that which he afterwards speaks of as growing upon the vine and wheat-blade. The offerings made at the celebration of the Eucharist in the time of our author, I conclude to have been no other than the productions of the earth, the creatures of God, which were believed to be sanctified by the invisible operation of the Spirit. Besides, his whole argument necessarily supposes the offerings of the Eucharist to be something distinct from the real body and blood, soul and

[1] Primitias earum quae sunt ejus creaturarum offerentes..... Hanc oblationem Ecclesia sola pura offert Fabricatori offerens ei cum gratiarum actione ex creaturâ ejus. Idem, cap. 34.
[2] Quomodo autem constabit eis eum panem in quo gratiæ actæ sunt, corpus esse Domini sui, et calicem sanguinis ejus, si non ipsum Fabricationis mundi Filium dicant etc. Ibidem.

divinity of Christ; for he argues that Christ is the Son of the Maker of the world, inasmuch as those things which are offered as his sacramental body and blood in the Eucharist, are the creatures of that Being who neither needs nor covets what belongs to another. (See above, Letter viii, p. 147–8.) Now, had he been a believer of the modern doctrine of the Mass, his argument would run as follows: Christ is the Son of the Maker of the world, because that which is offered in the Mass is the real body and blood, soul and divinity of Christ; which would not have been at all applicable to the point then in dispute, nor indeed of any force whatever, the whole argument being resolved into the proposition: Christ is the Son of the Maker of the world because he, who is offered, is the Son of the Maker of the world, which is a simple *begging of the question*.

CYPRIAN rebukes some of the rich women who came to the sacrament without bringing these oblations, as follows: "Thou comest into the house of the Lord without a sacrifice, and takest a part of that sacrifice which the poor hath offered."[D]

AUGUSTINE also reproves this covetous practice when he says: "Offer the oblations which are consecrated upon the altar; a man who is able ought to blush if he communicate another's oblation."[E]

From these passages it appears that the offerings of bread and wine made by the people, were indiscriminately called *sacrifice* and *oblation;* which are the terms applied to the offering of the consecrated Eucharist by the cleric.

But as the offerings made by the people for eucharistic purposes were confessedly bread and wine in their proper substance, so also were these

[D] Cyprian. de Operibus et Eleemos.
[E] Aug. Serm. xiii, de Temp.

made by the priest, as we may infer from the passages just cited from CYPRIAN and AUGUSTINE, where the more wealthy communicant is rebuked for taking what the poor *offers*, which would not be true, if what had been previously offered did not preserve its former nature and substance when sacramentally received.

Besides, the Fathers themselves expressly teach that what is offered in the Eucharist, is substantially bread and wine. IRENÆUS teaches that "Christ took that bread which is of the creature, and gave thanks, saying 'This is my body.' And in like manner the cup, which is, according to us, of the creature, he confessed to be his blood, *and he taught the new oblation of the New Testament, which the church receiving from the Apostles, offers to God in all the world.*"[1] And CYPRIAN says: "The cup which is offered in his memory, should be offered mixed with WINE. For when Christ says, 'I am the true vine,' the blood of Christ is then not water but wine." And a little after he argues, that Melchisedec was a type of Christ; "for," says he, "who is more eminently a priest of the Most High God than our Lord Jesus Christ? Who offered a sacrifice to God the Father; and offered this SAME that Melchisedec offered, that is, BREAD and WINE?"[2] From the fact, therefore, that the Fathers call the Eucharist a sacrifice and oblation, we can no more infer that they intended a true and proper sacrifice, than we can that they intended

---

[1] Eum qui ex creatura est panis, accepit, et gratias egit, dicens: Hoc est corpus meum. Et calicem similiter, qui est ex ea creatura, quæ est secundum nos, suum sanguinem confessus est, et Novi Testamenti novam docuit oblationem; quam ecclesia ab apostolis accipiens, in universo mundo offert Deo. Iren. adv. Hæreses, lib. iv, cap. 32.

[2] Cyprian, Ep. lxiii, ad Cæcilium.

such a sacrifice, when they speak of the offerings made by the people for sacramental use.

3. The Eucharist is called a sacrifice by the ancients, on account of those religious acts performed by the communicants. Thus, IRENÆUS speaking of the Eucharist says: "God would have us continually offer a gift at his altar; there is therefore an altar in heaven; for thither our prayers and oblations are directed."[1] AUGUSTINE, where he discourses on "a true and perfect sacrifice," after telling us that every work which is referred to God as the end of good, is a sacrifice; that man himself consecrated in the name of God and vowed to him, is a sacrifice, and that the congregation and society of the saints is offered to God through the great High Priest, as a universal sacrifice, thus concludes: "We being many are one body in Christ. This the church, also frequently performs at the sacrament of the altar, known to the faithful, where it is shown that in the thing which she offers, she is herself offered."[F] And in the Ordo Romanus, which is older than transubstantiation, the Eucharist is called a sacrifice of praise for our redemption, and for the hope of our salvation. "Remember, O Lord, thy servants and handmaids, and all that stand around, whose faith and devotion thou knowest, who offer to thee this sacrifice of praise for themselves and all theirs, for the redemption of their souls, for the hope of salvation; .... and to thee do they render their vows."[2]

4. The Eucharist is also called a sacrifice, because it is both a commemoration and representation of

---

[1] Iren. adv. Hæreses, lib. iv, cap. 33.

[F] Aug. de Civitat. Dei, lib. x, cap. 6.

[2] .... Qui tibi offerunt hoc sacrificium laudis pro se suisque omnibus pro redemptione animarum suarum, pro spe salutis.... tibique reddunt vota sua. Ordo Roman., p. 62.

the sacrifice of Christ upon the cross. The Jews called that the Passover which was only a memorial of it. So, also, may Christ be representatively sacrificed in the Eucharist as ST. AUGUSTINE says: "Was not Christ offered once for all? And yet he is daily immolated in the sacrament by the people; neither does he lie who says that Christ is immolated; for if the sacraments had not the similitude of those things of which they are sacraments, they would in no manner be sacraments, but from this similitude they often take the name of the things themselves." Which he thus explains: "That which is a memorial of anything does often take the name of that of which it is a memorial, on account of its similitude, as when the Pasch approaches, we say to-morrow or next day is the passion of Christ, when he has suffered once only many years ago; and on the Lord's day we say, to-day Christ rose again, for, on account of its similitude, it is called that day though it is not."[1] In another place he tells us that "a visible sacrifice is a sacrament of an invisible sacrifice, that is, a sacred sign;" and, "nothing else ought to be understood by a sacrifice, than a sacrifice which is preferred before it; because that which by all is called a sacrifice, is a sign of a true sacrifice."[G]

CHRYSOSTOM discourses at some length on the sacrifice of Christ once made, and delivers himself much in the same manner as his African contem-

---

[1] Nonne Christus semel oblatus est? Et tamen in sacramento quotidie populis immolatur, etc. Illud quod alicujus memoriale est propter similitudinem, sæpe ejus rei cujus memoriale est, nomen accipiat, ut appropinquante Paschate, dicimus cras aut perendie est passio Christi, cum semel tantum ante multos annos sit passus, et die dominicâ dicimus, hodie Christus resurrexit, propter similitudinem enim dies ille esse dicitur, quod tamen non est. Aug. Epist. cxx, ad Honorat.

[G] Idem, De Civitat. Dei, lib. x, cap. 5.

porary. In allusion to the multiplicity of the Jewish sacrifices, he remarks, that their "multitude show that they never make clean;" and are an "accusing of sins but not a deliverance from them; an accusation of infirmity, not a proof of their efficacy. For because the first availed nothing, the second was offered; and because this also availed nothing, again another; so that there was a proof of sins. Therefore, the making of an offering is a proof of sins, but always making such is a demonstration of their infirmity. But in regard to Christ, on the contrary, he was once offered, and that suffices forever." And he makes a fine illustration of this drawn from the healing art, where he says, that "an efficient medicine that procures health, and can change all the disease by a single application, proves its own power, by doing away with the necessity of a re-application; but if it is always applied, it is an evident sign that it has no virtue." How perfectly fatal is all this to what is called the sacrifice of the Mass, which is, by the Trent doctors declared to be a propitiatory sacrifice. Their frequent repetition demonstrates their inefficacy. He, a little after, adds: "The wounds being removed there is no longer need of the remedy;" and asks, "What then, do we not offer daily? We do indeed offer, but we recall his death to memory; and this memory is one, not many.... Our Chief Priest is he that offered a sacrifice which purifies us. We now offer that which was then offered and incapable of being expended. This is made for a memorial of that which was then made. For he says, 'Do this for a remembrance of me.' As the High Priest then did, we make not another, but we always make the same sacrifice, rather we make a remembrance of sacrifice."[11] By the expressions, "we always make

---

[11] Chrysost. Hom, xvii, § 3, in Epist. ad Heb.

the same sacrifice," and "we now offer what was then offered," he evidently means, we now offer one kind of sacrifice which is neither to be changed nor expended, in contradistinction from the varied sacrifices under the old dispensation, and we now make the same sacrifice commemoratively, as Christ originally made in reality. Such sentiments are quite fatal to the professed sacrifice of Romish altars, which is affirmed to be a sacrifice, not only of praise and thanksgiving, or a mere commemoration of the sacrifice made upon the cross, but also a propitiatory sacrifice, which ought to be offered for the living and dead, for sins, punishments, satisfactions and other necessities.[1] Of such a propitiatory sacrifice in the Eucharist, the ancient church had no idea, as we may farther learn from others.

"We always offer him," says THEOPHYLACT, "rather we make a remembrance of his offering.... Do we not always offer unbloody sacrifices? Yes, we make a remembrance of his death."[2]

EUSEBIUS expresses the same quite clearly: "He has delivered to us continually to offer a memorial instead of a sacrifice to God."[1]

It is also worthy of remark that the older schoolmen, who lived before the sacrifice of the Mass was understood in its present sense, and as taught by the Council of Trent, also teach that the Eucharist is called "a sacrifice and oblation, because it is a memorial and representation of a true sacrifice, and that holy immolation made upon the altar of the cross."[3] ST. THOMAS AQUINAS seems to have followed the author of the Sentences; for he says,

---

[1] Concil. Trident. Missæ, Canon 3.
[2] In Heb. x.
[1] Euseb. Demonstrat. Evang., lib. i, cap. 10.
[3] Ad hoc breviter dici potest, illud quod offertur et consecratur a sacerdote, vocari sacrificium et oblationem, quia me-

"Because the celebration of this sacrament is a certain image of the passion of Christ, and, because also by this sacrament we are made partakers of the fruit of the Lord's passion, it is fitly called the sacrifice of Christ, first indeed because, as AUGUSTINE to Simplicius says: Images are accustomed to be called by the names of those things of which they are images; as when we look upon a painted table or wall we say, that is Cicero, and that is Sallust; but the celebration of this sacrament is a certain representative image of Christ's passion, which is his true immolation.—In another manner as to the effect of Christ's passion, because by this sacrament we are made partakers of the fruit of the Lord's passion."[1]

5. The Jews and heathen reproached the early Christians for their want of altars and sacrifices in their worship as a great impiety. To this they replied in their apologies, that they had no proper altars, nor visible and external sacrifices, but in their stead, they offered the more spiritual sacrifices of praise and thanksgiving, of honest lives and virtuous actions, which were the sacrifices of Christians, and more acceptable to God than any others.

"We are not Atheists," says JUSTIN, as they were called, because they had not the visible worship of sacrifices, "but we worship the Maker of all things, who needs not blood and libations and incense, . . . with the word of prayer and thanksgiving, . . . giving him praise as much as we are able, counting this the

moria est et representatio veri sacrificii, et sanctæ immolationis factæ in ara crucis. Petr. Lombard., lib. iv, dist. 12.

[1] Tum quia hujus sacramenti celebratio, imago quædam est Passionis Christi, tum etiam quia per hoc sacramentum participes efficimur fructus dominicæ Passionis.... convenienter dicitur Christi immolatio, etc. Aquinat. Sum., Part iii, quæst. 83.

only honor worthy of him,... and we suppose that God needs no material offering from men."¹

Again, "prayers and thanksgivings made by those who are worthy, are the only perfect and acceptable sacrifices to God."ᴶ "We are charged with atheism," says ATHENAGORUS, "by many who measure their piety by the law of sacrifices; but what have I to do with your whole burnt-offerings which God needs not? But, we must offer him an unbloody sacrifice and bring him a rational worship."² The *rational worship*, in this passage, is explanatory of the *unbloody sacrifice*. In answer to the charge that the Christians did not sacrifice for the Emperors, TERTULLIAN replies: "Because we do it not for ourselves, it follows by the same reason that we should not sacrifice for others."ᴷ He afterward speaks of the sacrifice made by him as a rich sacrifice, to wit, "prayer from a chaste body, from an innocent soul, proceeding from the Holy Spirit."ᴸ "The Host to be sacrificed," says MINUTIUS, "is a good soul, a pure mind and a sincere conscience,..... these are our sacrifices, these are the sacred things of God."³ And when CELSUS objects that the Christians had no altars, ORIGEN replies: "Our altars are the sovereignty of each righteous man's mind, from which is truly and understandingly sent up sweet incense, prayers from a pure conscience."⁴ So also LACTANTIUS says: "The chief way of worshiping God, is praise directed to God

---

¹ Apol. ii.
ᴶ Dialog. cum Trypho.
² Athenag. Legat. pro Christ.
ᴷ Tertul. Apol. adv. Gentes, cap. 10.
ᴸ Idem, cap. 30.
³Cum sit litabilis hostia bonus animus et pura meus, et sincera conscientia—hæc nostra sacrificia, hæc Dei sacra sunt. Min. Octav.
⁴Origen. cont. Celsum, lib. viii.

from the mouth of a just man."[1] In view of these plain testimonies, it is more than improbable that those defenders of the Christian religion, should have thus replied to the objection made against them, that they had no proper sacrifice, nay, deny that such a sacrifice is to be performed, as does ARNOBIUS in his disputation against the nations,[2] had they entertained any such idea of an external sacrifice, as is now entertained by the advocates of the modern sacrifice of the Mass. How fitly might the argument of a modern Romanist have been urged, had those ancients believed as our contemporaries now do. They might have replied, "Why do you accuse us of an ungodly and atheistic religion? Instead of having no external sacrifice, we hold that 'without external sacrifice there is no complete system of divine adoration. Take away sacrifice, and God is no more served than creatures may be served; for every form of worship, with the exception of sacrifice, may be offered up within certain limits to creatures. Sacrifice, sirs, belongs to the Almighty alone, and that is the form of worship by which divine worship is to be distinguished; because external sacrifice is an offering to Almighty God of an external thing for the purpose of acknowledging his superior authority; acknowledging that we adore him with our whole man, and leave nothing for ourselves—that we have received every thing from him, and that it is proper we should offer up every thing to him. So if you will travel over all countries you will find no people that have not an idea of external sacrifice in some way or other..... Cicero, a Pagan, states this as an

---

[1] Summus igitur colendi Dei ritus est, ex ore justi hominis ad Deum directa laudatio. Lactant. de Vero cultu. lib. vi, § 25.

[2] Lib. vii.

argument for the belief of a God, that there never was a people known who did not admit the necessity of sacrifice, and who did not use external sacrifice; that you would sooner find a city without a sun than a people without an altar. Now, as the Almighty God required sacrifice and established its necessity—aye, and its very form, in the old law, shall Christians do less than Pagans and Jews, and exclude this essential form of worship? Shall not rather Christians, who have the most perfect system of religion, have the most perfect form of worship and sacrifice? Both reason and religion demand it."[1] So that you err exceedingly, sirs, in blaming us for having no external and formal sacrifice, since we abound in this kind of worship and have it in its most perfect form. You do indeed offer to your dumb gods your beastly sacrifices, but we offer upon our holy altars the glorified body and blood, the soul and divinity of the Son of God; a sacrifice infinitely superior to all the Jewish and Pagan sacrifices ever offered, a sacrifice propitiatory and profitable for sins, punishments, satisfactions and other necessities; nay, for the slumbering dead even; and we are ready to offer our external sacrifice for emperors whether living or dead; and if their spirits are lingering in the dreary regions of purgatory, our sacrifices of the Mass will help their souls and aid them in their escape from the iron grasp of the prince of darkness."

6. When the Fathers call the Eucharist a sacrifice they add such qualifying epithets, as plainly indicate that they did not regard it as a proper and material sacrifice. CYRIL of Jerusalem says: "Then after finishing this *spiritual sacrifice*, and the unbloody worship over this sacrifice of propitiation,

[1] Dr. Ryder, President of the College of the Holy Cross.

we beseech God for the common peace of the churches."¹ He afterward exhorts: "Preserve yourselves without any offence, lest you separate yourselves from communion, lest by the defilement of sin you deprive yourselves of these holy and spiritual mysteries."² By the term *spiritual* he evidently means to distinguish this sacrifice from all corporeal oblations, and makes it consist rather of those moral and intellectual exercises of prayer, thanksgiving and praise, than in the offering of the visible elements.

It is also called a spiritual sacrifice by EUSEBIUS, THEODORET, and others. As it is therefore evident that a spiritual sacrifice cannot be an external and visible one, so it is equally clear that these authors did not regard the Eucharist as a proper sacrifice, but rather as an oblation, representative and commemorative of the true and proper sacrifice of our Lord upon the cross. Thus Christ is said to be "sacrificed without being sacrificed;"ᴹ to be "offered in image;"ᴺ and in the Book of Sacraments attributed to AMBROSE, it is said to be done "in a *figure* of the body and blood of our Lord Jesus Christ." ᴼ If it be in a figure it cannot be in reality, but in commemoration, as AUGUSTINE says, "Christians by the most holy oblation and participation of the body and blood of Christ, celebrate the *memory* of the same sacrifice that has already been accomplished."ᴾ And EUSEBIUS in his Demonstrations makes the matter plain when he says, that "Christ being sacrificed with tokens of good, has offered to

¹ Catech. Mystagog. v, § 6.
² Idem, § 19.
ᴹ Diatypos Concil. Nicen. apud Gelas. Cyzic.
ᴺ Ambros. de Offic., lib. i, cap. 48.
ᴼ Lib. iv, cap. 5.
ᴾ Aug. contra Faustum, lib. xx, cap. 18.

his Father a wonderful sacrifice and an excellent victim for our salvation, and commanded us continually to offer to God a *memorial* instead of a sacrifice."Q If, therefore, the Eucharist be a *memorial* of the real sacrifice of Christ made upon the cross, it is not the same sacrifice as was then made; for the thing remembered, and the memorial by which it is remembered are not one and the same thing. "But the sacrifice acceptable to God is the separation of the body and its passions not to be repented of, which in reality is the true worship of God."R And "not unfitly do we honor God by prayer, and send up that best and most holy sacrifice with righteousness, giving honor to the most righteous Word, through whom we have received knowledge, giving glory for what we have learned by him. There is, therefore, amongst us here a terrestrial altar, to wit, the multitude of those who are devoted to prayer, having, as it were, one common voice and one knowledge .... For the sacrifice of the Church is the word which is exhaled from the souls of the saints, where the sacrifice and the whole understanding are together laid open to God."[1] CHRYSOSTOM says: "We no more offer sheep and cattle, nor blood and the odor of roasted flesh: all these are abolished, and instead of them a RATIONAL worship has been introduced. What is this RATIONAL worship? That which is performed by the mind and by the spirit, ... which has no need of a body, nor organs, nor places; such are gentleness, temperance, almsgiving, long-suffering, and holiness of mind."S Surely, our author could not have regarded external sacrifice as a Christian

Q Euseb. Demonstrat. Evang., lib. i, cap. 10.
R Clem. Alex. Stromat., lib. v, cap. 11, p. 686.
[1] Idem, Stromat., lib. vii, cap. 6, vol. ii, p. 848.
S Chrysost. in Ep. ad Heb., Homil. xi, § 3.

sacrifice, *par excellence*, for he adds: "Do you see by what sacrifices God is well pleased? Do you see also that the Jewish went out of use many years ago, but these took their place? These therefore we offer. Those were of the wealth of those who possessed, but these of virtue; those were *external*, these *internal;* those could be made by any one, these a few can perform. As much as a man is better than a sheep, so much is this sacrifice better than that, for thou offered thy soul a sacrifice."

EPIPHANIUS having spoken of the great number of sacrifices made by the Jews, says: "Henceforth God, by the advent of his Christ in the flesh, cut off all occasion of sacrifices, this one sacrifice, which is the sacrifice of Christ, having perfected all the preceding, because Christ our Passover has been sacrificed, according to the Scripture."[T]

From the foregoing it is certain that the modern doctrine, which affirms that the same offering is now made in the sacrament of the Eucharist that was made upon the cross, was unknown to the early church. And it is a matter of astonishment that men of reputed knowledge in the things of Christianity, are to be found advocating their corporeal and external sacrifice as a necessary mark of the true Church of God, and fulminating their curses against those who, better informed, demur at their material worship, and regard it as a grand novelty; nay, the prime heresy of the church which attempts to bear down Scripture, reason, and antiquity, in order to elevate a licentious authority upon their common ruin.

7. But a true and propitiatory sacrifice requires a duly authenticated priesthood; hence by the second of those canons above cited, the doctors of Trent declare that, by the words, 'Do this in remembrance

[T] Epiphan. adv. Hæreses, lib. i, tom. iii, p. 368.

of me,' Christ instituted his Apostles sacrificing priests. But if by these words the Apostles were made priests when they received the bread, as the Council teaches, then by the equivalent words 'Drink ye all of this,' they were again made priests at the delivery of the cup. From the words of institution, therefore, there is the same evidence that they were made priests *twice* as there is that they were made such *once*. But if they were not instituted priests *twice*, then they were not *once*.

Besides, these words were directed to the Apostles only, or to all Christians in general. If to the former only, then no lay Christian has any divine warrant for receiving the sacrament *in either kind*, but the priests only; but if to the latter, then all Christians are made sacrificing priests equally with the Apostles and all others of the clergy. Lastly, it has been above shown that no true and proper sacrifice was ever made before Christ offered himself upon the cross; and that there Christ offered himself once for all; therefore, the Apostles having power given them at the last supper to do only what Christ then did, they could not have been made such sacrificing priests as the Council of Trent affirms, but were authorized only, by the words under consideration, to commemorate his bloody passion with thanksgiving, and thereby 'show forth his death till he come.'

The Apostle affirms that Christ is a priest forever; (Heb. vi: 20;) and therefore can have no successors. And because he continueth forever, ch. vii: 24, he hath an unchangeable, or more expressively, an *untransmissible*—$\alpha\pi\alpha\rho\alpha\beta\alpha\tau o\nu$—priesthood—rendered in the margin, "which passeth not from one to another." And this testimony of an inspired Apostle is instead of all the unscriptural assumptions of the ages. Nay, what need of a sacrificing priest, since Christ has offered one perfect and sufficient sacrifice for the inhabitants of all time? "When Christ the Lord came," says Cyprian,[1] "concerning whom it was written in the chapter of the book, that he would, by his death, fulfill the will of the Father, SACRIFICES CEASED.... and of so great dignity was that one oblation of our Redeemer, that ONE sufficed to take away the sins of the world."

That which is perfect in its nature, infinite in its merits, and unceasing in its duration, admits of nothing additional. Does he, who trod the wine-press alone, who poured out his soul unto death, and proclaimed, in expiring agony upon his cross; IT IS FINISHED, does he require the aid of him whose breath is in his nostrils, a frail mortal, a worm, a sinner, to supplement his great propitiatory sacrifice?

We are amazed at the boldness that dares confront the authority of the Sacred Oracles, which clearly affirm, that *Christ does not offer himself often; for then must he often have suffered since the foundation of the world;* which unmistakably teaches that suffering is inseparable from a true sacrificial offering for sin; which is not true of the Mass; and therefore, it is no true or propitiatory sacrifice. *Without shedding of blood there is no remission;* (Heb. ix: 22,) therefore the unbloody sacrifice of the Mass procures no remission and is no proper sacrifice.

But, "I have no pleasure in you, saith the Lord of hosts, neither will I accept an offering at your hand. For, from the rising of the sun even unto the going down of the same, my name shall be great among the Gentiles; and in every place incense shall be offered unto my name, and a pure offering; for my name shall be great among the heathen, saith the Lord of hosts," (Mal. i: 10, 11.) This, of late years, has been put forward as a pro-

---

[1] De Ratio. Circumcis. p. 318.

phecy of the unbloody sacrifice of the Mass, by the advocates of the Roman Church. But the better interpretation of this prophecy, applies it to the more spiritual worship under the Christian dispensation, in contradistinction from the offerings of victims under the Jewish economy. In this manner several of the ancients understood it. Alluding to this prophecy of Malachi, IRENÆUS inquires: "What other name is there which is glorified among the Gentiles, than that which belongs to our Lord, through whom the Father is glorified, and man is glorified? And because it properly belongs to his Son, and by him he was made man, He calls it his..... Therefore seeing that the name of the Son is proper to the Father, and the church offers unto God Almighty through Jesus Christ, well is it said with respect to each; 'And in every place incense is offered in my name, and a pure sacrifice.' But John, in the Apocalypse, says that incenses are the prayers of the Saints."[1] Evidently the offerings made to God *through* Christ by the church, were the prayers of her saints, but not the body, soul and divinity of Christ in the sacrament. CLEMENT of Alexandria questions and answers as follows: "How therefore shall I sacrifice to the Lord? The sacrifice to the Lord, he says, is the contrite spirit. How then shall I crown or anoint him; or what incense shall I offer to the Lord? The odor of sweet smell to the Lord, he says, is the heart which glorifies him who made it. These are the CROWNS, the SACRIFICES, the AROMAS and FLOWERS of God."[2] More explicitly TERTULLIAN discourses: "When the sacerdotal law was appointed by Moses in Leviticus, we find it prescribed to the people of Israel that sacrifices should be offered to God in no place,

---

[1] Iren. adv. Heres., lib. iv, c. 33.
[2] 2 Clem. Alex. Pædag. lib. iii, p. 261.

except in the land of promise, which the Lord God
would give to the people of Israel and their brethren..... afterward the spirit predicted by the prophets, that it should come to pass, that in every
land, or in every place, sacrifices should be offered
to God, as he said by his messenger Malachi, one
of the twelve prophets: *I will not accept a sacrifice
from your hands, since, from the rising even to the
setting sun my name is renowned among all nations,
saith the Lord Almighty.* And in every place clean
sacrifices are offered in my name. Also in the
Psalms David says: '*Offer to God ye people of the
Gentiles,*' doubtless because in every land the
preaching of the Apostles was to go forth. Offer
to God renown and honor; offer to God the sacrifices of his name. Lift up the victims and enter into
his courts. For God must be appeased, not with
EARTHLY sacrifices, but with SPIRITUAL; so we read
that it is written: *The contrite and humble heart is
God's victim.* And elsewhere: *The sacrifices of God
are the sacrifice of praise; and render to the Most
High thy vows.* In this manner spiritual sacrifices
of praise are designated, and a contrite heart demonstrated to be a sacrifice acceptable to God.
Thus, therefore, carnal sacrifices are understood as
reprobrated, concerning which Isaiah also speaks,
saying: *What have I to do with the multitude of
your sacrifices, saith the Lord:* so that spiritual
sacrifices are declared acceptable, as the Prophets
announce. *Because also ye have adulterated my fine
flour,* says God, *your prayer is an abomination to me.*
And to this he adds: *Your holocausts and sacrifices,
the fat of he-goats and the blood of bulls, I will not.
Nor may you come to appear before me, for who hath
required this from your hands?* Concerning spiritual
sacrifices he adds, saying: *And in every place clean
sacrifices are offered in my name, saith the Lord.*[1]

[1] Tert. adv. Judæos, cap. v.

JEROME, commenting on the words of the Prophet, remarks: "Now therefore is this word fitly made to the priests of the Jews, who offer to the Lord the blind, the lame and the feeble, to be immolated, that they may know that to carnal victims should succeed spiritual victims; and by no means the blood of bulls and of goats, but incense, that is, the prayers of the Saints, should be offered to the Lord; and not in the one province of the land of Judea, neither in the one city of Jerusalem of Judea, but in every place oblation should be offered, and that by no means unclean, as among the people of Israel, but clean, as in the ceremonies of Christians."[1]

The interpretation of this beautiful prophecy of Malachi, by these Christian Fathers, contrasts remarkably with the partisan application of it to the sacrifice of the Mass by Bishops Hughes, Gibbons, Barrister French, and the rest. The interpretation of the former accords with the spirit and teaching of the New Testament, that of the latter, only with the dogma and institution of a much later age.

Besides, the Hebrew word, *mincha*, here used by Malachi, is the term elsewhere employed to indicate a thank-offering, but not a propitiatory sacrifice. It is the same as found in Gen. iv, 3, which signifies the thank offering of Cain, and consisted of the first ripened fruits of the earth. So that, if it could, by any degree of probability, be understood as applicable to the Eucharist, it would thus far only go to prove this sacrament to be an offering of praise and thanksgiving to God for his gifts, but not a sacrifice for sin. And this view is confirmed from the fact, that this offering was sometimes made in connection with the victim-offering, *Zebach*, as in the case of Abel; which shows that it did not, of itself, signifi-

---

[1] Com. in Mal. c. 1.

25*

cantly point out the sacrifice of redemption by our Lord Jesus Christ, and for that reason was not respected by God in the case of Cain. In a word, it was not a sacrifice representative of the shedding of blood; and hence its unsuitableness as a prototype of the Eucharist, which is the symbolical representation of the bloody passion upon the cross. We are therefore compelled in view, both of the extraordinary gifts of the Spirit prophetically revealed under the Old, and historically experienced under the New dispensation, and by just criticism, to accept the above patristic and Protestant interpretation of this prophecy of Malachi.

Yours truly,
E. O. P.

LETTER XVI.

WORSHIP OF THE SACRAMENT.

DEAR BROTHER:—Another consequence of transubstantiation, not inferior in importance to that last considered, is the practice, observed by your communion, of paying divine worship to the Eucharist. The Council of Trent authorizes this worship in the following language: "There is therefore left no room to doubt but that all the faithful of Christ should, in their veneration for this most holy sacrament, give it the worship of *latria* which is due to the true God, according to the custom always received in the Catholic Church. Nor is it therefore the less to be adored, because it was instituted by Christ our Lord that it should be eaten."[1] Again, "If any one should say that Christ the Only Begotten Son of God is not to be adored in the holy sacrament of the Eucharist with the worship of *latria* as also with external worship, and therefore not to be venerated with peculiar festive celebrity, nor solemnly carried about in processions according to the laudable and universal rite and custom of holy church, nor publicly presented to the people to be adored, and that its worshipers are idolators; let him be anathema."[2]

---

[1] Nullus itaque dubitandi locus relinquitur, quin omnes Christi fideles, pro more in Catholica Ecclesia semper recepto, latriæ cultum qui vero Deo debetur, huic sanctissimo sacramento in veneratione exhibeant; neque enim ideo minus est adorandum, quod fuerit a Christo Domino, ut sumatur, institutum. Sess. xiii, cap. 5.

[2] Si quis dixerit, in sancto eucharistiæ sacramento Christum unigenitum Dei Filium non esse cultu latriæ, etiam externo,

The manner of this worship is thus described by the Roman Missal: "Having uttered the words of consecration, the priest immediately adores the consecrated host upon his knees; he rises, shows it to the people, replaces it upon the corporale, and again adores it."[1] The same worship is also paid to the consecrated cup with similar rites. The priest having adored it, rises up and elevates the host and shows it to the people, who at the tinkling of the little mass-bell, fall down upon their knees and worship it as if it were God himself. They also pray to it as Jesus Christ "Lamb of God, who takest away the sins of the world, have mercy on us, Lamb of God, who takest away the sins of the world, have mercy on us, Lamb of God, who takest away the sins of the world, give us peace."[2] This practice we regard as having no foundation in Scripture, reason, or antiquity.

1. The Apostle says: "All Scripture is given by inspiration of God, and is profitable for doctrine, for reproof, for correction, for instruction in righteousness; that the man of God may be perfect, thoroughly furnished unto all good works." (2 Tim. iii: 16, 17.) I infer from this passage that all works of devotion not furnished by the letter

adorandum; atque ideó nec festiva peculiari celebritate venerandum, neque in processionibus, secundum laudibilem et universalem ecclesiæ sanctæ ritum et consuetudinem, solemniter circumgestandum, vel non publice, ut adoretur, populo proponendum, et ejus adoratores esse idololatras; anathema sit. Idem, cap. viii, can. 6.

[1] Prolatis verbis consecrationis, statim hostiam consecratam genuflexus adorat; surgit, ostendit populo, reponit super corporale, iterum adorato. Missale Rom. p. 212.

[2] Agnus Dei, qui tollis peccata mundi, miserere nobis. Agnus Dei, qui tollis peccata mundi, miserere nobis. Agnus Dei, qui tollis peccata mundi, dona nobis pacem. Idem, p. 219.

or spirit of the inspired Scripture, are not good and therefore forbidden.

So TERTULLIAN observes: "Scripture denies what it does not make known."[1] Now there cannot be found one word in all the inspired Scripture to authorize the worship of the sacrament; nor, so far as I know, have the ablest and most zealous advocates of this practice ever pretended to prove the orthodoxy of their usage from any Scripture command. This perfect silence of the Word of God in regard to a matter so practical and important in your church, is fearfully significant, and should, of itself, strike alarm to the conscience of every human being who bows the knee and offers supreme worship to the Eucharist.

But this practice is expressly forbidden by the second commandment. "Thou shalt not make unto thee any graven image, or the likeness of any thing that is in heaven above, or that is in the earth beneath, or that is in the water under the earth; thou shalt not bow down thyself to them, nor serve them; for I the Lord thy God am a jealous God." (Ex. xx: 4, 5.)

This command must be understood as embracing a general prohibition of the worship of any and every thing, except God himself, either with the heart, or by external acts of homage. It is here worthy of remark, that in this command, God presents himself as a spouse, united to his bride the Church, over which he watches with a jealous eye, knowing her disposition by nature to depart from Him, forget her bridal vows of chastity, and corrupt herself by adulterous acts of idolatry. He, therefore, expressly forbids her to form, serve, or even bow down herself religiously, to any thing bearing the marks of human formation, such acts

---

[1] Negat Scriptura quod non notat. De Monogamia, c. 4.

or affections being regarded as idolatrous. Hence all worship, and bowing down before the consecrated host, before pictures, or other representations, is strictly prohibited by the second commandment, as idolatrous.

"All the marks," says Elliott, "that the Scriptures give us of an idol, and all the reproaches they cast upon it, do as well suit the popish god in the sacrament, and as heavily light upon it, as any thing that was worshiped by the heathen. It is the mark and reproach of a heathen idol that it was made by men. And is not the god in the Mass as much the work of men's hands as any of the pagan idols were? Let none be offended when we say the Romanists *make* their god, or make the body and blood of Christ, for it is their own word and solemnly used by them. And one of the greatest reasons for which they deny the validity of Protestant ministers is, because in their ordinations they do not pretend to confer a power of MAKING *the body of Christ.*

Moreover, the Scripture not only describes an idol, but also exposes it to laughter and contempt, by reckoning up the many outrages and ill usages it is obnoxious to, and from which it cannot rescue itself. Now there is no abuse of this kind which they reckon up, but the god which the Roman Catholics adore in the Mass is as subject to as any pagan idol ever was. If Laban be laughed at for serving *gods which were stolen away,* (Gen. xxxi, 30,) are they not as much to be laughed at whose god has been so often in danger of being stolen by thieves, that they have been forced to make a law for its safe custody? If men are reproached for worshiping what at last may be *cast to the moles and bats,* (Isa. ii, 20,) are not the Romanists equally censurable for worshiping that which may become the prey of rats and mice, &c.? If it was a sufficient proof that the Babylonian gods were idols because they were *carried away captive*, will it not be as good an argument to prove the host of the Mass to be an idol? For they carry it about from place to place to be worshiped, and there is one day in the year set apart for that purpose, namely, Corpus Christi day. And if we may believe history, this host has been likewise taken from Christians and carried away captive by the Mohammedans.

In the forty-fourth chapter of Isaiah we have the following description of an idol: 'The smith with the tongs both worketh in the coals and fashioneth it with hammers, and worketh it with the strength of his arms. The carpenter stretcheth out his rule; he marketh it out with a line; he fitteth it with planes, and he marketh it out with the compass, and maketh it after the figure of a man, according to the beauty of a man, that it may remain in the house. He burneth part thereof in the fire; with part thereof he eateth flesh; and the residue thereof he maketh a god, even his graven image; he falleth down unto it, and worshipeth it, and prayeth unto it, and saith, Deliver me, for thou art my god.' The parallel between this and making the host and its worship, is very striking.

The farmer soweth wheat, it grows, it ripens, is reaped, and is threshed; it is ground at the mill, it is sifted with a sieve: with a part thereof the fowls and cattle are fed; another part is taken and baked by the baker, yet it is no god; it is brought forward and laid on the altar, and yet it is no god; the priest handles and crosses it, and yet it is no god; he pronounces over it a few words, when instantly it is the supreme God. He falls down before it and prays to it, saying: 'Thou art my God.' He lifts it up to the people and cries, 'Ecce Agnus Dei, qui tollit mundi peccata.—Behold the Lamb of God, that taketh away the sin of the world.' The whole congregation fall down and worship it, crying, *Mea culpa, mea culpa, mea maxima culpa—My fault, my fault, my very great fault.* How exact the parallel between popish and heathen idolatry."[1]

The transubstantiationist, however, vastly outdoes the heathen in extravagance and impiety; for no heathen ever supposed the materials of which he made his idol, to be substantially changed by the operation. Their gods were still the same gold, silver, wood and stone, as before; and they worshiped them not as their supreme gods, but rather as their images, or representatives. And if their idols were defaced, broken, stolen, or carried away captive, they were far from believing that the supreme object of their adoration was defaced, broken, stolen, or carried away captive. Such injuries might affect the image, but their gods themselves were above such casualties. Having made his god out of bread, the Papist not only worships it, but, what is unheard of in the follies of Gentile idolatry and repugnant to every feeling of humanity and true piety, he presently eats it. The Egyptians could worship the vilest of creatures, but they never dared to eat what they had once worshiped. But Romanists constantly cast this indignity upon the Lord Jesus Christ. Well might they be instructed by the words of a pagan, who said, "That among all the religions of his time, there was no man so foolish as to pretend to eat his god."[2] And to such we would say: either desist from this unscriptural practice, or cease to persuade reasonable men to become Christians.

[1] See Elliott on Romanism, vol. 1, pp. 297, 298, and following.

[2] Ecquam tam amentem esse putas, qui illud quo vescatur Deum credat esse? Cicero, lib. iii, de Natura Deorum.

WORSHIP OF THE SACRAMENT. 301

II. The Council of Florence decreed as follows, respecting the sacraments. "The sacraments of the new law are seven, namely, *baptism, confirmation, the Eucharist, penance, extreme unction, orders,* and *matrimony.* .... All these sacraments are perfected by three things, to wit, by things as to *matter*, by *words* as to *form*, and by the *person* of the minister who confers the sacrament with the intention of doing what the church does; if any of which be wanting, the sacrament is not perfected."[1]

In like manner the Council of Trent decrees: "whoever shall affirm that the sacraments of the new law were not all instituted by Jesus Christ our Lord, or that they are more or fewer than seven, to wit, *baptism, confirmation, the Eucharist, penance, extreme unction, orders,* and *matrimony,* or even that any of these seven is not truly and properly a sacrament; let him be anathema. And, whoever shall say that *intention* of doing at least what the church does, is not required in ministers when they perform and confer the sacraments; let him be anathema."[2]

---

[1] Novæ legis septem sunt sacramenta, videlicet, baptismus, confirmatio, eucharistia, pœnitentia, extrema unctio, ordo, et matrimonium .... Hæc omnia sacramenta tribus perficiuntur, vidilicet, rebus tamquam materiâ, verbis tamquam formâ, et persona ministri conferentis sacramentum cum intentione faciendi quod facit ecclesia: quorum si aliquod desit, non perficitur sacramentum. Decretum Concil. Florent. 1442.

[2] Si quis dixerit, sacramenta novæ legis non fuisse omnia à Jesu Christo, Domino nostro, instituta; aut esse plura vel pauciora quam septem, videlicet, baptismum, confirmationem, eucharistiam, pœnitentiam, extremam unctionem, ordinem, et matrimonium; aut etiam aliquod horum septem non esse vere et proprie sacramentum; anathema sit. Concil Trident, Sess. vii, canon 1. Si quis dixerit, in ministris, dum sacramenta conficiunt, et conferunt, non requiri intentionem saltem faciendi quod facit ecclesia; anathema sit. Idem, canon 11, 1547.

In the Roman Missal, bearing date Oct. 28th, 1834, and approved by the Archbishop of Baltimore, I find the following, "concerning the defects occurring in the celebration of Masses." "The priest about to celebrate must use all diligence, that nothing of those things requisite for the performance of the sacrament of the Eucharist be wanting. But defect may happen, on the part of the material to be consecrated, the form to be used, and the minister who performs. For whatsoever of these is wanting, that is to say, the due material, the form with intention, and sacerdotal order in him who performs, the sacrament is not made."

"*Of defect of the bread.* If the bread be not of wheat, or if of wheat, it be mixed with grain of another kind in so great quantity, that it remains not wheaten bread, or if it be in any other way corrupted, the sacrament is not made.

"*Of defect of the wine.* If the wine has become very sour, or putrid, or if it has been expressed from sour or unripe grapes, or if so much water is mixed with it that it has become corrupt, the sacrament is not made.

"*Of defects of form.* On the part of form, defects may happen if any of those things are wanting which are required to the integrity of the words in the consecration itself. But the words of consecration, which are the form of this sacrament, are these. *For this is my body;* and, *This is the chalice of my Blood of the new and eternal testament; the mystery of faith which was shed for you and for many for the remission of sins.*

"But if any one should diminish or change aught of the form of the consecration of the body and blood, and in that change of the words they should not signify the same thing, he does not perform the sacrament.

"*Of defect of intention.* If any one intends not to consecrate, but to act deceptively; also if any hosts remain upon the altar from forgetfulness, or if any part of the wine, or any host lies concealed, when he intends only what he sees; also if he have before him eleven hosts and intends to consecrate only ten, not determining which ten he intended to consecrate, in these cases he does not consecrate, because intention is required."[1] These are the most important, though but a few of the defects, liable to occur in the celebration of *Masses* so called.

Now admitting, for argument sake, that the doctrine of transubstantiation is true, it nevertheless follows, from the above-named contingencies, that no man can be certain that the change takes place in any particular case. For there are several intervening uncertainties which are perfectly destructive of anything like certain knowledge. No host-worshiper on earth can tell whether, in the succession of ordinations from the days of the Apostles to the present time, some consecrator has not wanted the requisite intention. Indeed, it is highly probable that some have wanted this intention; for it is

---

[1] *De defectu panis.* Si panis non triticens, vel triticens admixtus sit granis alterius generis in tanta quantitate ut non maneat panis triticens, vel sit alioqui corruptus, non conficitur sacramentum.

De defectu vini. Si vinum sit factum penitus acetum, vel penitus putridum, vel de uvis acerbis, seu non maturis expressum, vel ei admixtum tantum aquæ ut vinum sit corruptum, non conficitur sacramentum.

De defectu formæ. Si quis, aliquid diminuerit vel immutaret de forma consecrationis corporis et sanguinis, et in ipsa verborum immutatione, verba idem non significarent, non conficeret sacramentum.

De defectu intentionis. Si quis non intendit conficere, sed delusorie aliquid agere: item si aliquæ hostiæ ex oblivione remaneant in altari vel aliqua pars vini, vel aliqua hostia lateat, cum non intendat, consecrare nisi quas videt: item si quis habeat coram se undecim hostias, et intendat consecrare solum decem, non determinans, quas decem intendit, in his casibus non consecrat, quia requiritur intentio. Vide Missal. Rom. pp. 51-55.

well known that some of the Romish clergy have been infidels, simonists, &c., &c. If such intention were ever wanting in any consecrating bishop, no present priest can know that he has not received his orders through this vitiated succession of ordinations, coming directly from one destitute of any intention of doing what the church intends. "No celebrant can evidently know," says GABRIEL BIEL, "that he is a priest, because he cannot evidently know that he has been baptized or legitimately ordained."[1] And BELLARMINE assures us that "No man can be certain, by the certainty of faith, that he receives a true sacrament; because it is not performed without the intention of the minister; and no one can see the intention of another."[2] Hence, no man can know, with the certainty of faith, that transubstantiation takes place; and if it does not take place, then Christ is not there as an object of adoration; and he who worships the non-consecrated wafer, is guilty of idolatry. So that no host-worshiper can certainly know, that he does not commit an idolatrous act every time he worships the Eucharist.

Besides the defects already enumerated, which may confessedly occur in the *matter, form* and *minister* of this sacrament, there are several other contingencies which render the perfection of the sacrament still more uncertain: for, in solitary mass, and in the public processions in which the consecrated elements are carried through the streets in covered vessels, who can tell whether the bread were wheaten, or the wine expressed from sour and unripe grapes; or whether the consecrator canoni-

---

[1] Nullus celebrans, potest evidenter scire, se esse sacerdotem, quia non potest evidenter scire se fuisse baptizatum, aut legitimè ordinatum. Gab. Biel, in Epist. Can. Missæ.

[2] Sacramentum, non conficiatur sine intentione ministri, et intentionem alterius nemo videre possit. Bellarm. lib de Justificat. cap. 8.

cally uttered the words of consecration? He might, indeed, make an essential mistake without the knowledge of his attentive, although learned auditor; for it is the practice to utter these words in a low and indistinct voice. Who then can tell; for, "to err is human," that his priest does not frequently err in the utterance of the words of consecration?

Thus, my Brother, according to your own standards, you cannot be certain, as faith requires you should be, that you do not worship a piece of bread and a cup of wine instead of the adorable Saviour. But uncertainty in the things of religion is distressing, and doubt is damnable. The true worshipers who worship the eternal God, are subject to no such uncertainty; for, *We know what we worship.* (John, iv: 22.)

Be assured, the infinite and all-wise Jehovah has not subjected the adoration required by him to such a multitude of contingencies; and that the object of your worship is thus inseparable from the common accidents of earth, and the frailties of our humanity, is proof of its terrestrial origin.

Consider also: "If the consecrated host disappear either by some accident, or by the wind, or by a miracle, or be eaten by some animal, and cannot be found, then let another be consecrated."

"If any thing poisonous touch the consecrated host, then let the priest consecrate another and receive it as directed, and let the former be preserved in a tabernacle in a separate place until the species are corrupted, and then let the corrupted species be cast into the sacristy.

"If in winter the blood be frozen in the cup, let the cup be wrapped in warm cloths; if this does not suffice, let it be put in boiling water near the altar till it be melted, not permitting it to enter the cup.

"If by negligence any of the blood of Christ fall, either upon the ground or upon the table, it must be licked up, and the place sufficiently scraped, and the scrapings burned, but the ashes must be laid up in the sacristy.

"If the priest vomit the Eucharist, and the species appear entire, let them be reverently received, unless nausea be produced; for in that case the consecrated species must be carefully separated [from the vomit] and laid up in some sacred place until they are corrupted, and afterward cast into the sacristy; but if the species do not appear, let the vomit be burned and the ashes cast into the sacristy."[1]

So then we are taught by your infallible church, that the glorified body of our Lord Jesus Christ may be blown away by the wind, eaten by a mouse or rat, or some other animal, poisoned, frozen and thawed, and corrupted! These are doctrines too contradictory of plain Scripture and full of ab-

---

[1] Si hostia consecrata dispareat vel casu aliquo, aut vento, aut miraculo, vel ab aliquo animali accepta, et nequeat reperi; tunc altera consecratur.

Si aliquod venenatum contigerit hostiam consecratam, tunc alteram consecret, et sumat eo modo quo dictum est; et illa servetur in tabernaculo, in loco separato donec species corrumpantur, et corruptæ deinde mittantur in sacrarium.

Si in hieme sanguis congeletur in calice, involvatur calix in pannis calefactis, si id non profecerit, ponatur in fervente aqua prope altare, dummodo in calicem non intret donec liquefiat.

Si per negligentiam, aliquid de sanguine Christi ceciderit, seu quidem super terram, seu super tabulam, lingua lambatur, et locus ipse radatur quantum satis est et abrasio comburatur; cinis vero in sacrarium recondatur.

Si sacerdos evomet Eucharistiam, si species integrae appareant, reverenter sumantur, nisi nausea fiat; tunc enim species consecratæ cautè separentur, et in aliquo loco sacro reponantur donec corrumpantur, et postea in sacrarium projiciantur; quod si species non appareant, comburatur vomitus; et cineres in sacrarium mittantur. Rom. Missal, ubi sup. cit.

surdity, it would seem, to be credited by men of intelligent piety and cultivated reason. And yet this little wafer, so corruptible in its nature and subject to all the casualties of a morsel of bread, is believed to be the Saviour of the world, and adored as such!!!

III. Such adoration being unsustained by either Scripture or reason, let us examine the records of the ancient and primitive church, and see whether she divinely worshiped the Eucharist.

1. I argue that this sacrament was not anciently worshiped from the fact, that no one of those writers who have given us an account of the manner of celebrating the Eucharist in the early Church, has made any mention of such practice.

JUSTIN Martyr, in his Apology, speaks of the prayer of consecration, the response of the people, the impartation of the bread and wine by the deacons to each of those present, the qualification of those who are permitted to communicate, and the sending abroad of the elements to those not present; but he gives not the least intimation of any adoration paid to them.[1]

The Apostolic Constitutions also give us an account of the manner in which the ancients conducted their devotions at the celebration of this sacrament. Here we find the directions for the deacons to give the word for saluting one another with the kiss of peace; with fan in hand, to drive away small animals from coming near the elements; to watch men, women and children, in order to prevent disorder; and to bring water, even for washing the hands of the priests; but nothing is said of bowing down and worshiping the sacrament. The several prayers are given at length; and instead of finding them invoking a perishable morsel of bread

---

[1] Justin Martyr, Apolog. i. See above, p. 123.

and a cup of wine, we find them offering praying to God, "who is every where, and present in all things: who is not bounded by place, nor grown old by time; who is above all corruption, free from all change, and invariable by nature, who dwelleth in light inaccessible, the God of Israel."[1]

CYRIL of Jerusalem is still more minute, in the enumeration of the several parts of worship performed at the time of communicating, giving his newly initiated hearer directions even how to hold his hand when he receives the bread; but he says not a word about worshiping any except God himself.[2]

The oldest Liturgies that contain the manner of administering the Eucharist, make no mention of such supreme worship of this sacrament, either by the priest or people, as is now contained in the Roman Missal and Ritual; and no such prayer to it as that which bears the name of the "Litany of the Blessed Sacrament." In vain do we look for any thing of the kind in these ancient forms. More than a thousand years, from the advent of our Saviour, had passed, before the Christian world became sufficiently apostatized from the true faith to give countenance to this master-piece of creature worship, and allow it to disgrace their books of devotion.

Nor are we now to be required to produce from these ancient liturgies a rule against the adoration of the Eucharist. It is enough for our affirmation that they are silent on this point. We might, with equal propriety, be required to produce from them a prohibition against worshiping the water of baptism. The framers of these ancient formulæ contemplated rather what was done in their service,

---

[1] Lib. viii, cap. 15.
[2] Vide Cyril, Ierosol. Catech. Mystag. v.

than what was not to be allowed. They designed them more for a rule of positive action, than for a law of prohibition. And we can no more be required to produce from them a prohibition against this kind of worship, than we are to produce, from the ritual of any modern church, a law prohibiting the worship of beasts, or the invocation of devils. But, as silence in the latter is to be taken as proof, that no such practices now prevail in Christian communities, so the universal silence of the former in regard to the worship of the Eucharist, is to be taken as a sufficient proof of its non-existence in the ancient church. Nay, it must be admitted as a general rule, that, in all essential matters, of either doctrine or practice, a universal silence is equivalent to a prohibition; for it is utterly impossible, that the ancient universal church should have believed and practiced daily what they never mentioned in their writings. There ought, therefore, to be produced a positive injunction, or, at the least, an unquestionable example, of a given practice, before its prohibition can be demanded. We are not left, however, to conjecture what was the proper object of worship in the ancient church, when we hear them exclaim; *God be merciful to me a sinner*,[A] any more than we are, what is the object of worship of the modern Papist, when we hear him cry out to the Eucharist; *Supersubstantial bread—chalice of benediction—sacrament of piety;* and the like. *Have mercy on us.*[1]

2. Several practices, wherein the ancient Catholic church and the modern Romish church differ, go to show, that the earlier Christians held the consecrated elements in less reverence, than the present worshipers of the Eucharist do.

[A] Chrysost. Liturg.
[1] Litany of the Blessed Sacrament.

The ancients allowed private individuals, to take a portion of the consecrated elements home with them for their own private use.

CYPRIAN relates a very strange thing that happened to a man and woman who had unduly been to the sacrament, and brought some part of it home.[1] So also the bishops were accustomed to send the Eucharist to distant bishops, as a token of friendship and communion.[2] EUSEBIUS also delivers the account, given by Dionysius of Alexandria, of one Serapion who had lived an irreproachable life; but, in the weakness of his human nature had been induced to perform the heathen sacrifice, in a time of persecution. But as he approached his last end, he desired his *grandchild* to run and call a presbyter to come and absolve him. The boy did his errand. "But it was night and the presbyter was sick." "A small portion of the Eucharist" was, however, given to the lad, who was told "to dip it in water, and drop it into the old man's mouth;" which was faithfully done by the boy, and old Serapion immediately expired in peace and comfort.[3]

Contrary to ancient usage, your church does not allow the laity of her communion to take into his hand the element which he receives. The sacred emblem, which is believed to be no less than the body of the Son of God, is regarded as too holy for any one to handle except the divinely prerogatived clergy. The ancients, on the contrary, made the handling of the Eucharist by the communicants the occasion of exhorting them to keep those same hands from being defiled with idolatry, murder, rapine, and the like.

TERTULLIAN, reproaching the Christian Statuaries, represents the zealous believer as "lamenting that

[1] Cyprian de Lapsis.
[2] Euseb. Histor. Eccles. lib. v, cap. 24.   [3] Idem.

a Christian should come from idols into the church, from the workshop of the adversary into the house of God, and raise to God the Father those hands which are the mothers of idols; with those hands to adore without, those things which are worshiped against God, and to move to the body of the Lord those hands which make bodies for demons."[B] AMBROSE repelled Theodosius from the holy table, after the slaughter made by him at Thessalonica, with these words: "How wilt thou extend thy hands yet dropping with the blood of an unjust slaughter? How with those hands wilt thou receive the Lord's most holy body?"[1] NAZIANZEN inquires; "Should not those hands with which thou paintest that pensive beauty, shudder, when thou extendest them to the mystic feast?"[C] CLEMENS ALEXANDRINUS informs us that those "who distributed the Eucharist, as was the custom, permit each one of the people to take his portion."[D] Not long after him, DIONYSIUS of the same city, in a letter to Xystus Bishop of Rome, makes mention of one of his church members who had renounced his heretical baptism, and desired to be re-baptized, as having been for some time in the habit of "standing at the table, and extending his hand to receive the sacred elements."[2] And BASIL very expressly says: "In the church the priest delivers a portion, and the recipient takes it with all his ability, and so brings it with his hand to his own mouth."[E] These several

---

[B] Tertul. de Idolatria, cap 7, p. 107.
[1] Apud Theodoret. Hist. Eccles. lib. v, cap. 19.
[C] Greg. Naz. Carmen, lxiii, p. 152.
[D] Clem. Alex. Strom. lib. i, cap. 1.
[2] Apud Euseb. Hist. Eccles. lib. vii, cap. 9.
[E] Basil. Epist. 289, ad Cæsarium Patricium, vol. iii, p. 279. Vide et Origen, Hom. 13 in Exod. Cyril, Ieros. Catech. Myst. v, et Aug. Cont. literas Petil. lib. ii, c. 23.

passages are produced, not only as proof of an ancient usage, but also as condemnatory of that degradation to which the laity of your church are subjected, by being treated as unfit to handle the sacred emblems of their crucified Redeemer.

In connection with the foregoing, we may observe, that in the ancient church it was the practice to administer the cup in glass vessels, which, because of the danger from so fragile a material—*ob periculum quod immineret materiæ fragili*—is by no means allowed in the Romish Church since the establishment of transubstantiation.

"Nothing is richer," says JEROME, "than he who carries the body of the Lord in a wicker basket, and his blood in glass."[1]

It would be needless to multiply testimonies, since it is confessed by BARONIUS in his notes upon the acts of St. Donatus, that "glass chalices seem to have been in use from the times of the Apostles."[2] And he acknowledges that he can find no earlier prohibition of this use than that of the Council of Rhemes, which, he says, was held in the days of Charles the Great. The Canon Law enjoins that the cup and plate be, if not of gold, at least of silver, allowing pewter in cases of great poverty only; forbids the use of brass and copper; and will allow no one to celebrate Mass from a wooden or glass cup.[3] Such great caution consists well with your doctrine and the worship of the sacrament; but had the ancients believed and practiced thus, why did they not provide, in like manner, against this

---

[1] Nihil illo ditius, qui corpus Domini canistro vimineo, sanguinem portat in vitro. Hieron., Ep. iv, ad Rusticum.

[2] A temporibus Apostolorum vitreus calix in usu fuisse videtur. Notis ad Martyrol. Rom.

[3] Nullus autem de ligneo, aut vitreo calice presumat Missam Cantare. Can. ut calix, dist. 1, de Consecr.

WORSHIP OF THE SACRAMENT. 313

danger of spilling the adorable element? With all their care and veneration for the sacred gifts, they are greatly outdone by their professed successors at Rome.

It is difficult to reconcile with the full belief of a corporeal presence and the worship of the Eucharist, the practice of mixing this species with ink in writing documents of great importance. According to BARONIUS, about the middle of the seventh century Pope Theodorus dropped some of the sacramental wine into the ink, and with his own hand wrote the deposition of Pyrrhus the Monothelite.[1] At the fourth Council of Constantinople, A. D. 869, the Bishops are said to have subscribed the deposition of Photius, Patriarch of Constantinople, "not with mere ink, but dipping the pen into the blood of the Saviour, they thus deprived him of authority, and condemned him and all that had been ordained by him."[F] Also in the same age the agreement of peace between Charles the Bald and Bernard, Count of Barcelona, was confirmed and signed (between the king and count) with the eucharistic blood,[2]—*sanguine eucharistico*. I grant these last examples occurred when innovation in the Eucharist had already made considerable progress, but such a use of this element is quite inconsistent with the present belief of transubstantiation and that supreme worship of the sacrament now given it.

To the same effect we might notice the uses and disposition which were anciently made of the elements remaining after communion. By the rule of some churches, they were divided among the communicants;[3] by that of others, they were given to

---

[1] Vid. Baron. ad An. Dom. 648, sec. 14.
[F] Apud Concl. Labbe, tom. 8.
[2] Vide Baluz. notis ad Agobardum.
[3] Theoph., canon 8.

innocent children to consume;¹ and in the church of Jerusalem, in the fifth century, they were burnt.² Now, had they been host-worshipers, how must simple Christians have been scandalized in seeing the object of their supreme adoration thus treated. "And with what face," says Bingham, "could they have objected this to the heathen, that they worshiped such things as might be burnt, (which is the common argument used by ARNOBIUS, LACTANTIUS, ATHANASIUS, and most others,) if they themselves had done the same things?"³

The modern practice of elevating the Eucharist for the purpose of adoration, was unknown to the ancients. No one of the Greek Fathers who wrote of the ritual of the eucharistic service, makes any mention whatever of the elevation of the Eucharist for any purpose. And DALLIE affirms that he cannot find, among all the interpreters of ecclesiastical offices in the Latin Church, the mention of any kind of elevation before the eleventh age; which was subsequent to the first introduction of transubstantiation. GERMANUS, patriarch of Constantinople, first mentions the practice in the Greek Church for the purpose of representing "the lifting up of Christ upon the cross, his death upon it, and his resurrection,"ᵃ but not for the purpose of adoring it. Another reason given for it was, to invite the people to partake of it, as we learn from NICHOLAS GABASILAS, who says: "The priest receiving the sanctified things, turns to the people, and showing them the holy things, invites those who will to partake of them."ᵇ Hence it appears, that the

---

[1] Concil. Matiscon. ii, canon vi; et Evagrii, lib. iv, cap. 36.
[2] Hesych. Com. in Levit., lib. ii.
[3] Antiquities of the Church, vol. i, p. 806.
[a] In Bibliotheca Patrum, tom. ii.
[b] In Expos. Liturg., apud Biblioth. Patrum, tom. ii.

elevation of the Eucharist for the purpose of adoring it, is an innovation, and most probably proceeded from the new doctrine of transubstantiation as its legitimate consequence, the practice early following the adoption of the doctrine. And Bingham affirms on the authority of DALLIE that "the first writer that assigns the reason of the elevation for adoration is GULIELMUS DURANTUS, who wrote his *Rationale* about the year 1386. So that transubstantiation and adoration of the Eucharist, as mother and daughter, came within an age of one another."[1]

3. Several objections made by the ancient Christians against the heathen objects of worship, are incompatible with the adoration of the sacrament.

The early and most learned Fathers, charged the Egyptians and other heathen with the greatest folly in worshiping animals which were eaten.[I] And it was the opinion of a learned author, that God made the difference between the clean and unclean beast, to prevent this Egyptian and brutish folly in the Israelites who lived among them. "For this reason," says he, "he calls some animals unclean, and others clean, that abominating those that are unclean they should not deify them, nor worship those that were eaten; for it is the extreme of stupidity to worship what is eaten."[J]

If they regarded it as the extreme of stupidity to worship and eat the same *kind* of animal, what would these Fathers have said, had the heathen worshiped and afterward eaten the same *individual* animal? Most certainly, the ancient Christians could not have been guilty of doing essentially the

---

[1] Antiquities, Book xv, chap. v, sec. 4.

[I] (a) Origen, contra Celsem, lib. iv. (b) Tatian, Orat. contra Græcos. (c) Apim bovem adoratis et pascitis. Minut. Octav. p. 94.

[J] Theodoret., in Quæst. in Gen.

same thing they so bitterly condemned in others, and which they accounted for only, by a reference to the great stupidity of the heathen.

Had the ancient church worshiped the Eucharist, the Christian apologists never could have ridiculed the idols of the heathen, as being the work of the carver, or the painter, or as being such gods as were baked in the furnace of a potter;[1] or as being gods of brass and silver.[2] Nor could they have indulged their cutting satire against their impotent and senseless deities, because they were liable to be stolen by thieves.[K] "How much more correctly," says MINUTIUS, "do mute animals naturally judge of your gods, such as mice, swallows, and cranes; they know that they are senseless, they gnaw them, light upon them and sit; and unless you drive them away they build their nests in the very mouth of your god, and the spiders weave their web upon his face."[L] Had those Christians been believers of a real bodily presence, and worshipers of the Eucharist, they never could have employed such bitter invectives against the gods of the heathen, without having their own argument retorted upon themselves to their entire confusion. And this brings us to another consideration.

The ancient enemies of Christianity never slandered the doctrine of the Eucharist, nor accused the Christians of worshiping this sacrament, which they most certainly would have done, had the ancients believed and practised as Romanists now do. For "it is well known that the adversaries of Christianity took all possible occasions to reproach the faith and worship of Christians, and make their names odious. Nothing that looked strange and

---

[1] Arnobius, contra Gentes, lib. vi.   [2] Minut. Octav. p. 74.
[K] Lactant. Institut. lib. ii, c. 4.   [L] Minut. p. 75.

absurd in either, escaped the notice of such men as Celsus and Porphyry, Lucian and Julian, among the heathen, and Trypho among the Jews. They curiously examined and surveyed what they taught and practiced, and whatever they thought to be foolish and incredible, they with all their wit and cunning, endeavored to expose it. So they did with the doctrines of the Trinity, the eternal generation of the Son of God, his incarnation, his crucifixion especially, and our resurrection.

Neither were they less prying into the Christian mysteries and worship, which they could not be ignorant of, there being so many deserters and apostates in those times of persecution, who were well acquainted with them; and by threatening and fears of torment, if there were any secret things, were likely to betray them; thus Julian the Apostate, who had been initiated into the Christian mysteries, laughed in particular of their baptism, that Christians should fancy a purgation thereby from great sins."

To the reproofs of the Christians they did indeed object the worship of Christ, as homage paid to a finite creature.

"If Christians," said Celsus, "should worship no other except one God, they would perhaps have a valid reason against others. But now they worship this man [Christ] who has lately appeared; and nevertheless, they think they commit no offence against God, although his servant is worshiped."[1] Most certainly this learned and bitter enemy of Christianity would have objected against the Christians, the worship of the Eucharist, had they practised it, as an offset to their own idol worship. That neither he nor any other ancient infidel did so, is to be accounted for only from the presump-

[1] Origen, contra Celsum, lib. viii.

tion, that neither the doctrine of transubstantiation, nor the worship of the host, was known in the Church of God in the early ages. Indeed, soon after the Church of Rome set up this kind of worship, we find Averroes the Arabian philosopher, in the thirteenth century, giving this character of the Christians: "That he had found no sect worse or more foolish than the Christian. Because they divide and devour with their teeth the God which they worship."[1] A later historian and traveler relates, that it was a common reproach with the Turks and Mahomedans, to call Christians, God-eaters.[2] And in a book printed at Amsterdam, A. D. 1662, among other questions, this is put to the Christians; "If the Host be a God, why does it corrupt and grow covered with mould? And why is it gnawed by mice?"[3] But why was not this kind of taunt always cast into the face of Christians? Was Averroes more sagacious than Celsus, Julian, or Lucian, that the former should account this a most foolish thing, but the latter never say one word about it. Believe it who can—I never.

4. From several considerations we may further learn, that the early church did not worship the Eucharist. The Fathers frequently teach that none but God is to be invoked in prayer or worshiped;[4] but they never speak of the Eucharist as being an object of invocation, or as being God, we

[1] Nullam se sectam Christiana deteriorem aut ineptiorem reperire. Quem colunt Deum, dentibus ipsi suis discerpunt ac devorant. Apud Dionys. Carthus. in dist. 4.

[2] Bullæus Gultius in Itiner.

[3] Si Hostia Deus est cur situ obducta corrumpitur? Cur à gliribus et muribus corroditur? Lib. Quæst. et Respons.

[4] Vide Justin Martyr. Apol. i. Tertul. ad Scapulam c. 2. Origen. contr. Celsum, lib. v, et lib. viii. Cyprian ad Fortunat. Athanus. Orat. iii, cont. Arianos; et alios ubique.

therefore legitimately infer, that this sacrament was neither invoked nor adored by them.

AUGUSTINE tells us, that Christians adore an invisible God. "But now, brethren, we see not with our eyes him whom we adore, and yet we rightly adore. Much more is God commended to us as a being of power, because we see him not with our eyes. If we should see him with our eyes, perhaps we should despise him; for the Jews despised Christ seen; the Gentiles have adored him not seen."[1] Evidently the object of worship with AUGUSTINE was an invisible God; but not the visible bread and wine of the Eucharist.

In commenting upon the work written by one against ORIGEN's doctrine, that the Holy Ghost does not operate upon things inanimate, JEROME admired the profit the churches would derive from the work; "that they who are ignorant, being instructed by the testimony of Scripture, may learn with what veneration they ought to receive holy things, and perform the service of the altar; and that the holy cups and holy veils and other things that pertain to the worship of the Lord's passion, have not a sanctity such as things inanimate and wanting of sense, but from their fellowship with the body and blood of the Lord, are to be venerated with the same majesty with which his body and blood are venerated,"[2] so that, if the holy cups and

[1] Modò autem fratres, non videmus oculis quem adoramus, et tamen correcti adoramus. Multò magis nobis Deus commendatur potentior, quia eum non oculis videmus. Si eum oculis videremus fortè contemneremus. Nam et Christum Iudæi visum contempserunt, non visum gentes adoraverunt. Aug. Enar. in Psal. xlvi.

[2] Ut discant qui ignorant eruditi testimoniis Scripturarum, quâ debeant veneratione sancta suscipere et altaris servitio deservire; sacrosque calices et sancta velamina, et cætera quæ ad cultum pertinent Dominicæ Passionis, non quasi inanima et sensu carentia sanctimoniam non habere, sed ex con-

veils and other furniture are to be worshiped as God, then are the eucharistic elements also, but not without, JEROME being the judge. And the seventh Council of Constantinople declared that "Christ commanded to offer as his image a choice material, THE SUBSTANCE OF BREAD, not to make the form of a man; in order that idolatry might not be introduced."[M] If it would be idolatry to worship the image of Christ in the Eucharist or elsewhere, were it in the shape of a man, it cannot be less idolatry to worship that image in "the substance of bread," not having the form of man.

IV. Several passages have been cited from the Fathers, with a view to prove the practice of adoring the sacrament in their time; but they only prove, that they approached and received the Eucharist with humility, and reverence, like humble worshipers, sorrowing for their sins, and loving and honoring the Saviour.

In his laudatory oration, upon his sister Gorgonia, GREGORY NAZIANZEN tells, that she being affected with disease, and "rejecting all other remedies, fled to the physician of all; and observing the midnight hour, when her disease remitted a little, she cast herself before the altar, with faith, calling upon him who was honored upon it with loud cry and with all epithets, and reminding him of all those mighty deeds before wrought, (for she was wise in things both old and new,) she committed a certain unbecoming, yet pious and excellent act. She imitated the woman whose flow of blood was dried up by touching the hem of Christ's garment; she put her head upon the altar, with equal cries and tears, as one of old washed the feet of Christ,

---

sortio corporis et sanguinis Domini, eadem corpus ejus et sanguis majestate veneranda. Hieron. Ep. ad Theoph. Alex.
[M] Concil. Constanti. vii, act 6.

she threatened not to desist before she obtained a cure; then mingling with her tears, O marvellous! Whatever of the antitypes of the precious body or blood her hand had treasured up, and anointing her whole body with this medicine of her own making, she immediately received a cure and departed."[1] So quick and marvellous was the reputed cure of Gorgonia, by means of a eucharistic poultice, of a singular disease, as it seemed to the medical men of that age, whose skill had been employed to no effectual purpose; and for whose cure, the tears of her parents, and public prayers and supplications, had been unavailingly poured out. By the host worshiper, Gorgonia is supposed to have worshiped the Saviour under the form of the eucharistic elements, as it is said that she "called upon him who was honored upon the altar." But it is one thing to invoke the Eucharist as God, and another to call upon him who is honored by the celebration of this sacrament. The former is no less than idolatry, the latter, which is here mentioned, is a commendable and Christian act. There is not, in the whole passage, the remotest intimation, that the Eucharist was invoked by Gorgonia. On the contrary, the asserted fact of her taking the sacramental emblems which she herself had reserved for private use, mixing them with her tears, and applying the same as a medicine to her body, is wholly inconsistent with the belief of a real corporeal presence.

When we find CHRYSOSTOM saying, "Thou seest him upon the altar,"[N] we are to understand him as speaking figuratively, as does AMBROSE when he says, that "Stephen being upon earth touched Christ in heaven."[O] And when we meet with such

[1] Greg. Naz. Orat. xi, in laudem sororis Gorgoniæ.
[N] In I Ep. Cor. x.
[O] Ambros. Serm. lvi.

an expression as this, "that Christ is worshiped upon the altar,"[1] we are not to understand it as meaning that the Eucharist was worshiped there, but simply that Christ was worshiped in this sacramental act of devotion.

JEROME tells us of some "Christians who went to Jerusalem, that they might adore Christ in those places in which the Gospel first shone from the cross."[p] He "worshiped him in the grave, and Paula worshiped him in the stall."[2] With equal propriety may we be said to worship him upon the altar, or in the sacraments, without adoring any visible representation there employed.

The Fathers do indeed speak of coming to the sacraments in the manner of suppliants and worshipers,[q] for the purpose of honoring and adoring the Son of God, and offering him a lowly and submissive heart, but not for worshiping the elements used, for they believed them to be, not the real body and blood, but the symbolical body and blood of Christ.

It is true, however, without doubt, that some of the ancients considered the human body of Christ to be an object of adoration, on account of its union with his divine nature. AUGUSTINE found some difficulty in his Latin version of David's words, "*Adore his footstool;*" (Ps. xcix: 5,) and he endeavored to reconcile this with the command to worship and serve God alone. He says: "I inquire what is his footstool; and the Scripture tells me, *The earth is my footstool.* (Isa. lxvi: 1.) In doubt I turn to Christ, because I seek him here; and I find how

---

[1] Chrysost. Hom. xxiv, in I Cor.
[p] Ep. ad Marcel.
[2] Idem, ad Paul, et Eustoch.
[q] Chrys. Hom. vii, in Matt. Vide et Cyril, Hierosol. Catech. Mystag. v.

without impiety, the earth is adored, without impiety his footstool is adored. For he took earth from the earth; because flesh is from the earth, and from the flesh of Mary he took flesh. And since he walked about in this flesh, and has given us this flesh to be eaten for our salvation; but no one eats this flesh unless he has first adored [it]; it is found how such a footstool of the Lord is adored, and not only do we not sin by adoring, but we sin by not adoring."[1]

Referring to the sixth of John he goes on to speak of the unprofitableness of a carnal manducation; the foolishness of those who understood Christ to speak literally in this chapter; represents our Saviour as saying to them, that they should not eat his visible body, nor drink that blood which was soon to be shed by the spear of the soldiers; and as concluding by exhorting to a spiritual understanding of his words, and affirming, that although this sacrament is to be visibly celebrated, it must be understood invisibly.[2] That the worship of the Eucharist is not taught by St. AUGUSTINE in this passage, I gather from the following considerations: 1, The flesh of Christ to be adored, is that which was born of the Virgin. But our author

---

[1] Quæro quod sit scabellum pedum ejus; et dicit mihi Scripturæ: *Terra scabellum pedum meorum.* Fluctuans converto me ad Christum, quia ipsum quæro hic; et invenio quomodo sine impietate adoretur terra, sine impietate adoretur scabellum pedum ejus. Suscepit *enim* de terra terram; quia caro de terra est, et de carne Mariæ carnem accepit. Et quia in ipsa carne hic ambulavit, et ipsam carnem nobis manducandam ad salutem dedit; nemo autem illam carnem manducat, nisi prius adoraverit; inventum est quemadmodum adoretur tale scabellum pedum Domini, et non solum non peccemus adorando, sed peccemus non adorando. Aug. Enaratio in Psal. xcviii, § 9.

[2] See the closing part of this paragraph quoted above, p. 49.

elsewhere teaches that Christ, "according to his bodily presence is now above the heavens at the right hand of the Father,"[1] and therefore not upon earth in the sacrament. 2, He condemns the carnal apprehension of Christ's words by those who were offended and receded from him, and teaches a spiritual and invisible participation of his flesh and blood in the Eucharist. 3, He affirms that "no one eats this flesh unless he has first adored [it,]" which would be untrue if he intended, in the Romish sense, the real flesh of Christ in the Eucharist; for many ungodly persons, rejecters of Christ's divinity, and infidels, who worship not the flesh of the Lord in any proper sense, have always participated of the sacrament of the Lord's Supper. The meaning, therefore, of St. AUGUSTINE evidently is, that no one eats the flesh of Christ SPIRITUALLY in the Eucharist, unless he be a true believer, and has worshiped that Saviour who was born of the Virgin.

More than the words of St. AUGUSTINE does the language of THEODORET seem, at first sight, to favor the worship of the Eucharist, where he says: "The mystic symbols are understood to be what they are made, and are believed and venerated as being those things which they are believed to be."[2] The word we here render by the term *venerate* is the same as that which is commonly translated by the word *adore*. That this author does here mean veneration and not worship or adoration, in our acceptation of the term, is plain from the fact, that he did not believe the bread and wine to pass out of their former and proper substance, as the connection expressly declares. He means, therefore, that the elements are understood to be the sacramental

---

[1] Idem, Serm. cxx, de Diversis. See also above, p. 220.
[2] Theodoret, Dial. ii.

body and blood which they are made by consecration, and are reverenced as such.

2. The Greek προσκύνησις and its corresponding Latin *adoratio* do not, when applied to creatures signify, among the ancient writers, that highest degree of religious worship which is now affirmed to belong to the Eucharist.

"It is one thing to adore, and another to serve," [*i. e.* worship supremely,] says ORIGEN; "For he who serves idols with his whole soul, not only adores, but he also worships them. And he who acts hypocritically because of the heathen, does not worship, although he adores them." [R]

Again he says: "The abjurers of Christianity, at or before the tribunal, do not indeed worship, but they adore idols, taking the name of the Lord God in a vain and lifeless matter. And thus the people, who were defiled with the daughters of Moab, adored their idols, but did not worship them; therefore it is written in these words, *that they called them to the sacrifices of their idols, and the people ate of their sacrifices, and they adored their idols, and Israel was initiated to Baalpeor.* Observe, it is not said, *And they worshiped their idols*, for it was not possible, after such signs and wonders, that, in one moment of time, they would be persuaded by the women with whom they committed whoredom to think their idols were gods." [S] Also CYRIL of Alexandria makes "adoration, as it were, the gate and way unto acts of worship, being the beginning of the service of God." [T] From which we may infer that the ancients did not generally use the term προσκύνησις to express the supreme worship of God from the heart, but rather to indicate that kind of venera-

[R] Orig. Hom. viii, in Exod., No. 4.
[S] Idem, Exhortatio ad Martyrium, Op. vol. i, p. 277.
[T] Cyril, Alex., Com. in Joan. iv : 22, lib. ii, cap. 5.

tion expressed by external acts, and introductory to full and true worship. And when it is applied to sensible objects it expresses only that reverence which belongs to things esteemed sacred. Accordingly CONSTANTINE, in his Letter addressed to the bishops assembled at the Council of Ariminum, calls the law divine and προσκυνητοῦ;[1] ISIDORE of Pelusium calls the tomb of Christ προσκυνούμενον;[2] LEO II calls *Rome* the Apostolic throne προσκυνητὸν;[3] and JUSTINIAN affirms the same of baptism.[4]

By this word the Seventy translate the Hebrew, *shachah*, which means to *stoop* or *bow down*. Abraham bowed down, προσεκυνησεν, to the three angels in the plain of Mamre. (Gen. xviii : 2.) Lot performed the same act to the two angels at the gate of Sodom. (ch. xix : 1.) Jacob bowed down seven times to the ground to his brother Isaac, (ch. xxx : 3 ;) and Joseph's brethren bowed down to him. (ch. xlii : 6.) In these and other cases of the same character, too numerous to mention, civil respect to others, a deference to those superior in rank or circumstance, or a veneration for what is deemed sacred, is all that is intended. The application of this term, therefore, to the Eucharist, does, by no means, prove that the ancients worshiped this sacrament.

V. The abettors of transubstantiation and the worship of the sacrament, consistently with their doctrine and practice, argue a continued and perpetual succession of miracles in the Eucharist. Mr. Hughes says: "Of all the wonders operated by Jesus in the institution of his religion, the only one which a mere creature deputed by God *could* not accomplish, is that which subsists in the real pres-

[1] Apud Athanas., tom. i, part 2, p. 768.
[2] Isidor. Pelus. Epist., lib. iv, No. 27.
[3] Concil. sub Menna, Act. 5.
[4] Justinian, Novell. vi.

ence, in the Eucharist. This doctrine then is the shield of his divinity. He might have accomplished all the miracles that Protestants believe of him, and yet be nothing more than what Socinians represent; but to accomplish the miracle which we contemplate, not with the eye of the body, but with the eye of faith, in the mystery of the holy Eucharist, he must have been God. To *creatures* deputed by God some *power* was given, but to Christ ALL POWER both in heaven and on earth; and it was in the Eucharist alone that this ALL POWER was exercised."[1] Of the operation of *such* miracles, I find nothing among the ancient writers. Although some of them, in their rhetorical discourses, give glowing descriptions of the efficacy of the sacraments, by reason of the wondrous accession of divine grace, yet they do not speak of this as a miracle of POWER above and distinct from all other operations of the Godhead. At most, they regarded it as a miracle of grace.

On the other hand, CHRYSOSTOM argues the benefit of the discontinuance of miracles in the Church on the ground, that "in proportion as things are more evident and effectual in producing assent, in the same proportion is faith lessened, for this cause miracles are now discontinued; .... and therefore, by as much as a more evident miracle is set forth, by so much is the reward of faith lessened; so that if miracles were now to take place the same thing would follow."[u] That is, a lessening of the power and reward of faith.

Yours, in the true worship of God,

E. O. P.

---

[1] Controversy, No. 27, p. 220.
[u] Chrysost. in I Cor. Hom. vi, § 3, tom. x, p. 53.

LETTER XVII.

RISE, PROGRESS, AND ESTABLISHMENT OF THE DOCTRINE OF TRANSUBSTANTIATION.

DEAR BROTHER:—The assertion, that the doctrine of transubstantiation was not a doctrine of the early church, having been discussed at some length, and shown to be true, it only remains for me now to consider briefly the history of this dogma of your church.

On your side, "the impossibility of any change ever having taken place in the doctrine of the church, upon the subject of the real presence and transubstantiation," is argued from the asserted "fact;" "that no formal protest or opposition of whatever kind, was ever made by any part of the church, or any body of Christians during that, or any other period, when the change is said to have taken place; excepting JOHN SCOTUS, a man of very little repute for soundness of judgment, who had no followers, his error on the Eucharist broached toward the middle, expiring with him before the end of the ninth century; also excepting BERENGARIUS, arch-deacon of Angers, two hundred years after, whose error was condemned by all the learned men of that period, and condemned in many councils; and he himself died a sincere penitent A. D. 1088." In view of this representation you ask; "Would all Christians without exception and in a short time, have divested themselves of their natural and religious feelings, to admit a new doctrine, the most opposed to the senses and imagination that can be conceived? Would they have admitted it as a part of the divine revelation given by Christ to his Church, whilst it was to their own knowledge a mere novelty, and not a word had been heard of it before? Would they have adopted it without difficulty, without trouble, without opposition and protestation, as must be supposed in this case, since nothing of the kind can be discovered to have taken place in those times? And whilst the author, the rise and the progress of every heresy, even on much less important points, have been carefully noticed in every age, here on the contrary, by a strange reversal of the moral laws which govern mankind, both the fact and the circumstances of the supposed change of doctrine, were immediately buried in perfect oblivion." This argumentation proceeds, first, upon the assumption that Protestants affirm a sudden change, throughout Christendom, of the doctrine of the Eucharist; whereas, they affirm no such thing; and secondly, upon the assertion of what we suppose to be historically untrue; namely, that SCOTUS in the ninth century was alone in his belief, and in his opposition to the doctrine of a physical change; that BERENGARIUS died a sincere penitent, as represented, for opposing such a change; that no important opposition was made to transubstantiation before the Reformation. Were both the assumption and the assertion true, the reasoning which is based upon them would have weight; but should they be proved false, then the argument falls with the foundation upon which it rests.

It is supposed to be impossible that a change in the doctrine of the Eucharist should have occurred, without producing agitation in the church like that excited by the Arian, Pelagian and other heresies. This would be true, without doubt, were the change in dispute sudden as those more ancient errors, and proposed in as healthful and intelligent a state of

Christian society. But, that the Christian Church during the middle ages, was in a condition highly favorable to the introduction, progress and ultimate establishment of a change of the doctrine of this sacrament, will appear from the following considerations.

1. The Christian world was, for the most part, in a state of profound ignorance. "For many centuries," says Hallam, "to sum up the account of ignorance in a word, it was rare for a layman of whatever rank to know how to sign his name. Their charters, till the use of seals became general, were subscribed with the mark of the cross. Still more extraordinary it was to find one who had any tincture of learning." The Emperor Frederick Barbarossa could not read, nor John, King of Bohemia, in the middle of the fourteenth century, nor Philip the Hardy, King of France, although the son of St. Louis. With some honorable exceptions, "even the clergy were, for a long period, not very materially superior, as a body, to the uninstructed laity. An inconceivable cloud of ignorance overspread the whole face of the church, hardly broken by a few glimmering lights, who owe almost the whole of their distinction to the surrounding darkness..... Of this prevailing ignorance it is easy to produce abundant testimony. Contracts were made verbally, for want of notaries capable of drawing up charters; and these, when written, were frequently barbarous and ungrammatical to an incredible degree. For some considerable intervals scarcely any monument of literature has been preserved, except a few jejune chronicles, the vilest legends of saints, or verses equally destitute of spirit and metre. In almost every Council the ignorance of the clergy forms a subject for reproach. It is asserted, by one held in 992, that scarcely a single person was to be found in Rome itself, who

knew the first elements of letters. Not one priest of a thousand in Spain, about the age of Charlemagne, could address a common letter of salutation to another. In England, Alfred declares that he could not recollect a single priest south of the Thames (the most civilized part of England) at the time of his accession, who understood the ordinary prayer or could translate Latin into his mother tongue."[1]

2. Immorality kept pace with ignorance and extended to both clergy and laity, as a few passages from Mosheim will show. "That those who in this (eighth) age had the care of the church, both in the East and in the West, were of very corrupt morals is abundantly testified. The Oriental bishops and doctors wasted their lives in various controversies and quarrels, and disregarding the cause of religion and piety, they disquieted the State with their senseless clamors and seditions. Nor did they hesitate to imbrue their hands in the blood of their dissenting brethren. Those in the West who pretended to be luminaries, gave themselves up wholly to various kinds of profligacy, to gluttony, to hunting, to lust, to sensuality, and to war. Nor could they in any way be reclaimed, although *Carloman*, *Pepin*, and especially *Charlemagne*, enacted various laws against their vices." "The true religion of Jesus Christ, if we except the few doctrines contained in the Creed, was wholly unknown in this age, even to the teachers of the highest rank; and all orders of society, from the highest to the lowest, neglecting the duties of true piety and the renovation of the heart, fearlessly gave themselves up to every vice and crime."[2]

---

[1] View of the Middle Ages, pp. 459, 460.

[2] See Mosheim's Eccles. Hist. Cent. viii, ix, x, xi, and following

The same is true of succeeding centuries, as credible historians testify. Rancor, strife, sedition, rapine and murder; indulgence, lust, licentiousness and debauchery; fraud, perjury and simony are the terms by which the faithful historian is compelled to designate the common vices of those ages of mental darkness and moral depravity.

Such a state of immorality and general ignorance of the practical doctrines of Christianity, could not be otherwise than highly favorable to the production and growth of any error, however unreasonable or absurd. *But while men slept, his enemy came and sowed tares among the wheat, and went his way.* (Matt. xiii: 25.) "Ignorance and immorality," says Edgar, "are the parents of error and superstition. The mind void of information, and the heart destitute of sanctity, are prepared to embrace any fabrication or absurdity. Such was the mingled mass of darkness, depravity, and superstition which produced the portentous monster of transubstantiation." (Var. p. 369.)

3. Of all the superstitions which contributed to the establishment of this doctrine, an undue reverence for the clergy, and the belief of perpetual miracles, were perhaps foremost. After the first passage above cited, Mosheim adds: "Although these vices of the persons who ought to have been examples for others, were exceedingly offensive to all, and gave occasion to various complaints; yet they did not prevent the persons defiled with them, from being every where held in the highest honor, and being adored as a sort of deities by the vulgar."[1] It is but fair to assume that men of such character, would naturally foster the reverence paid them by the multitude, and encourage any belief which might serve their personal aggrandizement. Nothing

---

[1] Cent. viii, Part ii, c. 2.

could do this more effectually, than the belief of the doctrine of transubstantiation. Let the mind once be persuaded of the truth of this dogma, and the necessary mediation of the priest, and it is prepared to award to such agency the honors of something like a god-like superiority. This is not mere theory.

"The hands of the pontiff," said Urban, in a great Roman Council, "are raised to an eminence granted to none of the angels, OF CREATING GOD THE CREATOR OF ALL THINGS, and of offering him up for the salvation of the whole world." "This prerogative," adds the same authority, "as it elevates the Pope above angels, renders pontifical submission to kings an execration. To this the Synod replied, Amen."[1]

Cardinal Biel extends this power to all priests. "He who created me," says he, "if it be lawful to say it, has given to me to create himself; and he who created me without me, is created by my mediation." He makes a comparison by which he exalts the clergy even above the Virgin; and exclaims: "Consider, O ye priests, in what rank and dignity ye are placed."[2]

It is the profession of this extraordinary power, in making and conferring the sacraments of the Church, that has done more than anything else to elevate in the minds of the masses the importance of the sacerdotal office. Even at the present day, the priestly professor of this tremendous power is

---

[1] Dicens, nimis execrabile videri, ut manus, quæ in tantam eminentiam excreverunt, quod nulli angelorum concessum est, ut Deum cuncta creantem suo signaculo creent, et eundem ipsum pro salute totius mundi, Dei Patris obtutibus offerant. Et ab omnibus acclamatum est, Fiat, fiat. Hoveden, ad Ann. 1099, p. 268. See Dowling, p. 203.

[2] Canon Miss. Lect. 4. See above, p. 200.

viewed by the simple believer of transubstantiation as having ability to open and shut the portals of heaven; nay, to unbar the iron gates of purgatorial dungeons, and, by the means of masses said for the dead, wrest from the hands of the prince of darkness his tormented victims. The influence of such professions upon the untaught minds of the darker ages, may be easily understood. And the readiness with which a doctrine encouraging such prerogatives, would be admitted by men aspiring to the highest possible earthly influence and power, is easily accounted for. In view, therefore, of the ignorance of all, and the immorality and ambitious designs of the clergy of former ages, we may cease to wonder at the introduction of this most strange of all human opinions.

4. The importance to the authority of the clergy, which must have been early attached to this dogma, may be gathered from the persecuting measures adopted by the Romish priests, in order to silence those who dared to call it in question. A few examples from English history: Thomas Badby, a layman, was arraigned A. D. 1409, before the Bishop of Worcester, and convicted of heresy. On his examination he said, that it was impossible any priest could make the body of Christ sacramentally, nor would he believe it, unless he saw, manifestly, the corporeal body of the Lord to be handled by the priest at the altar; that it was ridiculous to imagine that at the supper Christ held in his own hand his own body, and divided it among his disciples, and yet remained whole. "I believe," said he, "the omnipotent God in trinity; but if every consecrated host at the altars be Christ's body, there must then be in England no less than twenty thousand gods.".... "When the king had signed the warrant for his death, he was brought to Smithfield, and there being put in an empty tun, was

bound with iron chains, fastened to a stake, and had dry wood piled around him..... The prior of St. Bartholomew's, in Smithfield, brought, with all solemnity, the sacrament of God's body, with twelve torches borne before, and showed the sacrament to the poor man at the stake. And then they demanded of him how he believed in it; he answered, that he knew well it was hallowed bread, but not God's body. And then was the tun put over him, and fire put unto him, ... till his body was reduced to ashes, and his soul rose triumphant to him who gave it."

Anne Askew testifies: "But this is the heresy which they report me to hold, that after the priest hath spoken the words of consecration, there remaineth bread still. They both say, and also teach it for a necessary article of faith, that after these words be spoken, there remaineth no bread, but even the self-same body that hung upon the cross on Good Friday, both flesh, blood, and bone. To this belief of theirs say I, Nay. For then were our common creed false, which saith, that he sitteth on the right hand of God the Father Almighty, and from thence shall come to judge the quick and the dead. Lo, this is the heresy that I hold, and for it must suffer death." With three others she was chained to the stake and suffered the death of an unyielding martyr in the midst of the flames. "One Bainham was seized and condemned for having said that Thomas Becket was a murderer, and damned if he did not repent; and that in the sacrament, Christ's body was received by faith, and not chewed with the teeth. Sentence was passed upon him and he was burnt."

"Frith was a young man much famed for his learning; and was the first who wrote in England against the corporeal presence in the sacrament. He followed the doctrine of Zuinglius. For his opinions he was seized in May, 1533, and brought before Stokesly, Gardiner, and Longland. They charged him with not believing in purgatory and transubstantiation." He was brought to the stake at Smithfield the fifth of July following; he "hugged the faggots with transport," and expired in the triumphs of faith.[1]

For opposing the doctrine of a corporeal presence, and other papal errors, Wickliff became the object of frequent persecution by the clergy, and would doubtless have fallen a victim to their exterminating violence, had he not been supported by the Duke of Lancaster and other powerful friends. But his grave did not protect him from the vandalism of the age.

Thirty years after his death, the Synod of Constance ordered his bones to be exhumed and reduced to ashes. This decree was subsequently executed, and his ashes are said to have been thrown into the river Swift at Lutterworth. "From thence," says Bonnechose, "to adopt the striking expression of Fuller, his remains were successively borne into the Severn, St. George's Channel, and the Atlantic, ... a veritable emblem of his doctrines, which were diffused from his province throughout the whole nation, and from his nation throughout all the kingdoms of the earth."[2]

From these specimens of papal persecution, we may infer, that the doctrine of transubstantiation has a very important connection with the authority of the Church of Rome. For it is well known that when her favorite auxiliaries, the dungeon, sword, and flame, have been employed, it has been to guard those doctrines which look to the perpetuation of her supremacy over the mind and conscience

---

[1] See Fox's Book of Martyrs, by Goodrich.
[2] Reformers before the Reformation, chap. vi.

of mankind. And as none of her dogmas has a more direct tendency to support her spiritual authority, than that of transubstantiation, its introduction and progress, in those ages when spiritual despotism and worldly ambition possessed the whole soul of priestly aspirants, is most satisfactorily accounted for.

5. The superstitious belief of false miracles in those dark ages, was highly favorable to the progress and establishment of this doctrine.

"Successive ages of ignorance swelled the delusion to such an enormous pitch," says Hallam, "that it was as difficult to trace, we may say without exaggeration, the real religion of the Gospel in the popular belief of the laity, as the real history of Charlemagne in the romance of Turpin. It must not be supposed that these absurdities were produced, as well as nourished, by ignorance. In most cases they were the work of deliberate imposture."[1] A single example will suffice to illustrate both the credulity and imposition of the times. A man whose occupation was highway robbery, was careful to address a prayer to the Virgin, whenever he set out on a predatory expedition. "Taken at last, he was sentenced to be hanged. While the cord was round his neck he made his usual prayer, nor was it ineffectual. The Virgin supported his feet 'with her white hands,' and thus kept him alive two days, to the no small surprise of the executioner, who attempted to complete his work with a stroke of a sword. But the same invisible hand turned aside the weapon, and the executioner was compelled to release his victim, acknowledging the miracle."[1] This miracle was reported in proof of the orthodoxy of the worship of the Virgin. The corporeal presence and worship of the host, have

[1] Middle Ages, p. 465.

also been dignified by similar miraculous interpositions.

PETRUS CLUNIAC, lib. 1, cap. 1, reports, "that a certain peasant of Auvergne, a province in France, perceiving that his bees were likely to die, to prevent the misfortune, was advised, after he had received the communion, to keep the host, and to blow it into one of his hives; and, on a sudden, all the bees came forth out of their hives, and ranking themselves in good order, lifted up the host from the ground, and carrying it in upon their wings, placed it among the combs! After this the man went out about his business, and at his return, found that this advice had succeeded contrary to his expectation; for all his bees were dead. Nay, when he lifted up the hive, he saw that the host WAS TURNED INTO A FAIR CHILD AMONG THE HONEY COMBS; and being much astonished at this change, and seeing that this INFANT seemed to be dead, he took it in his hands, intending to bury it privately in the church; but when he came to do it, he found nothing in his hands, for the infant had vanished away."

Nicholas de Laghi, in his book of the miracles of the holy sacrament, says, "that a Jew, blaspheming the holy sacrament, dared to say, that if the Christians would give it to his dog, he would eat it up, without showing any respect to their God. The Christians being very angry at this outrageous speech, and trusting in the Divine Providence, had a mind to bring it to a trial; so, spreading a napkin on the table they laid on many hosts, among which one only was consecrated. The hungry dog being put upon the same table, began to eat them all; but coming to that which had been consecrated, without touching it, he kneeled down before it, and afterwards fell with rage upon his master, catching him so closely by the nose, that he took it quite away with his teeth." The same which St. Matthew warns such like blasphemers, saying "Give not that which is holy unto dogs, lest they turn again and rend you." From other accounts we learn that bees, acknowledging their God in the sacrament, erected to him a little chapel of wax, with its doors, windows, bells, and vestry; and within it a chalice where they laid the holy body of Jesus Christ; and of asses falling upon their knees and adoring the sacrament when carried by a priest. Indeed, no less than seventy-three pretended miracles of reverencing the consecrated host by animals are contained in Father Toussain's collection. Such were the impostures practiced by artful monks and priests, in order to establish the popular belief in transubstantiation. "Some of them attested upon oath, swearing by their sacred vestments, that they had seen the blood trickle in drops, as it does from a human body, from the consecrated wafer held in the hands of the priests; and others, that they had received still more ocular demonstration of the reality of the change of the bread into the body of Christ, inasmuch as they had actually seen it thus changed into the Saviour himself, *sitting in the form of a little boy upon the altar.*" [1]

We conclude therefore, that, so far from a change in the doctrine of the Eucharist being morally impossible, as asserted by you and others, the ignorance and credulity of the masses, and the immorality and fraudulent practices, the ambition and spiritual despotism of the clergy of the dark ages, rendered such a change as we affirm comparatively easy with the multitude.

II. Let us see whether there are traces of a change in the doctrine of this sacrament.

[1] See Dowling's History of Romanism, pp. 198, 199.

That the ancient Fathers did not believe the dogma of transubstantiation, has been fully proved in former communications. Quite early, however, the sacraments were abused, by being exalted to an undue proportion in the Christian system. Instead of soberly explaining the figurative language of Scripture, writers of a warm imagination were inclined to go even beyond the original.

And when once an opinion had taken root that seemed to exalt the sacraments, it easily grew and spread; and the more so as enlightened piety gradually sank into the shadows of superstition and ignorance. Let the pious Christian compare the condition of the Christian Church in the days of the Apostles, with that which followed in subsequent ages, as delineated in the writings of the Fathers, and he will pass from the investigation, grieved that a formal ritualism, a cold and lifeless sacramentarianism, should so soon have taken the place of vital godliness. Accordingly, we find the Fathers sometimes employing expressions which, taken by themselves, were easily accommodated to favor, in after times, the doctrine of a physical change of the elements. Thus, JUSTIN Martyr says: "We do not receive these as common bread and common drink, but as our Saviour Jesus Christ, who was made flesh by the word of God, took flesh and blood for our salvation, so also, we have been taught that the food which has been blessed by the prayer of his word, and by which our flesh and blood are nourished in the change, is the flesh and blood of that Jesus who was made flesh."[1]

In a later age, CYRIL of Jerusalem says: "When Christ affirms and says of the bread, *This is my body*, who will henceforth dare hesitate? And when he confirms and says, *This is my blood*, who

[1] Justin Martyr, Apol. i.

then will doubt, saying that is not his blood? Water he once changed into wine by his nod, in Cana of Galilee, and is he not worthy of belief when he changes wine into blood? Being called to a corporeal marriage he wrought that wonderful miracle, and shall he not much more be confessed by the sons of the bridegroom when he gives the fruition of his body and blood?"[1] CYRIL does not here compare the one change to the other, but he argues from the energy of Christ to perform miracles transcending human power, his ability to change the bread and wine into his body and blood, by the addition of spiritual grace to these elements. This he considered a less exhibition of his power than that employed at Cana of Galilee, which illy agrees with transubstantiation. For the terms *much more* show, that he argues from the *greater* to the *less*. So that his argument is, If Christ wrought that greater miracle at Cana, *much more* can he operate this change of the elements into his body and blood, which requires a less exercise of divine power. Indeed this reasoning of CYRIL is fatal to transubstantiation; for its advocates, as we have seen, rightly place this, according to their theory, at the head of all the miracles operated by Christ.

2. But the doctrine of a physical change appears to have been first suggested by the heresy of Eutyches, who believed that in Christ there was but one nature, that of the incarnate word; and that the human nature was changed into the substance of the divine nature.

Availing himself of the phraseology of the ancient liturgies, though abundantly explained as to their real meaning, he made this the premises of his doctrines, which is well expressed by Theodoret

[1] Cyril, Hierosol. Catech., Mystagog. iv.

in the following argument of his Eranistes, the spokesman for the doctrine of Eutyches. "As then the symbols of Christ's body and blood are one thing before the invocation of the priest, but after the invocation, are changed and become something else; so the body of the Lord, after his assumption, is changed into the divine essence."[1] The heresy of Eutyches was met by Theodoret and Pope Gelasius in the fifth century, and by Ephrem of Antioch in the sixth. And the intimation in this passage by Eranistes of a physical change in the bread and wine, is immediately denied by Orthodoxus, the spokesman for the Catholic doctrine of that age.

3. The learned Tillotson observes, that "The doctrine of the *corporeal presence* of Christ in the Eucharist, was first started upon occasion of a dispute about the worship of images: in opposition whereto, the Synod of Constantinople, about the year 750, did argue thus: 'That our Lord having left no other image of himself but the sacrament, in which the substance of bread, &c., is the image of his body, we ought to make no other image of our Lord.' But the Council of Nice, in 787, being resolved to support the image worship, did on the contrary declare that the sacrament, after consecration, is not the image and antitype of Christ's body and blood, but is properly his body and blood."[2] So that the doctrine of the corporeal presence in the sacrament, was first introduced to support image worship. This refers to the introduction of the doctrine into the Greek Church. Still, however, though the doctrine received the sanction of a general council, and that, too, in direct contradiction of another general council, it was in a rude and undigested state.

[1] Theodoret, Dial. ii.
[2] Tillotson on Transubstantiation, Serm. xxvi.

4. In the ninth century, a warm controversy arose among the Latins respecting the *manner* in which the body and blood of Christ are present in the sacred supper. On this point the sentiments of Christians were various and contradictory; nor had any council prescribed a definite faith on the subject. Both reason and folly were hitherto left free in this matter, nor had any imperious mode of faith suspended the exercise of the one, or restrained the extravagance of the other.

But in the year 831, PASCHASIUS RADBERT, a Benedictine monk, and afterwards abbot of Corby, published a treatise "Concerning the Body and Blood of the Lord," which he presented enlarged and improved to the Emperor, Charles the Bold, in the year 845. The doctrine advanced by PASCHASIUS, may be expressed by the two propositions following: *First*, That after the consecration of the bread and wine in the Lord's supper, nothing remained of these elements but the outward figure, under which the body and blood of Christ were locally present. *Secondly*, That the body and blood of Christ, thus present in the Eucharist, was the same body that was born of the Virgin, suffered on the cross, and was raised from the dead. This new doctrine, especially the second proposition, excited the astonishment of many, and gave rise to a great dispute. This doctrine was opposed by RABANUS MAURUS, HERIBALD, and others, though not in the same manner, nor upon the same grounds. The Emperor Charles the Bold ordered BERTRAM and JOHN SCOTUS, two men of distinguished learning and talent, to give a true exposition of that doctrine which PASCHASIUS had corrupted. Though the views of BERTRAM are somewhat confused, yet the following passages, erased from his work by the papal censors of the sixteenth century,[1] plainly shows that he was no transubstantiationist. "It must also be considered," says he, "that in this bread is figured not only the body of Christ, but also the body of the people who believe in him. And hence it is that it is made up of many grains of wheat; because the whole body of believing people is united together, and made into one by the word of Christ. And therefore, as it is by a mystery that we receive this bread for the body of Christ, in like manner it is by a mystery also, that the members of the people believing in Christ are intimated. And as this bread is called the body of believers, not corporeally but spiritually, so also the body of Christ must be understood, not corporeally but spiritually. So also is it in the wine, which is called the blood of Christ, and with which it is commanded that water be mixed, it being forbidden to offer the one without the other; because as the head cannot subsist without the body, nor the body without the head, in like manner the people cannot be without Christ, nor Christ without the people. If, therefore, this wine which is sanctified by the office of ministers is changed corporeally into the blood of Christ, then the water which is mixed with it must also of necessity, be corporeally changed into the blood of the believing people; for where the sanctification is one, the operation is consequently one; and where the reason is equal, the mystery also that follows it is equal. But as for the water, we see that there is no such corporeal change wrought in it; it therefore follows that in the wine there is no corporeal transmutation. Whatsoever then of

---

[1] Non malè aut inconsultè omittantur igitur omnia hæc a fine paginæ: "Considerandum quoque quod in pane illo," &c.; usque ad illud multò post, "Sed aliud est quod exteriùs geritur," &c., in eadem pag. *Index Expurg. Belg.* an. 1571, *in Bertramo.* See Daillè on the Right Use of the Fathers, p. 91.

the body of the people is signified by the water, is taken spiritually, therefore, whatsoever of the blood of Christ is intimated by the wine must be taken spiritually.

Again, those things which differ among themselves, are not the same. Now the body of Christ which died, and was raised up to life again, dies no more, having become immortal; and death having no more power over it; it is eternal and free from further suffering. But this, which is consecrated in the church is temporal, not eternal; corruptible, not free from corruption; in its journey, and not in its native country. They differ from one another and are, therefore, not the same. If, then, they are not the same, how can this be called the true body of Christ, and his true blood? If it be the body of Christ, and if it may be truly said that this body of Christ is really and truly the body of Christ—the real body of Christ being incorruptible and impassible, and therefore eternal—consequently, this body of Christ which is operated in the Church, must necessarily be incorruptible and eternal also. But it cannot be denied that it does corrupt, since it is divided into parts and distributed to be eaten; and being ground by the teeth it is cast into the body."[1]

[1] Considerandum quoque, quòd in pane illo non solum corpus Christi, verum etiam corpus in cum credentis populi figuretur, unde multis frumenti granis conficitur, quia corpus populi credentis multis per verba Christi fidelibus augmentatur, (al. coagmentatur.) Qua de re sicut mysterio panis ille Christi corpus accipitur: sic etiam in mysterio membra populi credentis in Christum intimantur. Et sicut non corporaliter, sed spiritualiter panis ille credentium corpus dicitur; sic quoque Christi corpus non corporaliter sed spiritualiter necesse est intelligatur. Sic et in vino, qui sanguis Christi dicitur, aqua misceri jubetur, nec unum sine altero permittitur offerri, quia nec populus sine Christo, nec Christus sine populo, sicut nec caput sine corpore, vel corpus sine capite

JOHN SCOTUS, however, as being a philosopher, expressed his views perspicuously and properly, teaching that the bread and wine are *signs* and *representations* of the absent body and blood of Christ. Having no determinate opinion, the other theologians fluctuate, and assert in one place what they gainsay in another; and reject at one time what they presently after maintain. Among the Latins, therefore, in that age, there was not yet a determinate common opinion as to the *mode* in which the body and blood of Christ are in the Eucharist,

At this time also, no mention is made of the *worship* of the sacrament, much less contended for, and none maintained that the soul and divinity of Christ are contained in the Eucharist; which are

<blockquote>
valet existere, igitur si vinum illud, sanctificatum per ministrorum officium, in Christi sanguinem corporaliter convertitur, aqua quoque, quæ pariter admixta est, in sanguinem populi credentis necesse est corporaliter convertatur. Ubi namque una sanctificatio est, una consequenter operatio; et ubi par ratio, par quoque consequitur mysterium. At videmus in aqua secundum corpus nihil esse conversum, consequenter ergo et in vino nihil corporaliter ostensum. Accipitur spiritualiter quicquid in aqua de populi corpore significatur; accipiatur ergo necesse est spiritualiter quicquid in vino de Christi sanguine intimatur. Item, quæ à se differunt, idem non sunt; corpus Christi, quod mortuum est, et resurrexit, et immortale factum jam non moritur, et mors illi ultrà non dominabitur, æternum est, jam non passibile. Hoc autem, quod in ecclesia celebratur temporale est, non æternum; corruptibile est, non incorruptibile, in via est, non in patria. Differunt igitur à se quapropter non sunt idem. Quòd si non sunt idem, quomodo verum corpus Christi dicitur, et verus sanguis? Si enim corpus Christi est, et hoc dicitur verè, quia corpus Christi in veritate corpus Christi est, et si in veritate corpus Christi, incorruptibile est, et impassibile, ac per hoc æternum. Hoc igitur corpus Christi quod agitur in ecclesia necesse est ut incorruptibile sit, et æternum. Sed negari non potest corrumpi; quod per partes commutatum dispartitur ad sumendum, et dentibus commolitum in corpus trajicitur. Bertram. Presbyt. lib. de Corp. et Sang. Dom. Quoted by Daillé in the work cited, p. 90.
</blockquote>

additional proofs of the novelty of these doctrines. The testimony of RABANUS MAURUS, Archbishop of Mentz, A. D. 847, is worthy of notice. He says: "Some persons, of late, not entertaining a sound opinion, respecting the sacrament of the body and blood of our Lord, have actually ventured to declare, that this is the identical body and blood of our Lord Jesus Christ; the identical body, to wit, which was born of the Virgin Mary, in which Christ suffered on the cross, and in which he arose from the dead. This error we have opposed with all our might."[1]

5. During the tenth century there was little or no controversy on the subject of the sacrament of the Eucharist. Opinion seemed to be divided, keeping about the same bounds as in the ninth century. Some of the Latin doctors held that Christ's real body and blood are present in the Eucharist, while others believed the Lord's body to be not present, and to be received in the sacrament only by a holy exercise of the soul. "The moderation and forbearance manifested in this age respecting this holy sacrament, is not to be attributed to the wisdom and virtue of the age," says Mosheim; "it was rather the want of intelligence and knowledge, which rendered both parties indisposed and unable to contend on these subjects."[2]

As yet, the doctrine of transubstantiation was unknown to the English; it was, however, received by some of the French and German divines.[3] In the year 980, Heriger, an English abbot, composed a homily which was used in the churches in London in 990, as follows: "There is a great difference

[1] Raban. Maur. Epist. ad Heribald, c. 33. Cited by Elliott, vol. i, p. 277.
[2] Eccles. Hist. Cent. x, part 2, chap. 3, sec. 2.
[3] See note on the same place.

between the body in which Christ suffered, and that body consecrated in the host. The one was born of the Virgin Mary, consisting of flesh, bones, skin, nerves, human members, and a rational soul; but his spiritual body which we call the *host*, is made of many grains, without blood, bones, members, or soul. The body which once died, and rose from the dead, shall die no more, but is eternal and impassible; but the host is temporal, corruptible, distributed into various parts, ground by the teeth, and passes into the belly; lastly, this is a mystery, pledge and figure; but the body of Christ is truth itself. What is seen is bread,—what is understood spiritually is life."

6. In the beginning of the eleventh century, A. D. 1004, *Leutheric*, Archbishop of Sems, had taught, contrary to the more general opinion, that only the holy and worthy communicants received the body of Christ; but *Robert*, King of France, and the advice of friends, prevented him from raising commotion among the people by the doctrine. But toward the middle of the century, controversy was revived respecting the manner in which Christ's body and blood are present in the Eucharist. In the year 1045, BERENGARIUS, a canon and master of the school at Tours, and afterward Archdeacon of Angers, publicly professed his opposition to the doctrine of PASCHASIUS. He was a man of profound learning and acuteness, but wanting in moral courage to adhere unwaveringly to his profession. He was condemned for heresy by several councils. Leo IX, the Roman Pontiff, in the year 1050, caused his opinion to be condemned, first in a council at Rome, and then in one at Vercelli, and ordered the work of Scotus from which it was derived, to be committed to the flames. BERENGARIUS was not present at either of these councils. Two persons, whom he sent to the latter named council

to maintain his doctrine, were forced to be silent as soon as they had commenced. "A council held at Paris in the same year," says Mosheim, "by Henry, King of France, concurred in the decision of the Pontiff; and issued very severe threats against BERENGARIUS who was absent, and against his adherents who were numerous. A part of these threatenings were felt by BERENGARIUS, for the King deprived him of the income of his office. But neither threats, nor decrees, nor fines, could move him to reject the opinion which he had embraced.

This controversy now rested for some years, and BERENGARIUS who had many enemies, (among whom his rival Lanfranc was the principal,) and also many patrons and friends, was restored to his former tranquillity. But after the death of Leo IX, his adversaries incited Victor II, the new Pontiff, to order the cause to be tried again before his legates, in two councils held at Tours in France, A. D. 1054. In one of these councils in which the celebrated Hildebrand, afterward Gregory VII, was one of the papal legates, BERENGARIUS was present, and being overcome, by threats, undoubtedly, rather than by arguments, he not only gave up his opinion, but (if we may believe his adversaries who are the only witnesses we have) abjured it, and was reconciled to the church. This docility, however, was only feigned; for he soon after went on teaching the same doctrine as before, though perhaps more cautiously. How much censure he deserves for this transaction it is difficult to say, as we are not well informed of what was done at the council.

Nicolaus II being informed of this bad faith of BERENGARIUS, in the year 1058 summoned him to Rome; and in a very full council, held there in the year 1059, he so terrified him, that BERENGARIUS requested a formula of faith to be prescribed for him, which being accordingly done by Humbert,

BERENGARIUS subscribed to it and confirmed it with an oath. In this formula he declares, that he believes "what Nicolaus and the council required to be believed, namely, that the bread and wine after consecration are not only a sacrament, but also the real body and blood of Christ, and are sensibly, and not merely sacramentally, but really and truly handled by the hands of the priests, broken and masticated by the teeth of the faithful."[1] This opinion however was too monstrous to be really believed by such a man as BERENGARIUS, who was a man of discernment and a philosopher. Therefore, when he returned to France, relying, undoubtedly, upon the protection of his patrons, he expressed his detestation, both orally and in his writings, of what he had expressed at Rome, and defended his former sentiments. Alexander II, indeed, admonished him in a friendly letter to reform, but he attempted nothing against him; probably because he perceived him to be upheld by powerful supporters. Of course the controversy was protracted many years in various publications, and the number of BERENGARIUS' followers increased.

When Gregory VII was raised to the Papal chair, he also undertook to settle this controversy, and for this purpose, summoned BERENGARIUS to Rome in the year 1078. He seems to have been attached to BERENGARIUS, and to have yielded rather to the clamors of his adversaries, than to have

---

[1] Ego Berengarius, &c., consentio sanctæ Romanæ sedi, corde profiteor et ore, et—de sacramentis Dominicæ mensæ, eam fidem me tenere quam Dominus Papa Nicolaus et hæc S. Synodus authoritate evangelica et apostolica tenendam tradidit, mihique firmavit; silicet, panem et vinum quæ in altari ponuntur, post consecrationem, verum corpus et sanguinem Domini nostri Jesu Christi esse, et *sensualiter*, non solum sacramento sed veritate, manibus sacerdotum tractari, frangi et fidelium dentibus atteri. Apud Gratian, de Consecr. dis. 2, c. 42.

followed his own inclinations. In a council held
near the close of the year, he allowed the accused
to draw up a new formula of faith for himself, and
to abandon the old formula drawn up by Humbert,
though it had been sanctioned by Nicolaus II and
by a council; for Gregory being a man of discernment, undoubtedly saw the absurdity of that formula. BERENGARIUS, therefore, now professed to believe, and swore that he would in future believe
only, "that the bread of the altar after consecration is the real body of Christ which was born of
the Virgin, suffered on the cross, and is seated at
the right hand of the Father; and that the wine of
the altar after consecration is the real blood which
flowed from Christ's side." But his enemies, maintaining that this formula was ambiguous, were not
satisfied, and demanded that one more definite
might be prescribed for him. To their importunate
demands the Pontiff yielded. The following year
therefore, A. D. 1079, in a council held again at
Rome, BERENGARIUS was required to repeat, subscribe, and swear to a third formula, which was
milder than the first, but harsher than the second.
According to this, he professed to believe, "that
the bread and wine, by the mysterious rite of the
holy prayer, and the words of our Redeemer, are
changed in their substance, into the real and proper
and vivifying flesh and blood of Jesus Christ;" and
he also added to what he had professed by the
second formula, "that the bread and wine are,"
after consecration, "the real body and blood of
Christ, not only by a sign and in virtue of a sacrament, but in their essential properties, and in the
reality of their substance." But this forced profession was only feigned; for as soon as he returned
home he discarded and confuted by a book what he
had professed at Rome in the last council. Indeed,
Martine has published a writing of BERENGARIUS in

which he most humbly begs God to forgive the sin he committed at Rome; and acknowledges, that through fear of death, he assented to the proposed formula, and accused himself of error, contrary to his real belief. "God Almighty," says he, "the fountain of all mercy, have compassion on one who confesses so great a sacrilege."

It appears, however, that Gregory agreed with BERENGARIUS in his views of this sacrament, for just before the last council he addressed him as follows: "I certainly have no doubt that your views of the sacrifice of Christ are correct and agreeable to the Scriptures; yet because it is my custom to recur on important subjects, &c..... I have enjoined upon a friend who is a religious man—to obtain from St. Mary, that she would through him vouchsafe not to conceal from me, but expressly instruct me, what course I should take in the business before me relating to the sacrifice of Christ, that I may persevere in it immovably." And what was her response? He says, "My friend learned from St. Mary and reported to me, that no inquiries were to be made, and nothing to be held respecting the sacrifice of Christ beyond what the authentic Scriptures contain; against which, BERENGARIUS held nothing. This I wished to state to you, that your confidence in us might be more secure, and your anticipations more pleasing." Gregory, therefore, appears to have believed that we should simply hold what the sacred volume was supposed to teach, that the real body and blood of Christ are exhibited in the Eucharist, but should not dispute about the *manner* of it. Besides, he undoubtedly approved of the second formula drawn up by BERENGARIUS himself; for he neither punished his inconsistency, nor manifested displeasure at his recantation of the third formula which had been obtruded upon him, contrary to the inclination of the Pontiff. "He was constrained," says BERENGARIUS, "by the importunity of the buffoon—not bishop—of Padua, and of the antichrist—not bishop—of Pisa, to permit the calumniators of the truth in the last Quadragesimal council, to alter the writing sanctioned by them in the former council." Having experienced much opposition, BERENGARIUS at length retired to the island of St. Cosme near Tours, where he led a solitary life in prayer, fasting, and other devotional exercises, and bitterly repented of his want of firmness and his dissimulation, until the year 1088, when he reached the end of life and persecution. Like some of the Reformers, he appears to have been a consubstantiationist, as we infer from the second formula drawn up by himself, and from his language in a letter to Almannus. "It is evident," says he, "that Christ's true body is placed upon the table, but true spiritually to the interior man; because the incorrupt, untarnished, and unbruised body of Christ is spiritually eaten by those only, who are members of Christ;"[1] and from what his enemies attribute to him. Thus Guitmund observes: "But it is confirmed by the consent of the church universal, that the bread and wine of the altar of the Lord are substantially changed into the body and blood of Christ (not as BERENGARIUS raves, that they are only figures and shadows of the Lord's body and blood, or *cover Christ concealed within themselves.*")[2]

[1] Constat verum Christi corpus in ipsa mensa proponi, sed spiritualiter interiori homini verum, in ea Christi corpus ab his duntaxat, qui Christi membra sunt, incorruptum, intaminatum inattritumque spiritualiter manducari. Martine's Thesaur. tom. iv, p. 109. See Note 23 in Mosheim's Eccles. Hist. Cent. xi, part ii, chap. 3, sec. 18.

[2] Sed panem et vinum altaris Domini in corpus et sanguinem Christi substantialiter commutari, (non sicut delirat Berengarius corporis et sanguinis Domini figuras tantum esse

From the foregoing considerations we may remark, that in the eleventh age, the belief of the Romish Church, respecting the Eucharist, had not come to any fixed determination, as the three formulas of BERENGARIUS evince, beyond successful controversy; for they most manifestly disagree, not in words only, but in import.

Nicolaus II and his council decided, that the first formula which Cardinal Humbert drew up, was sound and contained the true doctrine of the church. But this was rejected, and deemed too crude and erroneous, not only by Gregory, but also by his two councils that tried the cause. For if the Pontiff and his councils had believed that this formula expressed the true sense of the church, they would never have suffered another to be substituted for it. Besides, the gloss upon the canon law says, "that, unless, we understand these words of BERENGARIUS in a sound sense, we shall fall into a greater heresy than that of BERENGARIUS; for we do not make parts of the body of Christ." As we have seen, Gregory supposed that the doctrine of this sacrament, was not to be explained too minutely, but that, dismissing all questions, as to the *mode* of Christ's presence, the words of the sacred volume were simply to be adhered to; and as BERENGARIUS had done this in his formula, the Pontiff pronounced him no offender. But the last council departed from the opinion of the Pontiff; and the Pontiff, though reluctant, suffered himself to be drawn over to the opinion of the council. Hence, the third formula, disagreeing with both the former ones."[1]

"In the commencement of the eleventh century," says Elliott, "Aelfrick, Archbishop of Canterbury, in his Saxon Homily, maintains the doctrine of

et umbras, aut intra se latentem Christum tegere) universalis Ecclesiae consensione roboratum est. Guitmundi, lib. iii, de Sacramento.

[1] See Mosheim's Eccles. Hist. in loco cit.

Bertram, and in nearly his words. In his letter to Wulfin, Bishop of Schirburn, he says: 'That housel (*i. e.* sacrament) is Christ's body, not bodily, but spiritually; not the body which he suffered in, but the body of which he spoke when he blessed the bread and wine to housel the night before his suffering, and said by the blessed bread, "This is my body.'" And in writing to the Archbishop of York, he said: 'The Lord halloweth daily, by the hand of the priest, bread to his body, and wine to his blood, in spiritual mystery, as we read in books. And yet notwithstanding, that lively bread is not bodily so, nor the self-same body that Christ suffered in.' From these quotations it appears that transubstantiation had not yet made much progress in England."[1]

7. Nor was this the settled doctrine of the Church in the twelfth century, as we learn from the following testimonies.

St. Bernard says: "Many things are done for their own sake only, others to designate something else; and these are called and are signs. A ring is given on its own account, absolutely, and then there is nothing signified. It is also given for investing some one with an inheritance; and then it is a sign; so that he who takes the ring may now say; the ring of itself is of no avail; but it is the inheritance which I sought. In this manner, therefore, did our Lord, when he approached his passion, take care that his disciples should be invested with his grace, so that, by some visible sign, his invisible grace should be afforded. For this end have all sacraments been instituted, and for this is the Eucharist to be received."[2] He also teaches, "that

---

[1] Vol. i, p. 278. See Usher's Answer, p. 79, and Bishop Taylor on the Real Presence, sec. 12, Id.

[2] ..... In hunc itaque modum, appropinquans passioni Dominus, de gratia sua investiri curavit suos, ut invisibilis gratia signo aliquo visibili præstaretur. Ad hæc instituta

the body of Christ is, in a mystery, the food of the mind and not of the body; it is, therefore, not eaten *corporeally;* for such as is this food, so it is understood to be eaten."[1]

Peter Lombard, Master of the Sentences, A. D. 1160, says: "If it be inquired what kind of conversion it is, whether it be formal or substantial, or of another kind, I am not able to define it; only I know that it is not formal, because the same accidents remain, the same color and taste. To some it seems to be substantial, saying, that so the substance is changed into the substance, that it is done essentially; to which the former authorities seem to consent. But to this sentence others oppose these things; if the substance of bread and wine be substantially converted into the body and blood of Christ, then every day some substance is made the body and blood of Christ, which before was not the body; and to-day something is Christ's body which was not yesterday; and every day Christ's body is increased, and is made of such matter of which it was not made in the conception."[2] In his time there "appear to have been four opinions permitted and disputed. The first was that of consubstantiation; the second, that the substance of bread is made the flesh of Christ, but ceases not to be what it was; another was, that the substance of bread is not converted, but annihilated; and a fourth was the doctrine of transubstantiation, confusedly held and variously defended and explained."

sunt omnia sacramenta, ad hæc Eucharistiæ participatio. Serm. de Cœna. Dom. in Joan. vi.

[1] Quod Christi corpus in mysterio cibus mentis sit et non ventris, proinde corporaliter non manducatur; sicut enim cibus est, ita et comedi intelligatur. Idem, Serm. de Purif. B. Mariæ.

[2] Lib. iii, de Euch., c. 23, sec. unum tamen. Sum. lib. iii, c. 20. See Bishop Taylor's Dissuasive, sec. iv, paragraph, *Now for this,* &c.

The opinions of Christian doctors concerning the *manner* in which the body and blood of Christ are present in the Eucharist were, therefore, somewhat various in the twelfth century; nor had the church determined, by any clear and positive decree, her precise doctrine on this point.

8. But it was Innocent III who pronounced the opinion that is now embraced by the Church of Rome. He summoned a council consisting of four hundred and twelve bishops in person, about eight hundred abbots and priors, and a large number of deputies of the absent bishops and of the chapters.

The council met in the Church of St. Saviour de Lateran, November, 1215. The Pope read seventy canons or decrees, already drawn up without any deliberation, debate, or voting on the part of the council. In proof of this statement, the language of Dupin, in his account of this council, may be quoted. "It is certain," says he, "that these canons were not made by the council, but by Innocent III, who presented them to the council ready drawn up, and ordered them to be read; and that the prelates did not enter into any debate upon them, but that their silence was taken for an approbation." These decrees, or canons, though not ordained by the council, obtained reputation by being inserted among the decretals of Gregory IX, which was done, not in the name of the council, but in the name of Innocent. They were first published under the name of the Lateran Council in 1538, by John Cochlæus. The decree on transubstantiation is as follows: "The body and blood of Christ are contained really in the sacrament of the altar under the species of bread and wine; the bread being transubstantiated into the body of Jesus Christ, and the wine into his blood, by divine power."[1] For this wonderful tran-

[1] Concil. Lateran iv, cap. i.

substantiation the following curious reason is assigned: "That we might receive of Christ's nature what he had received of ours." The word transubstantiation was first used by Stephen, Bishop of Augustodunum, and so pleased Innocent, that he inserted it in his decrees proposed to the council.[1]

From the foregoing it appears, that instead of the change in the doctrine of the Eucharist having been effected suddenly, as you suppose, it required centuries, for men so far to abandon their better reason and judgment, as to receive the dogma in question, as a doctrine of Christianity.

In conclusion, I have now performed the task imposed by your denial of the fact, that the Fathers of the first six or seven centuries after Christ, speak of the Eucharist as the *figure* of Christ's broken body and shed blood. In doing this, recourse has been had, in all possible cases, to the original documents of the ancient Church. And where I have been unable to consult the original author, I have availed myself of the productions of those only, in whom I could confide, as learned and reliable writers.

The evidence which has been adduced, both express and constructive, would seem to be sufficient, to satisfy any honest mind not so wedded to a system, as to be proof against the grounds of rational belief. All which is commended to your candid and prayerful consideration, as a fellow-traveler toward that final tribunal, where even the thoughts of the heart shall be laid open to the All-seeing eye of God.

With the continued and sincere regards of
    Your fellow-servant and Brother,
                      E. O. P.

---

[1] See Elliott on Romanism, vol. i, Book ii, chap. 4.

APPENDIX.

LETTER III.

^A *Spiritus est enim, inquit, qui vivificat; caro autem nihil prodest.* Tunc autem, quando hoc Dominus commendavit, de carne sua locutus erat, et dixerat: *Nisi quis manducaverit, carnem meam, non habebit in se vitam æternam.* Scandalizati sunt discipuli ejus quidam, septuaginta ferme, et dixerunt: *Durus est hic sermo; quis potest eum intelligere?* et recesserunt ab eo, ut amplius cum eo non ambulaverunt. Durum illis visum est quod ait, *Nisi, quis manducaverit carnem meam, non habebit vitam æternam:* acceperunt illud stulte, carnaliter illud cogitaverunt, et putaverunt quod præcisurus esset Dominus particulas quasdam de corpore suo, et datarus illis, et dixerunt, *Durus est hic sermo.* Ipsi erant duri, non sermo. Etenim si duri non essent, sed mites essent, dicerent sibi: Non sine causa dicit hoc, nisi quia est ibi aliquod sacramentum latens. Manerent cum illo lenes, non duri; et discerent ab illo, quod, illis discedentibus, qui remanserunt, didicerunt. Nam cùm remansissent cum illo discipuli duodecim, illis recedentibus, suggesserunt illi, tanquam dolentes illorum mortem, quod scandalizati sunt in verbo ejus et recesserunt. Ille autem instruxit eos et ait illis, *Spiritus est qui vivificat; caro autem nihil prodest: verba quæ locutus sum vobis, spiritus est et vita.* Spiritualiter intelligite quod locutus sum: non hoc corpus quod videtis, manducaturi estis; et bibituri illum sanguinem, quem fusuri sunt qui me crucifigent. Sacramentum aliquod vobis commendavi; spiritualiter intellectum vivificabit vos. Etsi necesse est illud visibiliter celebrari, oportet tamen invisibiliter intelligi.

^B Καὶ ἐνταῦϑα γαρ αμφοτερα περι εαυτου εἴρηκε σαρκα και πνευμα· και το πνευμα, προς το κατα σαρκα διεστειλεν, ινα μη μονον το φαινομενον αλλα και το αορατον αυτου πιττευσαντες μαϑωσιν, οτι και α λεγει, ουκ εστι σαρκικα, αλλα πνευματικα. Ποσοισ γαρ ηρκει το σωμα προς βρωσιν, ινα

και του κοσμου παντος τουτο τροφη γενηται; Αλλα δια
τουτο της εις ουρανους αναβασεως εμνημονευσε του υιου του
ανθρωπου, ινα της σωματικης εννοιας αυτους αφελκυση, και
λοιπον την ειρημενην σαρκα βρωσιν ανωθεν ουρανιον, και πνευματικην τροφην παρ' αυτου διδομενην μαθωσιν· α γαρ λελαληκα,
φησιν, ημιν, πνευμα εστι και ζωη· ισον τω ειπειν, το μεν
δεικνυμενον και διδομενον υπερ της του κοσμου σωτηριας,
εστιν η σαρξ ην εγω φορω· αλλ' αυτη υμιν και το ταυτης αιμα
παρ' εμου πνευματικως δοθησεται τροφη, ωστε πνευματικως
εν εκαστω ταυτην αναδιδοσθαι, και γινεσθαι πασι φυλακτηριον
εις αναστασιν ζωης αιωνιον.

LETTER IV.

^AΟυχ ηδομαι τροφη φθορας, ουδε ηδοναις του βιου τουτου·
αρτον του Θεου θελω αρτον ουρανιον, αρτον ζωης ο εστι σαρξ
Ιησου Χριστου του υιου του Θεου, του γενομενου εν υστερω εκ
σπερματος Δαβιδ και Αβρααμ· και πομα θελω το αιμα αυτου,
ο εστιν αγαπη αφθαρτος, και αενναος ζωη.

^BΔια τουτο ως νηπιοις, ο αρτος ο τελειος του Πατρος γαλα
ημιν εαυτον παρεσχεν, οπερ ην η κατ' ανθρωπον αυτου παρουσια,
ινα ως υπο μασθου της σαρκος αυτου, τραφεντες, και δια της
τοιαυτης γαλακτουργιας εθισθεντες τρωγειν και πινειν τον
λογον του Θεου, τον της αθανασιας αρτον, οπερ εστι το πνευμα
του Πατρος, εν ημιν αυτοις κατεσχειν δυνηθωμεν.

^cEtsi carnem ait nihil prodesse, ex materia dicti dirigen-
dus est sensus. Nam, quia durum et intolerabilem existima-
verunt sermonem ejus, quasi vere carnem suam illis edendam
determinasset; ut in spiritum disponeret statum salutis, præ-
misit, spiritus est qui vivificat. Atque ita subjunxit, caro nihil
prodest; ad vivificandum scilicet. Exequitur etiam quid
velit intelligi spiritum, verba quæ locutus sum vobis, spiritus sunt; vita sunt. Sicut et supra, qui audit sermones meos
et credit in eum qui me misit, habet vitam æternam, et in judicium non veniet, sed transiet de morte ad vitam. Itaque
sermonem constituens vivificatorem, quia spiritus et vita sermo eundem etiam carnem suam dixit; quia et sermo caro est
factus, proinde in causam vitæ appetendus, et devorandus
auditu, et ruminandus intellectu, et fide digerendus. Nam
et paulo ante carnem suam panem quoque cœlestem pronun-

ciarat, urgens usquequaque per allegoriam necessariorum pabulorum, memoriam patrum, qui panes et carnes Egyptiorum præverterant divinae vocationi. Igitur conversus ad recogitatus illorum quia senserat dispergendos, caro, ait, nihil prodest. Quid hoc ad destruendam carnis resurrectionem?

^DSed quam eleganter divina sapientia ordinem Orationis instruxit! ut post cœlestia, id est, post Dei nomen, Dei voluntatem, et Dei regnum, terrenis quoque necessitatibus petitioni locum facerat: nam edixerat Dominus; Quærite prius regnum, et tunc vobis etiam hæc adjicientur. Quamquam panem nostrum quotidianum da nobis hodie spiritaliter potius intelligamus, Christus enim panis noster est; quia vita Christus, et vita panis, Ego sum, inquit, panis vitæ, Et paulo supra; panis est sermo Dei vivi, qui descendit de cœlis. Tunc quod et corpus ejus in pane censetur: hoc est corpus meum. Itaque petendo panem quotidianum, perpetuitatem postulamus in Christo, et individuitatem a corpore ejus. Sed et quia carnaliter admittitur ita vox, non sine religione protest fieri et spiritalis disciplinæ.

^EPanem nostrum quotidianum da nobis hodie. Quod potest et spiritaliter et simpliciter intelligi, quia et uterque intellectus utilitate divina proficit ad salutem. Nam panis vita Christus est, et panis hic omnium non est, sed nostra est. Et quomodo dicimus pater noster, quia intelligentium et credentium pater est; Sic et panem nostrum vocamus, quia Christus, noster qui corpus ejus contingimus, panis est. Hunc autem panem dari nobis quotidie postulamus, ne qui in Christo sumus, et eucharistiam quotidie ad cibum salutis accepimus, intercedente aliquo graviore delicto, dum abstenti et non communicantes a cœlesti pane prohibemur, a Christo corpore separemur, ipso prædicante et monente: Ego sum panis vitæ qui de cœlo decendi; si quis ederit de meo pane, vivet in æternum; panis autem quem ego dedero caro mea est pro sæculi vita. Quando ergo dicit, in æternum vivere si quis ederit de ejus pane, ut manifestum est eos vivere qui corpus ejus attingunt et eucharistiam jure communicationis accipiunt, ita contra timendum est et orandum, ne dum quis abstentus separatur a Christi corpore, procul remaneat a salute; comminante ipso et dicente, nisi ederitis carnem filii hominis et biberitis sanguinem ejus, non habebitis vitam in vobis.

^FἈλλαχοθι δε και ὁ Κυριος εν τω κατα Ιωαννην Ευαγγελιω, ετερως εξηνεγκεν δια συμβολων· φαγεσθε μου τας σαρκας,

ειπων και πιεσθε μου το αιμα· εναργες της πιστεως και της
επαγγελιας το ποτιμον αλληγορων, δι ων η εκκλησια, καθαπερ
ανθρωπος, εκ πολλων συνεστηκυια μελων, αρδεται τε και
αυξεται, συγκροτειται τε και συμπηγνυται εξ αμφοιν· σωματος
μεν, της πιστεως· ψυχης δε, της ελπιδος, ωσπερ και ο Κυριος
εκ σαρκος και αιματος· τω γαρ οντι αιμα της πιστεως η
ελπις εφ᾽ ης συνεχεται, καθαπερ υπο ψυχης, η πιστις.

G 'Ο Λογος τα παντα τω νηπιω, και πατηρ και μητηρ, και
παιδαγωγος και τροφευς. Φαγεσθε μου Φησι, την σαρκα, και
πιεσθε μου το αιμα. Ταυτας ημιν 'οικειας τροφας ὁ Κυριος
χορηγει, και σαρκα 'ορεγει και αιμα εκχεει και ουδεν εις
αυξησιν τοις παιδιοις ενδει· ὦ του παραδοξου μυστηριου!
Αποδυσασθαι ημιν την παλαιαν και σαρκικην εγκελευεται
φθοραν, ωσπερ και την παλαιαν τροφην. καινης δε αλλης της
Χριστου διαιτης μεταλαμβανοντας, εκεινον, ει δυνατον, ανα-
λαμβανοντας, εν εαυτοις αποτιθεσθαι, και τον σωτηρα ενστερ-
νισασθαι· ινα καταρτισωμεν της σαρκος ημων τα παθη.
'Αλλ᾽ ου ταυτη· νοειν εθελεις, κοινοτερον δε ισως. Ακουε
και ταυτη· σαρκα ημιν το Πνευμα το αγιον αλληγορει. και
γαρ υπ᾽ αυτου του δεδημιουργηται ἡ σαρξ. Αιμα ημιν τον
Λογον αινιττεται· και γαρ ως αιμα πλουσιον, ὁ Λογος επι-
κεχυται τω βιω· ἡ κρασις δε ἡ αμφοιν, ὁ Κυριος, ἡ τροφη
των νηπιων· ὁ Κυριος. Πνευμα και Λογος· ἡ τροφη, τουεστι
Κυριος Ιησους, τουεστιν ὁ Λογος του Θεου, Πνευμα σαρκουμε-
νον· αγιαζομενη σαρξ ουρανιος· ἡ τροφη, το γαλα του Πατρος,
ω μονω τιθηνουμεθα οι νηπιοι.

H .... Ουτως πολλαχως αλληγορειται ὁ Λογος. και βρωμα,
και σαρξ, και τροφη, και αρτος, και αιμα, και γαλα απαντα ὁ
Κυριος, εις απολαυσιν ημων των εις αυτον πεπιστευκοτων.

I .... Οτι δε το αιμα ὁ Λογος εστιν, μαρτυρει του Αβελ
του δικαιου το αιμα εντυγχανον τω Θεω.

J 'Αρα και αιμα και γαλα, του Κυριου παθους και διδασκαλιας
συμβολον.

K Διττον δε το αιμα του Κυριου· το μεν γαρ 'εστιν 'αυτου σαρ-
κικον, ω της φθορας λελυτρωμεθα. το δε πνευματικον, τουτεστιν
ω κεχρισμεθα. Και τουτ᾽ εστι πιειν το αιμα του Ιησου, της
κυριακης μεταλαβειν 'αφθαρσιας.

ᴹ'Ει τίνυν το μεν γαλα, των νηπιων· το βρωμα δε, των τελει-
ων τροφη προς του Αποστολου ειρηται, γαλα μεν η κατηχησις,
οιονει πρωτη ψυχης τροφη, νοηθησεται· βρωμα δε η εποπτικη
θεωρια· σαρκες αυται και αιμα του Λογου, τουεστι, καταληψις
της θειας δυναμεως και ουσιας. Γευσασθε και ιδετε οτι Χριστος
ὁ Κυριος, φησιν· ουτως γαρ εαυτου μεταδιδωσι τοις πνευματικω-
τερον της τοιαυτης μεταλαμβανουσι βρωσεως.

ᴺ Si perfecta loquimur, si robusta si fortiora, carnes vobis
Verbi Dei apponimus comedendas.

ᴼ "Αρτον αγγελων εφαγεν ανθρωπος; κ. τ. λ 'Ο Σωτηρ φησιν·
εγω ειμι ὁ αρτος ὁ εκ του ουρανου καταβας. Τουτον ουν τον αρτον
ησθιον μεν προτερον αγγελοι, νυνι δε και ανθρωποι. Το εσθιειν
ενταυθα το γινωσκειν σημαινει· τουτο γαρ εσθιει νους ὁ δε γινωσκει,
και τουτο ουκ εσθιει ὁ ου γινωσκει.

ᴾ Ergo de litera quidem egredimur legis; infra virtutem
autem spiritalem legem constitui, spiritaliter celebrantes im-
plemus omnia quæ illic corporaliter celebranda mandantur.
Expellimus enim vetus fermentum malitiæ et nequitiæ, et in
azymis sinceritatis et veritatis celebramus pascha, Christo
nobiscum cæpulante secundum voluntatem agni dicentis:
Nisi manducaveritis carnem meam, et biberitis sanguinem
meum, non habebitis vitam manentem in vobis.

ᵠ In occultis enim et in azymis invisibilibus epulantur sinceritatis et veritatis: manducant etiam pascha immolatum
Christum pro nobis, qui dixit; Nisi manducaveritis carnem
meam, non habebitis vitam manentem in vobis.

Et per hoc quod bibunt sanguinem ejus verum potum, un-
gunt superliminaria domorum animæ suae, quærentes, non
sicut illi, ab hominibus gloriam, sed a Deo occulta videnti.

ᴿ .... Jesus ergo quia totus ex toto mundus est, tota
ejus caro cibus est, et totus sanguis ejus potus est; quia omne
opus ejus sanctum est, et omnis sermo ejus verus est. Propterea ergo et caro ejus verus est cibus, et sanguis ejus verus
est potus. Carnibus enim et sanguine verbi sui tanquam mundo cibo ac potu, potat et reficit omne hominum genus.

ˢ .... Est enim et in Evangeliis litera quae occidit, non
solum in veteri Testamento occidens litera deprehenditur.
Est et in novo Testamento litera, quæ occidat eum, qui non
spiritaliter quæ dicuntur advertit. Si enim secundum literam
sequaris hoc ipsum quod dictum est: Nisi manducaveritis

carnem meam, et biberitis sanguinem meum, occidit hæc litera.

ᵀ .... Αποδεικνυμεν οτι ουκ αν τοσουτον ανοητοι ησαν οι ακουοντες, ως υπολαμβανειν οτι προκαλειται ο λεγων τους ακροατας εις το προσελθειν, και εμφαγειν του σαρκην αυτου.

ᵁ Bibere dicimus sanguinem Christi, non solum sacramentorum ritu, sed rt cum sermones ejus recipimus, in quibus vita consistit, sicut et ipse dicit, verba quæ locutus sum, spiritus et vita est. Est ergo ipse vulneratus, cujus nos sanguinem bibimus, id est, doctrinæ ejus verba suscipimus.

ᵛ Μη γαρ την σαρκα, ην περικειμαι, γυμισητε με λεγειν, ως δεον αυτην εσθιειν, μη δε το αισθητον και σωματικον αιμα πινειν, υπολαμβανετε με προστατσειν .... ωστε αυτα ειναι τα ρηματα και τους λογους αυτου την σαρκα και το αιμα .... Ταυτα γαρ ουδεν ωφελει αισθητως ακουομενα, το δε πνευμα εστι το ζωοποιουν τους πνευματικως ακουειν δυναμενους.

ᵂ .... Και οτε παλιν ο Κυριος λεγει περι αυτου, εγω ειμι ο αρτος ο ζων, ο εκ του ουρανου καταβας. Αλλαχου το αγιον Πνευμα καλει αρτον ουρανιον λεγων, τον αρτον ημων τον επιουσιον δος ημιν σημερον. Εδιδαξε γαρ ημας εν τη ευχη εν τω νυν αιωνι αιτειν τον επιουσιον αρτον, τουεστι τον μελλοντα, ου 'απαρχην εχομεν εν τη νυν ζωη της σαρκος του Κυριου μεταλαμβανοντες καθως αυτος ειπε, και ο αρτος δε ον εγω δωσω η σαρξ μου εστιν υπερ της του κοσμου ζωης. Πνευμα γαρ ζωοποιουν η σαρξ εστι του Κυριου.

ˣ .... Εκεινοι μη ακηκοες πνευματικως των λεγομενων σκανδαλισθεντες, απηλθον εις τα οπισω, νομιζοντες οτι επι σαρκοφαγιαν αυτους προτρεπεται.

ʸ Ὁ τρωγων με, φησι, ζησεται δι' εμε· τρωγομεν γαρ αυτου την σαρκα, και πινομεν αυτου το αιμα, κοινωνοι γινομενοι δια της ενανθρωπησεως, και της αισθητης ζωης του λογου και της σοφιας· σαρκα γαρ και αιμα πασαν αυτου την μυστικην επιδημιαν ονομασε· και την εκ πρακτικης και φυσικης και θεολογικης συνεστωσαν διδασκαλιαν εδηλωσε, δι' ης τρεφεται ψυχη.

ᶻ Legimus sanctas Scripturas. Ego corpus Iesu, evangelium puto; Sanctas Scripturas, puto doctrinam ejus. Et quando dicit; qui non comederit carnem meam, et biberit sanguinem meum: licet et in mysterio possit intelligi, tamen verius corpus Christi, et sanguis ejus, sermo Scripturarum est doctrina divina est. Si quando imus ad mysterium: qui fidelis est, intelligit: si in maculam ceciderit periclitatur. Si quando audimus sermonem Dei, et sermo Dei, et caro Christi, et sanguis ejus in auribus nostris funditur, et nos aliud cogitamus, in quantum periculum incurrimus! .... Sic et in carne Christi, qui est sermo doctrinæ, hoc est, Scripturarum Sanctarum interpretatio, sicut volumus, ita et cibum accipimus. Si sanctus es, invenis refrigerium; si peccator es, invenis tormentum.

a Secundum tropologiam possumus dicere, omnes voluptatis magis amatores quam amatores Dei sanctificari in hortis et in liminibus quia mysteria veritatis non valent introire, et comedere cibos impietatis, dum non sunt sancti corpore et spiritu; nec comedunt carnem Jesu, neque bibunt sanguinem ejus. De quo ipse loquitur, qui comedit carnem meam, et bibit sanguinem meum, habet vitam æternam. Etenim pascha nostrum immolatus est Christus. Qui non foris, sed in domo una et intus comeditur.

b Si præceptiva est locutio, aut flagitium aut facinus vetans, aut beneficentiam jubens, non est figurata. Si autem flagitium aut facinus videtur jubere, aut utilitatem aut beneficentiam vetare, figurata est. Nisi manducaveritis carnem filii hominis, etc,—facinus vel flagitium videtur jubere; figura ergo est præcipiens passioni Domini esse communicandum, et suaviter atque utiliter in memoria condendum, quod caro ejus pro nobis crucifixa et vulnerata est.

c .... Hoc est opus Dei, ut credatis in eum quem misit ille. Hoc est ergo manducare cibum non qui perit, sed qui permanet in vitam æternam. Ut quid paras dentes et ventrem? Crede et manducasti.

d Denique jam exponit quomodo id fiat quod loquitur, et quid sit manducare corpus ejus, et sanguinem bibere. Qui manducat, etc. Hoc est ergo manducare illam escam et illum bibere potum, in Christo manere, et illum manentem in se habere. Ac per hoc qui non manet in Christo et in quo non manet Christus, proculdubio nec manducat [spiritaliter] carnem ejus, nec bibit ejus sanguinem [licet carnaliter et visibiliter premat dentibus sacramentum corporis et sanguinis Christi;] sed magis tantæ rei sacramentum ad judicium sibi manducat et bibit.

e Hunc locum veteres interpretantur de doctrina cœlesti.

f Και το μεν, εις πιστιν ευωχει, το κριμα . . . . ἧς οι κατα πιστιν μεταλαμβανοντες, αγιαζονται και σωμα και ψυχην.

g . . . . Ἐν τυπω γαρ αρτον, διδοται σοι το σωμα· και εν τυπω οινου, διδοται σοι το αιμα· ινα γενη, μεταλαβων σωματος και αιματος Χριστου, συσσωμος και συναιμος αυτου.

LETTER V.

A Ἡ αληθεια δε ουκ εν τω μετατιθεναι τα σημαινομενα ευρισκεται· ουτω μεν γαρ ανατρεψουσι πασαν αληθη διδασκαλιαν· αλλ εν τω διασκεψασθαι τι τω Κυριω και τω παντοκρατορι Θεω τελειως οικειον τε και πρεπον· κ'αν τω βεβαιων εκαστον των αποδεικνυμενων κατα τας γραφας, εξ αυτων παλιν των ομοιων γραφων.

LETTER VI.

A Loquebatur enim de præsentia corporis sui.

Nam secundum majestatem suam, secundum providentiam, secundum ineffabilem et invisibilem gratiam impletur quod ab eo dictum est; Ecce ego vobiscum sum usque in consummationem seculi! Secundum carnem verò quam verbum assumpsit, secundum id quod de virgine natus est, secundum id quod a Judæis prehensus est, quod ligno crucifixus, quod de cruce depositus, quod linteis involutus, quod in sepulchro conditus, quod in resurrectione manifestatus non semper habebitis vobiscum. Quare? Quoniam conversatus est secundum præsentiam quadraginta diebus cum discipulis suis, et eis deducentibus videndo non sequendo, ascendit in cœlum, et non est hic.

B Ουδαμου της των φυσεων διαφορας ανηρημενης δια την ενωσιν, σωζομενης δε μαλλον της ιδιοτητος εκατερας φυσεως, και εις ἑν προσωπον, και μιαν ὑποστασιν συντρεχουσης.

C Quoniam extra potentiam Dei nihil est, idcirco omnia potest. . . . . Omnia enim quæcunque voluit Dominus fecit, in cœlo et in terra.

Et quid voluit, licet figura panis et vini hic sit, omnino nihil aliud quàm caro Christi et sanguis post consecrationem credenda sunt.

Unde ipsa veritas ad discipulas.
Hæc, inquit, caro mea est pro mundi vita.
Et ut mirabilius loquar, non alia planè, quam quæ nata est de Maria, et passa in cruce, et resurrexit de sepulchro. Hæc, inquam, ipsa est, et ideo Christi caro est, quæ pro mundi vita adhuc hodie offertur.

ᴰ Planè nihil Deo difficile. Sed si tam abrupte in præsumptionibus nostris hac sententiâ utamur, quidvis de Deo confingere poterimus, quasi fecerit, quia facere potuerit. Non autem quia omnia potest facere, ideo utique credendum est illum fecisse, etiam quod non fecerit, sed an fecerit, requirendum. Potuit, ita salvus sim, Deus pennis hominem ad volandum instruxisse, quod et milvis præstitit; non tamen quia potuit, statim et fecit. Potuit et Praxeam, et omnes pariter hæreticos statim extinxisse; non tamen quia potuit, extinxit. .... Hac ratione erit aliquid et difficile Deo; id scilicet quodcunque non fecerit, non quia non potuerit, sed quia noluerit. Dei enim posse, velle est; et non posse, nolle.

ᴱ Και ουκ εις ατοπωτατην τε αναχωρησιν αναχωρουμεν, λεγοντες οτι παν δυνατον τω Θεω .... Φαμεν δε οτι ου δυναται αισχρα ὁ Θεος, επει εσται ὁ Θεος, ουκ εστι Θεος .... και ημεις λεγομεν, οτι ου βουλεται τα παρα φυσιν ὁ Θεος, ουτε τα απο κακιας, ουτε τα αλογως γινομενα· ει δε τα κατα λογον Θεου και βουλησιν αυτου γινομενα αναγκαιως ευθεως ειναι μη παρα φυσιν· ου παρα φυσιν τα πραττομενα ὑπο του Θεου, κ' αν παραδοξα ῇ; ἤ δοκουντα τισι παραδοξα. Ει δε χρη βεβιασμενως ονομασαι· ερουμεν, οτι ως προς την κοινοτεραν νουμενην φυσιν εστι τινα υπερ την φυσιν ἅ ποιησαι αν ποτε Θεος, υπερ τον ανθρωπινην φυσιν αναβιβαζων τον ανθρωπον, και ποιων αυτον μεταβαλλειν επι φυσιν κρειττονα και θειοτεραν.

ᶠ Patet quod ille modus est possibilis, nec repugnat rationi, nec auctoritati Bibliæ, imo est facilior ad intelligendum et rationabilior quam aliquis aliorum.

ᴳ Scotus dicit non extare locum ullum Scripturæ tam expressum, ut sine declaratione ecclesiæ, evidenter cogat transubstantionem admittere, et id non omnino improbabile.

ᴴ Alterum quod evangelium non explicavit expresse, ab ecclesia accepimus, scilicet, conversionem panis in corpus Christi non explicate habetur in Evangelio .... Non apparet ex Evangelio coactivum aliquod ad intelligendum hæc verba proprie, nempe, *Hoc est corpus meum;* imo præsentia illa in sacramento, quam tenet ecclesia, ex his verbis Christi, non potest demonstrari, nisi etiam accesserit ecclesiæ declaratio.

LETTER VII.

A Harum et aliarum ejusmodi disciplinarum, si leges expostules scripturarum, nullam invenies.

Traditio tibi prætenditur auctrix, consuetudo confirmatrix, et fides observatrix.

B Ad hoc malorum devoluta est Ecclesia Dei et sponsa Christi, ... ut ad celebranda sacramenta cœlestia, disciplinam lux de tenebris mutuetur, et id faciunt Christiani, quod Antichristi faciunt.

C 'Ουκ ως Πετρος και Παυλος διατασσομαι υμιν. 'Εκεινοι αποστολοι Ιησου Χριστου, εγω δε ελαχιστος.

D Nihil in his ut verbis meis credatur exposco, nisi testes idoneos dedero. Ipsum vobis Dominum, et Salvatorem nostrum Jesum Christum testem horum et auctorem dabo.

E Μηδε εμοι τω ταυτα σοι λεγοντι απλως πιστευσης, εαν την αποδειξιν των καταγγελλομενων απο των θειων μη λαβης γραφων· η σωτηρια γαρ αυτη της πιστεως ημων ουκ εξ ευρεσιλογιας, αλλα εξ αποδειξεων των θειων εστι γραφων.

F Quod genus literarum, non cum credendi necessitate, sed cum judicandi libertate legendum est . . . . Sed nullo modo illi sacratissimæ canonicarum Scripturarum excellentiæ coæquantur, etiam in quibuscumque eorum invenitur eadem veritas, longe tamen est impar auctoritas.

G Scio me aliter habere Apostolas; aliter reliquos tractatores; illos semper vera dicere; istos in quibusdam, ut homines errare.

H Erraverunt in fide alii, tam Græci quam Latini, quorum non necesse est proferre nomina, ne videamur cum, non sui merito sed aliorum errore, defendere.

I Σπουδαζετε ουν πυκνοτερον συνερχεσθαι εις ευχαριστιαν Θεου, και δοξαν· οταν γαρ συνεχως επι το αυτο γενεσθε, καθαιρουνται αι δυναμεις σατανα, και απρακτα αυτου επιστρεφει τα πεπυρωμενα βελη προς αμαρτιαν.

J .... ἕνα αρτον κλωντες, ὅ εστι φαρμακον ἀθανασιας, αντιδο-
τος του μη αποθανουν, αλλα ζην εν Θεω δια Ιησου Χριστου.

K Vos igitur mansuetam patientiam resumentes recreate
vosmetipsos in fide quod est caro Domini, et in charitate quod
est sanguis Iesu Christi. Nullus vestrum adversus proximum
aliquid habeat.

L 'Ου γαρ ως κοινον αρτον ουδε κοινον πομα ταυτα λαμβανομεν·
αλλ ὅν τροπον δια λογου Θεου σαρκοποιηθεις Ιησους Χριστος ὁ
Σωτηρ ημων, και σαρκα και αιμα υπερ σωτηριας ημων εχεν, ουτως
και την δι ευχης λογου του παρ' αυτου ευχαριστηθεισαν τροφην,
εξ ἧς αιμα και σαρκες κατα μεταβολην τρεφονται ημων, εκεινου
του σαρκοποιηθεντος Ιησου και σαρκα και αιμα εδιδαχθημεν ειναι...

M .... Οποτε ουν και το κεκραμενον ποτηριον, και ὁ γεγονως
αρτος επιδεχεται τον λογον του Θεου, και γινεται ἡ ευχαριστια
σωμα Χριστου, εκ τουτων δε αυξει και συνισταται ἡ της σαρκος
ημων υποστασις.

N Cum gratias egisset, tenens calicem, et bibisset ab eo, et
dedisset discipulis, dicebat eis. Bibite ex eo omnes.

O .... Sic enim Deus in Evangelio quoque vestro revela-
vit panem corpus suum appellans, ut et hinc jam eum intelli-
gas corporis sui figuram pani dedisse cujus retro corpus in
panem Prophetes figuravit, ipso Domino hoc sacramentum
postea interpretaturo.

P Sed ille quidem usque nunc nec aquam reprobavit Creatoris, qua suos abluit, nec oleum, quo suos unguit, nec mellis
et lactis societatem, qua suos infantat nec panem quo ipsum
corpus suum repræsentat; etiam in sacramentis propriis egens
mendicitatibus Creatoris.

Q Acceptum panem, et distributum discipulis, corpus illum
suum fecit, hoc est corpus meum dicendo, id est, figura corporis mei. Figura autem non fuisset, nisi veritatis esset corpus. Ceterum, vacua res, quod est phantasma figuram capere
non posset.
Aut si propterea panem corpus sibi finxit, quia corporis
carebat veritate: ergo panem debuit tradere pro nobis. Fa-
ciebat ad vanitatem Marcionis, ut panis crucifigeretur....
Itaque illuminator antiquitatum, quid tunc voluerit signifi-
casse panem, satis declaravit, corpus suum vocans panem.
Sic et in calicis mentione testamentum constituens sanguine

suo obsignatum, substantiam corporis confirmavit. Nullius enim corporis sanguis potest esse, nisi carnis. Nam et si qua corporis qualitas non carnea opponetur nobis, certo sanguinem nisi carnea non habebit. Ita consistit probatio corporis de testimonio carnis; probatio carnis de testimonio sanguinis.

^R Proinde panis et calicis sacramento jam in Evangelio probavimus corporis, et sanguinis dominici veritatem, adversus phantasma Marcionis.

^S Marcion phantasma eum maluit credere, totius corporis in illo dedignatus veritatem.

^T Διττον δε το αιμα του Κυριου· το μεν γαρ εστιν αυτου σαρκικον ῷ της φθορας λελυτρωμεθα· το δε πνευματικον, τουεστιν ῷ κεχρισμεθα. Και τουτ' εστι πιειν το αιμα του Ιησου της κυριακης μεταλαβειν αφθαρσιας· ισχυς δε του Λογου το πνευμα, ως αιμα σαρκος. Αναλογως τινυν κιρναται ὁ μεν οινος, τω υδατι· τω δε ανθρωπω, το πνευμα· και το μεν, εις πιστιν ευωχει, το κραμα· το δε, εις αφθαρσιαν οδηγει, το πνευμα· ἡ δε αμφοιν αυθις κρασις, ποτου τε και Λογου, Ευχαριστια κεκληται, χαρις επαινουμενη και καλη· ἧς οι κατα πιστιν μεταλαμβανοντες, αγιαζονται και σωμα και ψυχην· το θειον κραμα, τον ανθρωπον, του πατρικου βουληματος πνευματι και Λογω συγκιρνουντος μυστικως.

^U .... Ευ γαρ ιστε, μετελαβεν οινου και αυτος, και γαρ ανθρωπος και αυτος. Και ευλογησεν γε τον οινον, ειπων, Λαβετε, πιετε· τουτο μου εστιν το αιμα, αιμα της αμπελου. Τον λογον, τον περι πολλων εκχεομενον εις αφεσιν αμαρτιων, ευφροσυνης αγιον αλληγορει ναμα. Και οτι μεν σωφρονειν τον πινοντα δει δι ων εδιδασκεν παρα τας ευωχιας εδειξεν σαφως· ου γαρ μεθυων εδιδασκεν. Οτι δε οινος ην το ευλογηθεν, απεδειξε παλιν, προς τους μαθητας λεγων· Ου μη πιω εκ του γεννηματος της αμπελου ταυτης, μεχρις αν πιω αυτο μεθ'υμων εν τη βασιλεια του Πατρος μου.

Αλλ οτι γε οινος ην το πινομενον προς του Κυριου, παλιν αυτος περι εαυτου λεγει, την Ιουδαιων επονειδιζων σκληροκαρδιαν · · Ηλθεν γαρ φησιν, ὁ υιος του ανθρωπου, και λεγουσιν· Ιδου ανθρωπος φαγος και οινοποτης, τελωνων φιλος. Τουτι μεν ημιν και προς τους Εγκρατητας καλουμενους παραπεπηχθω.

^V Ει γαρ και το υδωρ οινον εν τοις γαμοις πεποιηκεν, ουκ επετρεψε μεθυειν.

APPENDIX. 371

w Οινω δε ολιγω χρω, τω Τιμοθεω υδροποτουντι, δια στομαχον σου, φησιν ο Αποστολος.

x Ειδ', ως ουτοι φασιν ασαρκος και αναιμος ην· ποιας σαρκος, η τινος σωματος, η ποιου αιματος εικονας διδους, αρτον τε και ποτηριον, ενετελλετο τοις μαθηταις, δια τουτων την αναμνησιν αυτου ποιεισθαι;

y Ubi vero tempus advenit crucis suæ, et accessurus erat ad altare ubi immolaret hostiam carnis suæ accipiens, inquit, calicem, benedixit, et dedit discipulis suis dicens; Accipite, et bibite ex hoc. Vos, inquit, bibite, qui modo accessuri non estis ad altare. Ipse autem tanquam accessurus ad altare, dicit de se; Amen dico vobis, etc.

z Ει δε παν το εισπορευομενον εις το στομα, εις κοιλιαν χωρει και εις αφεδρωνα εκβαλλεται, και το αγιαζομενον βρωμα δια λογου Θεου και εντευξεως, κατ αυτο μεν το υλικον εις την κοιλιαν χωρει, και εις αφεδρωνα εκβαλλεται· κατα δε την επιγενομενην αυτω ευχην, κατα την αναλογιαν της πιστεως, ωφελιμον γινεται και της του νοου αιτιον διαβλεψεως, ορωντος επι το ωφελουν και ουχ η υλη του αρτου, αλλ ο επ' αυτω ειρημενος λογος εστιν ο ωφελων τον μη αναξιως του Κυριου εσθιοντα αυτον. Και ταυτα μεν περι του τυπικου, και συμβολικου σωματος.

a . . . . Nam cum dicat Christus: Ego sum vitis vera; sanguis Christi, non aqua est utique, sed vinum. Nec potest videri sanguis ejus, quo redempti et vivificati sumus, esse in calice, quando vinum desit calici, quo Christi sanguis ostenditur. . . . . Nam quis magis secerdos Dei summi, quam Dominus noster Iesus Christus? qui sacrificium Deo patri obtulit, et obtulit hoc idem quod Melchisedech obtulerat, id est, panem et vinum, suum scilicet corpus et sanguinem. . . . . Cæterum omnis religionis et veritatis disciplina subvertitur, nisi id quod spiritaliter præcipitur, et fideliter reservetur, nisi si in sacrificiis matutinis hoc quis veretur ne per saporem vini redoleat sanguinem Christi.

LETTER VIII.

A Τα συμβολα της ενθεου οικονομιας τοις αυτου παρεδιδου μαθηταις την εικονα του ιδιου σωματος ποιεισθαι παρακελευομενος.

ᴮ Τουτου δητα του θυματος την μνημην επι τραπεζης εντελειν, δια συμβολων τουτε σωματος αυτου και του σωτηριου αιματος κατα θεσμους της καινης διαθηκης παρειληφοτες.

ᶜ .... Και οτι εν τη εκκλησια προσφερεται αρτος και οινος, αντιτυπον της σαρκος αυτου και του αιματος· και οι μεταλαμβανοντες εκ του φαινομενου αρτου, πνευματικως την σαρκα του Κυριου εσθιουσι.

ᴰ Εν τυπω γαρ αρτου, διδοται σοι το σωμα, και εν τυπω οινου, διδοται σοι το αιμα· ινα γενη, μεταλαβων σωματος και αιματος Χριστου συσσωμος και συναιμος αυτου.

ᴱ Μεταληψομεθα του πασχα νυν μεν τυπικως ετι, και ει του παλαιου γυμνοτερον. Το γαρ νομικον πασχα, τολμω και λεγω τυπου τυπος ην αμυδροτερος.

ᶠ Fac nobis hanc oblationem ascriptam, rationabilem acceptabilem quod est figura corporis et sanguinis Domini nostri Jesu Christi.

ᴳ Dupliciter vero sanguis Christi et caro intelligitur: spiritualis illa atque divina, de qua ipse dixit : Caro mea verè est cibus, et sanguis meus verè est potus: et, nisi manducaveritis carnem meam .... vel caro et sanguis, quæ crucifixa est, et qui militis effusus est lancea.

ᴴ De hac quidem hostia quæ in commemorationem mirabiliter fit, edere licet. De illa vera quam Christus in ara crucis obtulit, secundum se, nulli edere licet.

ᴵ In typo sanguinis sui non obtulit aquam, sed vinum.

ᴶ Cum adhibuit ad convivium in quo corporis et sanguinis sui figuram discipulis commendavit et tradidit.

ᴷ Dominus non dubitavit dicere, Hoc est enim corpus meum cum daret signum corporis sui.

ᴸ Tunc autem hoc erit, id est, vita unicuique erit corpus et sanguis Christi; si quod in sacramento visibiliter sumiter, in ipsa veritate spiritualiter manducetur, spiritualiter bibatur.

ᴹ Potest sacramentum adoptionis adoptio nuncupari, sicut sacramentum corporis et sanguinis ejus quod est in pane et poculo consecrato corpus ejus, et sanguinem dicimus. Non quod proprie corpus ejus sit panis, et poculum sanguis, sed quod in se mysterium corporis ejus et sanguinis contineant. Hinc et ipse Dominus benedictum panem et calicem, quem discipulis tradidit corpus et sanguinem suum vocavit.

ᴺPanis quia confirmat corpus, ideo Christi corpus nuncupatur; vinum autem, quia sanguinem operatur in carne, ideo ad sanguinem Christi refertur. Hæc autem duo sunt visibilia, sanctificata autem per Spiritum sanctum in sacramentum divini corporis transeunt.

ᴼLoco carnis et sanguinis agni, substituit Christus sacramentum carnis suæ et sanguinis in figura panis et vini.

ᴾDedit in cœno discipulis figuram sacrosancti corporis et sanguinis sui.

ᵠ Τον ενα γαρ και τον αυτον δι ὧν εφημεν και ψηλαφητην ουσίαν εχειν και αψηλαφητον ανεκηρυξε .... Αλλ ουδεις αν ειπειν δυναται νουν εχων ως ἡ αυτη φυσις ψηλαφητου και αψηλαφητου, και ορατου και αορατου. Ουτω και το παρα των πιστων λαμβανομενον σωμα Χριστου, και της αισθητης ουσίας ουκ εξιστάται. Και της νοητης αδιαιρετον μενει χαριτος. Και το βαπτισμα δε πνευματικον ὅλον γενομονον και ἓν υπαρχον, και το ιδιον της αισθητης ουσίας, του υδατος λεγω, διασωζει, και ὃ γεγονεν ουκ απωλεσεν.

ᴿDeus et homo Christus; Deus propter impassibilitatem, homo propter passionem. Unus Filius, unus Dominus, idem ipse proculdubio unitarum naturarum unam dominationem, unam potestatem possidens, etiamsi non consubstantiales existunt, et unaquæque incommixtam proprietatis conservat agnitionem, propter hoc quod inconfusa sunt [duo] dico. Sicut enim antequam sanctificetur Panis, Panem nominamus, divina antem illum sanctificante gratia, mediante sacerdote, liberatus est quidem appellatione panis dignus autem habitus est dominici corporis appellatione, etiamsi natura panis in ipso permansit, et non duo corpora, sed unus corpus filii prædicatur. Sic et hic divina, ενιδρυσάσης, id est, inundante corporis natura, unum filium, unam personam, utraque hæc fecerunt.

ˢCerte sacramenta quæ sumimus, corporis et sanguinis Christi, divina res est, propter quod et per eadem divinæ efficimur consortes naturæ; et tamen esse non desinit substantia vel natura panis et vini; et certe imago et similitudo corporis et sanguinis Christi in actione mysteriorum celebrantur.

Satis ergo nobis evidenter ostenditur, hoc nobis in ipso Christo Domino sentiendum, quod in ejus imagine profitemur, celebramus et sumimus; ut sicut in hanc, scilicet, in divinam transeunt spiritu sancto perficiente substantiam, permanente tamen in sua proprietate natura, sic illud ipsum mysterium principale, cujus nobis efficientiam virtutemque veraciter repræsentant, ex quibus constat propriè permanentibus unum Christum, quia integrum verumque permanere.

^T Τω μεν σωματι το του συμβολου τεθεικεν ονομα, τω δε συμβολω το του σωματος . . . . Ουτος τα ορωμενα συμβολα τη του σωματος και αιματος προσηγορια τετιμηκεν, ου την φυσιν μεταβαλων, αλλα την χαριν τη φυσει προσεθεικως.

^U . . . . Ου γαρ κατα τον αγιασμον το μυστικα συμβολα της οικειας εξισταται φυσεως· μενει γαρ επι της προτερας ουσιας και του σχηματος και του ειδους και ορατα εστι και απτα, οια και προτερον ἦν.

Νοειται δε απερ εγενετο, και πιστευεται και προςκυνειται ως εκεινα οντα απερ πιστευεται.

^V . . . . Quemadmodum enim qui est a terra panis percipiens invocationem Dei, jam non communis panis est, sed eucharistia, ex duabus rebus constans, terrena et cœlesti : Sic et corpora nostra percipientia eucharistiam, jam non sunt corruptibilia, spem resurrectionis habentia.

^W Ὑμεις δε μυρω εχρισθητε, κοινωνοι και μετοχοι του Χριστου γενομενοι. Αλλ' ὁρα μη υπονοησῃς εκεινο το μυρον ψιλον ειναι· ωσπερ και ὁ αρτος της Ευχαριστιας, μετα την επικλησιν του αγιου Πνευματος, ουκ ετι αρτος λιτος αλλα σωμα Χριστου· ουτω και το αγιον τουτο μυρον, ουκ ετι ψιλον, ουδ' ως αν ειποι τις κοινον μετ' επικλησιν, αλλα Χριστου χαρισμα.

^x . . . . Ὁ αρτος παλιν αρτος εστι τεως κοινος· αλλ' οταν αυτον το μυστηριον ιερουργηση, σωμα Χριστου λεγεται τε και γινεται. Ουτως το μυστικον ελαιον, ουτως ὁ οινος, ολιγου τινος αξια οντα προ της ευλογιας· μετα τον αγιασμον τον του πνευματος, εκατερον αυτων ενεργει διαφορως. Η αυτη δε του λογου δυναμις, και τον ιερεα ποιει σεμνον και τιμιον, τη κοινοτητι της ευλογιας της προς τους πολλους κοινοτητος χωριζομενον. κ. τ. λ.

^Y Και ὁ αρτος και το ελαιον αγιαζεται τη δυναμει του ονοματος, ου τα αυτα οντα κατα το φαινομενον οἷα ειληφθη, αλλα δυναμει

εις δυναμιν πνευματικην μεταβεβληται. Ουτως και υδωρ και το εξορκιζομενον και το βαπτισμα γινομενον, ου μονον χωρει το χειρον, αλλα και αγιοσμον προσλαμβανει.

LETTER IX.

A Postrema verba, quibus cavetur, ne octo Libri constitutionum Apostolicarum publicentur, apertè indicant, eas primis sæculis factas non esse, cùm primi sæculi Christiani sua lubentes Mysteria, ut vel ex Justino constat, enuntiarent.

B Acta de Mysteriis silentia non agebant Apostoli, nec catechumenos arcebant sacramentorum conspectu.

C Ex forma omnibus mysteriis selentii fides adhibetur.

D Ad baptisterium catechumeni nunquam admittendi.

E Το δε τρις βαπτιζεσθαι τον ανθρωπον, ποθεν; Αλλα δε οσα περι το βαπτισμα . . . . . Α γαρ ουδε εποπτευειν εξεστι τοις αμυητοις.

F Quid est quod occultum est, et non publicum in Ecclesia? Sacramentum baptismi, sacramentum Eucharistiæ. Opera nostra bona vident et pagani, sacramenta verò occultantur illis.

G Εχεις του μυστηριου τα εκφορα, και ταις των πολλων ακοαις ουκ απορρηται τα δε αλλα εισω μαθηση.

H Ευλογουμεν δε το τε υδωρ του βαπτισματος, και το ελαιον της χρισεως.

I Περι του μη δειν τας χειροτονιας επι παρουσια ακροωμενων γινεσθαι.

J Και ο μελλων χειροτονειν, και τας εκεινων ευχας καλει τοτε, και αυτοι επιψηφιζονται, και επιβοωσιν απερ ιασιν οι μεμυημενοι· ου γαρ δη θεμις επι των αμυητων εκκαλυπτειν απαντα.

K Και γαρ τα μυστηρια δια τουτο τας θυρας κλεισαντες επιτελουμεν, και τους αμυητους ειργομεν.

L Ταυτην δε την προσευχην ου τους αμυητους, αλλα τους μυσταγωγουμενους διδασκομεν. Ουδεις γαρ των αμυητων λεγειν τολμα, Πατερ ημων ὁ εν τοις ουρανοις, μηπω δεξαμενος της υιοθεσιας το χαρισμα. Ὁ δε της του βαπτισματος τετυχηκως δωρεας πατερα καλει τον Θεον.

M .... Ουδε γαρ δυνατον καλεσαι Πατερα τον Θεον, μη παντων εκεινων επιτυχοντα των αγαθων.

N Οτι γαρ πιστοις αὑτη ἡ προσευχη προσηκει, και οι νημοι της Εκκλησιας διδασκουσι, και το προοιμιον της ευχης. Ὁ γαρ αμυητος ουκ αν δυναιτο Πατερα καλειν τον Θεον.

O .... Και γαρ τα μυστηρια δια τουτο τας θυρας κλεισαντες επιτελουμεν, και τους αμυητους ειργομεν ουκ επειδη ασθενειαν κατεγνωμεν, των τελουμενων, αλλ επειδη ατελεστερον οι πολλοι προς αυτα ετι διακεινται.

P Οὐ χρη γαρ τα μυστηρια, αμυητοις τραγωδειν, ινα μη Ελληνες μεν αγνοουντες γελωσι, κατηχουμενοι δε περιεργοι γενομενοι, σκανδαλιζωνται.

Q Ταυτα τα μυστηρια νυν τι εκκλησια διεγειται τω εκ κατηχουμενων μεττβαλλομενω. Ουκ εστιν εθος εθνικοις διηγεισθαι. κ. τ. λ.

R De Iudæis autem præcepit S. Synodus, nemini deinceps ad credendum vim inferri. .... Qui autem jam pridem ad Christianitatem venire coacti sunt, sicut factum est temporibus religiosissimi principis Sisebuti, quia jam constat, eos sacramentis divinis sociatos, et baptismi gratiam suscipisse, et chrismate unctos esse, et corporis Domini et sanguinis existisse participes, oportet, ut fidem etiam, quam vi vel necessitate susceperunt, tenere cogantur, ne nomen Domini blasphemetur, et fides quam susceperunt, vilis ac contemptibilis habeatur.

s .... Οὗτος ὁ λογος της των αγραφων παραδοσεως. ως μη καταμεληθεισαν των δογματων την γνωσιν ευκαταφρονητον τοις πολλοις γενεσθαι δια συνηθειαν.

T .... Quia et si non eis fidelium sacramenta produntur, non ideo sit quod ea ferre non possunt, sed ut ab eis tanto ardentius concupiscantur, quanto eis honorabilius occultantur.

U Fidelibus loquor, si quid non intelligunt catechumeni, auferant pigritiam, festineant ad notitiam. Non ergo opus est mysteria promere; Scripturæ vobis intiment, quid est sacerdotium secundum ordinem Melchisedec.

LETTER X.

^A Το μυστηριον ουν του προβατου ὅ το πασχα θυειν εντεταλται ὁ Θεος, τυπος ἦν του Χριστου . . . . και ἡ της σεμιδαλεως δε προσφορα . . . . τυπος ἦν του αρτου της ευχαριστιας . . . . αλλα και το δωδεκά κωδωνας εξηφθαι του ποδηρους του αρχιερεως παραδεδοσθαι, των δωδεκα αποστολων συμβολον.

^B Εν τω παναγιω βαπτισματι τον τυπον ορωμεν της αναστασεως, τοτε δε αυτην οψωμεθα την αταστασιν· Ενταυθα τα συμβολα του δεσποτικου Θεωμεθα σωματος, εκει δε αυτὸν οψωμεθα τον δεσποτην.

^C . . . . De quo conficitur panis Domini, et sanguinis ejus impletur typus, et benedictio sanctificationis ostenditur.

^DDedit itaque Dominus noster in mensa in qua ultimum cum Apostolis participavit convivium, propriis manibus panem et vinum; in cruce verò manibus militum corpus tradidit vulnerandum ut in Apostolis secretiùs impressa sincera veritas, et vera sinceritas, exponeret gentibus quo modo vinum et panis caro esset et sanguis, et quibus rationibus causæ effectibus convenirent, et diversa nomina vel species ad unam reducerentur essentiam, et significantia et significata eisdem vocabulis censerentur.

^EImago veritate non usquequaqe adæquabitur; aliud enim est secundum veritatem esse, aliud ipsam veritatem esse.

^FNeque enim sibi ipsi quisquam imago est.

^GNemo potest sibi ipsi imago fuisse.

^H Ουκ ετι γαρ αν εικων ει δι' απαντων ἔιη ταυτον εκεινω.

^I Quid absurdiùs quàm imaginem ad se dici?

^J Figura non est veritas, sed imitatio veritatis.

^K 'Ο δε τυπος ουκ αληθεια, μορφωσιν δε μαλλον της αληθειας εισφερει.

ᴸ Pignus et Imago alterius rei sunt, id est, non ad se, sed ad aliud aspiciunt.

ᴹ Ἦν ποτε δικαιοσύνη, ἣν καὶ ὁπότης ἐπὶ Ἰουδαίων ἀλλ᾽ οὐ τῆς ἀληθείας, ἀλλὰ τοῦ τύπου ἡ δικαιοσύνη ἐκείνη. Τὸ γὰρ καθαρὸν εἶναι σώματι τύπος καθαρότητος ἦν οὐχὶ ἀληθεία καθαρότητος· τύπος δικαιοσύνης ἦν, οὐχὶ ἀληθεία δικαιοσύνης.

ᴺ Σμῆμα αὐτῆς καταδεέστερα, καὶ τοσοῦτον, ὅσον σημεῖον τοῦ πράγματος ὅπερ ἐστὶ σημεῖον.

ᴼ Hic umbra, hic imago, illic veritas. Umbra in lege, imago in evangelio, veritas in cœlestibus.

ᴾ Ascende ergo, homo, in cœlum, et videbis illa quorum umbra hic erat vel imago.

ᵠ Μετὰ γὰρ ὅτι τὴν αὐτοῦ παρουσίαν. οὐκ ἔτι χρεία τῶν συμβόλων τοῦ σώματος, αὐτοῦ φαινομένου τοῦ σώματος.

ᴿ Ἅγια δῶρα—Σύμβολα τῶν ἄνω καὶ ἀληθινοτέρων.

ˢ Σκιὰ γὰρ τὰ τῆς παλαιᾶς, εἰκὼν δὲ τὰ τῆς καινῆς διαθήκης, ἀλήθεια δὲ ἡ τῶν μελλόντων κατάστασις.

ᵀ Quod cùm per manus hominum ad illam speciem perducitur, etc.

ᵁ .... Si speciem visibilem intendas, aliud est, si intelligibilem significationem, eundem potum spiritualem biberunt.

ⱽ Recte etiam vini specie tum sanguis ejus exprimitur.

ᵂ In illum in quo fides non est præter visibiles species panis et vini, nihil de sacrificio pervenit.

ˣ Corporis et sanguinis sui sacramenta panis et vini substantia discipulis tradidit. .... Nihil ergo congruentius his speciebus ad significandam capitis et membrorum unitatem, potuit inveniri.

ʸ Non potest intelligi aqua sine humectatione, neque ignis sine calore, neque lapis sine duritia. Unita enim sunt invicem hæc; alterum in altero separari non potest, sed semper coexistere.

APPENDIX.

z Πασα γαρ ποιοτης εν ουσια εστι.

a Ης˜ [ουσιας] μη υπαρχουσης, ανυπαρκτον ειναι την ποιοτητα.

b Μη δυναται χωριζεσθαι καθ' υποστασιν απο της υλης ή ποιοτης.

c Αλλα καν λογω διακρινης το σχημα του σωματος, ή φυσις ου παραδεχεται την διακρισιν, αλλα συνημμενως νοειται μεθ' ετερου το ετερον.

d . . . . Οπου δ' αν συνδραμη τα ειρημενα την σωματικην υποστασιν απεργαζεται.

e Ουτω διαλεξομεθα το πνευμα το αγιον, ην των καθ' εαυτο υφεστηκοτων παντως υποθετεον, ή των εν ετερω θεωρουμενων ὦν το μεν ουσιαν καλουσιν οι περι ταυτα δεινοι, το δε συμβεβηκος. Ει μεν ουν συμβεβηκεν, ενεργεια τουτο αν ειη Θεου.

f Monstruosum enim et a veritate alienissimum est, ut id quod non esset, nisi in ipso [sc. subjecto] esset, etiam, cùm ipsum non fuerit, posse esse.

g Mutato subjecto, omne quod in subjecto est necessario mutari.

h Tolle ipsa corpora qualitatibus corporum, non erit ubi sint, et ideo necesse est ut non sint.

i Την λευκοτητα τυχον ή την μελανιαν . . . . αυτας που καθ' εαυτας αρ' υπαρχειν οιηση δυνασθαι; ουδαμως.

j . . . . αει γαρ παραπεφυκε ταις τοιαυταις ουσιαις τα εξ αυτων τικτομενα.

k Ubique totum præsentem esse non dubites tanquam Deum, et in eodem Templo Dei esse tanquam inhabitantem Deum, et in loco aliquo cœli, propter veri corporis modum.

l Sursum est Dominus, sed etiam hic est veritas Dominus. Corpus enim Domini in quo resurrexit, in loco esse oportet, veritas ejus ubique diffusa est.

m Secundum præsentiam corporalem simul et in sole, et in luna, et in cruce esse non posset.

n Σωμα δε ομως εστι την προτεραν εχων περιγραφην.

º Homo, aut aliquid ei simile, cùm alicubi erit; tum alibi non erit; quia illud quod est illic continentur ubi fuerit, infirma ad id natura ejus, ut ubique sit qui insistens alicubi sit.

ᵖ Deus totus in cœlo est, totus in terra, non alternis temporibus, sed utrumque simul, quod nulla natura corporalis potest.

ᵍ Quantumcumque sit corpus seu quantulumcunque corpusculum loci occupat spatium eundemque locum sic impleat, ut in nulla ejus parte sit totum.

ʳ Nec omnino potest esse aliquod corpus sive coelesti sive terrestre, sive aereum, sive humidum, quod non minus sit in parte quam in toto, neque ullo modo possit in loco hujus partis habere aliam partem.

ˢ Αγγειον γαρ μεδιμναιον, ου χωρησει διμεδιμνον, ουδε σωματος ενος τοπος, δυο η πλειω σωματα.

ᵗ Μετοχον εαυτου παντελως ουδεν.

ᵘ Αλλ' ετερον εν ετερω σκηνοι . . . . ουδεν γαρ εν εαυτω κατοικει.

ᵛ Corpus hominis non aliud intelligam quam quod videtur, quod tenetur.

ʷ Ασωματος ων, διο και αορατος.

ˣ Ποτερον σωμα [Θεος] και πως το απειρον, και αοριστον, και ασχηματιστον, και αναφες, και αορατον; . . . . ου γαρ αυτη φυσις σωματων.

ʸ Ουκ εστι σωμα ῳ το χρωμα, και το σχημα, και η αντιτυπια, και η διαστασις, το βαρος, και τα λοιπα των ιδιωματων ου παρεστιν.

ᶻ Semper quidem divinitate nobiscum est, sed nisi corporaliter abiret a nobis, semper ejus corpus carnaliter videremus.

ᵃ Unaquæque res ita permanet sicut a Deo accepit ut esset, alia quidem sic, alia autem sic. Neque enim sic datum est corporibus ut sint sicut spiritus acceperunt.

LETTER XI.

^A Pene quidem sacramentum omnes corpus ejus dicunt.

^B Ημεις δε τω του παντος δημιουργω ευχαριστουντες, και τους μετ' ευχαριστιας και ευχης της επι τοις οηθεισι προσαγομενους αρτους εσθιομεν σωμα γενομενους δια την ευχην αγιον τι και αγιαζον τους μετ υγιους προθεσεως αυτω χρωμενους.

^C Accepit in manus quod norunt fideles, et ipse se portabat quodammodo, cùm diceret, hoc est corpus meum.

^D Secundum quendam modum sacramentum corporis Christi corpus Christi est: sacramentum sanguinis Christi, sanguis Christi est.

^E Christus quodummodo ferebatur in manibus suis.

^F Si sacramenta quandam similitudinem earum rerum non haberent quarum sacramenta sunt, omnino sacramenta non essent. Ex hac autem similitudine plerumque etiam ipsarum rerum nomina accipiunt.

^G Fortè dicis, speciem sanguinis non video, sed habet similitudinem. Sicut enim mortis similitudinem sumpsisti, ita etiam similitudinem pretiosi sanguinis bibis.

^H Panis quia confirmat corpus, ideo corpus Christi nuncupatur; vinum autem quia sanguinem operatur in carne, ideo ad sanguinem Christi refertur.

^I Αυτου σωμα νομιζειν .... Το δε ποτηριον εν ταξει αιματος ηγγεισθαι.

^J Τι γαρ εστιν ο αρτος; Σωμα Χριστου. Τι δε γινονται οι μεταλαμβανοντες; Σωμα Χριστου. Ουχι σωματα πολλα, αλλα σωμα εν.

^K Accepto pane deinde vini calice, corpus esse suum ac sanguinem testatus.

^L Cùm panem consecratum et vinum discipulis suis porrigeret Dominus, sic ait, hoc est corpus meum.

^M Nos audiamus panem quem fregit Dominus deditque discipulis suis esse corpus Salvatoris.

ᴺ Ebrietati sacrilegium copulantes aiunt, absit ut ego me abstineam a sanguine Christi.

ᴼ Ita in sacramentorum communione se temperant, ut interdum tutius lateant; ore indigno corpus Christi accipiunt, sanguinem autem redemptionis nostræ haurire omninò declinant.

ᴾ Ipse Dominus benedictum panem et calicem quem discipulis tradidit, corpus et sanguinem suum vocavit.

ᵠ Hoc est corpus meum ; id est, in sacramento.

ᴿ Hoc panis est corpus meum.

ˢ Μηδεν πλειον του σωματος και του αιματος του Κυριου προςενεχθειη, ως και αυτος ὁ Κυριος παρεδωκεν, τουτ' εστι, αρτου και οινου ὑδατι μεμιγμενου.

ᵀ Hoc, eo jubente, corpus Christi et sanguinem dicimus, quod dum fit ex fructibus terræ sanctificatur et fit sacramentum, operante invisibiliter spiritu Dei.

ᵁ Sanctificare aliquid, hoc est, vovere Deo.

ⱽ Το αγιαζεσθαι λεγομενον, ουχι παντος αγιασμου μετεχον εσται, σημαινει δε μαλλον και το εις δοξαν ανατεθειμενον τω Θεω.

ᵂ Αγιαζεσθαι τον τοπον, ἢ τον αρτον, ἢ τον οινον, ἅ τω Θεω φαμεν αφοριζεσθαι, και προς μηδεμιαν κοινην ὑποφερεσθαι χρησιν.

ˣ Quod sanctificatur et offertur, eo quod offertur sanctificari incipit, ergo prius non erat sanctum.

ʸ Quod in Domini mensa est—Benedicitur et sanctificatur.

ᶻ Cùm suscipitis corpus Domini, cum omni cantela et veneratione servatis, ne ex eo parum quid decidat, ne consecrati muneris aliquid dilabatur.

ᵃ Ad distribuendum comminuitur.

ᵇ De agni immaculati corpore partem sumere.

ᶜ Qui creavit me (si fas est dicere) dedit mihi creare se, et qui creavit me sine me, creatur mediante me.

d Illa prolatis octo verbulis, *Ecce Ancella Domini, fiat mihi secundum verbum tuum*, semel concepit Dei filium et mundi Redemptorem, Isti a Domino consecrati, quinque verbis, eundem Dei virginisque filium advocant quotidie corporaliter. Attendite O sacerdotes in quo gradu et dignitate sitis constituti.

e Τo ὂν ὂυ γινεται, αλλα το μη ὂν.

f Nihil quod fieri habet, sine initio est, quin initium sit illi incipit fieri.

g Omne quod fit, antequam fiat non fuit.

h Quod fit incipit.

i Facere enim est quod omninò non erat.

j Fieri ejus solet esse proprium, qui nunquam ante subsisterat.

k Οὐ γαρ αν δηπου το ηδη ὂν εις το ειναι φεροιτο, αλλα το μη ὂν.

l Quæ orta jam fuerint, redire in id rursum non queant ut nova creatione generentur.

m Ει εποιησε, το μη ὂν παντως εποιησε.

n Ὁ αρτος παλιν αρτος εστι τεως κοινος· αλλ' οταν αυτον το μυστηριον ιερουργηση, σωμα Χριστου λεγεται τε και γινεται.

o Ὑποκυπτομεν και Αγιω Πνευματι ινα τουτο γενωμεθα οπερ εστι και λεγεται.

p Non omnis panis, sed accipiens benedictionem Christi, fit corpus Christi.

q Επικλησεως γενομενης, ὁ μεν αρτος γινεται σωμα Χριστου, ὁ δε οινος αιμα Χριστου.

r Hoc quod conficimus corpus ex Virgine est . . . . vera utique caro Christi quæ crucifixa est, quæ sepulta est. Veri ergo carnis illius sacramentum est.

LETTER XII.

A Aliud est demutatio, aliud perditio. Perebit autem demutata, si non ipsa permanserit in demutatione quæ exhibita fuerit in resurrectione. . . . . Quomodo ergo quod perditum est, mutatum non est, ita quod mutatum est perditum non est. Perisse enim, est in totum non esse quod fuerit; mutatum esse, aliter esse est.

B Nec videtur glorificatur nostra conditio unione Deitatis, sed potius esse consumpta, si non eadem subsistit in gloria, sed sola existente Deitate humanitas illic esse jam destitit. . . . . Per hoc non sublimata, sed abolita potius invenitur.

C Si transfigurationem et conversionem in transitum substantiæ cujusque defendis, ergo et Saul in alium virum conversus de corpore suo excessit.

D Το γινεσθαι ου παντως φυσεως σημαινει μεταβολην.

E Παντως γαρ ου εαν εφαψαιτο το Αγιον Πνευμα, τουτο ηγιασται και μεταβεβληται.

F Per ignem Spiritus Sancti omnia quæ cogitamus, loquimur ac facimus, in spiritualem substantiam convertuntur.

G Οιον γαρ αν ῇ τη φυσει το μετεχομενον, προς τουτο αναγκη και το μετεχον συμμετατιθεσθαι.

H Dico proprie loquendo, quod transubstantiatio non est mutatio.

I Discant naturam posse converti, quando petra aquæ fluxit, et ferrum aquæ supernatavit.

J Nonne claret naturam vel maritimorum fluctuum vel fluvialis cursus esse mutatam ?

K Εις χιονα μεταβαλλεσθαι.

L Τα στοιχεια την οικειαν αγνοησαντα φυσιν, προς το χρησιμον εκεινοις μεταβαλλοντο, και τα θηρια ουκ ετι θηρια ἦν, ουδε ἡ καμνος καμνος.

M Per iniquitatem homo lapsus est a substantia in qua factus est.

N Μεταστοιχειουσα προς τον υιον.

O Δει αλλαγηναι και μεταβληθηναι τας ψυχας ημων απο της νυν καταστασεως εις ετεραν καταστασιν και φυσιν θειαν.

APPENDIX. 385

P Μεταποιηθηναι τη φυσει προς το θειοτερον.

Q Demutati in atomo erimus in angelicam substantiam.

R Demutatio terrenorum corporum in spiritualem æthereamque naturam.

S Εις θειχην φυσιν απαντες μεταβαλλονται.

T Veniat, veniat ut carnem reparet, animam innovet, ipsam naturam in cœlestem commutet substantiam.

U 'Αλλο ζωης ειδος αυτης, της φυσεως ημων μεταστοιχειωσις.

V Caro mortalis convertitur in corpus angeli.

W Cum induerit incorruptionem et immortalitatem, jam non caro et sanguis erit, sed in corpus cœleste mutabitur.

X Μετα την αναστασιν το μεν σωμα μεταστοιχειωθεν προς το αφθαρτον.

Y Deus in hominem convertitur.

Z .... Unde rubet baptismus, nisi sanguine Christi consecratus?

a Δια της του πνευματος ενεργειας το αισθητον υδωρ προς θειαν τινα και αρρητον αναστοιχειουται δυναμιν.

b Statim baptizatus in agni sanguine quem legebat, etc.

c Asperges me aqua Filii tui sacro sanguine mixta.

d Ingreditur anima vitales undas, velut rubras sanguine Christi consecratas.

e Χριστον μεταπεποιημαι τω βαπτισματι.

f Susceptus a Christo, Christum suscipiens, non idem past lavacrum, qui ante baptismum fuit, sed corpus regenerati sit caro crucifixi; hæc commutatio dextræ est Excelsi.

g ..... Αγιαζει τε λοιπον τους εν οις αν γενοιτο.

h Το υδωρ επινοια μονον διαφοραν εχει προς το πνευμα, επει ταυτον εστι τη ενεργεια.

ᵢ Aqua nostra suscipit mortuas et evomit vivos, ex animalibus veros homines factos ex hominibus in angelos transituros.

ʲ Εν εαυτω ζητεται, παντως ολος εις εμε μεταστοιχειουμενος.

ᵏ Christi caro de utero virginis sumpta, nos sumus.

ˡ Non aliud agit participatio corporis et sanguinis Christi, quàm ut in id quod sumimus transeamus.

ᵐNullus debet moveri fidelium in illis, qui etsi legitimè sana mente baptizantur, præveniente velocius morte, carnem Domini manducare et sanguinem bibere non sinuntur propter illam, videlicet, sententiam Salvatoris qua dixit; Nisi manducaveritis carnem Filii hominis, etc. . . . . . Quod quisquis . . . . mysterii veritatem considerare poterit in ipso lavacro sanctæ regenerationis hoc fieri providebit.

ⁿ Πολλα δε αν και περι αυτου λεγοιτο του λογου, ός γεγονε σαρξ, και αληθινη βρωσις ἥν τινα ὁ φαγων παντως ζητεται εις τον αιωνα, ουδενος δυναμενου φαυλου εσθιειν αυτην κ. τ. λ.

ᵒ Dum non sunt sancti corpore et spiritu, nec comedunt carnem Jesu, neque bibunt sanguinem ejus, de quo loquitur; Qui comedit carnem meam, et bibit sanguinem meum habet vitam æternam.

ᵖ De ipso pane et de ipsa Dominica manu, et Judas partem et Petrus accepit.

ᵠ Illi manducabant Panem Dominum, ille panem Domini contra Dominum, illi vitam, ille pœnam.

ʳ Hujus rei sacramentum, id est, unitatis corporis et sanguinis Christi. . . . . in Dominica mensa præparatur, et de Dominica mensa sumitur, quibusdam ad vitam; quibusdam ad exitium. Res vero ipsa cujus et sacramentum est, omni homini ad vitam, nulli ad exitium quicunque ejus particeps fuerit.

ˢ . . . . Nam qui discordet a Christo nec carnem ejus manducat, nec sanguinem bibit; etiamsi tantæ rei sacramentum ad judicium suæ præsumptionis quotidie indifferenter accipiat.

ᵗ Cujus caro cibus credentium est.

APPENDIX. 387

u Caro ejus qui est esca sanctorum.

v Hic est panis vitæ.

w Ταυτης μεν τοι της τροφης μεταλαβων, ανωτερος εσται του θανατου.

x Sacramentum aliquod vobis commendavi: Spiritualiter intellectum vivificabit vos. Etsi necesse est illud visibiliter celebrari, oportet tamen invisibiliter intelligi.

y Tunc autem hoc erit, id est, vita unicuique erit corpus et sanguis Christi, si, quod in sacramento visibiliter sumitur, in ipsa veritate spiritualiter manducetur, spiritualiter bibatur.

z Ipse dicens, qui manducat carnem meam et bibit sanguinem meum, in me manet et ego in eo, ostendit quid sit, non sacramento tenus, sed revera corpus Christi manducare et sanguinem ejus bibere.

a Hujus sacrificii caro et sanguis ante adventum Christi per victimas similitudinem promittebatur, in passione Christi per ipsam veritatem reddebatur, post ascensum Christi per sacramentum memoriæ celebratur.

b Hoc est, benedicens etiam passurus, ultimam nobis commemorationem sive memoriam dereliquit. Quenadmodum si quis peregre proficiscens aliquid pignus ei quem diligit derelinquat, ut quotiescunque illud viderit, possit ejus beneficia et amicitias memorari, quod ille, si perfecte dilexit, sine ingenti desiderio non possit videre, vel fletu.

c Christus coram discipulis elevatus in cœlum, corporalis præsentiæ modum fecit.

d Christus ad Patrem post resurrectionem victor ascendens, ecclesiam corporaliter reliquit.

LETTER XIII.

A Ου γαρ δοκησει ταυτα, αλλ' εν υποστασει αληθειας εγενετο· ει δε μη ων ανθρωπος εφαινετο ανθρωπος, ουτε ὁ ην επ' αληθεια εμεινε πνευμα Θεου, επει αορατον το πνευμα, ουτε αληθεια τις ην αυτω· ου γαρ ην εκεινα απερ εφαινετο.

ᴮ Ecce fallit et decipit et circumvenit omnium occulos omnium sensus, omnium accessus et contactus. Ergo jam Christum non de cœlo deferre debueras, sed de aliquo circulatorio cœtu.

ᶜ Sufficit mihi hoc definire, quod Deo congruit, veritatem scilicet illius rei, quam tribus testibus sensibus objicit, visui, tactui, auditui.

ᴰ Jam Deum tuum honoras fallaciæ titulo, si aliud se esse sciebat, quàm quod homines fecerat opinari.

ᴱ Cur autem inspectui eorum manus et pedes suos offert, etc.

ᶠ Ne ipsi quidem occuli fallunt; non enim renunciare possunt animo nisi affectionem suam. . . . . Quem oculus recte videt; ad hoc enim, factus est ut tantum videat; sed animus perverse judicat.

ᴳ . . . . Si forte diceremus Thomæ oculos fuisse deceptos, at non possemus dicere manus frustratas, in resurrectionis enim manifestatione de aspectu ambigi potest de tactu non potest dubitari.

ᴴ Illud est quod Magiæ simile dicimini asserere, etc.

ᴵ Qui nisi dæmones, quibus amica fallacia est?

ᴶ . . . . Potest fortasse aliqua oculos caligo decipere, palpatio corporalis verum corpus agnoscat.

ᴷ Tollit stultissimam eorum termeritatem.

ᴸ Πως συλληφθεις σταυρουται, ὁ μη ὑπ' αφην ὑποπιπτων κατα τον σον λογον;—ου γαρ δυνασαι φαντασιαν οριζειν τον ὑστερον ὑπ' αφην πιπτοντα δεικνυμενον.

ᴹ Ποθεν ἡ χλασις του αρτου εγενετο.

ᴺ Cum sacramenta signa sint rerum, aliud existentia, et aliud significantia.

ᴼ Το βαπτισμα ημων ου τοις αισθητοις οφθαλμοις κατανοητεον, αλλα τοις νοηροις.

ᴾ Non debetis aquas illas oculis æstimare sed mente.

APPENDIX. 389

q .... Non ergo solis corporis tui credas oculis. Magis videtur, quod non videtur.

r Illa multo majora sunt quae non videntur quàm quae videntur: quoniam quæ videntur temporalia sunt, quae non videntur æterna.

s Μη ως υδατι λιτω προσελθε τω λουτρω· αλλα τη μετα του υδατος διδομενη πνευματικη χαριτι..

t Πειθωμεθα τοινυν τη αποφασει του Θεου· ὁ οψεως γαρ εστιν αυτη πιστοτερα.

u Ει δε και το φαινομενον ουκ εστι Χριστος, αλλ' εν τουτω σχηματι αυτος λαμβανει και προσαιτει.

v Οταν τι εστι μη φαινεται αλλ' οπερ μη εστι δεικνυται.

w .... ατε ου πλαττομενοι ουδε ψευδη λεγοντες.

x .... και γινεται ημων ὁ οφθαλμος ερμηνευς της παντοδυναμου σοφιας ....

y .... πασης εργασιας υφηγηται και διδασκαλοι γινονται, και της απλανους οδοιποριας οδηγοι συμφυεις και αχωριστοι.

z Ει μεν ουν εκ των προς αισθησιν και νοησιν εναργων αρξαιτο τις .... οντως αποδεικνυσιν.

a Αχρις αν εις τα εξ εαυτων πιστα αναδραμωμεν. κ. τ. λ.

b .... Non licet, non licet nobis in dubium sensus istos devocare, etc.

c .... qui nec vocabula ista in luce proprietatum suarum conservant.

d .... Quod ergo videtis panis est et calix, quod vobis etiam oculi vestri renunciant. Quod autem fides vestra postulat instruenda, Panis est corpus Christi, calix sanguis Christi. .... Quomodo est panis corpus est? Ista, fratres ideo dicuntur sacramenta, quia in eis aliud videtur, aliud intelligetur. Quod videtur, speciem habet corporalem; quod intelligitur, fructum habet spiritalem. Corpus ergo Christi si vis intelligere, Apostolum audi dicentem Fidelibus: Vos estis corpus Christi et membra.

33*

ᵃ Πειθωμεν τοινυν πανταχου τω Θεω, και μηδεν αντιλεγωμεν. κ. τ. λ.

LETTER XIV.

ᴬ .... Μια γαρ εστιν ἡ σαρξ του Κυριου Ιησου, και ἕν αυτου το αιμα το υπερ ημων εκχυθεν· εἷς και αρτος τοις πασιν εθρυφθη, και ἓν ποτηριον τοις ολοις διενεμηθη.

ᴮ Εστι δε οπου ουδε διεστηκεν ὁ ιερευς του αρχομενου· οιον οταν απολαυειν δεη των φρικτων μυστηριων· ομοιως γαρ παντες αξιουμεθα των αυτων· ου καθαπερ επι της Παλαιας, τα μεν ὁ ιερευς ησθιε, τα δε ὁ αρχομενος, και θεμις ουκ ἦν τω λαω μετεχειν ὧν μετειχεν ὁ ιερευς. Αλλ ου νυν· αλλα πασιν ἓν σωμα προκειται, και ποτηριον ἕν.

ᶜ Indignum est Domino qui mysterium aliter celebrat, quàm ab eo, traditum est. Non enim potest devotus esse qui aliter præsumit dare quàm datum est ab authore.

ᴰ Corpus Christi non est sacramentaliter sub specie vini, nec sanguis sacramentaliter sub specie panis, ergo, ut sacramentaliter sumatur Christus, necesse est ut sumatur sub duabus speciebus.

ᴱ Cum Pontifex corpus Christi sumpserit, Episcopus Cardinalis porrigit ei calamum, quem Papa ponit in calice in manibus Diaconi existente, et sanguinis partem sugit.

ꜰ .... Item ipsa sancta synodus decernit et declarat, super ista materia, reverendis in Christo patribus et patriarchis, et dominis, ut effectualiter puniant eos contra hoc decretum excedentis, qui communicandum populum sub utraque specie panis et vini exhortati fuerint.

LETTER XV.

ᴬ Οἱ ουν τοις προστεταγμενοις καιροις ποιουντες τας προσφορας αυτων, ευπροσδεκτοι τε και μακάριοι.

ᴮ Τον δημιουργον τουδε του παντος σεβομενοι ανενδεη αιματων και σπονδων και θυμιαματων.

ᶜ Offert Deo ei qui nobis alimenta praestat, primitias suorum munerum .... primitias Deo offere ex suis creaturis, etc.

ᴰ In Dominicum sine sacrificio venis, quæ partem de sacrificio, quod pauper obtulit, sumis.

ᴱ Oblationes quae in altari consecrantur offerte, erubescere debet homo idoneus, si de aliena oblatione communicet.

ᶠ Proinde verum sacrificium est omne opus quod agitur. .... Hoc est sacrificium Christionorum; multi unum corpus in Christo, Quod etiam sacramento altaris fidelibus noto frequentat ecclesia, ubi ei demonstratur, quod in ea re quam offert, ipsa offeratur.

ᴳ .... Nihil aliud quàm sacrificio sacrificium prælatum oportet intelligi: quoniam illud quod ab omnibus appellatur sacrificium, signum est veri sacrificii.

ᴴ .... Τουτο εις αναμνησιν γινεται του τοτε γενομενου.

ᴵ Μνημην ημιν παρεδωκε αντι θυσιας τω Θεω διηνεκως προσφρειν.

ᴶ Ευχαι και ευχαριστιαι υπο των αξιων γινομεναι τελειαι μοναι και ευαρεσται εισι τω Θεω.

ᴷ Sequitur ut eadem ratione pro aliis non sacrificemus, quia nec pro nobis ipsis.

ᴸ Ei offero opimum et majorem hostiam .... orationem de carne pudica, de anima innocenti de Spiritu Sancto profectam.

ᴹ Αμνον Θεου αθυτως υπο των ιερεων θυομενον.

ᴺ Offertur in imagine.

ᴼ Quod sit in figuram corporis et sanguinis Domini.

ᴾ Jam Christiani peracti ejusdem sacrificii memoriam celebrant sucrosancta oblatione et participatione corporis et sanguinis Christi.

ᵠ Θαυμασιον θυμα και σφαγιον εξαιρετον τω Πατρι καλλιερησαμενος υπερ της ημων ανηνεγκε σωτηριας, μνημην και ημιν παραδους αντι θυσιας τω Θεω διηνεκως προσφερειν.

R Θυσια δε ή τω Θεω δεκτη, σωματος τε και των τουτου παθων αμετανοητος χωρισμος, ή αληθης τω οντι θεοσεβεια αυτη.

S .... Παντα ταυτα λελυται, και αντεισενηνεκται αντι τουτων ή λογικη λατρεια. Τι δ' εστιν ή λογικη λατρεια; τα δια ψυχης, τα δια πνευματος. κ. τ. λ.

T Και λοιπον αποκοψη δια της ενσαρκου παρουσιας της του Χριστου αυτου το παν της υποθεσεως των θυσιων· της μιας θυσιας τελειωσασης τας προυπαρξασας πασας ή τις εστι θυσια Χριστου. Οτι το Πασχα ημων ετυθη Χριστος, κατα το γεγραμμενον.

LETTER XVI.

A Ὁ Θεος ιλασθητι μοι αμαρτωλω.

B Toto die ad hanc partem zelus fidei perorabit, ingemens Christianum ab idolis in ecclesiam venire: de adversaria officina in domum Dei venire: attollere ad Deum Patrem manus, matres idolorum: his manibus adorare quae foris adversus Deum adorantur: eas manus admovere corpori Domini, quæ dæmoniis corpora conferunt,

C Ουδε χερες φρισσοισιν, επην ες μυστιν εδωδην. Τεινεις αις συ γραφεις πενθιμον αγλαιην.

D Εκαστ'ον του λαου λαβειν την μοιραν επιτρεπουσιν.

E Και εν τη εκκλησια ὁ ιερευς επιδιδωσι την μεριδα, και κατεχει αυτην ὁ υποδεχομενος μετ' εξουσιας απασης, και ουτω προσαγει τω στοματι τη ιδια χειρι.

F Ου ψιλω τω μελανι τα χειρογραφα ποιουμενοι, αλλα.... εν αυτω του Σωτηρος τω αιματι βαπτοντες την καλαμον ουτως εξεκηρυξαν Φωτιον.

G Την επι του σταυρου υψωσιν, και τον εν αυτω θανατον και αυτην την αναστασιν.

H Ὁ δ' ιερευς μετασχων των αγιασματων, προς το πληθος επιστρεφεται, και δειξας τα αγια καλει τους μετασχεειν βουλομενους.

APPENDIX.   393

I (a) σεβειν, και εσθιειν τι προσκυνουμενων.
(b) θυεις προβατον, το δε αυτο και προσκυνεις.

J Δια τουτο τα μεν ακαθαρτα των ζωων λεγει, τα δε καθαρα, ινα τα μεν ως ακαθαρτα βδελυττομενοι μη θεοποιωσι, τα δε μη προσκυνωσιν εσθιομενα. Αβελτηριας γαρ εσχατης το εσθιομενον προσκυνειν.

K Deos vestros plerumque in prædam furibus cedere.

L Quanto verius de diis vestris animalia muta naturaliter judicant, mures, hirundines, milvi; non sentire eos sciunt, rodunt, insultant, insident, ac nisi abigatis, in ipso dei vestri ore nidificant; araneæ verò faciem ejus intexunt.

M Την εικονα υλην εξαιρετον, ηγουν αρτου ουσιαν, προσεταξε προσφερεσθαι, μη σχηματιζεσθαι ανθρωπου μορφην, ινα μη ειδωλολατρεια παρεισαχθη.

N Ορας εν θυσιαστηριω.

O Stephanas in terris positus Christum tangit in cœlo.

P Ibant Christiani Hierosolymam ut Christum in illis adorarent locis in quibus primum Evangelium de patibulo coruscaverat.

Q Σχημα ικετων και προσκυνητων εχωμεν.

R Αλλο προσκυνειν, και αλλο λατρευειν. Ὁ μεν γαρ εξ ολης ψυχης δουλευων τουτοις [sc. ειδωλοις] ου μονον προσκυνει, αλλα και λατρευει. Ὁ δε καθυποκρινομενος, και δια τα εθνη ποιων, ου λατρευει μεν, προσκυνει δε.

S . . . . Ου λατρευουσι μεν, προσκυνουσι δε τοις ειδωλοις . . . .

T Πυλη γαρ ωσπερ τις εστι, και οδος της εν εργοις λατρειας η προσκυνησις, αρχην εχουσα, δουλειαν την ως προς Θεον.

U "Οσω αν φανοτερα και αναγκαστικωτερα η τα γινομενα, τοσουτω τα της πιστεως ελαττουνται· δια τουτο σημεια νυν ου γινεται . . . . Ουκουν οσω αν φανερωτερον αποδειχθη το σημειον, τοσουτω της πιστεως ὁ μισθος ελαττουται. Ωστε ει και νυν σημεια εγενετο, το αυτο αν εγενετο.

www.ingramcontent.com/pod-product-compliance
Lightning Source LLC
Chambersburg PA
CBHW022120290426
44112CB00008B/747